VICE

One Cop's Story
of Patrolling America's
Most Dangerous City

SGT. JOHN R. BAKER

with Stephen J. Rivele

ST. MARTIN'S GRIFFIN
New York

www.stmartins.com

Design by Kathryn Parise

THE LIBRARY OF CONGRESS HAS CATALOGED THE HARDCOVER EDITION AS FOLLOWS:

Baker, John R., 1942–

Vice : one cop's story of patrolling America's most dangerous city / John R. Baker with Stephen J. Rivele.—1st U.S. ed.

    p. cm.

ISBN 978-0-312-59687-3

1. Baker, John R., 1942– 2. Police—California—Compton—Biography. 3. Crime—California—Compton. I. Rivele, Stephen J., 1949– II. Title.

HV7911.B26A3 2011

363.2092—dc22

[B]

2010037517

ISBN 978-1-250-00207-5 (trade paperback)

First St. Martin's Griffin Edition: April 2012

D 10 9 8 7 6 5 4 3 2

In loving memory of my mother,
Elisa Oviedo Baker,
whose unending devotion to my safety
made this story possible
—Sgt. John R. Baker

Contents

CONTENTS

Acknowledgments

Reconstructing my fifty-year odyssey in Compton has been an enormous undertaking, and I could not have done it without a great deal of help. First and foremost, I must thank my coauthor, Steve Rivele, whose crafting of the episodes has been brilliant, making for a compelling narrative. Among the surviving Compton police officers who contributed to the book, I would especially like to thank Malcolm Landry and Ramon Allen for their encouragement, Robert Orasco for providing rare photographs, and Tim Brennan and Robert Ladd for their help in researching gang culture. My enduring thanks go to my CPD colleagues, David R. Arellanes, Philip "Catfish" Bailey, Bernard Brown, Jeff Nussman, Richard L. Daniels, Jimmy Pearson, and John Wilkinson, who backed me up on the street and supported me in writing this story.

Special thanks go to Dominic Rutigliano, who advised me throughout the writing of this book. Rut's help was crucial in both my police career and in recalling many of the incidents described here. His continuing comradeship is one of my proudest possessions.

Michael Morales assisted in compiling statistics on Compton history and gang culture, Sara Davis helped in the initial phases, Keani Gaor assisted with the typing, and Jennifer Puccio did a magnificent job transcribing my tapes. I am indebted also to Jason Ashlock, our agent, and to Marc Resnick and his colleagues at St. Martin's Press for their enthusiasm and expertise. Bill Byron helped correct the text, and India Cooper's work in copyediting the manuscript was also an invaluable contribution.

—Sgt. John R. Baker

Foreword

I first met Rick Baker in the gym. Being a writer and therefore able to make my own schedule, I was in the habit of working out at odd hours when the place was not crowded. But there was one fellow who seemed always to be in the gym at the same time as me. He was of medium height with jet black hair cut in a military fashion, and he carried himself with an air of confidence and authority. He was not beefy or bulked up like some of the pump-junkies who haunted the place, but he was in solid shape, and he lifted with a concentration and efficiency that spoke of years of experience.

One day I noticed a friend of mine talking with him, and I inquired who the man was. "He's a retired cop," my friend said. Then he added, "From Compton."

That struck me as curious, since the man was white. Later, I approached him while he was doing curls with free weights. He watched me in the mirror waiting to speak to him. When he had finished his set, I said, "You must have some interesting stories to tell."

He glanced up at me and scowled. "Who the hell are you?"

I told him that I wrote books and films, and I suggested that he write down some of the more unusual cases on which he had worked. I would take a look at them, I explained, and see whether there might be a television show or movie in them. He said grudgingly that he would think about it.

I asked his name. "John Baker," he replied. "But everybody calls me Rick."

A few weeks later, Rick relocated to Las Vegas, and for two years I did not hear from him. Then, shortly before Christmas 2007, there was a knock at my front door.

It was a tall, blond, stunning young woman. "I'm Tiffany," she said. "My dad wanted you to have this." She handed me a square black metal box.

"Who's your dad?" I asked her.

She smiled. "Rick Baker."

The box contained a dozen CDs. In the previous two years, with an efficiency and thoroughness I have come to admire, Rick had recorded on tape nothing less than an oral history of Compton from 1951, when his parents moved there, until he left the city fifty years later.

Over the Christmas holidays I listened to Rick's CDs with growing excitement and even awe. They contained what was, quite simply, the most amazing story I had ever heard. It was a tale of devotion, of sacrifice, of frailty and strength, of humanity and inhumanity, but above all of heroism in the face of dangers the rest of us can only imagine. It was the story of a small group of intense, and intensely human, men and women who, against enormous odds, kept their city from dissolving into chaos.

Detective Sergeant John "Rick" Baker is the most highly decorated police officer in Compton history. He was president of the Compton Police Officers Association and an official of the International Conference of Police Associations. He made thousands of arrests, resolved hundreds of crimes, saved dozens of lives, received a score of commendations, and never had a single complaint sustained against him.

During his eighteen years with the Compton Police Department, Rick was part of a tiny cadre of men and women who risked their lives, their health, and their sanity to maintain order in the city where most of them had been born, and in which many lived and raised their families. The odds against them were always long—the radicals and criminals and gangsters they faced were much more numerous and sometimes better armed than they; and the politicians who were supposed to support them too often were corrupt or indifferent, or both.

Some of the situations in which Rick and his fellow officers found themselves could not have been invented; indeed, if one tried to invent them, they would be beyond belief. Likewise, the characters—cops and crooks alike—seem more properly the product of fiction than of fact. I realized at once that Rick's story, the story of the men and women of the Compton Police Department, needed desperately to be told.

This will be a controversial book. In some cases the methods the Compton police used defied procedure and redefined the meaning of law and order. However, as Rick argues, what he and his fellow officers were engaged in was not so much police work as urban warfare. It was a war they fought from street to street and from house to house, using whatever weapons, tactics, and resources were available. There were triumphs and tragedies, heroes and villains, and often it was difficult to tell the difference. Because Compton's cops were also its residents, they knew the criminals—had known them all their lives—and that fact was a source of their strength, and sometimes also of their weakness.

Still, no matter how uneven the odds they faced, no matter how demanding and dangerous their job became, no matter how vile and vicious the violence, the cops of Compton never lost sight of the fact that their sworn duty was to protect the innocent citizens of their city. They did so with the full force of their humanity, for better and for worse. It was this humanity, in all its complexity and contradictions, with all its brutality and beauty, that shone through Rick Baker's recordings. To be a cop in Compton in the sixties and seventies and eighties was to be a human being in the fullest sense of the term. It meant to be *real,* for in the unforgiving streets of Compton during those turbulent days, nothing—not valor or venality, not selflessness or honesty or courage—could be faked. That, too, blazed through Rick Baker's astonishing account.

The Compton of Rick Baker's memoirs is a reflection of America in its period of darkest political and social unrest—it was a city that, like the nation itself, was struggling for survival as it searched for its soul. That Compton did survive, that it did not descend into the anarchy that threatened to consume it, is a testament to the bravery and skill, to the heroism and unquenchable humanity, of the men and women who every day and every night put their lives on the line for the sake of the city they were sworn to serve.

This is their story, seen through the eyes of Rick Baker, and it has been my privilege to write it.

—Stephen J. Rivele

Preface

It was late in the summer of 2005 when I asked John Wilkinson what he thought would be our legacy as cops in the City of Compton. Wilkinson, who was known as Wilk to his fellow officers, had completed twenty-five years of service in the Compton Police Department, achieving the rank of field sergeant. He turned to me with a deadpan expression and said, "Rick, it doesn't matter if the public ever knows what we endured, because we know what we did."

I digested Wilk's statement. It meant that the public might never be told about the quality of the Compton PD, its camaraderie, its skill, and its sacrifices, and our apocalyptic thirty-year campaign of urban warfare against the criminal element of what a federal government report called America's most dangerous city. To me this seemed a travesty; an injustice not only to the men and women who served, but to the wider interests of history. So I became obsessed with the idea of relating to the public my fifty-year odyssey as a citizen and a cop in Compton.

Another incentive was the fact that two former street thugs, Kody Scott (a.k.a. Sanyika Shakur) and Stanley "Tookie" Williams, had written books depicting their lives as bona fide gangsters. These books, together with the scabrous lyrics of the gangsta rappers, told distorted, one-sided versions of the Compton story. It became my crusade to let the world know that there was another side to the story of that turbulent era of gangland violence—our side, the story of the men and women of the Compton Police Department.

In trying to characterize the war we fought against a criminal element that vastly outnumbered us in men and weapons, I often use as an analogy the epic story of King Leonidas and his three hundred Spartans holding at bay a Persian army of more than a hundred thousand. As with them, discipline and unity were our most important weapons—and like them, we were defeated finally not by the enemy we faced, but by treachery from behind our own lines.

In my effort to present accurately and in detail the Compton story as I lived it, I have been fortunate to be able to collaborate with Stephen J. Rivele, author and Academy Award® nominee. The skill and insight he has brought to this work have greatly enhanced its value, and I am extremely grateful to him.

It is all here as I remember it—the good, the bad, and the ugly—but it is as true an account as I could make it. My duty in writing this book was the same as it was when I wore the uniform of the Compton PD: to serve the interests of the public faithfully and with integrity. I have done my best here, as I did then, and I hope that you will find it enlightening and enjoyable.

—Sgt. John R. Baker

Authors' Note

All of the incidents in this book are real—none has been invented. In the absence of transcripts, some dialogue has been interpolated. A few of the names have been changed in the interest of privacy.

A policeman goes after vice as an officer of the law, and comes back a philosopher.

—Finley Peter Dunne

A Model Community

I was not born in Compton, but I grew up there.

My father moved to the Boyle Heights section of Los Angeles in 1927 from Tucson, where his father had lived. My original family name was Boulanger, which is the French word for a baker. My father's grandfather had served with the Emperor Maximilian's army in Mexico. After the defeat of the French by the Mexican army at the Battle of Puebla in 1862 (which is still celebrated as Cinco de Mayo), he relocated to Arizona, and his name was Anglicized from Jean Boulanger to John Baker. An industrious man, my great-grandfather worked at many trades, from rancher and barber to railroad man, saloon keeper, and prospector. Before long he owned several small apartment buildings, which he rented to the poorer folk of Tucson. When my father was ten years old, my grandfather moved his family of six sons and three daughters to Los Angeles in search of fortune and adventure.

My mother, the child of Mexican immigrants, was born in Silver City, New Mexico. Her parents relocated to Santa Ana, south of Los Angeles, when she was little; then, later, they moved into Boyle Heights in the southern L.A. suburbs. It was there, in 1940, that my mother and father met, fell in love, and married. Then the attack on Pearl Harbor thrust the United States into war, and my father was drafted and sent to Europe. He was in the third wave of the D-day invasion, fought across Europe to the Rhine, and was severely wounded.

After the war, my parents settled in the Aliso Village section of Boyle Heights, in a housing project that was built for low-income workers who could not afford to buy a home. As I recall, they paid twenty-six dollars a month in rent, and had a hard scrabble to find even that much. Aliso Village was one of the poorest neighborhoods in Los Angeles.

Boyle Heights, in the 1930s and '40s, was largely a Jewish community, with kosher butchers and orthodox synagogues and Hebrew schools, dominated by the organized crime mob of Mickey Cohen. I often saw his shiny black Packard parked outside his headquarters, a shoeshine parlor on Brooklyn Avenue. The hood was surmounted by a big chrome swan, and everyone in the neighborhood knew that you did not touch Mr. Cohen's car.

By the time my parents reached it, Boyle Heights was transforming. Latinos were moving from Mexico and Central America, as were blacks from the South, lured by the promise of cheap housing and jobs in the defense industries of Los Angeles. In a process I would see replicated later in Compton, the demographics of the neighborhood quickly began to change.

By the time I was born at White Memorial Hospital in 1942, Boyle Heights had become a tough and eclectic community. Life was a struggle, and everyone was out to make a living, make a killing, make a fast buck. There were legitimate small businessmen and hustlers, zoot-suited flash boys and big-band swingers, soldiers and sailors and their families eager to do their part and wishing the war were over—and Mickey Cohen's gangsters, who ran the betting pools and numbers games, promising to make you rich or break your legs.

In addition to the immigrant Jews, many ethnic groups and languages were represented in the neighborhoods, yet there was no sense of animosity. Everyone was in the same boat, and there was none of the hostility and territorialism that would later characterize Compton. All this was tempered, of course, by the wartime mentality. Both of my parents' families were caught up in the hurricane of war. Five of my uncles served in Europe, the oldest, Lefty Baker, being killed in the D-day invasion. His body remains in Normandy, the homeland of his ancestors. The war and the struggle against tyranny trumped everything else. No matter how different we were, no matter what our ethnic rivalries, we were all fighting the same enemy in a life-and-death struggle to save our civilization.

There was another constant in those days and in those neighborhoods: the police. It was the cops, and not the kids or the crooks, who controlled the streets of Boyle Heights. The police were strict and stolid, and you defied them at your peril. No matter how wild we kids ran, we knew that the absolute barrier to lawlessness was the LAPD. A blue-suited cop would grab you by the collar, shake the mischief out of you, smack you across the butt with his nightstick, or crack your skull if you got too far out of line. The police were the great common denominator of our hustling and hybrid neighborhood. What it lacked in homogeneity, the cops more than made up for with their authority. As a result, I learned to respect the police, and though I was careful not to cross them, I regarded them with admiration, and even awe.

I spent my first nine years in Boyle Heights, and that experience, seen now through the prism of adulthood, served me well later when I lived in Compton. In school and on the streets I learned to deal with every sort of person, from the sons of rabbis to black transplanted Alabama share-croppers to the "wetbacks" who had only recently risked their lives in the deserts along the border to reach America. Their children were my school-mates and my playmates, and from them I absorbed a level of tolerance and unthinking acceptance that proved later in my life to be a rare and valuable gift. In my personal relations and my choice of friends, I never saw color, never heard an accent, never assumed that anyone was any better or worse than me just because of the color of his skin or the way he talked. Boyle Heights was my preparation for my life in Compton.

In 1945, my father returned from the war in Europe with disabling injuries to his lungs, kidneys, and shoulder. He spent two years in a veterans' hospital before he was well enough to come home. During that period I rarely saw him, so much of the bonding experience I should have had with him was lost. My father remained for me a remote, nearly inaccessible figure, rarely affectionate and often critical. Whether it was his nature or the result of his wounds I never knew.

Through my mother's hard work and thrift, and with some help from the GI Bill, by 1950 my parents had saved enough money to buy a house. Boyle Heights and the surrounding areas proved too expensive, but they discovered that houses were affordable in the city of Compton to the south. At that time, Compton was 98 percent white, a tightly knit community dominated by Mormons. There were two Mormon temples in the city, and the mayor, Elder Del Clawson, later served in the U.S. House of Representatives.

Compton had a reputation as a progressive community that welcomed newcomers and valued its independence from Los Angeles. Modest individual houses were springing up in the western part of the city, which real estate agents advertised as being open to "veterans of all races." They were all of a plan, some with two bedrooms and some with three, and selling for nine to ten thousand dollars.

My parents found a house on the corner of 136th Street and Central Avenue in the heart of West Compton and made the down payment. The real estate agent, Mr. Davenport, warned them that the neighborhood was likely to undergo a transformation. He was quite up-front and honest about it, and told my parents that, while the eastern part of Compton was steadfastly white, West Compton was being touted as a future home for lower-middle-class blacks who were hunting jobs in the factories of South L.A.

"Things are going to change here, and soon," he told them as I stood in the parlor of the first real home we had ever owned. But I paid no attention to him. Across from the house, on what became Piru Street, was a helicopter testing ground busy with the exotic shapes of aircraft and the thrum of spinning rotors, and nearby on Central Avenue was a horse farm where cowboys taught kids to ride for fifty cents. After the cramped apartment in Boyle Heights, the prospect of airplanes and horses within walking distance was thrilling beyond my imagination. To my nine-year-

old mind, Compton was a fairyland, a place of wonder and adventure to
rival anything my grandfather had come to California to find.

In 1784, during the Spanish occupation of California, the new king,
Ferdinand VII, deeded seventy-five thousand acres of ranchland, called
Rancho San Pedro, to Juan José Dominguez. It remained a privately held
ranch until the Mexican War, after which American settlers began moving into the area in search of open land and a mild climate. In 1867, a
minister and pedagogue from Virginia named Griffith Dickinson Compton led a group of settlers to the area and created a town, which some
twenty years later was incorporated as a city named after him. Griffith
Compton had a vision of a community of farmers, householders, and schol-
ars that would serve as a model to the Southern California region. He established a school system and a library, as well as a college that grew over the
decades into Compton College, which I would one day attend.

From its founding in 1889 until the year we arrived, 1951, Compton
had been an almost all-white city. Originally an agricultural settlement,
it was a haven for people fleeing the urban sprawl to the north. Its open
fields, trim homesteads, ranches, and farms had proved irresistible to
those seeking a refuge from the increasingly oppressive crush and clamor
of Los Angeles. There had, however, always been a belt of black residents,
stretching along Central Avenue right down from South Central L.A. to
the city of Long Beach. Compton tolerated these hardworking middle-
class blacks, who confined themselves to one small district in the western
part of the city and showed little inclination to move beyond it until
the aftermath of World War II.

It was then that Compton real estate interests began to open up the
northwestern neighborhoods to black veterans and migrants from the
Deep South. What had once been meadows and farmland quickly developed into low-income tract housing, stretching through West Compton
from 127th Street at the southern L.A. border to Rosecrans Avenue along
Central Avenue. This was the very neighborhood into which my parents
moved.

Compton in those days was something like a model community; indeed, in 1952 it was designated an "All-America City" by the National Civic League. It consisted of tidy, well-planned streets and boulevards with palm trees and pin-striped lanes, and single-family houses with landscaped yards, resembling a precocious child's layout of a train platform. Burris, Sloan, and Poinsettia avenues off Compton Boulevard framed a neighborhood of luxurious homes with broad lawns and wrought-iron gates, which came to be known as Compton-Hollywood. The downtown shopping district was lined with trees and fronted with prosperous small businesses, and in the pedestrian walkways there was piped-in music to entertain passersby. To this day I have never heard of another urban commercial district that plays music for the enjoyment of shoppers.

There were two theaters and the only drive-ins in southeastern Los Angeles. The city had its own college, which was prized not just for the quality of its education but for its football teams as well. Compton College was considered to be a farm school for the University of Southern California, since its coach, Hall of Famer Tay Brown, was said to be able to get any Compton College player into USC on his recommendation alone. When I attended the college, my tennis coach was Ken Carpenter, who had won a gold medal in discus at the 1936 Berlin Olympics.

Compton got its nickname "the Hub," because the city was equidistant from Los Angeles and Long Beach, and most of the commercial traffic between the ports of those cities had to pass through. This gave Compton, despite its small size—a mere nine square miles—a cosmopolitan flavor. It was, for example, a center of country and western music. Cowboy bars drew sailors from the naval base at Long Beach, and a local celebrity, Spade Cooley, became a national figure through his televised hootenanny, which was broadcast from a studio in Compton.

Music was always part of the life of the city. In addition to the piped-in music of the downtown district, there were amateur performers on the street corners and in the clubs and malt shops experimenting with new sounds and new dances, a practice that was to flourish in later years. Even in the fifties, Compton was a cradle of musical movements. A local group called the Six Teens scored a nationwide hit with the song "A Casual

Look," and another Compton combo, the Hollywood Argyles, who worked at Bishop's malt shop on Long Beach Boulevard, produced the doo-wop hit "Alley Oop." Later, the fusion group War developed in Compton, spawning such hits as "Low Rider," "Cisco Kid," and "Why Can't We Be Friends?"

It seemed that all the kids of Compton were into some kind of music. My friends and I used to meet on the corner of 134th and Central Avenue to harmonize impromptu doo-wops and "ham bones." One of my best buddies was a bright Hispanic kid named Jesse Sida who lived on Slater Street, a stone's throw from my parents' house. Jesse knew all the latest dances, and he taught me his moves in the local clubs and at the Pike on the pier in Long Beach. We wore three-quarter-length jackets and roll-cuff Levi's, and we slicked our hair into a "waterfall." We bought our bell-bottoms and lavender shirts at Sy Devore's on Melrose (they had to be lavender because of *West Side Story*) and did the Slob, the Stroll, the Watusi, the Bristol Stomp, and the Slauson Shuffle. I became a pretty good dancer, and I learned very quickly that dancing was a great way to meet girls.

One of the girls I met was Lorraine Mayor. I was burning up the floor at the Cinnamon Cinder in Hollywood one night when she asked if she could dance with me. She was a cute little blonde who lived in the exclusive L.A. suburb of Hidden Hills, and she drove her daddy's new white Cadillac to the popular dance clubs. She told me she had never seen a boy who could dance as well as I, and soon we were partnering and winning trophies together. Her father was wealthy, and Lorraine gave me her gasoline credit card so that Jesse Sida and I could drive out to Hidden Hills in my '55 Chevy to pick her up and go dancing.

Above all, Compton was autonomous. It had its own city government, its own police force, its own water and power. Its Mormon fathers were so proud of the city's independence that when the first shopping mall was proposed for the southern Los Angeles region the city council turned it down, fearing that it would detract from the downtown shopping district and draw in too many outsiders from L.A. Still later, when the adjacent city of Carson asked that Compton annex it so that Carson could share in

Compton's prosperity, the city fathers again refused, though Carson was twice the size of Compton and offered a huge potential for expansion of its revenue base. So confident was Compton in those days, and so sure of its integrity and of its future, that it played the role of the unobtainable princess who remained aloof, though courted by suitors from across the Southland.

My family moved into our new house in time for me to enroll at St. Leo's school in the Watts section of Los Angeles. My parents were determined that I would receive a Catholic education, and St. Leo's was the closest parochial school to our home. The irony of this was, of course, that Watts was an almost entirely black community, and I was one of the few white kids at St. Leo's. As I had in Boyle Heights, I again found myself thrown into a culture other than my own, compelled to learn a new jargon, new habits, a new way of thinking. Ironically, however, I met with no discrimination at St. Leo's. This was due, I think, to the fact that the majority of students were Creoles, whose families had migrated to Los Angeles from Louisiana and Mississippi, and who shared my French heritage. To them I was not John Baker but Jean Boulanger, and they accepted me in a way they might not have accepted most white kids.

The other thing that we had in common, of course, was the strictures of the school. Catholic education was not then what it is today. The Sisters of Notre Dame wore the traditional milk bottle habits, with stiff white linen and yards of black crepe, and rosary beads that jangled ominously from their broad leather belts. As with the police, you crossed the nuns at your own risk. Their discipline was total and intolerant, and they enforced it with a level of violence that would be unthinkable today. Stern and iron-faced, the sisters administered beatings with righteous enthusiasm. Yes, they taught us to read and write and respect our elders, but they also put the fear of God into us, a fear that has never quite left me.

Unlike the kids at the local public school, at St. Leo's we developed a respect for authority that became a permanent part of our personalities. To us, disobedience meant sinfulness, and sinfulness would be punished by the nuns in this life, and by the Almighty in the next. So better to shape up now than to face that temporal and eternal retribution.

While I was at St. Leo's, I served as an altar boy. In those days this was a privilege accorded to students who had a record for good behavior and good grades, and who could master and memorize the Latin Mass. We wore black cassocks with starched white surplices, and around our necks we buttoned a tall cellulose collar clasped with a gold stud and tied with an ample black silk bow. Our hair had to be slicked with military precision, our nails scrupulously clean, and we bowed to the Blessed Sacrament on the altar like the minions of a great and silent king.

We also assisted at weddings and funerals and all the other milestones of the Catholic life, and I often was present at the wakes held in the local funeral parlors. Clutching my golden candlestick, I gazed down at the corpses as mute and unmoving as they. Those wakes were my first experience of death, swathed in satin, hung with floral wreaths, and fragrant with the musk of holy incense. It was an image of death that would be violently altered later in my life on the streets of Compton.

Though nearly all my friends at this time were black, few of them were from Compton. Since St. Leo's was in Watts, I began to identify with that neighborhood as much as with my own. In fact, as I grew older, I spent most of my free time in Watts, going to its movie theaters and soda shops, because my pals did not feel comfortable traveling to the all-white commercial district of Compton. In this way, I naturally began to feel closer to the black culture of South Central than to the white world of Compton. It was my black friends in L.A. who first started calling me by my middle name, Ricardo, or Rick, and it has stuck with me ever since.

One thing I learned from my friends in Watts was that the blacks in L.A. had a disdain for the blacks of Compton. They considered themselves to be superior, living as they did in an all-black neighborhood in Los Angeles. The Compton blacks, in their view, had sold out, moving southward in search of escape from the ghetto of Watts. This attitude would later play an important role in the development of the gang cultures in Watts and Compton.

At that time, Watts was about 10 percent Hispanic, and there were sharp divisions between the black and the Latino cultures. It was for this reason, given the fact that I associated almost exclusively with blacks, that the first racial animosity I felt directed at me came from Hispanics. They taunted me in Spanish, not realizing that, since my mother was Latina, I spoke Spanish almost as well as they, and they often challenged me to fight.

The first confrontation was with a kid named Rudy Diaz. He was bigger than me and had a reputation as a wannabe tough guy. He picked some pretense and we "locked asses," and I whipped him pretty soundly. When his older brother Augie saw this, he marched over and started in on me. At that moment, a Creole kid from St. Leo's named Jean Lamoureux stepped in between us. "Rick took your brother fair and square," he told Augie. "So if you're feelin' froggish, I'll stand in for him." Augie backed off, and through Jean, I became adopted by the Creole faction at St. Leo's.

Even in grade school I understood that bullies had to be dealt with quickly and in a language they could not misunderstand, so by the time I was in eighth grade, I was a seasoned street fighter. I began to take boxing lessons at the Boys' Club on 120th and Central, and that gym became my playground. It was there that I developed the confidence that I could hold my own in any one-on-one confrontation. As my boxing skills improved, I participated in backyard smokers, which were impromptu bouts staged by local gamblers in which the fighters did not wear the Boys' Club protective gear. Smokers were bloody, no-holds-barred affairs fought in vacant lots near the club. They were perhaps the best training I could have had for what I would later encounter in the streets of Compton.

Though I was attending school in Watts, I was still living with my parents in Compton, which was even then in transition. As more and more black families moved into the western part of the city, whites began moving out. Some fled to East Compton, which remained a whites-only stronghold, and before long, Central Avenue had become the dividing line between the two halves of the city. All this meant nothing to me, however, since Boyle Heights and Watts had accustomed me to mingling with all types of people. I was neither white nor Hispanic nor black, but in some way, I was all of them. So I counted among my friends and playmates black children, white children, and Latinos.

Among them were many individuals who would later play a role in my career, some for better and some, like Rex and Eddie Pope, Jesse Torres, Luis Lasoya, and Sylvester Scott, for worse—far worse. These were the children with whom I grew up, ran the streets, played stickball, and saw in church every Sunday, and who later became Compton's judges and politicians and leading criminals.

I was a natural athlete and played almost every sport. My real passions, however, were baseball and track. My father was the coach of the Little League team, and when I was old enough, I expected him to let me play. Instead, for reasons I have never understood, he would not even allow me to try out for the team. Though I begged and pleaded and argued, he remained steadfast—I was not going to play Little League ball.

Like many others of his generation, my father was not a hands-on parent, and he rarely supported or expressed approval of me. My mother, on the other hand, was my biggest fan. She attended all my track meets and framed my medals. My father's refusal to let me play baseball broke my heart, though, and marked a turning point in our relationship. It was in protest of that decision that I first began boxing at the Boys' Club in Watts, where I took out my resentment and frustration on the heavy bag and on the other boys I met in the after-hours smokers.

I became something of a star in track and field at St. Leo's, excelling at the high jump and the long jump. I also ran the hundred-yard dash and the 220, and I anchored the 440 relays. This was unusual since I was the only white kid on the team, but I was the fastest of all, and that was why I was chosen to run the final leg. In fact, at one meet, when I brought the baton in first, the judges gave the winners' medals to another team, assuming that, since I was white, I was not running for St. Leo's. Later the meet officials sent a letter to St. Leo's congratulating the team and apologizing for their mistake.

I also played football, both at school and in the rough-and-tumble pickup games in the sandlots of West Compton. Often during those games a scrawny black kid some ten years younger than me would watch longingly from the sidelines. He was too young and too small to play, and so most of the kids ignored him. I felt sorry for him, however, and after the games I stayed behind to throw the ball to him. Every time he caught a pass he would beam with a broad, gap-toothed smile of delight. Sometimes I took him down to the corner to sing doo-wop and jive with my friends. He lived on Piru Street, one block over from my parents' house on Central, and his name was Sylvester Scott. Many years later, he would found the most violent of Compton's black gangs.

Because of my success in track, I was offered a scholarship to Junipero Serra High School in the nearby city of Gardena. Serra was an old and prestigious academy run by the Marist fathers, and the opportunity to attend it free of charge was a great boon to my family. As usual, my mother was thrilled, and my father was guarded in his praise. The summer before my freshman year at Serra, a friend and I were cruising down Central Avenue on his motor scooter when he ran into a truck. I was thrown clear, but my ankle was broken. That was the end not only of my track and field days but of my scholarship at Serra High as well.

In my sophomore year, my parents enrolled me in St. Anthony High School, which was on 7th Street in the southern part of the City of Long Beach. St. Anthony's was a prep school noted for its success in placing its graduates into good colleges around California. My parents were anxious that I have such an opportunity, and though it meant a lengthy bus and trolley ride across Compton and Long Beach, I continued high school at St. Anthony's. It was, I soon discovered, 95 percent white, the mirror image of St. Leo's, and so once again I underwent a cultural shock, having to relate to a whole new class of people and to adjust my values and my behavior accordingly. Since I appeared to be white, I was accepted by the majority students, but most of my friends were black, and I was by heritage Hispanic. So once again my life became a sociological case study in blending different cultures.

On my first day at St. Anthony's, a big, buck-toothed Irish kid named O'Higgins challenged me to a fight. It was, I knew, an initiation into the new school that I had to accept, so I agreed to meet him in the gym at the YMCA in Long Beach. He was all swinging arms and no style, and I dissected him scientifically. When he was bloodied and on his back, I offered him a hand-up. He shook the cotton wool out of his head and gave me a crimson grin. We ended up at the Pike malt shop, where he bought me a root beer float and introduced me to Dick Dale and the Deltones and their surfer music. We remained friends throughout high school.

It was at about this time, the mid-1950s, that the first gang in Compton appeared. The gang formed in the growing black neighborhood of West Compton, and called themselves the Farmers because they wore overalls, a sort of precursor to the later gang gear. They were also called Gasheads, since they processed their hair in the fashion of the time, conked and smeared thick with Vaseline. They were bullies who migrated into Compton from Watts to terrorize the kids in my neighborhood along Central Avenue. Their headquarters were in Will Rogers Park on 103rd Street.

One day, as I was on my way home from school, three of the Farmers confronted me at the corner of 134th and Central and demanded money. There was a chain-link fence behind me, so I backed up against it to prevent them surrounding me. I had no choice but to fight, and though it was three against one, I was determined that, if I was going to go down, I would take one or two of them with me. I dropped my book bag and raised my fists, challenging them to come on.

Just at that moment I heard a voice from nearby. "Lay off him." It was a black kid, a little older than me. The Farmers turned to look at him. He was not big, but there was a calm determination about him that got their attention.

"Whatever you have with him, you have with me," he said. "So just lay off, and everything will be cool."

The three gangbangers hesitated, and then they walked away. I thanked the kid and asked why he had intervened.

"I see you around when I go to visit my godfather," he told me. "Mr. Garcia." The Garcias were the only other Hispanic family on my block. "My name's Howard Edwards." He put out his hand and I shook it.

"Thanks," I told him.

"C'mon, man," he said, "I'm going your way, I'll walk you home."

I came to know Howard Edwards very well. He was a bright, hard-working kid who had big ambitions for himself. A Creole whose family had moved south from the Crenshaw District of Los Angeles, he had hazel eyes and wavy brown hair, and his complexion was so light that he could have passed for Latino. We became friends, and the stories of our lives in Compton intertwined.

As Compton continued to change, more gangs sprouted up. By the late fifties, in addition to the Farmers, the Slausons and the Huns had appeared. The Slausons formed in South Central L.A. along Slauson Avenue, and like the Farmers, they began raiding down into Compton, preying on the local kids. The Huns were also a South L.A. gang, larger and much more aggressive than the Farmers.

These early black gangs took as their model the older Latino gangs of Los Angeles, affecting their gangland style, wearing baggy pants and beanies, adopting their jargon, and tagging the gang's territory with graffiti. Among the expressions the blacks borrowed from Spanish was *"chinga tu madre,"* which they reversed and translated as "motherfucker," and it entered black gang culture permanently. As the gangs proliferated and their numbers swelled, they became more territorial, and more violent.

As Compton shifted from white to black, racial tensions grew. The gangs were part of this, but race hostility was not confined to the streets. In 1955, the Compton Unified School District, which was dominated by whites, created Centennial High School in an effort to prevent the blacks of northwest Compton integrating Compton High. As the black population increased, however, this proved to be impossible. More blacks began enrolling at Compton High, and it was there, in 1959, that the city experienced its first race riot. The trigger seemed innocent enough: the selection of the homecoming queen.

By late 1958, Compton High was three-quarters white and one-quarter black. Every year, the student body voted for a girl who would preside over the homecoming celebrations, and every year they chose a white girl. In the voting for the 1959 queen, four white girls and one black girl competed for the honor. The entire black student body voted for the black girl, while the white girls split the majority vote. The result was that the black girl was narrowly elected. Almost immediately, racial tensions flared. White student body leaders began urging their fellow students to boycott the homecoming dance, and someone painted the words NOBODY ATTEND

THE JUNGLE HOP on the front wall of the school. Fights began to break out, and it was not long before the gangs got involved, some even coming from South L.A. to join in. The entire school became a battleground, and the police had to be called in.

The problem did not end there. White gangs began to invade Compton from South Bay in response to the homecoming riot. Calling themselves the Spook Hunters, they were openly racist thugs from surrounding white cities who attacked and brutalized black kids and working people in the parks between the west side and South Central L.A. As their violence spread toward the northern border, the Spook Hunters came into conflict with the Huns, and the first interracial gang brawls erupted.

Instead of dealing with the growing problem of racial hostility, the city council and the school district decided to further separate the races. In the aftermath of the riot at Compton High, they built a third high school, Dominguez Compton, on the far eastern edge of the city, where the population was still entirely white. As a result, many of the white students at Compton High moved over to Dominguez, and their places were taken by more and more black students.

The lines of demarcation between the races in Compton were now being drawn for everyone to see: West Compton was becoming a black area, while East Compton was fortifying itself as a white stronghold. It was a pattern that would dominate the life of Compton for decades, and determine its character and its destiny.

White Flight, Black Rage

By 1960, Compton was in flux. Blacks had expanded out of their northwest enclave and had moved toward Rosecrans Avenue and even farther south to Compton Boulevard. By 1963, the black area had crossed Central Avenue and extended as far east as Wilmington. Within the space of twelve years, since my family had relocated to Compton, the city had gone from 95 percent white to nearly 40 percent black. This fact precipitated one of the most important sociological events in Compton history: white flight.

Before 1963, it was not illegal to discriminate in housing in California. Blacks and other people of color had no right to buy houses in neighborhoods where they were not wanted. This changed when the Rumford Fair Housing Act, sponsored by the first black to be elected to the state legislature from Northern California, was signed into law. Though it met with sharp opposition, the Fair Housing Act was upheld by the courts, and every neighborhood in the state was suddenly opened to minorities. This fact had a powerful impact on the city of Compton.

Until this time, the families and real estate agents in East Compton, protected by legal discrimination in housing, had worked diligently to keep blacks out of the east side neighborhoods. Now that that protection was gone, a kind of panic set in. Real estate agents began sending flyers to homeowners warning that if they did not sell, and sell quickly, the value of their properties would plummet. This practice, called blockbusting, had an immediate effect. White families rushed to sell their homes, and to flee the city for the newly incorporated areas of Bellflower, Paramount, and Santa Fe Springs. The dam began to burst in 1964, and the Watts riots of the following year turned the flow into a flood.

Another turning point occurred in 1967 when the first black family moved into Compton-Hollywood. Dr. Ross Miller Jr. was a well-known surgeon and civic leader who became the first black president of the Los Angeles Surgical Society. He and his wife and children had not been in their new home a week before they were awakened in the middle of the night by shouts, jeers, and the lurid glow of flames. When Dr. Miller went to the window, he saw a massive cross burning in his front yard. Masked white men hurled curses and rocks at the house until the police arrived. Dr. Miller was a courageous man, though, a pioneer in spirit, and he refused to be intimidated. He stayed in his home, and in later years became an important community leader and political reformer in Compton.

One group that was immune from the panic was the Latinos. Never a large population in Compton, they were confined mostly to a northern part of the city known as the Latino Corridor. When white flight started, and black families began moving into West Compton, the Hispanics remained where they were. In one of those ironies of racial perceptions, blacks chose to move only into white neighborhoods, believing that culturally and linguistically they had more in common with whites than they did with Hispanics.

This created a Latino buffer zone between Compton and South Central L.A., a fact that helped prevent the Watts riots of 1965 from spreading into Compton. When the violence broke out in South L.A., some one hundred to one hundred and fifty rioters attempted to cross Mona Boulevard and enter Compton. To do this they had to penetrate the Latino Corridor between Watts and the black areas of Compton. By that time the Hispanics of Compton had formed their own gangs, the most notorious of which was Largo 36. As the rioting threatened to spill over into Compton, the police were tipped off to the fact that the Latino gangbangers were planning to ambush the rioters when they crossed over Mona. Knowing that they did not have enough officers to stop it, the CPD did nothing to prevent the ambush. The Largos met the black rioters with guns and knives, and several of them were killed before they retreated back across Mona into Watts. It was largely for this reason that Compton, unlike Watts, was not burned to the ground.

In 1961, I enrolled at Compton College, where I majored in sociology. This was a deliberate choice on my part, since I was seeing my city being transformed, and I wanted to learn about the forces that shaped such a transformation, and its possible outcomes. My goal was to acquire a master's degree in sociology and become a social worker in Compton. I was determined that if my city was undergoing a radical change, I wanted to be able to help manage that change.

Even Compton College itself soon proved to be a field of study. The year that I matriculated, black students endeavored to integrate the campus fraternities and were turned away on the grounds that only frat members could invite new pledges. When the college administration ordered the fraternities to admit blacks, they held a rally at which their leader, a student named John Foster, announced that, rather than integrate, they would move off campus. The state legislature responded by passing a law eliminating the practice of joining a fraternity by invitation only. Foster made good on his threat, and the white frats left campus. As a result, racial tensions rose inside the college.

One of the student leaders who attempted to mitigate this hostility was Howard Edwards, the boy who had saved me from a beating by the Farmers. A skillful negotiator and a powerful speaker, Edwards became a leading advocate for compromise within the student body. On the other side of the issue was a fiery black girl named Shondra Givens. A sociology major like me, Shondra was a radical who combined idealism with extremism on just about every subject. Because of this I found her fascinating, and I cultivated a friendship with her. We were both excited about the changes taking place in Africa and the United States. We talked of joining the Peace Corps together and working in the Third World, and we dated for a few months.

Another of my friends at Compton College at that time was a boy named Jimmy Mansfield. Jimmy was a black student who had come to Compton from Philadelphia, and though he was bright and well-intentioned, he had difficulty fitting in. He was a nerd who was not able to adapt to the language and culture of the new world of Compton. I knew what it was like to find yourself thrust into an alien environment, and so I made a point of befriending him. I even convinced Jesse Sida and my other dancing buddies to take him with us to the clubs in Hollywood to meet girls.

While I was in college, I worked part-time at the Compton Drive-In, which was located on the far eastern side of the city. Because of this, I was able to experience firsthand the panic and disruptive effects of white flight. The racial division of the city was becoming absolute. The entire time I worked at the drive-in, not a single black was hired, and I never saw a black person welcomed in to watch a movie. It was becoming clear to me that the situation within Compton could not go on for much longer. The blacks were moving inexorably east, displacing white families who had lived there for generations. The whites, on their side, were either abandoning the city altogether or fighting to preserve their own enclaves within it.

There was a cultural war brewing, and it sometimes erupted into violence. The neighborhoods were becoming more isolated from one another, the gangs were growing, and the population was in flux, further destabilizing the cohesiveness of the city. All this strengthened my determination to undertake a career in social work, in the hope that I might be able to help prevent the city from collapsing into chaos.

By 1963, when I graduated from Compton College, that chaos was already beginning. The Compton Cup, an invitational track meet featuring some of the best athletes from around the country, had to be canceled because of crime and racial violence at the stadium. The Compton Christmas parade, which my family had attended every year since 1951, began to suffer from the same sort of disruption. Eventually, the parade was abandoned altogether when the float carrying Santa Claus was fired upon by gang members, and the man portraying Santa was shot. Thus, two major events in the life of Compton became victims of the tension and instability that were ripping the city apart.

The nation, likewise, was undergoing profound change. The assassination of President John F. Kennedy was a blow to everyone who embraced his youthful spirit and his vision for an America that would be a more humane society and a force for world peace. I was an avid student of African liberation movements, and I thought that I could see in my own city some of the possibilities as well as the pitfalls of the sudden and radical social change. When the Belgians pulled out of the Congo in 1960, for example, they left a vacuum in qualified leadership that threw the new nation into anarchy. Indigenous leaders who flooded into the vacuum were either extremists or corrupt, and the country quickly dissolved into civil war. I feared that something like this might happen in Compton if the transition from a white dominated culture to a black one was not managed skillfully.

I enrolled at Long Beach State University in 1964 to continue my sociology studies. By this time the racial balance in Compton was beginning to tilt toward the blacks. Whole neighborhoods were being broken up, and in the wake of white flight the economic infrastructure of the city was deteriorating. Sears Roebuck, for example, long a pillar of Compton's economy, and the chain's second most profitable store, was forced to close because of the rising crime rate. Other major chain stores such as Penney's and Woolworth's, and many white-owned businesses like the row of auto dealers on Long Beach Boulevard, also began to disappear, eroding Compton's tax base and lowering its standard of living. What had once been a city that was so prosperous it could turn down outside businesses was now starving for them. Compton was becoming a fragmented and often frightening place.

With the murder of President Kennedy, I lost my desire to serve in the

Peace Corps. At the same time, America's involvement in the war in Vietnam began to escalate, and I felt the need to do something to help defend what I saw as my country's interests. Consequently, I put my education on hold and volunteered for the Marine Corps Reserve. From Peace Corps to Marine Corps in just one year—my life was changing as surely as was the life of my city.

I joined the 23rd Regiment, 4th Marine Division, which was stationed on North Alameda Street just south of the border with Watts. In addition to doing my patriotic duty, I thought that the Corps would teach me the discipline and focus I needed to better serve the future of my city.

In the summer of 1965 I was at boot camp in San Diego, and I returned often to Compton to visit my family and friends. My girlfriend at the time, Judy Ward, lived in the Bell Gardens–Cudahy section of Los Angeles, which we called "Billy Goat Acres" since most of the residents, including her family, were from Oklahoma. Judy was my first serious romance, and I saw her as often as I could. She had long raven hair and amber eyes, and she was bright and funny and shared my passion for dancing.

We soon became regulars at all the hot dance clubs, like the Buddha, the Peppermint Twist, and Gazzari's in Hollywood. Our favorite hangout was the Knight's Club in South Gate, where we did all the latest dances to doo-wop hits such as "Earth Angel," "Only You," "Da Doo Ron Ron," and "Duke of Earl." Judy and I were a natural couple, and we won nearly every competition we entered. When the Beatles and the British invaded in 1964, we adapted our style to their music and had even more fun. It did not take very long for me to realize that I was in love for the first time in my life.

In August of 1965 I was on duty with the Marines at Camp Pendleton north of San Diego, and I returned home for a few days' leave. Judy was dancing in a go-go cage at the Knight's Club, and I drove straight there to see her. When she spotted me walking into the club in my khaki trops, she was so excited that she jumped out of the cage and threw herself into my arms. Every minute that I did not spend at my parents' I spent with Judy, either in the dance clubs or at her family's home.

It was while I was visiting Judy at her parents' house on August 11, 1965, that the Watts riots broke out. From the backyard we could see the towers of smoke rising from the neighborhoods to the north. The news on television was cataclysmic: It seemed as though the entire southern portion of Los Angeles had gone mad and was devouring itself in a storm of manic violence.

The National Guard was mobilized, and my marine unit was ordered to report to its duty stations. I jumped into my '55 Chevy and raced down the Long Beach Freeway to the border of Compton, where I was stopped by a National Guard roadblock. The freeway from that point on was under siege, one of the Guardsmen told me, and no cars were being allowed through. I explained that I was a marine and that I had to report to the reserve headquarters on Alameda.

"No cars means no cars," the Guardsman answered.

I told him that if I didn't report I would be considered AWOL. "And the marines aren't giving anybody any freebies," I added.

The Guardsman opened the barricade and let me pass, with a warning to be on the lookout for snipers on the rooftops. "Be sure to keep your lights out," he told me. "Good luck."

The 710 Freeway was dark, deserted, and eerily quiet. I drove carefully but quickly, watching for any suspicious or sudden movements along the route. I got off at Rosecrans and made my way across East Compton toward Alameda. The streets were busy with cars, many of them "hogs," the hulking Roadmaster Buicks that were the favorite ride of the gang-bangers. They were heaped with stolen goods—televisions, furniture, rugs—which had been looted from the storefronts across the border in Watts. As I made my way into the heart of the city, a shot rang out over my head, and a bullet smacked into the sidewalk. I ducked and speeded up. A few blocks farther on, another shot whizzed by my windshield.

Before reporting in to headquarters I had to swing by my house to pick up my gear, so I crossed Alameda and headed for Central. As I did, a car cut in front of me. I was sure I was about to be hijacked, since mine was the only white face on the streets. A figure jumped out of the car and hurried toward me, waving and yelling, "Hey, Rick! Rick!"

It was Rex Pope, my neighbor and sandlot buddy. He was excited, gesticulating, juiced by the mayhem. "If you need anything, TVs or clothes or anything, I got it!" he shouted. I told him I had to get to my parents' house. "Just let me know, man; whatever you need, you can have it right now."

I thanked him quickly and drove on.

Central Avenue, where I had lived most of my life, seemed like a different place. Ghostly with lurid light from the fires, the cinders pouring down like a demonic snowfall, the neighborhood was now an armed camp. Residents sat on their porches or stood in the streets, all of them with guns, all prepared to defend their homes against the rioters. As I drove up to my house, several of them approached my car.

"What the hell you doing out driving around?" they wanted to know. I explained as quickly as I could. "Well, you're as like to get shot by us as them," I was told. "Get in your house and stay there."

I wished that I could, so that I might help these people to protect my parents from the violence that was raging fourteen blocks away. Instead, after making sure that my mother and dad were all right, I gathered up my gear and ran outside again.

I backtracked to Alameda and turned north toward the reserve headquarters. Not far ahead was El Segundo Boulevard, the border between Watts and Compton. The whole area north of El Segundo was flaring with a dirty white and yellow light from the fires that had already consumed much of the neighborhood. Against their primal glow I could see the silhouettes of rioters, most carrying clubs and looted goods, many with guns. It was like a scene of a pagan ritual from a Hollywood B movie— but this was real, and it was terrifying.

When I reached the reserve headquarters, most of the unit had already assembled. The first thing I noticed was how heavily armed the marines were. In addition to their issued M-14s, they were carrying shotguns, .38s, .45s. and .44 Magnums. Later I learned that, on their way to the headquarters building, they had bought out all the gun shops in the surrounding areas, and, in some cases, had looted extra ammunition. We also broke into our own armory and appropriated all the weapons, as well as 7.62

armor-piercing rounds for the M-14s. We were determined that if we were ordered into the streets to confront the rioters, we would outgun them even if we could not outman them.

By now the riot had begun to spill across the border into the extreme northeast section of Compton. The first target that the rioters attacked was the Safeway supermarket on Tamarind Avenue across the street from our building. We could see them smashing the windows and looting the place, and we knew that it was only a matter of time before they set fire to the building. This fire would not only spread to the adjacent structures, it would attract the attention of the rioters still in Watts, a signal for them to move south.

No one had ever seen anything like this. Our captain, whose name was Bosworth, had no idea what to do, and so a handful of the marines, all of whom were from Compton, went up onto the roof of the building armed with M-14s. While the rest of us manned the windows with rifles and pistols, these marines took up sniper positions and began firing into the Safeway store. Some of the rioters had guns, and they returned the fire, peppering our building with bullets. For a few horrible moments a gun battle raged across Tamarind, between the supermarket and the Marine Corps headquarters. Soon, however, the rioters had had enough, and they retreated back into Watts.

To this day I do not know whether anyone was hit, but it is entirely possible. The official death toll from the six days of violence was thirty-four rioters killed by police and National Guard, out of a total of fifty dead. Thus, sixteen deaths were never accounted for. It is possible that some of those at least were shot by marines of the 23rd Regiment who had taken it on themselves to protect their city.

The Watts riots were the worst in Los Angeles history, and their exact cause has never really been determined. Poverty, poor housing, and high unemployment clearly played a role in fueling racial resentment in the all-black community. When on August 11 three black residents were arrested by the Highway Patrol, that resentment boiled over into the streets.

From my perspective in the marine fortress on the perimeter, it was clear to me that the lead in the violence was being taken by criminals, especially by gang members from the Slausons and the Huns. These thugs took advantage of the racial tensions and swarmed into the streets, beating innocent bystanders, creating mayhem, and setting fires. Behind them, other criminals fanned out across the area to loot businesses and settle old scores. In my view, it was a case of social injustice providing a cover for widespread criminal activity.

The riots made a powerful impression on me. Nearly a thousand buildings had been destroyed, and some fifty people were dead. If Los Angeles, with all of its resources, could not prevent or even control such an outbreak of criminality, I thought, what did the future hold for Compton? Ours was a small city—scarcely seventy-five thousand people—with a mere 130 policemen. Already, the gangs of Compton far outnumbered the police, and the stew of racial tension and rising crime had been brewing for years. If Compton were ever to explode as Watts had done, I realized, the violence might well destroy the city.

The Watts riots upset my idealistic plans for my future. In their wake I found myself uncertain about what I ought to do. I considered going back to college, getting a degree, and teaching high school history. I had always loved history, especially of the Greeks, the Romans, and the wild warrior tribes that swept across Western Europe. What was more, I was in love with Judy Ward, although I was also dating a young Jewish girl named Kitty whom I had met through one of my cousins.

I held a few odd jobs before going to work for the post office in Compton. It paid well, but I was uncomfortable with the bureaucracy and the routine, and the prospect of having to work for forty years before I could retire on a government pension was not appealing to me. The job did have one important advantage, however: I was a special delivery mail carrier, which took me into virtually every neighborhood in the city. Before long I knew all the boulevards, streets, and alleys in Compton and had met most of the business owners, as well as hundreds and hundreds of residents.

I had made up my mind to marry Judy, but before I could ask her, Kitty informed me that she was pregnant. It broke my heart, but I told Judy that I felt I had to do "the honorable thing" and marry Kitty, which I did in

1966. She was just eighteen, and neither of us was ready for marriage, let alone for parenthood. Then, in an ironic and tragic twist, Judy told me that she, too, had been pregnant, but had terminated the pregnancy when I got married. The news devastated me, for Judy was, and remains, the love of my life—and now she was gone.

Kitty and I rented an apartment on Santa Fe Avenue on the east side of Compton. Her father was an LAPD sergeant, and I spent a lot of time talking with him about his job and about the challenges of police work. In the meantime, my old pal Howard Edwards had joined the Compton PD and was also a sergeant. Because of my relationships with these two men an idea was forming in my mind: I began to consider becoming a policeman.

Three events made my decision for me. The first was the assassination of Martin Luther King Jr. and the heightening of racial tension that provoked. The second was the murder of Senator Robert Kennedy, for whom I had just voted in the California primary. The third was the birth of our daughter, Michelle Christine. I felt not only that I had to do better than a postal worker's salary to support my new family but also that I had to do something to help my city. I had survived the rigors of the Marine Corps; I was a fairly good boxer; I was impatient with routine and the predictability of a conventional job. I craved adventure; I thirsted for a challenge. I wanted to test myself—my courage and my commitment—and I wanted to serve my city.

So, in June of 1968, I applied and was accepted as a recruit by the Compton Police Department. It was a decision that would change my life forever.

Part of the Uniform;
The Golden Garter

Until 1967, the city of Compton had its own police academy. Considering that there were never more than 150 officers in the CPD, this was an amazing fact. The LAPD, the L.A. Sheriff's Office, and all of the local police forces in the area made use of three police academies, while Compton recruits attended their own. Then the Compton Academy was closed, and all future cadets were sent to the Sheriff's Academy in East Los Angeles. When I joined, therefore, I was in only the second group of Compton cadets to attend the LASO training facility.

The program lasted sixteen weeks and included law and judicial procedure, weapons and tactics, physical and mental training, chain of command, criminology, basic psychology, and community relations. It was rigorous, and of the nearly two hundred cadets who enrolled with me, about a quarter dropped out. My military training served me well, and I got through the first ten weeks. Then I was called to report for my regular reserve duty with the Marine Corps.

The police department appealed the summons on the grounds that I was midway through my training, but the marines do not wait. I left the academy and reported to Camp Pendleton. When I got back, the rest of my class was far ahead of me. For a time it looked as if I would have to begin over again with the next class, but a veteran Compton detective, Lieutenant Richard Bidwell, came to my aid.

Dick Bidwell had conducted the background check on me when I applied for the force. In the course of it, he had befriended my mother, and had remained in touch with her. He had gone so far as to pick her up at our home one morning and drive her to work in Los Angeles to ask how she felt about her son becoming a Compton policeman. It was a gentle gesture by a cop who had a reputation as one of the toughest on the force. When Bidwell found out about my dilemma, he offered to catch me up on my training personally. For nearly three weeks, in his spare time, he taught me hand-to-hand combat, baton work, and how to shoot and qualify on the firing range. He was my private tutor, and I could not have had a better one. Because of him I graduated with my class, and though Dick Bidwell was not there to see it, having accepted a job with a small department in the San Joaquin Valley, I owed my success to him.

While I was waiting to return to the academy, I enrolled in a mini training course at the Compton police station under Dick Bidwell's supervision. This was my first hands-on experience of police work, and while it was invaluable preparation, it proved to be a mixed blessing.

Los Angeles Airways operated a helicopter shuttle service between L.A. International Airport and Disneyland. Each chopper could carry as many as twenty-five people on the fifteen-minute flight. On the morning of August 14, 1968, I was doing a ride-along with Dick Bidwell near Lueders Park when the Disneyland shuttle passed overhead. Suddenly there was a loud pop, a rotor blade went spinning off, and the chopper plummeted into the park. Instantly it burst into flames. Bidwell and I raced to the scene.

The front section of the chopper lay in the middle of the park near the playground. It was completely engulfed, the 100-octane gasoline burning ferociously. I could see the pilot lying half out of the cockpit, his head on fire. He was still alive, but it was impossible to get to him. He was a hero: Despite the lost rotor, he had managed to steer the chopper into the only open area in the neighborhood. No one on the ground was injured, but it was clear that everyone inside the helicopter must be dead.

The chopper's tail section lay at the edge of the park. Two police officers spotted a stewardess lying in the wreckage. She seemed to have survived the crash—her blond hair was not even ruffled—but when they pulled her free of the twisted metal, only the top half of her body came out. One of these two officers was a second-year patrolman named Dominic Rutigliano, whom I would shortly meet.

When the fire trucks had finally extinguished the flames, and we were able to move closer to the wreck, we found a scene of pathetic horror. Twenty-one people had been killed—most burned to death. Many were still strapped in their seats, among them more than a dozen children. The smell of burning flesh was overpowering, but what was even worse was the sight of tiny body parts, severed and smoldering.

Though I was not yet on the force or even in uniform, Dick Bidwell assigned me to cordon off the crash site and keep away the curious. For the next few hours I patrolled the perimeter with uniformed Compton cops, telling people to stay back and shooing away the packs of dogs that kept darting into the mangled wreckage to seize bits of smoking flesh. It was my introduction to police work, and I could not have had a grimmer, more melancholy one.

It had been a point of pride with the L.A. Sheriff's Office that one of their cadets always graduated first in the class. This was almost inevitable, since in any given class over 150 cadets were LASO recruits, while the rest came from Glendale, Pasadena, Torrance, Beverly Hills, and other communities. In my class, only seven of us were from Compton. Yet, when the final point tallies were taken, one of our cadets, Grover Cleveland Boden, a blond, blue-eyed ex-marine, graduated at the top of the class. It was the first time in the history of the academy that a sheriff's deputy had not taken the top prize. Sheriff Peter J. Pitchess was so impressed with "Sonny" Boden's accomplishment that he presented him with a nickel-plated .45 automatic and offered him a job as a sheriff's deputy in any district he chose in Los Angeles County. Having been a member of the elite Recon Marines, Sonny told Pitchess, "No thank you, sir; I prefer to serve in a war zone."

Calling Compton a war zone was not overstating the matter. It was a time of great upheaval in the country, and these changes were being reflected in Compton. Black consciousness was on the rise, and the image of black people in the popular culture was changing radically. Gone were Amos and Andy and Stepin Fetchit, to be replaced by Shaft and Super Fly. Young blacks were demanding a level of respect that was strange and threatening to the white establishment. This demand found its most public and militant forms in the Black Power movement, Black Nationalism, and the Black Panther Party.

The Panthers had formed in Oakland in 1966 under the leadership of Bobby Seale and Huey Newton. Their political program called for autonomy for black neighborhoods, which meant, among other things, self-defense against the white-dominated police forces. To enforce this self-defense, the Panthers armed themselves heavily, and in 1967 they marched into the state capitol in Sacramento brandishing rifles, shotguns, and pistols to protest a proposed ban on citizens carrying weapons. This was a direct challenge to the white power structure that achieved much publicity and encouraged many young blacks to join the Panthers. By the time I started with the CPD, the party's membership had grown to over five thousand, and it had spread to a dozen cities across the nation. With its majority black population, Compton was bound to become fertile ground for the Panthers. This fact would play a large part in my early career as a police officer.

I joined the Compton Police Department on June 20, 1968, but I was still an active member of the Marine Corps Reserve, and the war in Vietnam was very much a part of our lives. During that summer, the Tet Offensive was raging, and President Lyndon B. Johnson decided to send a hundred thousand additional troops to Vietnam, including sixty-two thousand reservists. My unit got the call, and it looked as if my career as a police officer might end before it had begun. By this time I was a platoon sergeant, in charge of thirty-six men. We were inoculated against dozens of diseases, issued our ammunition, and told to report to the Port of Long Beach for transshipment to Vietnam.

When word of the troop increase leaked out, it set off a chain reaction of public protest and even violence that boiled over from the streets into the halls of power. Candidates opposed to the war sprang onto the political scene, and demonstrations shut down universities, government buildings, and even Washington, D.C., itself. All this convinced President Johnson not to seek reelection, and it also resulted in the cancellation of our orders. So, at the last moment, I was spared a trip to Vietnam, and I returned to Compton to begin my training duties.

The Compton Police Department that I entered in 1968 was overwhelmingly white and made up almost entirely of officers who were longtime residents of the city. Of the 130 policemen in Compton, fewer than ten were nonwhites. This minority was split about evenly between black and Latino officers. Although the city was now 50 percent black, the mayor, the city council, the city manager, the police chief, and the upper ranks of the department were still white. In fact, there was only one black police lieutenant, my old friend Howard Edwards. There were no women on the force, and there had only ever been one, an Officer Stroud, who had worked in the Juvenile Division and had not been allowed to wear a uniform.

Like any other organization, the CPD tended to be divided into cliques, which originally followed the lines of the work shifts, though later they would form along racial and political lines. The day shift, from 8:00 A.M. to 4:00 P.M., was made up of older veterans of the force, men who were settled and had families, and who preferred the hours when relatively little was happening. Likewise, the graveyard shift, from midnight until 8:00 A.M., was mostly comprised of senior officers nearing retirement, who chose to work the quietest hours of the day. It was on the P.M. shift, between 4:00 and midnight, that most of the violent crime took place and an officer was likely to see the most action. It was the ambition of many of the rookies, myself included, to be assigned to the P.M. shift.

This shift was made up exclusively of white officers. They formed a kind of club, which was variously known as the Cowboys, the Rough Riders, or, most commonly, the Dirty Dozen after the hit movie of the time. Their leaders were Sergeant Walt Hartman and Sergeant Bob Stover, and among their ranks were some of the most famous, or notorious, officers of the CPD: Frank Brower, John Soisson, Paul Herpin, Julio Hernandez, Bob Kuhel, Dave Hall, Barry Case, Larry Merchant, and Bill St. Onge.

St. Onge, a small, compact, tightly wound veteran officer, was a member of the CPD's French mafia. It was amazing how many Compton cops were of French descent, either Creoles from the Crenshaw district of L.A. or Cajuns from Louisiana, many of whom spoke French, some fluently. The fact that my name was originally Boulanger and that I spoke a little French gave me an advantage.

Bill St. Onge had a reputation as one of the most aggressive, physical cops on the force. He had trained in the traditional French fighting art of savate, and he used his feet and his elbows as his primary weapons. Because of his reputation he was often challenged by would-be tough guys; more often than not, he would knock them out with one blow from an elbow.

St. Onge was known as one of the few cops who could walk alone into Sonny's Pool Hall at 500 West Rosecrans Avenue. Sonny's was like a level of Dante's hell, a dark, claustrophobic, stench-thick place where the worst of Compton's criminals congregated. There were fights, stabbings, and shootings at Sonny's nearly every night. When Bill St. Onge strode in, though, everything stopped; the creeps put down their drinks and pool cues and lined up to be frisked. One night I went into Sonny's with St. Onge to do a routine check. As usual, everyone spread-eagled against the wall—except this time, a huge black man named John Bonner, who styled himself "the baddest dude in Compton," refused to move. St. Onge ordered him to get up.

"If you didn't have that uniform on," Bonner growled, "I'd kick your white ass."

St. Onge never took his eyes off Bonner as he removed his badge, belt, and shirt and handed them to me. Stripped to the waist, he said to Bonner,

"Come on, motherfucker . . . outside." They went into the alley behind Sonny's while the rest of the thugs watched from windows in the back. In less than half a minute, St. Onge had knocked Bonner unconscious.

The real leader of the Dirty Dozen was Dominic Rutigliano, one of the officers who had pulled the severed body of the stewardess from the Disney chopper crash. A big, thickset, taciturn Italian, he had a reputation as one of the best cops in Compton, and like St. Onge, he commanded absolute respect from the city's criminals. Though he was solicitous, even soft-hearted toward citizens, Rutigliano, known as Rut, was absolutely ruthless with bad guys. It was Rut who set the style and tone of the Dirty Dozen, and I knew from my first day on the force that I wanted to be part of his crew.

I was in luck, since the training partner to whom I was assigned was Frank Brower. Brower had been on the force for only a year and a half, but he had become part of the Dirty Dozen, and he threw me in at the deep end by taking me for my training rides on the P.M. shift. This was my chance, and I was determined not to blow it. I asked him what I had to do to be accepted by the Dozen, and he explained very matter-of-factly that I had to prove two things: that I was tough, and that I could keep my mouth shut.

"Keep it shut about what?" I asked him.

He shrugged. "Maybe you see something that isn't exactly department procedure," he replied. "Something that could get a guy into trouble. You keep your mouth shut about that."

It was my introduction to the cops' code of silence, which, though unwritten, was ironclad.

On my first day of duty, I arrived early at the station so that I would have plenty of time to change into my uniform. I double-checked myself in the mirror, making sure that my buttons were shining and my hat was straight. As a newcomer, I was not yet entitled to crush the brim in the style of the veterans, so it haloed my head like a decorative blue saucer. As I regarded myself in the mirror I could not help but think, *I'm a cop, or at least I look like one. I'm a real cop going on patrol.* I was more than a little anxious;

I wanted to prove myself, to do a good job, and above all, not to do anything stupid.

I walked with Brower to our car, unit 3, assigned to the east side. I asked him what I should do, how I should handle myself.

"Pay attention," he grunted, "and don't say anything. Just do what I do. If I get out of the car, you get out. If I walk up on somebody, you back me up. Don't say anything to anyone on the street; don't touch the radio. And ask questions. If you don't understand something, don't guess."

I asked if there was anything else.

"Yeah," he said. "Listen. Listen and follow instructions. That's where most rookies screw up. If I tell you to do something, do it exactly as I tell you, when I tell you to do it."

By this time we had reached the car, a black-and-white '66 Chevy. As Brower opened the driver's door, he added one more thing—"car integrity."

"What's that mean?" I asked.

"Whatever happens inside this car, whatever anybody says or does in here, stays in here. You got it? You never, *never,* discuss what goes on inside your patrol unit."

That first night on patrol is a blur to me now. I tried to watch and listen and absorb everything I could. Brower was a brilliant cop; indeed, to me he seemed like Superman. We did not have many calls, but he handled them with a confidence, even an insouciance, that I thought miraculous. I endeavored to carry myself like him, to affect that careful yet careless authority that seemed to elicit respect automatically. It was a quality I had been told about in the academy called "command presence"—the ability to walk into any situation and take control.

By the end of our shift, I was exhausted but happy.

When we turned in the car, Frank Brower remarked, "You did okay."

That was all I needed to hear.

I was too excited and wrought up to go home and sleep, so I drove into the neighboring city of Gardena and stopped at the first bar I came to. I went in and sat down alone and ordered a drink to celebrate. As I sipped it, feeling flushed and satisfied with myself, I looked around at the other midnight patrons also ending their shifts, or just looking for a clean, well-lighted place, and I thought, *If you only knew what I did today.*

I was a cop.

Frank Brower had told me about the CPD's code of silence, which was as strict as the omertà of the Mafia. He had said that proving you could keep it was a key to being a cop, and a prerequisite for joining the Dirty Dozen. I was eager to prove myself, and it was not long before the chance was given to me—in fact, forced upon me.

One night, early in my training, some of the P.M. cops recovered a stolen Buick in South Park on the east side of Compton. It had been abandoned by joyriders who had stripped everything of value from it. The procedure in recovering a stolen car was to fill out a 180 form, which listed the condition of the car and its contents, before a tow truck was called. Usually, even though it was illegal to remove anything from a stolen car, the cops went through it first and took whatever it contained that they wanted—money, tires, radio, a gun.

In this case, there was nothing left in the car except a few eight-track tapes in the glove box. Dominic Rutigliano was the senior officer on the scene, and he removed these tapes and considered them a moment. Then he turned to me. "Here," he said, "these are yours."

He kept his eyes on me as he handed them over. It was an intimidating gaze. The tapes were of very little value, a few bucks each, and I had no use for them. Nevertheless, I knew what the gesture meant: *Can you keep your mouth shut?* If I took them, I would be breaking both the law and department regulations. If I refused, I might never be accepted by the cops of the P.M. shift.

I took the tapes and said nothing.

Rutigliano told me to fill out the 180, which I did back at the station, leaving out the eight-tracks. Then, on my way home that night, I dropped them into a trash can. I had passed my first test.

There were other practices, I learned, that fell under the code of silence. For example, there were four tow yards in the city that we could call to remove stolen or wrecked vehicles. Every such call meant business for these yards, and so, when the officer taking the report put in the call, he was doing the owner of the yard a favor. In return for this favor, the tow truck owner was expected to put money into the officer's pocket. Then, at Christmas, the tow companies all chipped in and bought cases of liquor or other gifts for the police association.

There was, too, the matter of the jail. Compton had its own jail in the basement of police headquarters, which was highly unusual since there were only three other jails in Southern California that were certified by the state to hold inmates. As a rookie I was assigned to jail duty every weekend, which meant processing prisoners and calling bail bondsmen. Like the tow truck companies, the bail bondsmen were dependent on the police for their business. Kickbacks on jail duty were simply accepted as part of the routine, and any effort to thwart the practice would have meant ostracism within the department, or worse.

These were all petty offenses, but they served two purposes. First, they helped supplement the officers' income, which was always inadequate, and, second, they cemented the bonds of trust and loyalty among them. Just as with the eight-track tapes, even if you did not want the money or the gifts, you took them, since to do otherwise would jeopardize your standing among your peers, as well as their chance to make a little additional money for their families. As one officer told me, "It's part of your uniform."

I was proud of my uniform. The Compton PD's uniform was designed by Sergeant Hartman's father; a Compton High track coach, he had emigrated from Germany and his design reflected the fact. The uniform was dark blue, like the LAPD's, but ours had gold buttons (which had to be polished every day), and there was a chain attached to the epaulet that carried a whistle. The hat was especially distinctive. LAPD and other police departments in the Southland wore hats of the old "jarhead" style, with stiff round tops and a badge on the front. Ours had a crest and a broad-winged eagle, and, as the veteran officers wore it, the top was slouched or turned down at the sides, giving it a rakish quality. However, as issued, the top was stiff and round like those of the other departments. It was not long before I learned that the slouch was a sign that a rookie had been accepted by his peers. Crushing the brim was a rite of passage, a privilege you had to earn, and it did not come easily.

One night I was riding with Officer Dave Shepherd on the west side. Frank Brower had told the others that I was all right, so Shepherd decided that it was time I "made my bones."

"There are two things you can't be," he told me as we cruised down Wilmington Avenue, "a rat and yellow." I had already proved I was not a rat; now Shepherd wanted to see if I was yellow.

He stopped the patrol car outside a bar called the Epicure Room, which was known as a hang-out for criminals and drug dealers. It was opposite Park Village on Alondra Boulevard and owned by a character named Joe Ropo, whose daughter had caught my eye. She worked at a Skippy's Burgers on Compton Boulevard, and I had a fervent, boyish crush on her.

"Go in there and search for weapons," Shepherd said.

I had no search warrant and no probable cause, but I knew that meant nothing. I got out of the car while Shepherd waited, and I walked in.

If the term "den of thieves" has any meaning at all, it referred to the Epicure Room. The place was cramped and dimly lit, and it smelled of cigarette smoke, liquor, urine, and dope. I walked to the center of the semi-circular bar, and everything stopped. I was not regarded with hostility so much as with a curiosity bordering on bemusement.

"Time to get up against the wall," I announced.

I had no idea what to expect, and I kept my hand near my sidearm. There was a long moment of silence, and then the characters at the bar stood and walked across the room. I had to hide my amazement. I told them to put their hands against the wall, and I moved along the line, patting them down for weapons. I found several—knives and blackjacks—and I confiscated them.

I stepped back, feeling much cockier than when I came through the door. "I'll be around," I told them. "If I find any of you assholes with a gun, I'll pop you." Then I turned and walked back to the car.

Shepherd seemed satisfied but said nothing. I threw the weapons onto the backseat and got in. "Any trouble?" he asked.

"None," I said as casually as I could.

The weapons, of course, meant nothing; Shepherd merely wanted to see if I had the guts and the command presence to walk into a place like the Epicure Room alone and start ordering people around. It was my second test, and I had passed it.

The third came a few nights later, when I was riding with Officer Dave Hall. Hall was the biggest man on the force, a giant at six foot seven and 290 pounds. No one messed with Dave Hall, whose nickname was Baby Huey, and when he and Rutigliano were partnered together, as they usually were, they made a formidable team. We were patrolling the east side along Rosecrans Avenue, and Hall pulled up outside the Slick Chick. It was, I knew, one of two bars where drugs were dealt after hours. The Chick was run by a big, tough gangster named Peter Gunn, who terrorized anyone who crossed him.

"Go in there and shake Pete Gunn down," Hall told me. I asked him on what grounds. "Just tell him you want to see some ID. And put these on." He handed me a pair of black fingerless gloves. They were sap gloves, the knuckles of which were lined with powdered lead. Punching someone with sap gloves was the equivalent of hitting him with a blackjack. Neither regulation nor legal, they were forbidden to LAPD and the sheriff's deputies, but all members of the Dirty Dozen wore them.

Once again I went in alone. This place was slightly more upscale than the Epicure, but the clientele was a notch below. Some of the worst elements in Compton frequented the Slick Chick, lorded over by Peter Gunn, who was nearly as broad as the bar. When I walked in, scarcely anyone bothered to look. I went straight up to Gunn and told him I wanted to talk to him. He turned droop-lidded, bloodshot eyes on me and demanded to know why.

"I want to see some ID," I answered.

He looked at me in stony silence a moment. He was over six feet tall, and his shaved head glowed dully in the blue light over the bar. He was what we called a 148er, which referred to the statute for resisting a police officer. He had tangled with more than one of us.

Gunn could tell from the shape of my hat that I was a rookie. He looked at me as if I were crazy, and then he broke into a laugh. "You gotta be shittin' me!"

I told him that he could either show me his ID, or he could come to the station with me.

His gaze turned lethal. "Who the fuck are you?" he growled.

I was terrified, but I knew that if I backed down in the slightest, if I showed any hesitation at all, Gunn and the other thugs in the bar would never respect me. I pointed to my badge. "You can see *my* ID, asshole," I answered. "Now I want to see yours. That, or you come with me."

Gunn glowered at me a long moment; then he reached beneath the bar. Instinctively I put my hand on my revolver. He saw the gesture and hesitated. Then he slowly brought his wallet out and held it up for me to see. He removed his driver's license and dropped it on the bar.

I glanced at it, then at him. "Expired," I remarked. "Get a new one before I come back."

He continued to stare at me as I walked out; I could actually feel his murderous gaze between my shoulder blades.

Dave Hall was waiting on the sidewalk. "How'd it go?" he asked.

"I'll come back in a couple of weeks," I replied. "If he hasn't renewed his license by then, I'll cite him."

Hall actually smiled. He just wanted to see if I would go up against a known thug like Pete Gunn. I had passed my third test. I was no raw rookie anymore.

Compton was divided into six police districts. Districts 1 and 2 were the west side, Districts 3 and 4 were on the east side, District 5 was in the northern part of the city, and District 6 was a floating assignment reinforcing the others in emergencies. Each district was assigned two patrol cars, a primary and a backup. The cars were designated according to the district they patrolled; car 1 patrolled District 1, car 2, District 2, et cetera. The backup cars had ten added to their numbers, so that the backup car in District 1 was car 11, in District 2, car 12, in District 3, car 13, and so on.

The allocation of officers on each shift to the various districts was often a matter of internal politics. If you were a member of the "in crowd," such as the Dirty Dozen, you could pull an assignment in Districts 3 and 4, which were relatively low-crime areas. On these patrols an officer was likely to get four or five calls a night, and few would be high-risk incidents, such as murder, armed robbery, shots fired, or man down. Those not so favored were likely to be assigned to Districts 1 or 2, where you could expect fifteen to twenty calls a night, many of them high-risk. The real punisher was District 5. This was a mixed black and Latino area, in which crime was endemic and most of it was violent.

District 5 included a section known as "Fruit Town" because the streets were named after fruit trees: Fig, Peach, Pear, and the like. In the sixties, Fruit Town was the breeding ground of the Latino gangs, and along its edges, the black gangs were gaining strength.

Clashes between opposing gangs were frequent and often bloody, and since the gangbangers far outnumbered the four to six officers assigned to the district, working District 5 was like walking into a battle zone almost single-handed. While LAPD and the sheriff's office could rotate their officers through good districts and bad—two nights in Watts, for example, followed by two in Malibu or Catalina—there was no respite in Compton. For us, every night on the streets was a night in hell.

Because of this, and the fact that the criminals in Compton were so much more numerous than the cops, CPD regulations allowed us to carry any weapons we chose. While LAPD officers were required to carry their issued .38 revolvers, Compton police carried .45 caliber and 9 mm automatics, .357, .41, and .44 Magnums, and even massive .50 caliber Desert Eagle pistols. I preferred the Smith & Wesson Model 27 .357 Magnum with a six-inch barrel, which I kept loaded with hollow-point ammunition for maximum stopping power.

We also were the only department in California that carried Gonzales saps. These were nine-inch-long blackjacks, covered in deerskin filled with mercury. Mercury was both a dead and a deadly weight. It allowed the force of the blow to be distributed over a wide area, whether it was the buttocks, the back, or the skull. Getting clobbered by a Gonzales sap was like being hit by a five-inch-long shotgun slug. The state had made them illegal for anyone to carry, cop or civilian—but Compton was a special place.

Though all the patrol units were equipped with a shotgun, some also carried MAC-10 submachine guns. They were completely illegal but small enough to conceal inside the cars, and, though inaccurate, their rapid rate of fire—a thousand rounds per minute—more than made up for it. Because of this, the CPD never had a SWAT team; the entire department *was* a SWAT team. Whenever LAPD or the L.A. sheriffs faced a man-with-a-gun call or a barricade situation on the edges of Compton, they called for CPD backup. In contrast, we handled all of our calls ourselves; CPD never asked for outside assistance.

In practice, most patrol officers were rotated through the districts, spending two nights in 1 or 2, then two in 3 or 4, and one in District 5. In this way, in any given workweek, we had at least two relatively quiet nights. On those nights on the east side, we would often cruise up and down Long Beach Boulevard near Rosecrans where clubs and bars proliferated, and where there were plenty of police groupies. These were girls who loved cops, and if you were single, or even if you were not, you could always find a date.

I have often thought about these teenaged girls who haunted Long Beach Boulevard at night in their halter tops and cutoffs, with too much lipstick and too little concern for their safety. What were they after? An authority figure, an older man to protect them, to make them feel special, to give them prestige? They were after adventure, too, I suppose, and exploring the mystery of sex. In any event, they were always willing to flirt or to meet you at a bar after your shift was over, and I had no such philosophical thoughts about them at the time. To me it was a heady experience having girls seek me out because I wore a blue uniform, because I carried a gun, because I owned the streets, which was their second home.

I was married at this time, and Michelle was a toddler, but I was also twenty-five. Kitty was only nineteen, scarcely more than a kid herself. Though I was determined to be a good husband and father, I soon found myself as a member of the elite P.M. shift with all the perks that entailed. The groupies were among the most important of these, and our main hangout, the nirvana of the Dirty Dozen, was the Golden Garter Saloon.

The Golden Garter was an old-fashioned strip bar on Long Beach at Rosecrans, owned by a high school friend of mine named Vito Pasquale. The son of transplants from back east, Vito had grown up in the Lincoln Heights section of L.A. His neighborhood was called "Pizza Valley" because it was overwhelmingly Italian. In fact, Dominic Rutigliano grew up on the same block of Workman Street as Vito, and as kids they had earned a reputation as good street fighters, the terror of Pizza Valley.

Nearby was my former neighborhood, Boyle Heights, where many of my friends still lived. To get from Boyle Heights to the Boys' Club where we boxed, we had to cross through Pizza Valley. This meant running the gamut of the Italian street thugs who guarded their territory jealously, and we often found ourselves having to fight our way through. I think it is likely that among the kids we battled in Pizza Valley were Rut and Vito. Later, Vito attended St. Anthony's, and he and I became friends.

Vito was a tall, broad-chested, black-haired son of immigrants. He wore his hair in the popular waterfall style, and he sang in a doo-wop group called the Continentals. His family was rumored to have mob connections, and whether it was true or not, he traded on the fact judiciously. You did not mess with Vito, because his boisterous gestures and explosive laugh concealed a ferocious temper, like a cloudburst before a tornado. I think that Vito Pasquale was the only man in Compton who could have gone toe-to-toe with Rutigliano and lived to tell about it.

The Golden Garter combined Old West decor with Jersey Mafia kitsch. It had a long, carved bar overhung by a gilded mirror, and red vinyl booths with checkered tablecloths. There was a small stage for live music, and at the end of the bar hung a red velvet curtain. Through that curtain burst some of the most beautiful and shameless women in southern Los Angeles County.

The Garter was a topless bar, which meant that the female bartenders and the waitresses all greeted you bare-breasted. To gain the privilege of offering topless alcohol service, which was rare in L.A. at that time, Vito had gone all the way to the state liquor board in Sacramento, where he no doubt greased palms as liberally as he glad-handed. The real draw at the Garter, though, was the strippers. They were good-looking girls who did not stop at topless—they went all the way as they danced to a raucous combo out among the tables and booths. As a result, the Garter became our watering hole, the after-hours place where we congregated when our shift was over.

I soon became a fixture at the Garter, since both Rut and I had known Vito most of our lives. Many nights, on the way home, we would stop by to have a few drinks, take in the sights, and flirt with the girls. Often we did more than flirt. Some of the Garter girls were married and had children, and they knew where to draw the line. Others were cop groupies like the teenyboppers on the boulevard. They would go into the back with you, or to the cheap motel next door, for fifteen minutes or for a couple of hours, depending on how much you had to spend and they had had to drink. I became such a common sight at the Garter and on the boulevard that I soon earned the nickname "Rosecrans Rick," which became my handle in the department.

Of course, none of this was good for my marriage, which began to suffer—but I was young and I was a cop, and this was Compton, which, like the Garter, retained some of the wild flavor of the Old West. In fact, in some ways Compton was reverting to a frontier town, with its growing lawlessness, its streets filled with bandits and guns, and its residents deserting in droves. The one constant, the primary source of stability, was the police.

By 1970, white flight was devastating Compton. The black area had expanded across Wilmington Avenue into the east side, and the whites were being slowly backed up against the Long Beach Freeway. There was simply no place left to go, and so white residents began deserting the city altogether, many moving down to Orange County. The exodus was so rapid that by 1971 Compton was 75 percent black. This sudden shift in demographics had profound repercussions for all of us who lived and worked in the city. The police department was no exception.

Apartheid, Détente, and the Great Penile Duel

Before white flight tilted the demographics of Compton from largely white to largely black, the police department was almost entirely white, and most officers were either Compton natives or Compton residents. One enormous advantage of this was that the officers knew the city intimately, and we also knew its criminals. If a call went out that a crime had been committed and a description of the perpetrator was given, we usually knew who it was immediately. This made us much more effective than a police force recruited from other locales, whose members did not live in the city they served. Later, however, it would give rise to accusations that the Compton PD was too close to the criminal element and, because of that, it must be corrupt.

As the black population grew, the city authorities understood that it was becoming necessary to bring more blacks into the department. Thus, for the first time, the CPD began recruiting black officers, both from within and from outside the city. As the number of black officers began to grow, changes were occurring within the department that in some ways mirrored those that were taking place in the city. The department was dividing up into areas of interest, with lines of separation that were more or less plainly defined. For this reason, two groups of white officers developed in response to the increasing black presence. We referred to one as the "apartheid" group and the other as the "détentes."

The apartheids were led by John Foster, the former Compton College student who had taken the fraternities off campus to protest integration. They made no secret of the fact that they resented jobs being taken away from qualified white candidates from within the city and given to outsiders who were black. They were also determined to hold on to the power they had always exercised within the department, and they resisted the call to relate to the community in a different way.

I sided with the détentes. These officers simply accepted the reality that was taking form around us. We knew that it was inevitable that the old white power structure would eventually give way, and we also understood that we could not expect to interact with the community as we had previously done. A different kind of thinking was called for, with altered attitudes and new ways of structuring the department, and so we preferred to try to adjust to the changes in the city, and to work with the new officers rather than shun them.

On the other side, the black officers who were entering the department tended to group themselves into three categories. The first was what we called the "bourgeois." These were officers who had grown up on the west side of Los Angeles, and who had attended college and were pursuing a career in law enforcement as a means to higher ends. Some wanted to move into city administration or into politics or the law, and many of them were taking after-hours college courses. The second group was the "militants." These young officers had been influenced by social and political trends already apparent in society. They believed that racial injustice had given them a disadvantage in life, and they were determined to use their positions as policemen to redress this and other grievances. The third group was the "jocks." These recruits were successful high school and college athletes who joined the police force out of a sense of adventure, and to pursue a career that would enable them to use their physical skills.

The bourgeois group tended to hold itself aloof from the whites, and even from the other blacks. The militants kept strictly to themselves and disdained the rest. The jocks seemed to be able to get along with just about anybody.

In a wider sense, a division between whites and blacks within the department was beginning to become apparent. This meant that the third group, the Latino officers, became the wild card in police politics. There were never many Latino officers in the CPD, but the division between blacks and whites gave them an influence beyond their numbers. When a procedural policy change or a shift in internal affairs was proposed, the Latino officers often held the deciding vote. Once again, I found myself on all sides of the divide. Being white from a Latino background, and having grown up in Watts and on the west side of Compton, I was both accepted and viewed with suspicion by all the groups. As time went on, they began to regard me as a sort of intermediary or peacemaker, and this tended to make me a political figure whether I wanted to be or not.

One fact that united us, however, was the situation we had to face in the streets. Crime was rising and becoming more violent, and despite the color of our skin, we were all cops. Time and again I saw this demonstrated: When the chips were down and officers' lives were at stake, there were no divisions among us—all of us were blue.

I saw an example of this shortly after I finished my training.

I was partnered with John Foster in car 2, which was the primary patrol car in District 2 on the west side. It was at the end of the P.M. shift, and we had had a tough night, including two stabbings, a shooting, and a vicious domestic violence call in which a woman was nearly killed. We were exhausted when we got back to the police station, and looking forward to going home. As we walked to the front door, though, a black man hurried up to us and told us that he had heard sobbing from the apartment next to his. It was a woman, he said, and he and his wife were very concerned.

It was midnight, our shift was over, and we had paperwork to do before checking out. Foster was perfectly entitled to tell the man to go to the sergeant inside and have him dispatch a patrol unit from the graveyard shift to deal with it. Instead, he asked the man to give us the address.

Our backup had already turned in for the night, and so we notified the primary car from the next shift and drove to the apartment building. As I started up the stairs, I could hear a woman's voice pleading, "Please . . . please don't hurt me. Please don't rape me . . ." Though our backup had not yet arrived, we knew we had to act. Foster and I threw ourselves against the front door and broke it down.

Inside, the place was dark, but we could see two men on the bed, raping a teenaged girl, who lay on her back moaning and crying. One of the men saw us and jumped up, naked, and ran into the bathroom. The other was so preoccupied that he did not even pause but continued hammering at the girl as if we were not there.

While Foster started pounding on the locked bathroom door, I pulled the rapist off her. He must have been high on drugs, because he immediately started fighting me, punching, kicking, trying to bite me. I took out my baton and began hitting at him, but it had no effect. His penis was still rigid, flailing around in the air between us. It was enormous, half the size of my baton, and so I swung at it, and for a few seconds, we were actually fencing, penis to baton.

He finally had had enough, and he collapsed onto the floor. Meanwhile, our backup had arrived, and while one officer helped me subdue the rapist, the other broke in the bathroom door with Foster. The man was hiding in the shower wrapped in the curtain, and so they dragged him out, curtain and all, threw him on the floor next to his friend, and cuffed him.

It was John Foster who comforted the victim, a young black girl who could not have been more than eighteen. He covered her with a blanket and held her until the ambulance arrived and took her to the hospital. Yet this was the man who styled himself as the leader of the apartheid group, the onetime opponent of college integration.

It was four more hours before Foster and I were able to close up the scene, return to the station, file the paperwork, and go home. We had done a shift and a half, and though we need not have taken the call, and despite the fact that the man who originally came to us was black, John Foster had responded as a cop. Because when he or any of us were on the job, color and race, nationality, and sexual orientation meant nothing. We were there to enforce the law in what I learned was called "Compton Style." Everyone was treated the same way: A crook was a crook, and a victim was a victim, and it mattered not at all who or what else they were.

The Compton Style of police work was a direct result of the fact that the CPD was always outnumbered by the criminal element. As the tide of violence rose and the gangs began to flourish, it became necessary for us to take matters into our own hands, often dispensing justice on the streets, since the courts were badly overburdened. We had some very good judges in Compton, like Commissioner Homer Garrett, who had been the first black highway patrolman in California; Cecil Mills, who gave up a chance to be a captain in the U.S. Marshals Service to become a judge in his hometown; Harry Shafer, the bane of automobile thieves, since his own prized Cadillac had been stolen; and Ralph Biggerstaff, a crew-cut WASP who was markedly propolice. They were tough, fair judges, but the epidemic of crime in the city clogged their courtrooms and brought the justice system almost to a halt.

A few statistics will serve to make the point. In 1950, there were no homicides in Compton; in 1970, there were 24. The incidence of rape had increased from 17 in 1950 to 120 by 1970. Robberies grew from 42 to 629; aggravated assaults increased 9,900 percent from 8 in 1950 to nearly 800 in 1970. Burglaries spiraled from about 400 to over 3,000, and auto theft likewise shot up from about 100 to 4,500.

On average this meant an increase in major crimes in that twenty-year period of nearly 3,500 percent. By 1970, the median age of a resident of Compton was 20.6. Crime was rising on a tidal wave of youth. With it all, not a single officer was added to the complement of 130 Compton police.

Although there was a lot of crime in Compton, there were few mysteries. I and most of the cops had grown up with the people who were now committing the crimes. We knew who they were and where and how they operated. Usually when a call came over the radio, we could tell just from the location and the type of crime who the perpetrator was likely to be.

So, in order to even the odds and preserve the justice system for the truly serious crimes, we dealt with many of the routine crimes in our own way—Compton Style.

Among my first ride-along partners as a rookie was a three-year veteran named John Sutton, and he was a prime example of the Compton Style. Like me, Sutton had grown up on the west side, and he knew the city and its crooks intimately. He was a big, burly black officer whose nickname was Shaft. He was not one of the Dirty Dozen, but he worked the P.M. shift and was widely respected. As a rookie, I learned a great deal from him.

One night, Sutton and I were called to the scene of a robbery, a liquor store on the west side. By the time we arrived, the robber had escaped with a bag full of cash. The owner said the man had threatened him with a gun. Sutton recognized him from the store clerk's description—a kid from the neighborhood who, Sutton knew, would never carry a real gun. He also knew that the kid hung out at the Glenmore Hotel, a sleazy joint off Tamarind on the north side, where hookers and dope were cheap.

We drove to the Glenmore, and while I went to the desk, Sutton waited in the alley at the back. Within moments the kid appeared and, seeing me at the front door, took off. As he turned the corner, he ran straight into John Sutton, all six foot two of him, with a deadly scowl on his face.

That was enough for the kid. He dropped to his knees and held the bag of money over his head. "Please, Mr. Sutton," he begged, "just take it. I'm sorry for what I did. Please, just give me a whoopin' and let me go!" Sutton took the bag, smacked him on the head, and told him to get lost. We returned the money to the store owner, and no report was filed.

Incidents like this not only served to save the city and the courts countless hours and taxpayer dollars, they also established without doubt the relationship between the CPD and the criminals. If you committed a crime and we knew who you were, we were coming after you to settle the matter quickly and privately—no lawyers, no bail, no plea bargains. You got what was coming to you, and if you were smart, you learned a lesson. If not, you got it again. That was police work Compton Style.

On another occasion, Sutton and I were patrolling District 5, and we stopped at the Glenmore, since there was always something going on there. As we checked out the corridors, we could smell the reedy odor of marijuana coming from one of the rooms. We had no probable cause and no search warrant and were not likely to get one quickly. Sutton walked to the door and knocked on it.

"Who's that?" a voice called.

Sutton answered, "It's me—Willy!"

"Willy who?"

Sutton bellowed, "Willy, man. Just open the damn door. You know it's Willy."

The door opened a crack, and we slammed into it, breaking the chain and barreling into the room. The place was thick with ganja smoke, and four men were sitting on the floor with piles of grass, rolling cigarettes. They were so stoned that they did not resist, and we took the lot of them into custody and confiscated the marijuana.

Later, when we filed our report, Sutton wrote that we had observed one of the men walking along the street with "a green leafy substance in a plastic bag" and had followed him to the room at the Glenmore, where we suspected illegal activity was taking place. The men pleaded guilty for possession with intent to sell, and again the taxpayers and the courts were saved the trouble and expense of a trial.

As businesses and longtime residents fled the city, the tax base shrank, social services deteriorated, and real estate values fell. Many white families who moved out could not sell their homes without a loss, and so, instead, they chose to rent them to the incoming black families. Often these families were Section 8 renters. Section 8 was a government subsidy program that paid the difference between what the family could afford and what the landlord required. As a result, low-income people were drawn to Compton as renters, not as homeowners. This meant that properties deteriorated and neighborhoods began to decay.

By the early seventies, downtown Compton had been devastated. Where once there had been big chain stores, family-owned boutiques, and piped-in music, there was now urban blight. Old established shops were boarded shut, and fly-by-night businesses sprang up in their places, generating very little revenue for the city. Bars and cheap clubs, liquor stores, and fast-food joints proliferated along Compton Boulevard, and the criminal element soon took over. Eventually, it became dangerous just to walk the downtown streets. All of this happened within a period of about five years, between 1965 and 1970.

Drugs also became a big problem. Several of the bars that suddenly appeared were little more than fronts for drug trafficking. The Texas Playhouse at 134th and Wilmington on the west side was the haunt of the three Allen brothers, the enforcers for Judge Williams and Eddie Pope, who were major pushers. The Gun Kit and the Slick Chick were two dives on the east side that did an active business in psychedelics, marijuana, and hash. Three white brothers named Lassiter frequented these bars; they were tough characters who were often arrested for being under the influence. Clem's Bar and the Golden Pheasant were the hangouts of Dave Connelly and the Merritt brothers, also users.

But the biggest dealer on the east side was Phil Lee, a homegrown criminal whose mother owned a beauty salon on Rosecrans. He looked like Elvis Presley and, like him, dressed flamboyantly, wearing oversized rhinestone sunglasses even at night. His motto was "When you're cool, the sun is always shining." He operated out of several of the east side bars, and word quickly spread that he could get you anything you wanted: grass, hash, Seconals, black beauties, cocaine, and heroin. Phil Lee became a target of the CPD, but he was a very careful and clever criminal, and he managed to avoid arrest. After I learned that he was selling drugs to kids, I promised myself that I would bust him one day.

As the drug business grew, crime escalated and became more violent. Armed robberies, assaults, beatings, stabbings, shootings, and murders became part of the everyday life of the city, and so part of our lives. This was driven home to me one night on the P.M. shift early in my career.

I was patrolling with John Sutton when we got a call of a man down on Chester Avenue off Rosecrans. When we pulled up to the scene I saw a black man lying on the sidewalk with something sticking out of his chest. As I approached, I could not make out what the weapon was—it was long and slender and seemed to shine in the streetlight. Then it hit me: It was a chrome car antenna, embedded deep in the victim's body.

Nearby, another man was standing by the Cadillac from which the antenna had been torn, apparently unfazed by what had happened. He was smoking, and, though a body lay bleeding at his feet, he seemed to be perfectly unconcerned, almost nonchalant. When we walked up to him, he scarcely noticed us.

While Sutton questioned him, I knelt next to the man on the ground. He was lying on his back, the stub of the antenna protruding from his shirt about eight inches. It had been driven nearly through his body, and there were other bloody holes to indicate that he had been stabbed several times. He was still alive, still breathing.

"I'm gonna get help," I told him. His eyes were glazed over, and I was not sure he had heard me. I squeezed his arm. "You hold on," I said.

I ran back to the car and called for an ambulance. By the time I returned to tell the man that help was on the way, he was dead, his face rigid, his empty eyes staring straight up at me.

In the meantime, Sutton had cuffed the other man and was patting him down. Still he gave no indication that anything out of the ordinary had happened.

I stood over the victim until the coroners arrived. This was not the peaceful death lit by candles and wound in satin and wreaths that I had seen as an altar boy at wakes; this was brutal death, callous death, lying on the sidewalk in the yellow glow of streetlights, with a metal shard stuck in its chest. There was nothing natural about it, nor anything solemn—no dirge or dignity. Strangers stood by gaping at the corpse; a few children tittered. When the coroners hefted the body, it sagged in the rubber sheet like a soiled carpet, the eyes still gazing open.

It was not merely death, it was murder—my first murder—and it brought home to me the real nature of the change in my city. Compton was no longer the childhood dream of cowboys and drive-ins and music piped into the streets; it was becoming the crime capital of California. That murder made me realize that my career as a cop was not just an adventure or a sociological experiment: It was a life-and-death reality that was going to test my humanity and strength, and demand everything I had.

As the coroners drove off, ideas were beginning to churn in my mind. I was in a very dangerous situation; I could be killed at any time on any shift, just as this man had been killed, suddenly, with whatever came to hand, by someone who neither cared nor was moved by his death. If I was going to survive, if I was going to do some good, I would have to use all the training I had received in the academy and on the streets, and all the resources of courage, cleverness, and compassion I possessed. I was beginning to understand what it meant to be a cop.

I had one vital advantage that might make the difference between success and failure, life and death: the fact that I was a Compton boy and knew the city and its personalities so well. I think that if I had come in cold, from the outside, I would have drowned in those first few years on the force.

A few nights after the murder, I was patrolling on the west side with my former training officer, Frank Brower. When Frank walked into a crime scene, it was clear who was in charge. He radiated authority. He also radiated charm. He had a girlfriend on the east side named Kathy, and occasionally, when we were working together, Frank would drive to Kathy's house and have breakfast with her and her family. I waited in the car in case there was a call, and if there was, I honked the horn, and Frank would come running out.

On one of these occasions, we got a call about a disturbance on West Poplar Street off Rosecrans near the San Antonio Bakery. When we arrived, a diminutive black man in his forties named Willie was sitting on the front porch of the house smoking a cigarette. Brower and I approached him; he clearly was expecting us.

"She's in there" was all he said.

While Brower stayed with Willie, I went inside. What I found was horrific.

Lying on the floor of the living room was a huge white woman, over 250 pounds. She was facedown in a pool of blood and matter, and there was a trail of gore leading from the kitchen to where she lay. I knelt and spoke to her, but all she could do was make burbling sounds, the blood frothing against the threadbare rug. I tried to turn her onto her side, but when I did, her face seemed to stick to the floor, thick mucus strings and blood clots peeling from it.

She had taken a shotgun blast in her face, and it was the remnants of it that I saw smeared from one end of the house to the other. By the time she had crawled to the point where I found her, nearly nothing was left. Where her features had been was now a tangle of flesh, bones, and blood embedded with lead pellets, like a livid sliced pomegranate studded with seeds.

"Ma'am . . . ?" was all I could manage.

As I held her by her shoulder, shaking at the sight, I felt her bloated body go limp.

I went outside and told Brower that we had to call the coroner; Willie's wife had been shot dead. While he made the call, I asked Willie what had happened.

He shrugged. "I told her to make me my black-eyed beans," he answered. "She knew how I liked 'em made. And she didn't do it. So I took the gun down from the ceiling and I shot her."

That was all: He had blown his wife's face off with a shotgun because she had failed to cook his beans the way he wanted.

It was first-degree murder. The shotgun had been hidden in the ceiling tiles, and Willie had had to tear half the ceiling apart in order to get it. He had had plenty of time to think about what he was doing. I assumed that he would be given life in prison. Instead, because the courts were so overburdened, he was able to plead down to manslaughter, his lawyer arguing that his wife was twice his size and had abused him. Willie was given two and a half to three years. That was justice Compton Style.

When I first joined the force, Chester Crain was the mayor of Compton, but by 1970 the white political establishment was being challenged by the representatives of the growing black population. Compton's first black city councilman, Douglas Dollarhide, ran against Crain and became the first black elected mayor in California history, and among the first in the nation. The racial makeup of the city council was changing, too, and Dollarhide filled his administration with blacks. The municipal government was thus beginning to reflect the changing nature of the city's population. We knew that it would not be long before this change would make itself felt in the leadership of the police department.

As the pressure of rising crime on the patrol officers increased, the CPD began to experience its own form of white flight. Officers with several years' experience on the street began to leave for other, less stressful departments. In their new jobs, more often than not, they were both promoted and given substantial increases in pay, because the saying among Southland police forces was that five years in Compton was worth twenty years anyplace else. Compton officers were highly prized and even courted by other departments, including LAPD, the Highway Patrol, and the Huntington Beach PD.

As veteran white officers transferred out, the CPD undertook an aggressive recruiting effort. Not only did we look for promising new prospects from across the country, we actively sought out experienced officers who had had less than stellar careers in other departments. We were not looking for misfits or malcontents, but rather for solid cops who had been guilty of minor infractions, and whose careers were therefore stalled. These included, for example, officers who had taken too many sick days, or who had physical problems that were not debilitating, or who had been guilty of some form of moral turpitude, such as having an affair or being accused of a petty offense. We also sought out cops who were bored with their jobs, and we found them among the Department of Motor Vehicles personnel and the airport police, LAPD, and LASO, and in cities such as Vernon, in which there was very little to do.

Such cops readily accepted an offer from Compton, since we would put them right onto the street and promote them regularly for good work. The CPD thus gained the reputation as the place you went to if you wanted a new start or better prospects for advancement, or if you were looking for action. We became the Foreign Legion of police work.

Rut, Crosby, and the Rise
of the Gangs

Of all the veteran officers I knew as a rookie, the one I most wanted to impress and to emulate was Dominic Rutigliano. Rut was all cop, as tough as he was fair, as honest as he was effective. He was as scrupulous about his reputation as he was about his uniform. Every day before his shift, after he had changed, he wrapped a piece of adhesive tape around his fingers and went over his uniform shirt to remove lint. His brass was polished, and his leather belts were waxed. He had that vital quality I had seen in Frank Brower, the most important asset a cop can possess: command presence. Command presence was a combination of style and will. It had to do with how you looked, how you carried yourself, and your ability to project your intention to take control of any situation. While it could be acquired with years of experience, some people never learned it, and a few were born with it. Rut was born with it.

He exuded authority and a calm determination to impose his will regardless of who or what confronted him. Besides being big, muscular, and intimidating, nearly as wide as he was high, Rut had a gaze that could fix you with its intensity and its intelligence. He wore his hair long, as was the fashion in the seventies, and sported a broad mustache, which had the effect of softening his appearance. Though he was poised and thorough, careful about citizens and solicitous of victims, when it came to bad guys, he was ferocious, and he always acted decisively. As a result, citizens respected him and criminals feared him. Sometimes it was enough for Rut to appear on the scene for tensions to be defused, and for the bad guys to surrender.

Rut was a cop first and foremost. Though he wielded his authority to great effect, he himself was totally unimpressed by authority. He treated everyone equally, whether it was a homeless person, a fellow officer, a captain, or the chief of police. He was not a political animal; indeed, he had no patience for the internal politics of the department. This was, perhaps, his only failing as a cop: He refused absolutely to play the game. By contrast, I learned quickly that police work was by its very nature political, whether you liked it or not. In order for a cop to be truly effective, he had to know how to work both the streets and the system. This is something that Rut refused to acknowledge—his job as he saw it was to protect the citizens and nail the crooks, and he went about it with an almost religious fervor. His was a single-minded devotion to duty.

Rut was a complex personality, a man of many moods. When he was in a good humor, no one was more gregarious and fun to be around. He joked and drank, and flirted with the girls at the Garter, and, just as in the Dirty Dozen, in a social situation he instantly became the leader. When his mood was dark, though, it was best to avoid him. He could become sullen and uncommunicative, and downright brutal in his speech and his behavior. I saw all these aspects of his character, and I respected them, but the thing that was most important to me was that Dominic Rutigliano was perhaps the best police officer I have ever known.

Rut's cases formed part of the mythology of the CPD. There was the time, for example, when he responded to the scene of a murder at the home of the houseboy of a municipal judge. The young man was a Latino and known to be gay. He lived in a second-floor apartment above a garage, which he had decorated in a nautical motif. Among the artifacts was a pair of crossed harpoons over the sofa. When Rut arrived, he found the houseboy hanging from the wall by one of the harpoons. His lover, in a jealous rage, had stabbed him through the chest with such force that his body was lifted off the floor and pinned to the wall. By the time Rut arrived, the boy was dead, his feet and lower limbs grotesquely swollen with settled body fluids.

Rut called for the coroner and Special Investigation team and, not having eaten lunch, asked his rookie trainee to run down the street and get him some fried chicken. When it arrived, Rut sat down on the sofa and hung his helmet on the end of the harpoon. Now, at this time, the district attorney's office had just begun a policy of having DAs report to the scenes of major crimes, and a young DA was dispatched to investigate his very first murder. When he walked into the apartment, he found the distended corpse pinned to the wall, and Rut sitting on the sofa gnawing a chicken leg, his helmet dangling from the end of the murder weapon. The young DA took in the scene with a horrified glance and fainted.

On another occasion, Rut responded to the scene of a busted drug deal in which a supplier had shot one of his distributors in the head with a 12-gauge. It was at such close range that the victim's skull was shattered, and his brain was blown out onto the sidewalk. As the SI team was photographing and documenting the scene, a dog dashed past and snagged the brain, which was a vital piece of evidence. Rut chased the dog several blocks, trying to get the brain away from it. Finally, the dog darted under a car and began making a meal. Another cop ran up with his gun drawn, intending to shoot the dog. Rut stopped him: There were too many spectators, and while they were used to murders, he knew they would never forgive the police department if they shot a dog.

Rut's impromptu style of police work sometimes backfired. While assigned to jail duty as punishment for some offense to the hierarchy, he found himself trying to restrain a middle-aged Mexican man who was wailing and crying hysterically. He had been caught in a drug sweep and was being charged with possession with intent to distribute. He had no prior record, and he kept howling that he had disgraced his family and wanted to die. Rut took away his belongings, including his belt and shoelaces, before locking him in. The man begged him to return his belt so that he could hang himself. Rut told him that he could not for that very reason. Still the man pleaded, sobbing that he wanted to kill himself. He made such a racket that, to shut him up, Rut finally snapped, "God damn it, just tear your shirt into strips and tie them together."

It seemed to have worked. For the next hour, the man was quiet, and peace returned to the jail. Rut went to lunch, and when he came back, he routinely checked the prisoners. He found the Mexican hanging from the cell door, the shreds of his shirt knotted around his neck, stone dead.

Rut turned furiously on the cop who had taken over while he had been at lunch. "How the hell did you let this happen?!"

The cop shrugged. "I thought you gave him the okay," he said.

It was Rutigliano who had taken down John Clutchette, who would become notorious as one of the "Soledad Brothers," along with the Panthers' George Jackson and Fleeta Drumgo. Clutchette had been born and raised in Compton, and he had been a lifelong troublemaker. When Rutigliano and some other members of the Dozen caught Clutchette for armed robbery, they gave him a good old-fashioned Compton asswhooping and sent him to the state prison at Soledad. It was there that in January 1970 Clutchette, Jackson, and Drumgo allegedly orchestrated the murder of a prison guard in retaliation for the shooting of a black inmate. (Drumgo and Clutchette were later acquitted of the guard's murder.) Several months later, Jonathan Jackson, George's seventeen-year-old brother, broke into Judge Harold Haley's court in Marin County heavily armed. Jackson gave guns to three prisoners who were in the courtroom, and took the judge and four other people hostage, demanding the release of his brother, Clutchette, and Drumgo. Images of one of the prisoners with his finger on the trigger of a shotgun taped to Judge Haley's neck as they hustled the hostages out of the courthouse were broadcast around the world. Shots were fired, and the judge, Jonathan Jackson, and two of the prisoners were killed.

One legendary incident involved Rut breaking down the door of a Black Panther safe house, only to find himself staring into the twin barrels of a sawed-off shotgun. It had been a setup; the Panthers were determined to "do" a cop. A vicious thug named Oscar Johnson, who wore a necklace of bullets, shoved the gun under Rut's chin, shrieking that he was going to blow his head off. Every time Rut tried to grab the shotgun, Johnson shoved it harder against his jaw. Rut's backup arrived, Stan Pate, a full-blooded Crow Indian. He drew his pistol and pointed it at Johnson.

"I'm gonna kill the motherfucker!" Johnson screamed, forcing Rut's head back with the snout of the sawed-off. There was nothing Pate could do.

"Listen to me," Rut told him calmly. "If this fucker kills me, I want you to shoot him in the fucking head, and then I want you to blow his dick off. Then I want you to go to the autopsy, and when they cut open his chest, I want you to take a shit in it, so that he goes to his grave with cop shit inside him."

Pate nodded. "You got it," he said.

Between Rut's threat and Pate's cold-eyed reply, Johnson had had enough. He lowered the shotgun. Rut took him prisoner and whipped him with his own gun.

Rut had trained with the legendary patrolman Carl Crosby. Crosby was known throughout Southern California as the toughest cop in Compton. A big, corn-fed Georgia farm boy, he had hands like rakes and the character of a grizzly bear, and like one, he was absolutely fearless. Seventh Fleet sailors used to come to Compton from the Port of Long Beach just to challenge him to fight, and Crosby never refused. They would meet at the Spade Cooley studio, Crosby would take off his badge and gun, and they would adjourn to the alley behind. Crosby never lost, and when he was done with the sailor, he would hang him by his neckerchief from one of the hooks in the studio's backstage dressing room.

There were four old-fashioned police call boxes located throughout the city, and Carl Crosby kept a fifth of Jack Daniel's in each. They were what he called "my breakfast." I worked with Crosby twice in my rookie year.

The first time, we responded to a house in the Richland Farms district on a report of a domestic disturbance. I had been to the house before, and knew that the owner was what we called an "Adam-Henry," or an asshole. Crosby and I walked to the screen door and shouted, "Police!" The man appeared on the other side in his underwear, drunk and surly. When Crosby asked him to open the door so that we could check on his wife, the man replied by spitting at him through the screen. I had my Gonzales sap, but before I could yank open the door, Crosby bolted a punch through the screen, ripping part of it away and embedding it in the man's forehead. When the ambulance arrived, the man was still unconscious, the black grille stuck to his flesh. The paramedics had to pry it off, leaving a livid crosshatched scar.

On the second occasion, I was riding with Crosby when we received a call of a man by the flagpole at Compton College beating a school security guard. When we arrived, there was an audience of students gathered around the pole watching the assault. A huge black man had the guard half off his feet and was dancing like Bruce Lee, fists raised, delivering one roundhouse kick after another.

Crosby and I waded through the crowd. "This one's mine," I told him. It was my old college, and a chance for me to show my stuff before the student body.

I took out my Gonzales sap as the man knocked the guard down and began pummeling him with his fists. As I made my way to him, though, Crosby stepped between us. The man turned, assuming his most fearsome karate stance. Crosby scarcely paid attention. He lashed out with the *back of his hand*, caught the man under the chin, and sent him flying to the pavement. When I approached, the man was unconscious, knocked out cold.

"God damn it, Carl," I protested. "I told you I had this one!"

He shrugged. "It's time for my breakfast," he said. He adjourned to the call box on campus, unlocked it, and took out the Jack Daniel's.

I learned much later that Carl Crosby drank because of an incident that had occurred in the late fifties when he was working in the juvenile division. He responded to a call of a robbery at a liquor store, and snagged a fifteen-year-old boy named Ruben Verra who had stolen a Hershey bar. The kid had no priors, so Crosby gave him a lecture and let him off. He monitored the kid from time to time, making sure he kept out of trouble. Whenever Ruben Verra saw Crosby's car, he ran up to it to chat with him. Crosby developed a liking for the kid.

Some months later, the owner of a metal smelting plant on Douglas Street off Alameda began complaining of vandalism taking place at night. His employees' cars were being stripped of radios and hubcaps, he reported, and scrap metal was disappearing from the piles in the yard. Since it was probably kids from the Latino Corridor, the juvenile division sent a car, together with a patrol unit, to stake out the plant. Crosby was one of the juvie detectives.

Long after midnight, the cops heard noises inside the fence. It was dark, but they could see shadows moving among the scrap heaps. One of the patrol officers yelled a warning, and the figures turned. The officer, who was young and nervous, caught a glint of chrome in a hand and fired. Crosby fired as well. In the echoing silence that followed, there was a slender figure lying on the gravel. It was Ruben Verra; he had been shot several times. When the boy saw Crosby, he crawled toward him, leaving a thick trail of blood. "Please, Mr. Crosby . . . ," he moaned. "You didn't have to shoot me. I don't have a gun."

He collapsed and died at Crosby's feet. In his hand was a pair of nickel-plated pliers.

As a detective in the juvenile division, Crosby was making more money and was in line for promotion to sergeant, but he requested a transfer back to patrol. He never worked detectives again, and he refused every offer of promotion. Carl Crosby was haunted by the boy's death for the rest of his life; Jack Daniel was the friend who helped him deal with his grief. He retired while I was still a rookie and became an alcoholic. He drank himself to death at the age of sixty-three, another victim of life on the streets of Compton.

I have already related how Rutigliano put me through my first test as a trainee, but the initiation did not stop there. Riding with Rut was always a kind of midterm exam, in which your character, your courage, and your comradeship were tested. He was tough on rookies and did not try to hide his disdain for them. As a boxer and a former marine, I was not inclined to take this kind of intimidation, and, as a result, my relationship with Rut could be tumultuous.

On one of my first solo shifts after I had finished my training, I was called to the scene of an armed robbery. As happened so often, when the victim described the crook, I had a pretty good idea who he was—a gang-banger known as High Pockets, because he habitually pulled his pants up to the middle of his chest. I cruised the neighborhood until I spotted him walking down the street, his cuffs at half mast above his white socks. I pulled over, and immediately he took off.

I radioed that I was going in pursuit; then I chased High Pockets on foot a couple of blocks until I was close enough to tackle him. We both went sprawling to the sidewalk. While I was trying to turn him over to cuff him, he managed to pull a switchblade knife from his pocket. I heard the metallic snap of the blade before I actually saw it, and for a few seconds we struggled over the knife. Finally, I managed to twist his arm up behind him in a hammerlock, and pry the switchblade from his hand. I cuffed him, half dragged him to my car, and threw him into the cage.

When my backup arrived, it was Rutigliano. He saw that I had everything under control and grunted his satisfaction. I was proud of the arrest, and I could not help showing Rut the knife I had taken away from the man. It was an impressive weapon, with a pearl handle and a seven-inch blade. He asked to see it, and I handed it to him. I knew he collected knives and was something of a connoisseur. He examined the knife a long moment, nodding admiration.

"I'll give you three knives from my collection for it," Rut offered.

The knife was evidence that the banger had tried to kill me, so I told him no, thanks.

Rut closed the blade and put the knife into his pocket. "I'm keeping it," he said.

I was stunned. It was my arrest and my evidence. I half hoped he was joking, and asked for it back.

"I told you," he answered, "I'm keeping it." Then he turned and got back into his car.

I watched him drive off in disbelief. The crook had been armed and had tried to stab me, and the knife was an important part of my report.

Now it was gone. All I could think was that one day I would get even with Rut for this.

Because Rut and I hung out at the Garter, we sometimes dated the same girls. By this time, my marriage to Kitty was over and I was on the prowl, earning my handle Rosecrans Rick. Sometimes Rut and I would take girls from the Garter out to the desert for camping trips and target practice, or to Redondo Beach for bodysurfing. I was dating a girl named Candy, whose nickname was Ferocious, because she had a vicious temper and could take care of herself. Rut was seeing her best friend, Pam, who also worked at the Garter. One night, after the P.M. shift, Rut and I stopped in to see the girls and have a few drinks.

In the Garter that night was a local character called Chickie, a young black dude who fancied himself a ladies' man. Chickie was always trying to make it with the Garter girls, and his utter lack of success did nothing to dampen his desire. Rut and I were sitting at a corner table when we saw Chickie huddling with Rut's girlfriend, Pam, at the bar. We watched in amusement as Pam pointedly ignored him. Chickie persisted, and finally Pam told him to get lost. Then, suddenly, Chickie reared back with his arm and slapped Pam across the face, almost knocking her to the floor.

Before I could even react, Rut was across the room. He grabbed Chickie from behind, swung him around, and leveled him with one punch to the jaw. Then, as the bar cleared, Rut knelt on Chickie's back, pulled his arm behind him, and forced his hand up to the back of his head. By the time I got to them, I could see that Chickie's arm was nearly broken, and that Rut was beside himself with fury.

"Rut, let him go!" I said. "You're gonna break his arm, man."

Rutigliano was so incensed that he did not hear me. I tried to pull his grip away, but his hands were enormous and too powerful. "Let him go, Rut," I said again. "This is an easy solver. We'll get him for assault."

I could see that Chickie was slobbering, drool pouring from his mouth. Rut had a death grip on the back of his throat. Then Chickie's foot began to shake uncontrollably, a sign that he was going into shock, maybe even dying. Finally Vito and I both grabbed Rutigliano and pulled him off.

Chickie lay half unconscious on the floor, his arm still twisted grotesquely up behind his back.

Rutigliano stood and stretched his thick neck and shoulders, calming himself. "Get outta here," he grumbled to Chickie, "and don't ever let me see you again."

I helped Chickie to his feet and hustled him out the door. When he was able to stand on his own I told him, "Man, you just got the best break of your life." He was too out of it to reply, and he staggered off down Rosecrans.

The rumors that Rutigliano's family was mob-connected were widespread in the department. He had grown up in New York, and it was said that every year on his birthday his godfather had sent him an envelope full of cash, even after his parents had moved to Southern California. This practice continued until Rut became a cop, and then the money stopped.

In addition to collecting knives, Rut was an avid biker. He owned a Harley-Davidson, of which he was immensely proud, and everyone in Compton knew that you did not touch Rut's hog. Though he never joined a motorcycle gang, he often rode with the Hell's Angels, where his best buddies were characters nicknamed Grumpy and Beautiful Buzzard. This connection with bikers came in useful more than once in his police work.

Across the city limits in L.A. County was a strip bar called the Cat Patch. It was a hangout for bikers, who preferred it to the Garter and its clientele of cops. The owner was a member of the Hessian motorcycle club, a big, bulky Irishman named Brady. Brady stole a couple of strippers from Vito Pasquale, and when Vito called him on it, Brady put a contract on Vito's life. Through his buddies in the Angels, Rut soon heard about it.

Vito knew that Brady's threat was serious; he was now a marked man. Any night, it was likely that someone would drive by the Garter and take a shot at him while he was closing up. Vito told Rut and me that he was going to bring some guys in from Vegas, where his family had connections, but we assured him that we would deal with it.

When our shift was over, Rut and I changed out of our uniforms and got into Rut's car. It was a cold December night, and we wore heavy overcoats. We drove over to the Cat Patch, parked, and walked straight in. The place was crowded with bikers, but we shoved past them to the bar, which Brady was tending. He had reddish-brown hair and a freckled face, which might have given him a boyish look were it not for the tattoos and chains he wore. He asked us what we wanted, and we told him we had come to talk. He looked between us a moment, then motioned us toward the back room.

Rut did not move. "What we have to say, we'll say right here," he told Brady.

"If it's about that asshole Pasquale," Brady said, "he's a dead man."

"No," Rut said, "it's about you."

We both opened our overcoats. Rut was carrying a .41 Magnum, and I had my .357.

"You want some of this?" Rut told him. "'Cause I'll give it to you right here in your own place." The man stared at the guns and said nothing. "You're gonna behave," Rut went on quietly. "You ain't gonna do shit to Vito. If you do, you can go home and kiss your wife good-bye, 'cause you'll be a dead man. You understand?"

The place had gone silent. Brady's eyes were still fixed on the guns in our waistbands. Rut repeated, "Do you understand?"

"Yeah," Brady muttered. "Yeah, I got it."

"Good," Rut said. "So you'll tell Vito it's okay."

Brady nodded, and we left.

The next day, Brady called Vito and assured him that there were no hard feelings. He apologized and offered to return the two girls he had lured away from the Garter. With that the matter ended. It had been an example of keeping the peace Compton Style.

During the early seventies, drugs were becoming a greater and greater problem in Compton. Heroin and cocaine were readily available on the streets, and they served as the principal source of revenue for the gangs, which were growing in number and violence. Drugs were pouring into Compton not just from L.A. but from abroad as well, and a lot of our time and energy went into trying to stem this tide.

We knew who most of the dealers were and where they hung out. One such hangout was the Golden Pheasant bar on Alondra Boulevard. I knew that Phil Lee, the flamboyant son of the matronly hairdresser, who drove a garish Roadmaster Buick and wore shades and an opera cape, used the Pheasant to distribute his stuff, which often ended up in the hands of kids. One night I stopped in at the Pheasant and spotted Dave Connelly, one of Phil Lee's runners. I waited until he left the bar, and then I pulled him aside. He wanted to know why.

"You appear to be drunk," I said. It was not true, but I needed some probable cause to search him. Sure enough, I found a bag with forty Seconals in his pocket.

"Oh, this is bullshit, man," he protested. I told him that with his record it was more like two years in Folsom. Connelly looked around and lowered his voice. "Look, Rick, man, I'll give you a bigger pop if you let me go." I asked him how big. "Phil Lee," he answered.

I had wanted to arrest Lee since I first joined the force, and this was my chance. I gave Connelly my word that if I got Lee, I would forget about the reds. Back at the station I told Frank Brower what was going down; he agreed that it was big.

That night, I had Dave Connelly call Phil Lee and tell him he was out of product. They agreed to meet behind Clem's Bar on Compton Boulevard, where Lee would replenish his supply. Brower and I staked out the bar, and, as it was Rut's and Dave Hall's district, they backed us up. Connelly waited in the alley, and before long Lee's Roadmaster pulled in. Lee got out in his signature shades and opera cape and opened the trunk. The moment he handed over the drugs to Connelly, Brower and I walked up on him. We had our guns drawn since we knew that Lee was probably armed and that he was crazy enough to shoot, but it was over for him. His face in the dirty light from the back of Clem's Bar showed how shocked he was.

I told him to put his hands on the car, and I patted him down. Meanwhile, Brower, Hall, and Rutigliano went through the car. It was loaded with drugs: bricks of cocaine and hash and bags of Seconals and black beauties.

Brower put Lee in the back of the unit, and I told Rutigliano that I was going to turn Dave Connelly loose.

"Hell you are," he said. "I'm putting the forty reds in with this stuff and popping them both." I told Rut that I had given Connelly a pass if we got Phil Lee. "Fuck you and your pass," he said, and he threw Connelly into the back of his car.

There was nothing I could do about it that night, but later, when Dave Connelly appeared for his hearing and I was called as the arresting officer, I could not remember a single thing about the incident. Judge Mills looked at me sidelong and then dismissed the charges against Connelly. They released him, and he reported back on the street that Rick Baker was a cop who kept his word. I had saved my credibility and had gotten even with Rut.

On the other hand, when I testified against Phil Lee, every detail was clear in my mind. It had been a big bust, and it brought with it the satisfaction of nailing Phil Lee. He was sentenced to four years in Folsom.

The next day when I reported for work, I wore the top of my hat crushed down. I was now a full-blooded Compton cop.

When we think of the gangs in Compton in the seventies and eighties, it is the Crips and Bloods that come to mind. But the history of the gangs is more varied and goes back much farther than that.

In 1848, after the war with Mexico, Hispanic residents of the Southwest were offered U.S. citizenship. Most accepted, but a minority refused to acknowledge that the United States had, in fact, conquered their territory. Many of these disgruntled Hispanics lived in the Pueblo of Los Angeles, which they still considered to be their territory. Then gold was discovered in California, and the flood of American immigrants quickly overwhelmed them.

Nonetheless, there remained a hard core of Latinos who had no desire to be absorbed into American culture. They were determined to retain their own language and traditions and to guard their territory, which had been the land of their ancestors. Inevitably, these people came into conflict with the growing Anglo population, which viewed them as aliens who would do better to return to their homeland. On their side, the Latinos insisted that they *were* home and that the Anglos were interlopers. The more isolated these Latinos became, the poorer and more put-upon they grew. It was this combination of cultural, political, economic, and sociological factors that gave rise to the first Hispanic street gangs.

In the early years of the twentieth century, Hispanic youths in Los Angeles began to form into loose confederations for mutual protection and to defend their territory. At this time, there was a flourishing drug and prostitution traffic from northern Mexico through El Paso, Texas, to Los Angeles. The early L.A. gangbangers emulated the dress, behavior, and speech of these Mexican drug dealers and pimps, called cholos, and it was from this that the So-Cal gangland style evolved. In fact, it was the El Paso gangbangers who invented and popularized the zoot suit style, called by the Mexicans *pachuco,* which became the rage in Los Angeles in the forties.

The earliest Hispanic gang in L.A. was the Maravillas, named for the housing project in East Los Angeles where they formed in the mid-1940s. Before long, other projects spawned rival gangs, and each claimed and marked its territory. It was in this way that graffiti, originally brought from El Paso, made its way into Los Angeles. A turning point for the Hispanic gangs occurred in 1943 when a member of the 38th Street gang was murdered, probably by a rival gang. In the retaliation that followed, twelve members of 38th Street were convicted of murder and sent to state prison, where they established a pattern of behavior that was to become a permanent part of gang culture. They kept to themselves, never mingling with the white and black prison populations. They were scrupulous about their clothing, they never complained though they were given the worst jobs, and they refused to allow the prison authorities to break them. When the gangbangers' convictions were later overturned and they were freed, they became folk heroes in the Hispanic community. Gangs and the gang mentality were here to stay.

After World War II, gangs proliferated, turf battles became more violent, and guns were used for the first time by returning veterans with a knowledge of firearms. Gangs coined the term "drive-by" for the practice of firing at rivals from moving cars. Also, inmates in state prisons were given bandannas to wear at work. The Southern California gangs chose blue bandannas, while those from the north chose red. This precedent of identifying gang affiliation by color would later be adopted by the Crips and Bloods.

By the time my family moved to Compton in 1951, Hispanic gang culture had already crossed the border from L.A. and taken root. I have mentioned some of the proto-gangs, like the Farmers and the Huns, but eventually these were superseded by larger and more violent organizations.

The west side was dominated by the 155th Street gang, which formed between 151st and 155th along Central Avenue in a strip of land called the Nestor Tract, which had been ceded to Compton by the County of Los Angeles. Compton officials, eager to expand the city's tax base, were only too happy to accept the new neighborhood. What they did not realize, however, was that with it came the largest and most violent of Latino gangs, the 1-5-5.

In response to the absorption of 1-5-5 into Compton, other Hispanic gangs sprang up to defend their territories. In the northeastern part of the city a vicious group calling itself CV Tres, or CV3, appeared in the early sixties. The CV stood for Compton Barrio, which the Latinos pronounced "vario," and the *tres* referred to the fact that it was an amalgamation of three smaller gangs, the Dead End, Largo, and Tortilla Flats, which had united to challenge the 1-5-5. Across the railroad tracks from CV3 another gang took shape, the Largo 36. Largo was the street on which the gang was formed; the number three stood for the third letter of the alphabet, *C,* which denoted Compton; the six was for the letter *F,* which stood for *firma,* meaning "signature."

All of these gangs had at least two things in common: They jealously guarded their territory, and they resented the police, whom they saw as the enforcers of the Anglo establishment that had displaced their culture. Nonetheless, they were *Compton* gangs, and when the Watts riots broke out just across the border, it was Largo 36 that kept the rioters out of the city. The decision to do so was taken spontaneously by their leader, an obese, bald-headed killer nicknamed Ditto. That he and his homeys did so was, perhaps, the ultimate act of defending their territory.

There were black gangs in Compton during this period, but they were loosely organized and never very large. That changed in the late sixties, however, as the city's population changed.

The Slausons were a black gang that had existed in South Central L.A. for some years. By the early seventies, the Slausons had affiliated with the Crips of Los Angeles, founded by Stanley "Tookie" Williams and Raymond Washington, and together they began making incursions down Central Avenue into Compton. Whenever a party was given to which the Slauson/Crips were not invited, they would drive by and shoot up the house. It was becoming clear that, before too long, the Crips were going to establish themselves in Compton.

To counter this, a gang formed in the neighborhood in which I had grown up, along Piru Street, which intersected Central Avenue just north of 136th. The leader of this gang was the scrawny kid with whom I had thrown a football in my sandlot days, Sylvester Scott, now known as Puddin'. Scott had joined forces with four other Compton boys, A. C. Moses, Larry Watts, known as Tam, Vincent Owens, and Lorenzo Betton, called Low, to create the Piru gang.

Originally the Pirus were affiliated with the Crips, but after a series of internal battles, they split off. Since the Pirus were vastly outnumbered by the more established Crips, Sylvester Scott began to pull together the smaller black gangs in the border areas of north Compton. The most important of these "sets" was the Family, a gang based on Central Avenue across the street from Centennial High School. Together they coalesced into a criminal confederation that eventually became known as the Bloods.

Just as the Hispanic gangs had done, the Crips and the Bloods adopted colors, jargon, and symbols of their own. Since the Crips used the color blue, the Piru/Bloods adopted red. Graffiti flourished, marking territory for the Crips and other outside gangs to see. Since the Bloods were a much smaller gang than the Crips, to compensate they quickly became more violent. They needed weapons and plenty of them, and so, in order to acquire them, the Bloods of Compton emulated the Crips and other

L.A. gangs by going into the drug trade. In this way, little Sylvester Scott, the kid no one wanted to play with, became not only one of the biggest drug traffickers in Compton but the leader of its most violent gang as well.

The rise of the gangs represented yet another dividing line in Compton. Kids who had grown up in the same neighborhoods, who had gone to school and played sports together, who dated one another's sisters, and danced at the sock hops in Cressey Park, were taking sides across a barrier that separated criminality and the law. Though Sylvester Scott and I had known each other all our lives, there could not have been a greater distance between us; he in his Bloods, and I in my Dirty Dozen. Central Avenue had become more than a dividing line between sections; it was a dividing line between souls.

Some of the cocaine that the Bloods were importing into Compton came from the Brazilian mafia via the Southeast Asia–Marseille–Rio de Janeiro route run by the French Connection. One night we got word that the Bloods had brought in a big shipment of Brazilian coke. Frank Brower was working undercover narcotics at that time, and he arranged to make a buy from the Brazilians at their safe house in Inglewood, near Los Angeles Airport.

The plan was for Brower, who was scruffy and bearded, to drive to the house followed by Rutigliano and me. We would watch the house while he went inside. During the deal, he would stand with his back to the window. If he turned, that meant there was trouble. Rut and I waited in an unmarked car across the street.

At first, everything was going as planned. Brower stood in the window, his back to the street. When he came out with the goods, we would rush in and make the bust. As we waited, a car carrying three men came slowly toward us, circling the block. We knew they were lookouts, Brazilians doing security for the deal, and we also knew that they carried submachine guns, and even a Browning Automatic Rifle. That BAR was capable of ripping open our car with us in it. As their headlights swept over us, Rut and I crouched down under the dashboard. The car passed us and disappeared around the corner.

"You think they made us?" I asked Rut as he squeezed his big bulk below the steering wheel.

"I dunno."

We both took out our guns.

I peeked over the dash. "We can't leave Brower in there."

"See what he's doing," Rut said.

I carefully raised my head and looked at the house. "He's facing the window."

"Shit," Rut grunted. It was the signal to go in. "If those fuckers come back, we're dead."

We were still wedged in under the dash, and before Rut sat up I said, "If we're gonna get killed, there's something I need to tell you."

Rutigliano glanced at me. "What?"

"I've never liked you," I said.

Rut screwed up his face. "You asshole."

We shoved the doors open and rushed the house. There was no sign of the surveillance car. By the time we broke in the front door, Brower had his gun out, and the three of us, shouting and waving our guns, took the gangbangers by surprise.

We confiscated over a million dollars' worth of cocaine and made half a dozen arrests. The surveillance car never came back.

The last patrol I did with Rutigliano occurred several nights later. We were assigned to District 1 on the west side of Compton. It was not an area Rut usually worked. A call came over the radio of a domestic abuse situation with a woman down and bleeding in the front yard of a house on Haskins Lane.

"Where the fuck is that?" Rutigliano said. He grabbed the street map from the glove box and began unfolding it. "Haskins . . . I never even heard of it . . ."

I knew that Haskins Lane was on the far edge of the west side; in fact, only a block of it was in Compton, the rest being in an unincorporated area of L.A. County. "It's over by the 110," I said.

Rut was still fumbling with the accordion of the map, fuming and cursing. "Where?!" he demanded. "Do you know where it is?!"

"Yeah," I remarked. "I used to deliver mail over there."

He was starting to panic. "Well, for Christ's sakes, tell me!" I said nothing. His face began to glow purple. "Is this about that fucking knife?!" he bellowed.

I just looked at Rut in silence. He exploded. "All right! Shit! I'll give you the fucking knife! Just tell me where the damn street is!"

"Go down to McKinley and turn left," I said. Then I added, "And you can keep the fucking knife."

Rutigliano threw the map out the window and jammed the car into gear. I sat back, satisfied. I was even.

It was not long after that that Rutigliano's career took a strange and unexpected turn. As did mine.

As bad as things were getting in Compton, in 1970 we had an intimation of worse to come. A radical group called the US Organization moved into the city and established a base on Atlantic Avenue on the far eastern side. US had been founded by Ron Karenga, a onetime member of the Black Panthers.

Karenga, a follower of Malcolm X, had a master's degree in political science from UCLA. He had discontinued his PhD studies after the Watts riots and had broken with the Panthers in order to create US, a Black Nationalist group that militated for separatism and community pride. A centerpiece of their platform was the declaration of Kwanzaa as an alternative to Christmas. US was summarily denounced by the Panthers, who claimed that their initials stood for "United Slaves."

In 1971, Karenga, another man, and a woman were convicted of the kidnapping, beating, and torture of two female US members. The tortures included stripping the women, whipping them with an electrical cord, and forcing a hot soldering iron into one's mouth. The creator of Kwanzaa served four years in state prison.

The principals in the Compton US clan were the four Benson brothers and the three Widby brothers. Far from being revolutionaries, we knew they were nothing more than local thugs who used the US label to terrorize the neighborhood. We had had many run-ins with the Widbys, including one time when I had arrested Joe Widby for a string of robberies and assaults. Joe had refused to talk, and so, while my partner Roland Ballard looked on, I had beaten a confession out of him using sap gloves.

One night Mario Widby went out on the balcony of the brothers' apartment on Atlantic Avenue with a .44 Magnum revolver. Across the alley was one of the last country and western bars in Compton, a remnant from the old Spade Cooley days, which was frequented by seniors who still came for the music. At around 2:00 A.M., an old hillbilly crooner stepped out into the alley for a smoke, and Mario Widby shot him. There was no provocation, no cause at all; he simply put a bullet into the old man's back and killed him. He was arrested, tried for murder, and sentenced to life without parole.

After that, Larry Widby went on a rampage of robbing local businesses. One night he hit the Milk Palace on Compton Boulevard, where he killed an Asian clerk and emptied the register. Five minutes later he walked into Gus's Liquor Store with his .44. The owner, an elderly Korean man, had been robbed so many times that he always carried a gun. When he saw Widby he started shooting, and Widby returned fire. The Korean was hit, but so was Widby.

Officer Philip "Catfish" Bailey and I were first at the scene. While Catfish secured the parking lot, I entered the store, where I found Larry Widby bleeding in one of the aisles. I thought he was a victim, but when I tried to help him, he reached for his gun. I wrestled with him, took the gun away, and arrested him.

US did not last long in Compton. The organization was neither well organized nor well funded, and its membership consisted almost entirely of criminals. As we began to round them up and send them to prison, US mutated into its true form, evolving into the Atlantic Drive Crips, an affiliate of the Crips of South Central.

This evolution from a so-called radical group into a gang foreshadowed a much more sinister trend; namely, from gangs to self-styled political parties. At the forefront of this menacing trend were the Black Panthers.

Panthers, Water Way, and the Standoff in Victory Park

During my first two years with the CPD, a radical change was taking place in the gang population. The Black Panthers had moved into South Central L.A. from their base in Oakland, and they immediately set about recruiting among the gangs.

While the Panthers had a political agenda that was much admired in chic left-wing circles, the fact was that they were a criminal conspiracy that used criminal methods. It was not long before the Panthers had virtually absorbed the Slauson gang, as well as several other smaller sets: the Huns, the Gaylords, the Gladiators, and the Brims.

All of these groups exchanged their traditional gang regalia for the black leather jackets and black berets of the Panthers, but their behavior remained exactly the same. Among other things, this meant narcotics trafficking. Though the Panthers' platform denounced drug use, it was only the drug trade they did not themselves control to which they objected. So the gangs of South Central continued their traffic in drugs, using the revenue to support the Panthers, some of whose leaders, such as Huey Newton, were addicts themselves.

To us, this was an ominous development. By now we estimated that there were some ten thousand criminals living in Compton—more than a tenth of the population—most of whom were gang members or were gang affiliated. The Panthers' success in uniting the gangs of South Los Angeles, therefore, posed the prospect of the gangs of Compton merging into one supergang that would be aligned with those in L.A. If this happened, we knew, it would be impossible for us, 130 cops, to maintain control of the city. To combat such a monolithic criminal organization, either the National Guard or federal troops would have to be brought in.

From our perspective in the CPD, this was the real threat posed by the Panthers: uniting the city's gangs into a massive criminal conspiracy under the guise of political activism. We were facing a tsunami of crime and trying to hold it back with a picket fence. We could not wait for the wave to hit; the question was how to prevent it.

The most common accusation that has been leveled against the Compton Police Department is that we were "too close to the criminals." In fact, given how badly outnumbered we were, our knowledge of the criminal element was one of our chief assets. We used this knowledge and the ability it gave us to be proactive and to even the odds. Our struggle against the Black Panthers' attempt to infiltrate Compton and organize its gangs is perhaps the most important case in point.

I had grown up with Sylvester Scott, and I had known the other founders of the Bloods most of my life. So when we began to see the Panthers' first incursions into Compton, I decided to have a talk with Puddin'.

One night I picked up an unmarked car and drove over to the west side with Officer Bernard Brown. I had chosen Brown carefully. He and I had grown up in the same neighborhood, and just a block away from Sylvester Scott. Brown was one of the "jocks" in the department, a former Centennial High athlete who held the high jump and long jump records and had run a 9.8-second hundred-yard dash. I wanted a black officer with me, and though Roland Ballard was my partner at the time, he was not physical enough, while Joe Ferrell, who hated bangers and never missed a chance to jack them up, could be too brutal, living up to his handle, Flashlight

Joe. So it was Bernard Brown I wanted behind me when I talked to the leader of the Bloods.

We turned off North Parmelee Avenue into Piru Street, where Scott still lived, and pulled over. We were only one block from my parents' house. Crime in my old neighborhood had become so prevalent, and shots were being fired so often, that my father had had to cement over the windows that faced Central Avenue. As I drove by the house that night, I could see their outlines through the newer stucco. It was a sad sight, like the swollen eyes of a domestic violence victim. There were bars on the other windows and on the doors, too, and not just in my house—the entire neighborhood seemed to have become an armed camp, the houses like medieval fortresses sealed against barbarian invasions.

We waited in Piru Street until I saw Scott leave his house and start toward Central Avenue. He was no longer a skinny little kid; he was tall and muscular, and the red 49ers jacket he wore made him seem even bigger. I kept the lights off and pulled over to the sidewalk.

Scott turned, scowling, and reached into his pocket. Then he saw me behind the wheel. "Hey, Johnny," he said, using the name that people had called me in childhood. I told him that we needed to talk and asked him to get into the back. He hesitated a moment, and then he climbed in.

Just off 134th Street near the intersection with Parmelee is an alley called Water Way. It is so small and secluded that many of the local people did not even know it was there, but some of the cops, like Rutigliano and myself, used Water Way for meetings we did not wish to advertise. It was also a convenient spot to settle scores and set people straight. Water Way was used by a rug cleaning company, and the only thing in it was a series of gigantic racks from which Oriental rugs were hung to be washed and dried. These hanging rugs gave the alley an even more private quality, which I thought would be indispensable for this meeting.

When I turned into the alley, Scott stiffened. "I thought you wanted to talk, Johnny," he said.

"That's all we're gonna do for now," I answered.

I pulled to a stop behind one of the broad, soaking rugs and got out of the car. While Bernie Brown waited, I opened the back door and asked

Sylvester Scott to take a walk with me. Again he seemed wary, but he had known me since he was a kid, and he trusted me. He got out and followed me into the maze of carpets down to the end of the alley.

We stopped between two of the hanging rugs. We were as isolated as if we were on the dark side of the moon; no one could see or hear us. Scott was armed, and I knew it; he could not go anywhere without a gun. Normally I would have patted him down before I put him in the car, and the fact that I had let him get this far with his gun was a deliberate signal to him.

"What you want, Johnny?" he asked. He had a full Afro, intelligent eyes, and clean-cut features. He could have gone to college and been anything he wanted. Instead, he was one of the most dangerous criminals in America's most dangerous city.

I said that I supposed he knew what the Panthers were up to.

"So?"

I told him that the Panthers were really nothing but the Slausons, who wanted to move into Compton and take over. "They want your turf, your girlfriends, and your trade." I said that the Panthers had already absorbed some of the smaller Crips sets, and it was only a matter of time before the Crips and the Panthers aligned. That meant a Panther move into Compton would be nothing less than an invasion by the Crips. "When Huey Newton and Tookie Williams join forces," I concluded, "it'll be a whole new ball game."

Scott heard me out in silence. "So what you want from me?" he asked. I was sure he already knew, but he wanted to hear me say it.

"You and I have the same interest in common: keeping the Panthers out of Compton. I want you to help us do that."

He thought about it a moment. Despite the deep shadows of the alley I could see that his face was serious, even solemn, and I thought that I could still see in it the lonely kid I had thrown the ball to a dozen years ago. "What you gonna do for us?"

It was the quid pro quo, and I was prepared for it. "We'll back off you till this business is over," I answered.

"How far off?"

"Not completely," I said, "but far enough." I knew that if I promised too much, he would not trust me, and if I offered too little, it would not be worth it to him.

"Who you talking for, Johnny?" he wanted to know.

"It's me, and it's Bernard. You know us, you know who we are. You know we'll keep our word." Then I brought down the hammer; he was expecting it, and I had to do it. "And you know that if you don't help us, if you even think about throwing in with the Panthers, we'll do whatever we have to do to stop it."

There was the faintest flicker of surprise in his eyes. "Whatever?" he repeated.

I was talking about killing him, and he knew it. "Whatever," I said.

He mulled it over a long moment, studying me closely, gauging how serious I was, how much this meant to me. I think if it had been any other cop, any social worker or city official, Scott would have laughed in his face, or just shot him on the spot. Instead, he nodded at me. "Yeah, okay," he said at last.

Brown and I drove him back to Piru Street, and he got out of the car.

"Don't forget," I called after him. "We got a deal."

Scott smiled. His smile was oddly shy, almost childlike. "Yeah, Johnny," he answered. "You and me, we always got some kinda deal."

I watched him walk into his house, the house where he had grown up and lived his twenty-three years. It was a life as brutal and violent as it was brief, and brilliant in its twisted way. In just a few years, he had succeeded in organizing a criminal conspiracy that was now a vital part of the life of his city, and he led it without fear and without remorse. As he quietly closed the barred door, I had to wonder why.

Maybe it was because no one would play with him as a kid, or maybe because, in his own way, he wanted to change things as much as I did. There was a depth of hurt and anger and a need for power and respect in this young man that was almost unfathomable. Whatever the cause, Sylvester Scott was now one of the most important people in Compton. Yet I could not help but feel that he was still a sad, lonely, and resentful little boy.

The strategy worked, just as it had done during the Watts riots. Unwilling to allow any outsiders into their territory, the Bloods, in effect, became our principal ally in the fight to keep the Panthers out of Compton. I have often thought that it was not only self-interest that motivated Sylvester Scott to decide to help us, but also the fact that I was one of the few people he trusted, because I had been kind to him as a child.

There was another line that we pursued against the Panthers, again using our knowledge of the city's criminal element. After I succeeded in putting Phil Lee in prison, his drug business was taken over by Joe Pagano, an Italian who ran with the blacks and was known as Super Fly. Before we could bust him for trafficking, Pagano was murdered by a member of his own crew. That left a vacuum in the leadership of the drug trade.

The west side trade was dominated by a kid from my neighborhood, Judge Williams. In addition to the usual stuff—Seconals, black beauties, hash, and grass—Williams was selling cocaine and heroin. His muscle men were the three Allen brothers, who worked out of Sonny's Pool Hall and the Texas Playhouse, and his chief distributors were Rex and Eddie Pope, who had grown up across the street from me. Rex Pope was the looter who had offered to get me anything I wanted during the Watts riot. Eddie, his stepbrother, worked for a disposal service, and it was with his garbage truck that Williams distributed his narcotics.

As I had done with Sylvester Scott, I arranged through Rex Pope to meet with Eddie to enlighten him about his self-interest where the Panthers were concerned. I pointed out that the Panthers' platform called for an eradication of the dope business—unless they themselves controlled it—and that would mean a war with the Williams-Pope syndicate. With the South Central gangs behind them, it was not a war they were likely to win. Williams and Pope got the message, and they agreed, as the Bloods had done, to help keep the Panthers out of Compton. In return, though we knew the drop-off points of Eddie's garbage truck, we stayed away from them.

Enlisting the aid of Judge Williams and Eddie Pope was one of the most difficult decisions I had yet made as a cop. They were scum—drug pushers who did not scruple to sell to kids, and whose trade was undermining the fabric of the community. Nevertheless, I had to make a value judgment: work with Williams and Pope long enough to neutralize the Panthers, or let the Panthers move into Compton and organize the gangs into a massive criminal conglomerate. I chose the former. The Panthers had to be dealt with now; the pushers could wait.

It was a policy of divide and conquer, like the one Caesar had used with the local tribes in the Gallic wars. As long as we could play the criminals off against one another, we had a hope of retaining control of the streets. We were striking a delicate balance, and a dangerous one. At any moment, Sylvester Scott or Judge Williams might see through our strategy and throw in their lot with the Panthers. Then the Crips and Bloods would unite, overwhelming us utterly. On the other hand, in order to hold up our end of the bargain, we had to be careful in our dealings with them. Too many raids or too big a bust might tip the scales against us, and that could mean anarchy in Compton.

Still, we never lost sight of the fact that these, our temporary allies, were criminals, and the worst kinds of criminals. So we walked a very fine line between maintaining order and losing control, between upholding the law and breaking it. Given our small numbers and the sheer size of the criminal element, the best we could hope for was to keep the lid on Compton as Caesar had done in Gaul. At one time in my life I had wanted to teach high school kids about the barbarian tribes that had swept across ancient Europe—now I was engaged in a struggle with them myself.

The Panthers were not the only radical group we had to deal with during my first years on the force. Another called itself the Malcolm X Foundation. It was headed by Malcolm X's cousin, Hakim Jamal, who came to California from Boston. In 1968, my rookie year, he established the Foundation in the Victory Park housing development off Wilmington Avenue in East Compton. A white enclave when Jamal arrived, Victory Park was a cluster of gray-sided town houses built by the Navy in World War II for personnel stationed at the Port of Long Beach. It was a labyrinth of narrow, curving, neatly landscaped streets surrounded by a black iron fence tipped with spear points.

Jamal had seen the Panthers' attempt to move into West Compton fail because of opposition from the Bloods and the Pope-Williams drug syndicate. Instead of making the same mistake, he chose to house his foundation in a white neighborhood in East Compton, and, ironically, that enabled him to gain a toehold in the city. Jamal's warlord and enforcer was a tall, fiery, rail-thin radical named David Hutton, and together they built their organization slowly and carefully, keeping a low profile.

As soon as the Black Muslims moved into Victory Park, the whites began fleeing in panic, their houses bought or rented by Muslims from the Bay Area and back east. Before long, the Malcolm X Foundation owned nearly every house in Victory Park, which had become an armed and isolated camp. To this point Jamal and Hutton had been careful and quiet, building their base, strengthening their stronghold, spreading their influence, but in late 1969 they made their first overt move to announce their presence in Compton. It was potentially an explosive one, triggered almost by chance.

It began with a pursuit on the 91 Freeway. A California highway patrolman, Sergeant Haggard, was chasing a young black woman in a car as it careened toward Compton. When the car reached Wilmington Avenue, it veered off the freeway and into the heart of the city. As the highway patrolman followed, the woman drove straight into Victory Park, where she finally stopped. Haggard got out of his car with his gun drawn and confronted the woman. She began screaming for help, and almost at once, members of the Malcolm X Foundation were pouring out of the surrounding houses. Before he knew it, Haggard was surrounded by an angry and jeering crowd.

This was nearly the same situation that, four years before, had ignited the Watts riots: a white CHP officer arresting a black suspect in an all-black neighborhood. What was even more serious now was the fact that this incident was occurring in the stronghold of an armed and organized radical group. As Haggard tried to get the woman out of her car, more and more Muslims crowded around, many carrying weapons—blackjacks, truncheons, knives, and guns—and within a few minutes, both Hakim Jamal and his warlord, David Hutton, had joined them.

Sergeant Haggard gave up his attempt to arrest the woman and instead called in to his station to ask for reinforcements. The crowd was pressing in on him as he sat in his patrol car with the windows rolled up and the doors locked. By now, David Hutton was whipping up the crowd, and the scene was becoming increasingly ugly. The dispatcher told Haggard that the nearest backup was fifteen to twenty minutes away, so CHP contacted Compton police headquarters to ask for assistance.

That night I was patrolling the district with Officer Willie Mosley, a Marine Corps reservist with whom I had gone through the academy. Mosley, who had been born in Mississippi, was a member of the militant faction, but he was a good, solid cop, short, thickset, and absolutely fearless.

When the call to assist a CHP officer came in, Mosley and I rolled to Victory Park, where we found a near riot in progress. There were by now fifty or sixty Muslims; they had both cars surrounded and were protecting the woman driver while at the same time threatening to smash in Sergeant Haggard's windows. Mosley and I drove to the iron gate at the Compton Boulevard entrance. When we reached the scene, David Hutton was shouting at the top of his voice that the crowd should attack the CHP car and "kill the pig" inside. Mosley and I knew we had to take control, or we might have another Watts riot erupting right there in Victory Park.

I got out of my unit and demanded to know who was in charge. Hakim Jamal stepped forward, backed by Hutton. Jamal was tall and wiry, with narrow eyes, a bulbous Afro, and a thin mustache and goatee. "I am," he said.

"Get these people off the street," I told him. "This is a police matter."

He sneered at me. "Police," he said, "you're nothing but a gang of thugs like the Slausons. They got their turf, you got yours. What's the difference?"

I refused to be baited. I told him that the crowd would have to disperse, and the CHP officer must be allowed to make his arrest.

"Fuck that!" David Hutton yelled. "Fuck you, and fuck the CHP!"

Instead of answering, I walked over to the woman's car, yanked open the door, and ordered her to get out. She did, and Mosley and I arrested her. This sudden action seemed to stun the crowd. While they watched, we took the woman over to Haggard's car and put her inside. There were only three of us facing down a crowd that had swollen to some seventy-five people, but instead of backing us up, Sergeant Haggard started his engine and, without a word, drove off. Now Mosley and I were left alone to deal with the mob. They were yelling and screaming again, urged on by David Hutton. We were completely cut off.

"What you gonna do now, pig?" Hutton demanded. "We're gonna fuck you up."

Mosley and I took our guns out and stood back-to-back. "I tell you what we're gonna do," I answered. "Anybody makes a move on us, we're gonna blow his fucking head off."

Hutton laughed. "There's plenty more of us than you."

"Yeah," I said, "but the first ones that come at us we're gonna kill. We're gonna take twelve of you down." I pointed my gun at Hutton's face. "And I'm starting with you, motherfucker."

For a moment, nothing happened, but it was a moment in which anything *could* have happened. They could have rushed us, the shooting would have started, we would have been killed, and Victory Park would have become the epicenter of a conflagration that might threaten the whole city. David Hutton seemed unsure what to do. Maybe it was my gun in his face, or maybe the fact that Mosley was black. Then a voice came from the edge of the crowd. "Make that twenty."

It was Officer Joe Flores, our backup in the district. He also had his gun out and pointed at the crowd. With Mosley and me back-to-back and Flores on the outside, the Muslims knew they were in trouble. After a few more moments' hesitation, they began to back off.

A path was clearing to our car, and Mosley and I started toward it, backing away with Flores behind us. It looked like the situation had been defused, but just as we reached the car, two of the Muslims made a lunge for us. One carried a straight razor, and the other had a knife. The man with the razor threw himself on me and slashed at my neck. I swung out with my revolver and smashed it against his head. He went down in a heap. I snatched the razor away and cuffed him. Meanwhile, Flores and Mosley had wrestled the other man to the ground. While Jamal and Hutton looked on, we jammed both of them into our car.

I turned back to what was left of the crowd. "Get the fuck out of here!" I yelled. "Go home!"

Slowly, sullenly, they dispersed. Their leaders had been challenged and forced to back down; they had been humiliated. Headless, the mob lost its heart. In a few more minutes, the street had been cleared. Mosley and I got into our car and Flores into his, and we drove back to headquarters.

There was blood dripping down under my collar, staining the blue sleeve of my uniform. "Rick, you better get that looked at," Mosley said.

"Deal with these assholes first," I answered.

We booked the two men for assaulting police officers, and the one who had cut me, a radical from South Central named Masika Jamaka Tatum, for attempted murder. Then I was driven to the hospital to have my neck attended to.

That was not the end of the incident, however. Hakim Jamal followed us to police headquarters, where he demanded that his men be released, and that charges be brought against Mosley and me for threatening him and David Hutton. The watch commander that night was Lieutenant Robert Conway, who was the senior officer of the Dirty Dozen, and he heard Jamal out in silence.

"Well," demanded Jamal, "what are you gonna do?"

Conway, who prided himself on keeping his cool, replied that he would speak to the officers involved.

"What you wanna talk to those two fuckers for?" Jamal shot back. "They're nothin' but two pachuco assholes and a fucked-up Uncle Tom."

Conway regarded him a moment longer, seething. "You get the fuck out of my face," he snarled. Jamal was stunned and tried to protest, but Conway exploded. "You got no business with me! Now grab your sorry ass and shag it out of here!"

Later that night the Muslims held a rally in Victory Park. Over a hundred people showed up, shouting antipolice slogans, led by Jamal and Hutton. The fury was fueled by alcohol and indignation, and when officers of the P.M. shift showed up, the crowd began showering them with projectiles. The Dirty Dozen had come armed with helmets, shields, and batons. They formed a phalanx and moved in echelon into the park.

The leaders of the shift that night were Dominic Rutigliano and Bill St. Onge. While St. Onge and his men held the protestors at bay, Rut made straight for David Hutton. "Get the fuck out of here," he ordered. Hutton defiantly refused. Rutigliano raised his baton. "Get over that fence or I'll bust your ass and drag it to jail."

Faced with Rut behind his mask and a three-foot-long truncheon in his fist, Hutton realized he had no choice. "I'll leave," he said, "but by the front gate, not the fence."

"You're goin' over the fucking fence," Rutigliano growled, and he shoved Hutton backward. Rut knew that if he could force Hutton to leave in this humiliating fashion, his credibility would be shattered.

Hutton knew it, too, and he stood his ground. "Fuck you, pig. I ain't movin'."

It was the wrong decision. Rut struck out with his baton and smacked Hutton on the hip. Hutton nearly collapsed. "Get over that fucking fence," Rut repeated, and he raised his baton again. This time Hutton capitulated.

While the Muslims watched, David Hutton pulled himself up painfully and hobbled toward the black iron fence. As he did, Rutigliano kicked him in the backside so hard that Hutton was lifted off his feet. He fell to his hands and knees. Rutigliano kicked him again, and then began prodding him with his baton across the grass. "Over it!" he shouted.

Hutton looked at him with a lethal rage in his eyes. "This ain't finished, pig," he grumbled.

"Damn straight," Rut answered with a grin. "And next time I see you, you better have a fucking gun."

He gave Hutton another whack on the backside with the baton. Hutton scrambled up and over the fence, landing headfirst on the far side.

St. Onge then formed up the men and marched toward the protestors.

He was livid, scarcely under control. Leading the phalanx, he slashed out savagely with his baton, smashing arms and skulls until they had forced the protestors off Alondra Boulevard back into Victory Park.

In one night, the Malcolm X Foundation had suffered three serious setbacks: our arrest of the woman in the park, Lieutenant Conway's refusal to be intimidated by Jamal, and David Hutton's humiliation at the hands of Rutigliano.

Later that night, when I was released from the hospital, I joined Rut, St. Onge, and the Dozen at the Golden Garter for a celebration. It had been a victory not so much of police work as of urban warfare. We had met the enemy on his home turf, and we had regained control of it. The CPD as a whole had established its command presence, asserting its will and proving that it was stronger than that of the insurgents.

We had damaged the Malcolm X Foundation, but we had not silenced it. Hakim Jamal and David Hutton knew that if they did not strike back, their hope of becoming the dominant force in the streets of Compton was dead. They therefore determined to get revenge on the CPD. When they tried, they did it in the most cowardly and vicious way possible.

Bullets in the Laundromat, Shondra, and the Bomb

A few nights after the demonstration in Victory Park, there was a football game at Compton High stadium. Such events always called for extra security, since members of rival gangs were likely to show up. We had several units stationed around the stadium and a few officers inside. I was again on duty with Willie Mosley, and we cruised up and down Compton Boulevard looking for troublemakers.

What we did not know was that several Black Panthers had slipped into the stadium, and at halftime one of them, a young kid, put on his black beret and began striding up and down the sidelines with a bullhorn urging people to "Organize, and off the pigs!"

One of our officers, Hourie Taylor, who because of his size was ironically known as Huggy Bear, grabbed this kid by his neck and began kicking him in the backside in front of the entire stadium. Then Taylor dragged him off the field as the students jeered and laughed.

"Next time I'm gonna do more than kick your ass," Taylor shouted, furious.

The young Panther was nearly in tears. "I'm gonna tell Ma what you did!" he whined.

The kid was Hourie Taylor's younger brother. Taylor hauled him out through the gate and shoved him into the street. "You get your ass home and stay there!" he shouted as his brother slinked off.

Apart from that, things were pretty calm until near the end of the second half. We had a senior officer, Burt Weingarten, patrolling the parking lot in an antiquated three-wheeled motorbike, enforcing the parking regulations. Burt was a big, heavyset veteran of twenty years on the force who was looking forward to retirement. At one point he spotted a car illegally parked on the far side of Compton Boulevard, and he drove his motorbike over to ticket it. Inside were four members of the Malcolm X Foundation.

As Burt approached, one of the Muslims shoved a carbine out the back window and fired several shots at him. He swerved away, but a bullet caught him in the back of the neck, just below his skull. Weingarten pitched forward onto the hub of his bike, which careened into a parked car. He was badly wounded, but as the Muslims sped off, he was able to reach his Motorola radio and put out an alert.

Mosley and I were the closest unit to the scene, and when we got Burt's call that he had been shot, we raced over. We found him slumped across the handlebars, losing blood and consciousness. He described the car and told us the direction it had taken. By this time other units were arriving, so we left Burt to be taken to the hospital and we set off in pursuit.

It was not long before we spotted the car dodging in and out of traffic on Compton Boulevard. I had my gun out, but I could not shoot because there were pedestrians on the sidewalks. This did not stop the Muslims, however. They were firing pistols and carbine rounds from both sides of the fleeing vehicle. People were dropping to the ground and cars were screeching to a halt as the one-sided gun battle continued down the boulevard. It was maddening, frustrating, but there was nothing Mosley and I could do except swerve in and out of traffic after them.

Then another patrol car screamed past us, shots firing from its passenger-side window. It was Officer Bruce Hutton, a bespectacled, scholarly-looking cop not usually known for his aggressiveness. Now, however, his .41 Magnum blasted over Compton Boulevard, the sound echoing off the storefronts. One of his shots blew out the rear window of the Muslims' car, which fishtailed onto the sidewalk and crashed through the windows of a Laundromat. As it smashed to a stop among the bricks and broken glass, the four men bailed out and hid behind the washing machines.

Mosley and I pulled up across the street, and the Muslims immediately began firing at us. We jumped out of our car, ducked behind the doors, and fired back. Then Bruce Hutton and his partner rolled up, and for a few frantic minutes, a gunfight blazed across Compton Boulevard.

While I was huddled behind the car door returning the Muslims' fire, I heard a voice shouting at me, "Rick! Hey, Rick!" It was my old pal from my dance club days, Jesse Sida, crawling toward me across the sidewalk. "Gimme a shotgun, man, and I'll help you out."

I yelled at him to get back, but he made his way toward the car on all fours as bullets went flying overhead, shattering the windows.

"Just toss me a shotgun, man," he called back, "and I'll help you charge those guys over there. Look, I can see 'em running."

It was true—the Muslims were darting toward the back of the Laundromat. At that moment, Bruce Hutton stood up from behind his car and fired off a quick couple of rounds. One hit a Muslim in the hip, and he went down. The others grabbed him and disappeared into the back of the store. We did not know where they were, so we moved in cautiously. By the time we had cleared the scene, the Muslims were gone. We learned later that they had made their way to David Hutton's house, where they hid overnight before escaping out of the state.

Burt Weingarten survived his wound, but afterward he suffered from such debilitating migraines that he had to take early retirement. Our sources within the community gave us the names of the shooters, and we put out a nationwide alert for them. It was not until two years later that the man who had shot Burt Weingarten was finally found in a little Texas town near the Louisiana border. Texas Rangers surrounded the house where he was holed up, and when he refused to surrender and began firing at them, they shot him dead.

After the shooting at Compton High, we put together a task force that swept the houses in Victory Park for weapons. We confiscated several dozen rifles and handguns, together with a good deal of ammunition. At that time it was not illegal to keep an unregistered weapon in the home, so we were not able to make any arrests, but we did take the guns back to the station. That night, Hakim Jamal marched on police headquarters with his followers.

Our sources in the neighborhood had warned us that the demonstration was going to take place, and so every cop in Compton had been summoned to headquarters. There were now 120 police in full riot gear—helmets, shields, shelter faces, and batons—confronting some 150 Muslims and Black Panthers outside the headquarters building. I was in the front rank, and I could see that many of the Panthers and some of the Muslims had guns.

Jamal demanded that we return their weapons, claiming that we had seized them illegally. The spokesman for our side was Captain Harold Lindemulder, the community affairs liaison, a slim, spectacled, soft-spoken man. As Jamal and Hutton ranted, the negotiations became more tense and vituperative, and with each passing minute, the standoff grew more ominous. If the Muslims opened fire, the results on both sides would have been catastrophic. One drug-addled brain, one brainwashed fanatic, one nervous finger would have been sufficient to provoke a massacre.

While Lindemulder and Hakim Jamal exchanged accusations and threats, I ran my eyes over the front rank of the mob, peering through the plastic of my visor. Some of the faces I recognized; some were new to me. Then my gaze fixed upon a woman standing nearly opposite me in the black leather jacket and beret of the Panthers, her face set in a grim determination, a revolver in her hand. It was Shondra Givens, my former classmate and girlfriend from Compton College. I straightened inadvertently and pointed my baton at her. The gesture caught her attention, and she scowled back, and then I saw her expression change—startled recognition at first, followed by a trace of a smile. From behind my face shield I winked at her.

The standoff lasted for another half hour, when Lindemulder agreed to give the Muslims back their weapons. They had a point, after all: We *had* confiscated them illegally, and we knew the court would eventually order us to return them. Half a dozen of our men went into the evidence locker, unloaded the rifles and pistols, and began turning them over. I grabbed a shotgun and walked up to Shondra Givens. "Be careful with this," I said with a smile.

"Fuck you, pig," she spat back for the benefit of her friends.

"You bet," I said.

As I handed the sawed-off to her, I passed her a note telling her that I wanted to meet her later that night.

When my shift ended at midnight I drove to the Compton Hotel, a dive frequented by junkies, winos, and hookers. It was no romantic hide-away, but it was inconspicuous. Shondra was waiting for me. We took a room and spent several hours together. She had become an addict, combining Seconals with "bombers," huge marijuana cigars. Once plastered, she began talking about Hakim Jamal and his plans. Jamal was determined to position himself as a black messiah, she told me, the embodiment of black pride and black consciousness. He had dreams of becoming the spiritual leader of the entire black liberation movement. His goals were grandiose, she said, and he would stop at nothing to achieve them. What was more, as the standoff at the police station had shown, he was attempting to forge an alliance with the Panthers. Shortly after telling me this, she passed out.

If what Shondra had told me was accurate, the information was as important as it was explosive. Hakim Jamal was going to try to use Compton as the base for initiating a whole new phase in the radical movement. Already he had succeeded in aligning the Malcolm X Foundation with the Panthers, at least to the extent that they had joined his demonstration at police headquarters. I could only assume that, having failed to penetrate the gang culture, the Panthers were looking for new avenues of infiltration into Compton and saw one in the foundation. It was not long before my assumption proved correct.

Soon after the demonstration, following Jamal's example, the Panthers opened an office on Compton Boulevard *east* of Long Beach. This move came as a complete surprise to us; we had not expected them to try to establish themselves in the remaining white neighborhoods of the far east side. It was an audacious tactic, and the Panthers very quickly made sure that we could not ignore it.

They kept guards in uniform outside their office, defying us to make a move against them. Every time a patrol car drove by, which was often, they taunted and challenged the cops, and made no secret of the fact that they kept guns inside the office and were prepared to use them. In response, those of us who worked the P.M. shift began looking for some pretext to enter their headquarters and let them know who controlled the street.

It was not long before we found that one of their lieutenants had several warrants outstanding against him. That night, Rutigliano and I pulled up outside the office and walked in with our guns drawn. The Panthers were so shocked that at first they did nothing. We arrested the lieutenant and started to drag him out to the car. A couple of the Panthers produced guns, but we faced them down.

"If you want to get it on with us," I told them, "we're ready."

They could see that we meant it, and so, while we backed out with the prisoner, they made no attempt to stop us.

After this, the Panthers became even more determined. They stepped up their narcotics traffic, and they began bringing in recruits not only from L.A. but from the Bay Area as well. We knew that they were also increasing their stock of weapons and ammunition, and we could only guess what they had in mind. It was not long before we found out.

One night Officers Julio Hernandez and Johnny Cato responded to a call of shots fired in a house on Fig Street in Fruit Town. Two brothers named Bender lived at the address, longtime criminals who, like many others, had adopted the Black Panthers' radical ideology as a cover for drug dealing. A year previously, Officer Warren Selby and I had arrested Columbus Bender for armed robbery. He had resisted so fiercely that we had had to break several of his ribs with our sap gloves. I knew the Benders were dangerous characters, so when I heard the call over the radio, I drove to Fig Street as backup.

The Bender brothers were sitting on the front porch of the tiny frame house with AK-47 rifles, laughing and firing into the palm trees across the street. By the time Hernandez and Cato arrived, they had run out of ammunition.

"What the fuck are you doing?" Hernandez demanded as he and Cato took away the weapons and cuffed the men. "Are you high?"

The brothers said nothing. They seemed smug, even pleased with themselves. Hernandez told them they were going to search the house.

"Go ahead, man," Columbus Bender replied.

His smirking expression stopped Hernandez. "You're going inside with us," he said, and he and Cato shoved the brothers toward the front door.

They froze. "You can't go in that way," Columbus sputtered.

Hernandez peered at him. "Why not?"

"You just can't," he repeated.

"We are, and you're going in first."

The brothers started to panic. "No, man, don't do that! You got to go in the side."

Hernandez and Cato led them down the narrow driveway and told Columbus Bender to open the side door. He pushed it with his shoulder. "Go on in," Hernandez ordered.

The door led into a pocket-sized kitchen, the floor of which was covered by a ragged throw rug. While Cato watched the brothers, Hernandez peered into the parlor. It was a moment before he understood what he was looking at.

Directly inside the front door was a mousetrap from which two slender wires ran along the parlor floor and under the kitchen carpet. A second trap, cocked and ready to be sprung, sat at the back door.

"What the fuck is that?" Johnny Cato asked.

Hernandez turned to the brothers. "What the hell you got in here?" he asked. Again they said nothing. He carefully slid the shag rug aside with the toe of his boot. The wires from both traps disappeared between the floorboards.

"What is it, Hoo?" Johnny Cato said, using Hernandez's handle.

Hernandez knelt down and ran his fingers across the boards. One gave way slightly. He took out his pocket knife, opened a blade, and slid it into the crack. The board pried up. Hernandez curled his fingers underneath and lifted it. An entire section of floorboards came away. "Trapdoor," he said.

By this time, I had arrived on the scene. I walked up the driveway to the side door and poked my head in.

"Careful!" Hernandez called to me. "We got a situation here."

He was balancing the floorboards on his fingertips. My eyes traced the wires from the opening to the mousetraps at the front and back doors. Hernandez glanced at me. "Booby trap," I said.

"Shit," said Johnny Cato.

I moved carefully into the parlor, where Cato was guarding the Benders. "What you boys been up to?" I asked Columbus. He lowered his eyes and said nothing.

Hernandez shined his flashlight under the boards. "There's a tunnel," he said.

"I'll call for the bomb squad," I told him, and I walked back to my car.

In the kitchen, Hernandez lifted the trapdoor clear. Beneath it was an opening just wide enough for a man. He stood and began stripping off his jacket.

"What are you doin'?" Johnny Cato asked anxiously.

"I'm goin' down."

"Wait for the bomb squad, Hoo."

Hernandez sat on the edge and gingerly slipped his legs into the hole. The Benders looked on, ready to bolt.

"You ain't gonna go down there," Cato said.

"Why? You wanna go first?"

"No fuckin' way."

"Okay," Hernandez said. "I'm goin' in. You keep an eye on them. Make sure they stay right there." He scowled at the Benders. "Anything happens to me is gonna happen to you."

While Cato and the brothers watched, Julio lowered himself into the tunnel. He was a big man, and it was a narrow squeeze as he wriggled down into the dirty darkness. The tunnel turned 90 degrees, and Hernandez doubled himself over and slithered in. He crawled on hands and knees until he came to a van-sized excavation beneath the house.

The first thing he saw in the narrow beam of his flashlight was a dozen MAC-10 submachine guns. Around the walls were thousands of rounds of ammunition, still in their packing crates. At the center of the chamber was a stack of bricks of what looked like pink modeling clay. Hernandez knew at once what they were: C-4 plastic explosive. C-4 was deadly in small amounts; here was enough to destroy the entire neighborhood.

In the spectral glow of his light, Hernandez could see that the wires from the mousetraps terminated in a pipe bomb beneath the pink bricks. Had he and Cato broken down the front or back door, they would have sprung the traps and detonated the pipe bomb, exploding the C-4. That would have killed not only them but people in the houses on either side. He backed off. The whole house was a bomb, rigged to explode.

Hernandez crawled out of the tunnel gingerly. When he got back up to the kitchen, he was filthy, and furious.

"What was it, Hoo? What's down there?" Cato asked.

Hernandez walked up to the Bender brothers. "You lousy motherfuckers," he growled. "You were shooting them fuckin' AKs just to get us out here. It was a setup."

The bomb squad defused the pipe bomb and removed the C-4. The Benders admitted that the weapons and explosives were to have been used against the police. If the stash had been found, the plan was to kill as many "pigs" as possible. The message was unmistakable: The Panthers had declared war on the CPD and were determined to begin killing cops.

We knew that we had to act, and act quickly.

One night deep into the P.M. shift, a fire broke out at the Panther headquarters on Compton Boulevard. Someone had climbed up onto the roof of the building and dropped Molotov cocktails into the ventilator shafts. Dave Hall and Dominic Rutigliano called the fire department but told them to take their time. It was twenty minutes before the firemen arrived, and by that time, the building had been gutted. When the Panthers showed up the next morning, there was nothing left.

Between our discovery of their weapons cache and the destruction of their headquarters, the Panthers got the message. Never again did they try to establish themselves in Compton.

The late sixties and early seventies were a time of radicalism of all sorts. The war in Vietnam had alienated many of the young people of the nation, and poverty, social injustice, and civil rights were at the forefront of America's consciousness. While most people who took an active role in trying to change the nation's course did so in peaceful ways, there were a few who used more violent methods. Compton was not spared this kind of extremism.

While we were dealing with the Panthers and the Malcolm X Foundation, another radical group appeared: the Mao Tse-tung Organization. This was a Communist cabal, never very large, but extremely violent. In 1969 they opened an office on Alondra Boulevard and, in addition to using it to distribute their propaganda and *The Little Red Book,* built a bomb factory in the basement. They were determined to compensate for their small numbers by a very large demonstration of their presence. Their first target was Compton police headquarters.

Around noon on a Sunday in October, one of the Maoists, a kid named Tommy Harper, left their office carrying a satchel of explosives rigged with a timer. He made his way along the Southern Pacific Railroad tracks to the east side of our building, where there were few windows, and where the embankment would hide him from view. His goal was to get the bomb onto the roof, so that its downward explosion would cause the maximum of damage and injury.

Tommy set the timer and threw the satchel toward the roof. It struck the eave and fell to the ground. According to witnesses, he ran to it, picked it up, and heaved it a second time. This time it hit the roof but slid off and dropped back at his feet. Determined, the Maoist picked up the satchel of explosives a third time, but before he could throw it, it exploded in his hands.

The blast rocked the building, shattering glass but doing little other damage. However, Captain Lindemulder, the community liaison officer who had negotiated with Hakim Jamal, was sitting at his desk below one of the windows, and the explosion threw him across the room, injuring his back. By the time I reported for work that evening, the mess had been cleaned up, and CSI people were combing the Southern Pacific tracks looking for pieces of the bomber. Ultimately, all that was found was a thumb, lying on top of the embankment across Willowbrook Avenue.

In the aftermath of the attempted bombing of CPD headquarters, the LAPD stationed a twenty-four-hour-a-day guard on the roof of its nearby 77th Precinct building. With our chronic shortage of manpower and our stagnant budget, we did not have the luxury of such a precaution; all that we were able to do was to replace the plate glass windows of the station house with a cinder-block wall. We did, however, move quickly against the Mao Tse-tung Organization, raiding their office, cleaning it out, and putting its members on notice that they were not welcome in the city. They quickly disappeared and were never heard from again.

The day after the bombing, I walked into the locker room to find Rutigliano and other members of the Dirty Dozen singing a song they had made up to the tune of "Old MacDonald Had a Farm."

Tommy Harper had a bomb, e-i, e-i-o; Tommy Harper came to town, e-i, e-i-o/ With a Tommy here and a Tommy there . . . a little bit of Tommy everywhere . . .

It was the sort of macabre humor that characterized the P.M. shift. I laughed along with them, but to me it seemed unnecessarily callous and cruel. Tommy Harper had been a misguided kid, a wannabe revolutionary with more ideology than brains. I had flirted with the radicals myself in college, and I understood how easy it is for ivory-tower professors and professional troublemakers to lead young minds astray. What Tommy had done was more stupid than malign—a muddleheaded act of self-importance, more a function of immaturity than of evil—and though we did not deserve to die for his foolishness, I could not help but feel that neither did he.

As incidents such as the bombing, the near riot in Victory Park, and the standoff outside headquarters proved, in Compton all of us were living on the edge. Each of us knew that at any moment a gun would go off or a bomb would explode, and that would be the end. All we could do was try to be prepared and, in the face of such lethal pressure, to retain some semblance of humanity, no matter how raw.

The Panthers had left Compton, and the Mao Tse-tung Organization had disappeared. That left only the Malcolm X Foundation, which had won a kind of victory by compelling us to return their weapons. They still had their enclave in Victory Park, and Hakim Jamal was embarked on his program of declaring himself to be the black messiah. We felt that if we could discredit him, we could neutralize the Muslims once and for all. The opportunity to do so came almost by chance.

The CPD's budget allowed for only a small intelligence unit, but LAPD had a large and sophisticated one. It was modeled on J. Edgar Hoover's FBI, and it kept secret dossiers on anyone and everyone of interest to the department. This included criminals, politicians, and radical leaders. We knew they must have something on Hakim Jamal since he was a high-profile activist; the question was how to get the information.

I had heard that every Thursday night members of the intelligence squad had a party at the L.A. Police Academy near Dodger Stadium. It was by invitation only, and it featured alcohol and girls brought in for the evening from among the LAPD's groupies. A few of us from the Dirty Dozen managed to get ourselves invited to one of these parties, and while we were drinking and swapping war stories with the L.A. detectives, I brought up the subject of Hakim Jamal.

The response was immediate. The L.A. unit had been compiling information on Jamal since he had moved to Southern California, and their sources extended from Boston and Oakland to Washington, D.C., and Europe. As the liquor flowed, so did the information. I learned that Jamal had a history of mental illness and heroin addiction, and that he had been institutionalized for two attempted murders. The most important information they gave me was that Jamal, the would-be black messiah, was having an affair with the daughter of a member of the British Parliament, and that he also was a lover of the actress and model Jean Seberg.

I took this information back to Compton and shared it with Shondra

Givens, who began spreading it around the west side: Hakim Jamal was preaching black and sleeping white. It had the effect I intended—Jamal was disgraced and discredited. His rivals began to gang up on him; there were threats against his life. He left Compton and never returned. The Malcolm X Foundation was decapitated.

There was, however, one more problem to settle, and that was the alliance we had been forced to make with the Pope-Williams drug organization. So long as they were useful to us in keeping the Panthers out of the city, we had tolerated their activities, and this was a fact that deeply disturbed me and other members of the Dirty Dozen. Once the Panthers were gone, we began to crack down again on Williams and Pope.

Eliminating them proved no easy task. Every time we got word of a big drug deal and planned a raid, it seemed as though Judge Williams knew about it, and when the officers showed up, the deal had been moved. This happened again and again, making Williams appear to be invincible. He became more defiant, and we became more determined to take him and his organization down. It all came to a head one night when Officer Vince Rupp, an old schoolmate of mine, chased a car driven by two of the Allen brothers, Judge Williams's strong-arm boys.

It was a minor traffic violation, and Rupp had no idea who he was pursuing. He followed the Allens down a blind alley and boxed them in with his unit. As he got out of the car, the brothers jumped him. They tried to take away his gun, but he held on to it, so they grabbed his baton and began beating him savagely. In fact, they would have beaten him to death had it not been for the fact that we were no longer allowed to wear our traditional slouch hats but were required to wear helmets instead. That helmet saved his life.

A female passerby saw what was happening and called the police. Within seconds backup cars began to arrive. They found Rupp bleeding but conscious on the ground, still clutching his gun. He had been beaten so viciously that his helmet had been split nearly in two. There were now half a dozen cops on the scene. The Allen brothers were trapped in the alley, and, knowing they did not stand a chance, they surrendered.

The cops could easily have shot and killed the Allens and no one would have questioned it, but that was not the way we did things in Compton. They grabbed the brothers and beat them just as badly as they had beaten Vince Rupp, before taking them into custody. They did so out of revenge, of course, but also to send a message. If we had allowed the Allens, or anyone else, to assault a police officer with impunity, all of our lives would have been in danger. We had to make it unmistakably clear that anyone who attacked a cop in Compton would receive worse in return. The courts could not have delivered that message to the streets; the beatings did.

We had no doubt that Judge Williams was behind the attack on Vince Rupp. The Allen brothers would never have assaulted a police officer without their boss's permission, and it sent shock waves through the department and the community.

We were now more determined than ever to rid Compton of Williams and Pope, but no matter how our narcotics squad tried, it seemed that they were always one step ahead of us. In frustration, we called in the federal authorities. DEA agents set up a sting in which a huge heroin deal was raided, and Williams and Pope were arrested. It was while they were in custody that they told the Feds that they had a mole in the Compton PD—a young black woman working in the records section who was tipping them off to our surveillance. We arrested her, too, and she, Williams, and Pope all went to prison. The era of the Panthers, the Muslims, the Maoists, and Judge Williams was over.

After Judge Williams and Eddie Pope were sent to prison, there was a vacuum in the drug trade, and it was quickly filled. Glenn Poole had been a small-time dope dealer operating out of the Golden Pheasant alongside Phil Lee. He was an enormous, brutal block of a man who lisped incongruously from a beating he had received from Bill St. Onge, which knocked out his front teeth.

Poole specialized in pushing Benzedrine and Seconals. Bennies were an upper, and reds a downer, and when the two were taken in succession they caused a roller coaster of chemical highs and lows the addicts called "cartwheeling." Like Williams and Lee, Poole did not hesitate to sell drugs to kids, and before long there was an epidemic of cartwheeling among teenagers on both the east side and the west side. What was more, Poole made a point of pushing Seconals to thirteen- and fourteen-year-old girls whom he would lure to his house. Once the girls were high on the reds, Poole and half a dozen of his friends would rape them.

CPD made a special target of Glenn Poole, but he was as smart as he was big. He kept his stashes in his house only briefly, never dealt directly with his customers, and was carefully "lawyered up." As a result, we were not able to get our hands on him, and he clearly enjoyed the fact, defying us to take him down.

One night at the end of the P.M. shift I was patrolling the west side and saw smoke rising above the rooftops on 132nd Street. It was not in my district, and the fire department was on its way, so I drove back to the station, turned in my car, and stopped as usual at the Garter. Rutigliano and Dave Hall were hosting a celebration, surrounded by several members of the Dirty Dozen. I walked over to the table, and Rut spread his arms magnanimously. "Sit down, Rick; have a beer. It's on me."

I asked what we were celebrating. Rut hoisted his mug. "We fucked up Glenn Poole pretty good tonight," he declared. "Hall and me."

I assumed they had caught him in a sting or given him an ass-whooping. "Fucked him up how?" I asked.

Dave Hall smirked, smug and massive, and said nothing. Rut took a long pull at his beer and wiped his thick mustache. "We burned down his house," he said.

Over the next couple of pitchers I got the whole story. Rut and Hall had received a tip that Poole was about to make a big sale, so they staked out his house during their shift. When Poole left, they broke in and searched the place. There was a sizable stash of bennies and reds, as they had expected. Rut walked to a nearby gas station, filled two cans with gasoline, and lugged them back to the house. He and Hall heaped all the drugs together in the living room, doused them with gas, and set them on fire. Once again, it was a while before the pumpers arrived.

When Poole came back to find his house a smoking ruin, Rut and Hall were waiting for him. "The next house you move into, we're gonna do the same thing," Rut told him. "Except next time, you're gonna be in it."

Glenn Poole knew he was beaten. He told Rut and Hall that he was leaving town.

Rutigliano raised his glass in a toast. "Here's to Glenn Poole," he said. "May he sleep in a fucking ditch tonight!"

We all drank. Williams, Pope, the Panthers, the Muslims, the Maoists, Phil Lee, Glenn Poole . . . It was worth celebrating. Maybe we were winning after all.

We were not the only ones who felt this way. At about this time, a cartoon appeared in the *L.A. Times* that showed five suspects against a wall and four LAPD officers holding them at gunpoint. In the next panel were eight suspects being held by five sheriff's deputies with guns drawn. In the last panel, ten suspects faced the wall, and behind them, holding them all at bay, was one lone Compton police officer.

That said it all.

Rape, Politics, and Other Crimes

I have spoken about the lines within the department that tended to divide the officers into cliques, except when the chips were down. There was another such line, and it had to do not with race or politics but with position.

The patrol officers in CPD operated out of the first floor of police headquarters; the second floor belonged to the detectives. It was a class distinction, not unlike those of the old British Empire, and while it was not formally declared, it was informally understood and observed. Street patrolmen went up to the second floor only when they were invited, and detectives, once they were promoted from patrol, avoided their old haunt on the first.

One night I was patrolling with Officer Willard Williams, a veteran who had been recruited from Alabama to help replace the white officers who were leaving. We received a call of a burglary, and when the dispatcher gave us the address, we were both shocked. It was the office of Dr. Hugh Penworthy, the affable physician who served as the CPD's medical consultant. We all knew and liked Dr. Penworthy; he gave us our physicals and tended to officers who were injured or sick, and he did so amiably and generously. He was very popular, not only with the police department but with the city government as well. We all appreciated and admired him.

His office, which was located in his home, was only a few blocks from police headquarters, and Willie and I raced over there. What we found could not have been more tragic.

Dr. Penworthy's home and office had been ransacked, his eighty-two-year-old mother lay unconscious on the floor, and his teenaged daughter was tied up, terrified, and bleeding. When she had calmed down sufficiently, she told us that her father was away on vacation, and that she had been alone in the office when a young Latino man broke in armed with a knife. He threatened to kill her, and then tied her up. When her grandmother came in, he hit her savagely over the head with a lamp, knocking her unconscious. Then he tore the house and office apart looking for money and drugs. He found both, as well as Dr. Penworthy's .32 automatic. He had gotten what he wanted, but instead of leaving, he turned on the girl.

She began screaming, so he put the gun to her head and threw her onto the floor, threatening to kill her if she resisted. Weeping, helpless, she told the man that she was a good girl, and she begged him not to take her virginity, because she wanted to be a virgin when she married. With tears pouring from her eyes, she recounted how he had obliged her, forcing her over onto her face and sodomizing her. While he was doing so, clutching the gun, it went off and shot off his right index finger. We found it lying on the floor. Even that did not stop him, ferocious and frenzied as he was. When at last he was done with her, he gathered up the money and drugs and left.

The girl broke down several times while telling us the nightmare story. Her face was contorted in an agony of memory; there were welts on her arms and back, and blood on the towel she had wrapped around herself. She was the most pitiable sight I had ever seen, scarcely eighteen, trembling, devastated, wounded to her soul.

When we reported the incident at headquarters, the outrage among the Dirty Dozen was deep and determined. Every one of them wanted to get onto the street and find the animal that had raped Dr. Penworthy's daughter. However, once the field report was filed, the case went to the detectives upstairs. Their chief, Captain Art Thomas, promised he would clear it within twenty-four hours. We knew that the detectives did not have the informant network we had, and so we doubted that this would happen.

The next night, Dominic Rutigliano was on duty, and he took matters into his own hands. From the girl's description of her attacker, and the nature of the drugs that he had stolen, Rut was pretty sure he knew who the rapist was—an addict from CV3 turf.

We knew that the rapist had fled in Dr. Penworthy's white Porsche, so Rut drove up to District 5. His contacts in CV3 told him that the man he was looking for was a heroin junkie who had committed at least a dozen other rapes. Rut cruised the neighborhood until he spotted the Porsche and pulled it over. When he walked up on the car, the driver was fumbling between the seats. Rut could see that he had toilet paper wrapped around his right hand, which was preventing him from reaching the gun he had hidden there. Many cops would have shot him dead on the spot, but Rut wanted him alive. He reached in, grabbed the man's shirt, and dragged him out through the window.

"Did you do it?" he demanded. "Did you rape her?"

"Rape who, man?! I dunno what the fuck you're talkin' about."

Rut shoved him to the street and put a choke hold on him with his forearm. The man struggled and gasped against the hold, his severed finger oozing blood. "Tell me," Rut growled, "or I'll break your fucking neck, I swear to God."

Face purple and eyes bulging, the man admitted that he had raped Dr. Penworthy's daughter. Rut put the cuffs on him and threw him into the car. He retrieved the doctor's gun, the drugs from his office, and the stolen cash, and brought all of them in.

He booked the man for burglary, assault, grand theft auto, rape, and sodomy. Then he stormed upstairs to the second floor. Half a dozen detectives were sitting at their desks doing paperwork or shooting the breeze. When Rut's enormous figure appeared, everything stopped.

"While you assholes have been sitting here drinking coffee and smoking cigarettes," he declared, "I nailed the guy that raped Dr. Penworthy's daughter."

The detective in charge was a sergeant named Joe MacAuliffe. He got to his feet. "What the hell are you doing up here?"

"Your fucking job!" Rut shot back. "You didn't see that girl; I did. Maybe you don't give a shit, but I do. Just make sure you don't fuck up the evidence and let that asshole get off." With that he turned and went back down the stairs.

Rutigliano's rage at Sergeant MacAuliffe in front of a room full of detectives was a stunning affront, a humiliation MacAuliffe would not forget.

One of the reasons that we had such good connections among the Latino gangs of North Compton was that many of us had grown up with the people who had founded them. As I had moved back and forth from home to school or to the Boys' Club boxing gym, I had often ridden the Red Bus with these kids. We had played in the sandlots together, or had run in track meets against one another. When I was in college, I had joined the Latin Imperials car club, which was headquartered in the north side's Latino Corridor. During Imperials meets I stayed at the home of my pal Andy Salcido on Peach Street in Fruit Town. Next door to him lived a scrawny Chicano kid named Santos Padilla. Years later he became a prominent member of the infamous Largo 36 gang. Though our lives took radically different paths, the fact that the gangsters had grown up with me and many others of the Compton police remained a constant.

From my youth, for example, I had known Jesse Torres, a notorious shooter for the 1-5-5; other gang members whom I knew were Tony Pimentel, known as Tony the Tiger, Bobby Quinzola, the Lopez brothers, the three Armijo brothers, and the four Carbajal brothers, all of whom were stone-cold killers. I could picture these gangbangers as children; yet now they were capable of the worst acts of violence, although their families still lived and worked in the neighborhoods in which we had played together.

In some ways, the 1-5-5 was unique. Although it was a tightly knit Latino gang that guarded its territory jealously, it counted among its members a number of outsiders. There were the Holmes brothers, for example, blond-haired, blue-eyed white kids who had grown up in the Nestor Tract and had been part of the gang from the beginning. Too, it included a group of Samoans, among them characters called Saber, Pineapple, and Coconut, who lived in the Samoan enclave of Park Village off Wilmington. Park Village was known as "White Island," the last stronghold of the Mormons who once had dominated the city's politics. Finding themselves surrounded by blacks, the Mormons decided to leave. Instead of selling their homes, however, they brought dozens of families from their missions in Samoa and rented the houses to them. Ironically, these Samoans once again found themselves living on an island, this time in the City of Compton.

Perhaps because the Holmes brothers and the Samoans were cultural misfits in the gang, they developed a reputation for being its most vicious members. The Samoans in particular were almost casual killers. They would habitually fire over the fence at Park Village into the black neighborhood along Wilmington Avenue, picking targets at random and shooting black people for sport.

When the Nestor Tract was ceded to Compton by Los Angeles, it permanently altered the criminal landscape of the city. In an attempt to balance the power of the 1-5-5, the Latinos formed themselves into gangs, giving rise to the Compton Barrio Tres and the Largo 36. The turf wars among the "Fifth," the "Tres," and the Largo gang were continual and violent—but with the appearance of Sylvester Scott's Bloods in West Compton, the situation became more complex and much more dangerous.

From their inception the Bloods were fighting an uneven battle with the Crips of L.A. Far outnumbered, they attempted to balance the scales with violence, yet they could not afford to be seen attacking the Crips directly. As a result, some of the Bloods sets, such as the 151st Street Bloods, began to contract with the 1-5-5 for attacks on the Crips, paying for the hits with drugs. A frequent target was the 166th Street Crips, known as the NBC, or Neighborhood Blocc Crips. (The spelling of "Blocc," ending with "cc," reflected the fact that the letters "ck" meant Crip Killer.) A carload of shooters from the Fifth would drive up to South Central spraying gunfire from the windows, killing known or suspected Crips and innocent by-standers as well. In return, the Crips retaliated against the Latinos, invading Compton in their low-riders and peppering sidewalks and houses with automatic fire. These attacks escalated tensions among the Latino gangs.

Things came to a head in the summer of 1969. A Latino girl named Sara Fimbres invited Chris and Johnny Lopez to attend a party at her home on the north side of Santa Fe Avenue. The Lopez brothers were members of the 1-5-5. Sara's husband and two uncles were all in the CV3. When the Lopez brothers arrived, the Tres immediately jumped them and beat them brutally. Sara's husband and his brothers dragged their unconscious bodies out onto Santa Fe Avenue and dumped them, half dead, on the sidewalk.

A few nights later, a low-rider roared into the Dead End, a blind alley that was the headquarters of CV3. Three Fivers—two of the Carbajal brothers and Big John Davila—climbed out and hosed the street with gunfire. There was chaos as bangers and residents ran for cover. Cholos from the Tres began shooting back, and a gun battle raged up and down the blind alley. The Carbajals and Davila scrambled back into the car, but as it swung around, a door flew open and Big John tumbled out. The Carbajals took off, leaving Davila behind. The Tres bangers jumped him and beat him nearly to death. Then a few of them climbed into their cars and ran back and forth over his battered body.

The next day, all-out war was declared between the Fifth and the Tres.

Almost every night for the next five months we were receiving calls of shots fired, man down, in North Compton, east and west. On the heels of the Panthers and the Muslims, the last thing we wanted was a widespread gang conflict, yet every week the violence seemed to be escalating. Two or three carloads of 1-5-5ers would roll into CV3 territory with guns blazing out the windows. Everyone—women, children, old people—was at risk as the gangbangers fired indiscriminately into rival territory. Then the CV3 would retaliate in kind, cruising down Central Avenue in search of prey. Soon the neighborhoods of North Compton began to resemble the Old West, with gun battles rattling the streets at all hours of the night.

Then, one Sunday morning, a twelve-year-old boy and a thirteen-year-old girl were gunned down on the steps of Sacred Heart Church on Winona Street as they left Mass, caught in the crossfire of a gang shooting.

Something had to be done, and quickly.

Dominic Rutigliano and his partner Dave Hall hit on a plan that was unorthodox to the point of being bizarre. The night following the murder of the kids, they cruised the strongholds of the two gangs, looking for their leaders. In the Dead End they found Joe Annette, a wiry Latino kid, and at 155th and Central, they collared the big Samoan, Pineapple, of the 1-5-5. They snatched them off the street and locked them in the backseat of the patrol car. The two gang leaders turned their backs on each other. Rut and Hall drove them to a deserted stretch of railroad tracks along South Alameda Street.

When they reached the tracks, Rut turned to the backseat and told them that the killings had to stop. Annette and Pineapple pointedly ignored him.

"You listen to me," Rut said. "Either you settle this thing, or we're gonna do you both right here." He and Dave Hall pointed their pistols at them. "You decide."

They knew what he meant: Rutigliano and Hall would kill them both and dump their bodies. The murders would be seen as gang killings.

Annette and Pineapple asked Rutigliano what he wanted.

"You're gonna fight this out one-on-one," Rut told them. "No guns, no knives; just a fair fight. Whoever wins, there's gonna be a truce—no more shootings, no more killings."

The two gang leaders did not have much choice. They agreed.

Rutigliano and Hall let them out of the car and walked them to the middle of the tracks. I was working District 5, so they called me in as backup. While Rut and Hall refereed the fight, my job was to make sure that no one interfered.

Rutigliano gave each of the gang leaders half a brick and told them to go at it. Annette and Pineapple squared off under the lurid mercury lights of the railroad, and the fight began. It lasted over twenty minutes, with neither man managing to gain an advantage. Annette knocked Pineapple down, and then, bloodied and furious, the big Samoan tore into Annette, sending him to the tracks. Back and forth it went as Rut and Hall kept things clean. Pineapple was the bigger of the two, but Joe Annette refused to quit. After fifteen minutes, both were battered and tiring, and the bricks had been reduced to dust; both had been down several times, but they were still on their feet. At last, Pineapple caught Annette with two vicious shots to the ribs, then smashed a huge fist into his mangled face, and he went down.

Even so, the Latino kid was not finished. He staggered to his feet and charged Pineapple, and they tumbled to the dirt. For another five minutes they wrestled and pummeled each other until they were exhausted. They were on their knees, bloody, panting, covered in bruises, neither able to continue. Rut declared the fight over, and he and Hall dragged them to their feet.

"Truce?" Rut said.

The two gangbangers nodded yes.

Pineapple was put into Rut's car, and Annette into mine. Each boy was told that he had won, so that neither would lose face, and we spread that word in their respective turfs after we had dropped them off.

The truce lasted for six months, during which there was relative peace in North Compton; gang incidents fell off sharply, and the murder rate dropped to zero. Rutigliano and Hall had accomplished what no other police force, no gang specialty unit, no state or federal program had been able to do. For six months there were no shootings, no killings, no families and homes at risk. It had been done outside the law—Compton Style.

There was only one serious threat to the truce, and that came from a character called Debo.

Debo was a Crip who lived with his mother in the "Front Hood." The Front Hood was a strip on the west side between Wilmington and Central where Front Hood Crip turf and West Side Piru turf met. The dividing line between them was the shallow concrete trench of the Compton Canal. It was like the Alsace region between Germany and France in the early twentieth century, a flashpoint of disputed territory. Crip or Piru, you crossed the canal only with an army, for to do so was to invite a war.

Debo was the leader of the Front Hood Crips, a huge, muscular killer who feared nothing. He had shown no hesitation to mix it up in street fights, or to use guns or knives, or to assault a cop. He was as volatile as he was unpredictable.

One day in the locker room, Dominic Rutigliano said to me, "That Debo's a crazy motherfucker." Coming from Rut, it was a dark compliment.

"What's he done now?" I asked.

Rut told me that the word on the street was that Debo had crossed the canal alone, gone to the house of a West Side Piru who lived on Tajauta Avenue, a killer nicknamed Bartender, and pounded on the door. When Bartender opened it, Debo bitch-slapped him—hit him with the flat of his hand across the cheek like he was a bad-mouthed whore. He had then calmly walked back across the canal.

It was a bold and dangerous provocation, and I knew that it could have devastating consequences. I also knew that the only way to avoid those consequences was to take Debo down.

In L.A., or any other city, moving on an OG—an original gangster—like Debo would have meant assembling a SWAT team, surrounding his house, and raiding it with riot gear and shotguns. This was Compton, though, and that was not the way we did things.

I went through the files until I found an old warrant on Debo and drove to his mother's house on 131st Street. I walked to the front door in civilian clothes and knocked, my gun in its holster inside my jacket. Debo's mother insisted that she did not know where her son was, had not seen him in days. I stepped to the window beside the door and looked in. A pair of sneakers was protruding from behind the couch. I went back to the door, pulled it out of his mother's grasp, and elbowed her aside.

Debo was six foot three and over two hundred pounds, so I knew I was in for a tough fight. I also knew that if a fight lasts more than a few seconds, it means trouble. You have to make it as short as possible, getting in the first shots if you can.

I walked to the end of the couch and told Debo he was under arrest. He got up and charged at me. I sidestepped and hit him with two or three quick body shots that took the wind out of him. He doubled, and I nailed him with a left hook to his ear. He went down to his knees. I moved on him, reaching for my sap, but he scrambled back to his feet, threw a shoulder into my rib cage, lifting me off the floor, and drove me against the wall. The whole time his mother was screaming her head off at the front door.

Debo had me pinned against the wall. I got out my sap and gave him three or four sharp blows across the back, and he staggered. I shoved him off at arm's length and threw the hardest right hand I could. Blood spurted from his nose, and he sprawled backward onto the couch. I flipped him over and cuffed him.

His mother was shrieking, "Police brutality! They killin' my baby!" A knot of people appeared on the sidewalk. I dragged Debo to his feet as his mother yowled at me, "You honkey motherfucker! Cocksucker, you let go of my child!"

I had called for backup, a unit with a cage, since I could not put Debo into the back of my unmarked unit. Officer Ron Malachi arrived, and he limped into the house. Several years before he had lost a leg in a traffic accident, but he was so tough that he had fought for his job and gotten it back.

"What the fuck you got yourself into, Rick?" he asked.

I could not answer, still winded from the fight. Malachi put his gun to Debo's head, and for a moment I had visions of him blasting Debo's skull open, splattering me with brains. "I got it! I got it!" I panted. Malachi put his gun down.

We had to get Debo to the car, and I did not know what was waiting for us outside. If it was his Crip brothers, we might have to shoot our way out. I took out my gun and shoved Debo out the door. By now a crowd had gathered, and I quickly scanned the figures. None was wearing blue. We kept our guns at our sides as we maneuvered Debo through them to Malachi's patrol car and folded him into the backseat. Malachi got in front and took off.

I booked Debo for assaulting a police officer, and that, together with the outstanding warrant, was enough to keep him off the streets for a while. However, it was not the end of the incident. Rut told me later that the news of Debo's solo incursion into Tajauta Avenue had come from one of his casual informants, a Piru by the name of Sterling Lewis, who had a gripe against him. That personal grudge would come back to haunt both of them. It would haunt me as well.

For decades, the Latino population of Compton had remained constant, a tiny minority—no more than 5 percent of the total—confined to the northwestern and northeastern sections of the city. In the early seventies, that began slowly to change. As more Hispanics migrated to L.A. County looking for work and housing, the low rents in Compton became a magnet that drew them to the city. In ones and twos, and then in slowly increasing numbers, Latinos began moving into the central part of Compton, for the first time integrating those black neighborhoods. It was a demographic change that would grow as the years went on and would have an impact on the city almost as great as the black influx that filled the vacuum created by white flight.

With the arrival of more Latinos in central Compton, another vacuum began to be filled. Since their inception in the fifties, the 1-5-5, the CV3, and the Largo gangs had been separated by the strip of land into which the Latinos were now moving. As a result, a new Latino gang appeared. Calling itself the Setentas, or the Seventies, it was founded by the Baruque brothers, two hardened criminals who lived off Almond Street behind the police station. As the older Latino gangs had done, the Setentas compensated for their small size with viciousness. Their most important shooter was Jake Guerina and he acted quickly to establish the gang as one of the most dangerous in the city.

One afternoon, a low-rider cruised down 155th Street, the heart of the Fifth, Jake Guerina in the backseat. It was a deliberate provocation. A Fiver named Mario Amijo saw them, picked up a brick, and threw it at the car. It glanced off the trunk, but the low-rider continued slowly rumbling down the street. Amijo picked up another brick and chased after it. At that moment, Guerina leaned out the back window with a .41 Magnum and fired one shot. It hit Amijo in the head, killing him instantly. The Setentas had put the Fifth on notice that they were for real.

A few nights later, it was the Largos' turn. One of their OGs, Jason Pompa, was invited to a party on San Vincente Avenue on the extreme east side. He showed up alone, dressed to dance—but it was an ambush.

When Pompa walked up to the house, two Setentas jumped him. They beat him with baseball bats, then forced him to kneel on the front lawn. One put a gun to the back of his head and fired. Pompa pitched onto his face, but he was still alive. The 7-0s attacked him again with the bats, and shot him in the head a second time.

When I arrived at the scene I found a horrific sight. Pompa lay on the sidewalk, his brain blasted out of his shattered skull, his body battered and bloody, nearly all of his bones broken. It had been as savage and premeditated a murder as I had ever seen, a demonic declaration to the Largo gang, and to us, that a new source of evil had appeared.

Because so much attention has been focused on Compton's black gangs, it is not widely known that, although the Latino gangs made up only about a fourth of the total gang population, during the seventies and eighties they accounted for about 40 percent of the killings. It was a forlorn fact that as the Hispanic population grew and Latinos began to perceive themselves as a minority oppressed by the black majority, young Latinos turned their frustrations inward. For the vast majority of those murders were Latinos killing Latinos.

This gradual population shift from black to Latino, and with it, from the predominance of black gang violence to Latino gang violence, foreshadowed the future of Compton.

Most Compton police patrolled alone. The field sergeants and the Special Investigation units were solo, and though the P.M. and graveyard shifts had two-man cars, it was customary for the senior officer to leave his partner at the station after an arrest to file the report while he went back out alone. Though this was largely due to the shortage of manpower, it had become a point of pride in the department: A real Compton cop worked alone.

One night I was assigned to District 5, the mixed black and Latino section of the north side, and, my partner being on vacation, I was on my own. It had been a relatively quiet night, and so, around midnight, I went "Code 7," which meant that I would be leaving the patrol car to eat lunch. In fact, we never went far from our cars so that we could continue to monitor the radio. While I was eating, a call came through of an alarm at the Paradise Liquor Store.

I knew the location; two weeks before I had arrested two young Hispanics who had robbed the owners of sixty dollars at gunpoint. It had been only the latest in a string of holdups at the store, which was owned by an elderly Latino couple. I was going to take the call, but Officer Frank Millhouse, knowing that I had not yet eaten, offered to take it for me. Millhouse was a twenty-seven-year veteran who was close to retirement.

Within a few minutes, I heard an urgent call over the radio. "Shots fired at Paradise Liquor. Units please respond." I ran back to my car and turned on the siren and lights. All the way over, I had a mental image of Frank Millhouse lying dead in the street, killed on a call I should have taken.

When I arrived I found Paul Herpin, Bill St. Onge, and Dominic Rutigliano already on the scene, and a Special Investigation team collecting evidence. Other officers were restraining the owners, who stood weeping and wailing in the alley. Nearby was Frank Millhouse, pale and trembling. When he saw me, he hurried over. "Rick . . . ," he stammered, "Rick . . ." I asked him what had happened. "The kid . . . I shot the kid . . ."

The back door of the liquor store was ajar, and from beneath it, I could see a pool of crimson-stained white liquid, like an abstract painting on the dirty linoleum. Millhouse was nearly in shock, so I walked to the door, which bore a single bullet hole, and nudged it open. A teenaged boy lay on the other side. Thick blood clotted his curly black hair; one side of his skull had been blasted out. Bits of blanched bone were scattered like nutshells across the floor of the storage room. A broken bottle of milk was clutched in one hand, a chrome-plated .22 revolver in the other. He was wearing shorts and a tank top, and his feet were bare. He was clearly not a burglar.

Millhouse staggered up to me. "I killed him, Rick," he said, his eyes big and desperate. "You gotta help me. My pension . . . I can't get fired . . ."

At that moment, Bill St. Onge strode over to us. "Baker," he barked, "the kid shot first, into the ceiling. Go up on the roof and look for a round." I glanced at Millhouse. Though he said nothing, he was pleading with me to find an expended bullet.

I climbed the ladder to the roof and made a careful examination, hoping to discover the bullet that would make this a "good shooting." While I did so, I heard a muffled gunshot from inside the store below. That was when I knew that I would find nothing.

Later, Rut told me what had happened.

Millhouse had pulled into the alley alongside the store and walked to the back. As he did, he saw the door open, and he drew his revolver. A young Hispanic man appeared at the half-open door. Millhouse challenged him to freeze, and when he showed a gun, Millhouse ducked and fired through the door, striking him in the head.

It was the grandson of the owners. They had no milk for breakfast, so the boy, no more than fifteen, had offered to go downstairs to fetch it. Knowing that the store had been robbed several times, he took his grandparents' gun. He let himself in, setting off the silent alarm, got the milk, and then heard Millhouse's car pull into the alley. He tried to get back to the apartment, which was across the darkened alley, but Millhouse had already gotten out of his car. Seeing him, and not realizing he was a cop, the kid brandished his gun and ducked back into the store. That was when Millhouse fired.

When St. Onge and Herpin arrived, they realized they had a very delicate situation on their hands. The kid had had a gun, but when they examined it they saw that it had not been fired. Millhouse had made a split-second decision, reacting somewhere between panic and self-defense, but while the facts were still unclear, the kid was lying dead. When I came on the scene, they immediately sent me onto the roof to look for a round that they knew had never been fired.

While I was up there, the detectives arrived. Herpin and St. Onge explained the situation to them. Millhouse was still in shock, his eyes pleading.

"Get a can of coffee," one of the detectives told Millhouse. He looked back at him, uncomprehending. "A big can of coffee," the detective repeated.

Millhouse went into the store and returned with the unopened can. The detective took the .22 from the dead boy's hand, pointed it at the lid, and fired. That was the shot I had heard. He handed the can to Millhouse. "There's your pension," he said.

The investigation that followed concluded that Frank Millhouse had acted in self-defense. As proof, they had the spent round, which Herpin and St. Onge testified that I had found on the roof. When I was questioned, I did not contradict them. It was the code of silence. "Maybe you saw something that could get a guy in trouble," Frank Brower had told me my first night on the job. "You keep your mouth shut." It was one of the hardest decisions I had to make, but there was really no choice.

There would be no indictment, no trial, no multimillion-dollar lawsuit. It had been a tragic accident, and now the case was closed.

In addition to his passion for motorcycles, Rutigliano also owned a horse, which he kept in the Manville Tract up in Dominguez Hills. At that time, in the early seventies, Dominguez Hills was still largely an area of farms, horse corrals, and bridle paths. Paul Herpin, whose nickname was the Mummy because he had served on the force so long, also owned a horse in the Hills, and he and Rut often went riding together.

The ranch on which they kept their horses belonged to a Compton police sergeant named Scofield, who also boarded a horse there. When Sergeant Scofield died in a motorcycle accident three weeks after his retirement, his widow told Herpin that if he took care of her husband's horse, she would transfer the deed on the property to him when she died. What the Mummy did not know was that developers from New York were eyeing the land, one of the last open parcels in the area. They wanted to build an industrial tract on it and had entered into preliminary negotiations with the city. It was therefore an extremely valuable piece of property.

One Sunday afternoon, an Indian drove into the corral where Rut and Herpin kept their horses, towing a new, unfinished horse trailer behind his pickup. He told them that the trailer was for sale, and he offered it to them for four hundred dollars, a good price. The next day, Rut and Herpin each gave the Indian two hundred in cash, and they drove the trailer to the police station parking lot. When the chief ordered them to move it, they took it to a shop to have it finished.

Sometime later, a man reported that the trailer had been stolen and that he had spotted it at the shop by accident. He did not want to file a report, he said; he just wanted the trailer returned. Chief W. K. Ingram insisted. He had a long-standing grievance against Paul Herpin, and he saw this as an opportunity to get rid of him. CPD had no internal affairs division, so Ingram ordered Captain Art Thomas, the head of detectives, to open an investigation.

The trailer was seized, and Herpin and Rutigliano were suspended pending the results of the investigation. Captain John Start, the commander of the Dirty Dozen, knew that the whole affair was bogus, and he requested authority to open an investigation of his own. Captain Thomas blocked it, arguing that there could not be two competing investigations at the same time. When Thomas reported his conclusions to the DA, Herpin and Rut were formally charged with receiving stolen property.

It was a setup. The city and the developers wanted the property, but Scofield's widow had refused to sell, having promised the deed to Herpin. When she heard about the charge against him, she changed her mind and sold the land to the developers.

Though the conspiracy had been aimed at Herpin, Joe MacAuliffe saw an opportunity to get his revenge on Rutigliano for humiliating him over the Penworthy rape arrest. Even though Rut had had no idea that the trailer was stolen, and had, in fact, parked it in the police department lot, MacAuliffe demanded that he resign. Rut refused. MacAuliffe pointed out that the trailer had no serial numbers on it, arguing that Rutigliano and Herpin must have cut them off. Rutigliano immediately denied it. MacAuliffe then announced that he had found two witnesses who would testify that they had, in fact, removed the serial numbers. Rut was furious. We had no lie detector equipment in Compton, so he demanded that he be taken to the Long Beach PD and given a test. Chief Ingram refused.

We knew that Rut was innocent and the Police Officers Association backed him to a man. Nevertheless, as the legal process ground forward and indictments neared, the pressure on Rutigliano to resign increased. He and Herpin were suspended pending trial, and both faced thousands of dollars in lawyers' fees.

Finally, Captain Start, whom Rut regarded as a second father, called him into his office. "Rut," he said, "they've got you by the balls."

"Bullshit," Rutigliano grunted.

"What about MacAuliffe's witnesses?"

"That's bullshit, too."

"They're going to take this to trial," Start assured him, "and whatever happens, it won't be pretty."

"Let 'em try," Rut said.

"Think of your family," the captain responded. "Think of your wife and kids." Rut was adamant. "Think of your reputation," Start added, knowing this meant everything to Rut. "If you go to trial and you lose, do you really want to go out with this on your record?"

The prospect of disgrace stopped Rut. It was the one thing he could not abide.

Captain Start promised Rut that if he resigned, the next day he would find him a job with another police force—any one he chose. He slid a letter of resignation across his desk. "Think of the department," he said. "You've got to take this one for the team."

Resigning was the last thing Rut wanted. It violated every instinct in his body, it affronted his pride, and it canceled out all that he had accomplished as a cop. The promise of a transfer to another department was not much of an incentive. Earlier that year, Rut had been offered a job with much better pay and benefits in Huntington Beach. When he did a ride-along with the HBPD, though, all he saw was a citation for two-on-a-bicycle and a report of a stolen lawn mower. The experience, he told me, "did not rise to the level of chicken shit."

Like many of us, Rut thrived on the adrenaline and the sense of accomplishment that Compton represented. It was in his blood, it was part of his soul, it was what made it worthwhile to get up every day and go to work. To be a cop in Compton meant to be a cop in the most real and vital sense: a man with pride and purpose who made a critical difference in people's lives.

In the end, though, he signed. To spare his family the disgrace of a trial, to spare himself a possible humiliation, Rut turned in his badge and gun and resigned.

Dominic Rutigliano, the best cop I ever knew, the heart and soul of the Dirty Dozen, was no longer a member of the Compton Police Department.

The next day, Rut asked Captain Start for a letter of recommendation so that he could apply for another job. At the urging of Sergeant Mac-Auliffe, Chief Ingram overruled Start and refused to provide it. Start protested to the chief and was turned down. Rut would not work as a cop again.

A few nights later, we gave Rutigliano a going-away party at the Golden Garter. All the members of the Dirty Dozen were there, and other veteran cops who had worked with and learned from Rut as well. It was a riotous affair, with Vito Pasquale presiding, and naked women dancing and hanging all over us. The beer and liquor flowed like Yosemite Falls, and by midnight, we all were so drunk we could barely stand or speak. At last, Paul Herpin pulled out his .45 auto and declared, "I can shoot off that fucking doorknob." He was pointing across the bar at the door to the men's room.

"Hell you can," Rut answered. "You're too fucking drunk."

"Bullshit," the Mummy retorted, and he took wavery aim. The shot exploded through the bar and blew a hole in the door a fist wide. We all laughed.

"Herpin!" Rut bawled. "Gimme that damn gun!"

When Herpin handed it over Rut announced, "I'm just as fucking drunk as you are, but I can hit the damn doorknob." He aimed and fired, and the knob exploded with a metallic clang like a bell bashed with a hammer. We broke into applause.

By now the other patrons in the bar were making for the exit, as were some of the girls.

"I can put out those damn lights, too," Rut bellowed, and he fired at the fluorescents in the ceiling overhead. They exploded in blue sizzling flame. He challenged, "Who else can put out the fucking lights?"

The rest of us took out our guns. Now the Garter was emptying out, terrified, stumbling barflies and half-naked girls streaming to the doors. When they were all gone, we locked the place up and began shooting at the lights, blasting ceiling tiles, and blowing fixtures off the walls. At last Vito, who was also drunk, banged on the bar with a beer bottle. We ceased firing and turned to him, expecting him to demand that we stop shooting up his club.

"You fuckers think you're so hot," he slurred. "I can outshoot any of you!" He took a .38 from under the bar and fired at a photo of Mario Lanza on the far wall. It shattered and fell to the floor. It was a signal to continue our shooting spree, which we did until we heard a pounding on the front door. It was a rookie cop whom we scarcely knew.

"I know you guys are in there," he yelled, "and you better clear out—the A.M. field sergeant's on his way."

The next afternoon, at the time Rutigliano would normally have reported for duty, he came to clear out his locker. We watched him in silence, unable to believe what was happening. He said nothing, simply took out his clothes and personal possessions, and the roll of tape with which he had so scrupulously brushed his uniform, and packed them neatly into a box.

Whenever a Compton cop reached what we called his EOW, end of watch, there was a ritual he was expected to perform. Like a warrior on his deathbed, he parceled out his equipment to his friends. One by one we walked to him, and to each of us he gave something he had carried during his career—his belts, his whistle, his nightstick or sap gloves. When my turn came, I told him that he did not have to give me anything; I felt help-less that I had been unable to prevent his leaving.

"That's okay," he said. "There's nothing left."

On his way out of the building, Rut did something characteristic: He walked up the stairs to the second floor.

Sergeant MacAuliffe was on duty, and Rut called across the room to him. "MacAuliffe!"

The sergeant turned, hesitating when he saw him. "What?"

"I want to make you a promise," Rutigliano said. "Whatever happens, I swear to you, I will piss on your grave." MacAuliffe said nothing. Rutigliano glared at him a moment, and then left the station.

Paul Herpin, who had refused to resign, was put on trial for receiving stolen property. On the first day of the trial the judge threw the case out, declaring that the charge was completely unsubstantiated. Herpin's sus-pension was lifted, and he returned to duty with full benefits and back pay. When Rutigliano heard about it, he demanded his job back on the grounds that he, too, would have been exonerated. At Sergeant Mac-Auliffe's urging, Chief Ingram refused.

I understood early in my career that politics played an important part in police work, and vice versa. My mother had for many years been politi-cally active, helping to elect Ed Roybal as the first Latino congressman from California since 1879. I thus did not take the view of Rutigliano and others that policemen should be above politics, even disdaining it. In-stead, I was drawn toward it.

There had been a police association in Compton when I joined the force, but it was little more than a social club. It sponsored poker games and toy drives, distributed turkeys to poor families at Thanksgiving, and held its meetings in bars and strip clubs. It was in no sense a union. In fact, it was forbidden to use the word "union"; instead, it had to refer to itself as a benevolent society. Though the membership dues of eight dollars a month were mandatory, the Compton Police Officers Association had ab-solutely no political clout. If ever there was a paper tiger, it was the CPOA.

This was the inevitable result of the fact that the police chief was a political appointee, chosen by the city manager and ratified by the city council. When contract time came around, the chief took his requests for raises or for more personnel or new equipment to the city manager—the man who had hired him and had the power to fire him. In response, the city manager would dictate the terms of the new contract according to the spending priorities of the council. There was no meaningful negotiation, and no recourse from his decision. The CPD simply took what the city offered.

I realized from the beginning that this system was untenable. Police officers had no say in their working conditions, and, as Rutigliano's case proved, we had no power to protest, and no right of appeal. Nonetheless, given the department's unofficial code of omertà, no one publically challenged this state of affairs. As a result, by the early 1970s, the Compton Police Department had fallen far behind other agencies throughout the state in salaries, in the ability to recruit qualified officers, and in the quality of its equipment.

Yet by this time Compton had become the crime capital of California, and our officers were taking more high-risk calls than the LAPD and the sheriff's office combined. The fact that we were earning much less than either of those departments, and that our recruit pool was slowly drying up, was a disgrace.

I was still relatively new to the force, so I hesitated to bring up such subjects at the association meetings. I did hear a lot of disorganized grousing about pay and conditions, however, and when at last Joe Banovic, the association president, raised the question of the new contract at a meeting, I took the opportunity to speak my mind.

I pointed out the disparity in salary between ourselves and other departments, and the fact that the Police Officers Association had a responsibility to address the issue before the city council. There were groans of skepticism. It had been tried in the past, I was told, and every time, the effort had met with the same roadblock: The chief owed his job to the city manager, and the council could and would fire him if he made a fuss. Though I was still scarcely more than a rookie, I persisted. The argument became more heated, since there was one thing about which everybody agreed: We were putting our lives on the line for pay that would not have been accepted by hotel workers.

"Then we have to do something," I said.

"What?" Frank Brower demanded.

I hesitated. "We have to go public."

The suggestion was met with silence. No Compton police officer had ever gone to the press about anything involving the department. To do so would not only violate the code of silence, it might jeopardize everything the code was meant to protect: the way we did our jobs, the solidarity that kept us fused as a single unit despite our differences, the very practice of Compton Style policing itself. Breach that dam of silence, and God only knew what floods might overwhelm us.

The alternative was political impotence, I argued. We were, and would remain, at the mercy of the city government, with no power to promote our interests or even to protect ourselves if the political climate turned against us.

The situation was complicated by the fact that Mayor Dollarhide headed the first black-dominated administration in Compton's history. Since the police force was still largely white, any attempt to oppose the administration was bound to be met with charges of racism. We had to do it, though. Crime was rising exponentially, yet nothing was being done to strengthen the police. Our efforts to protect the city were being bought at a cut-rate price, our lives being offered cheaply, and that was a direct result of the fact that we had no political influence at all. It seemed to me—and I said so—that it was a question of trading our code of silence for our salaries and our survival.

In the weeks following the meeting, officers began to come up to me privately and voice their support for my position, though there was still widespread reluctance to take our grievances to the press. Doing so was simply not in the culture of the department.

In the meantime, the chief had been informed by the city council of the terms of the new contract. We were being offered a 2 percent raise in pay and two new cars—no improvement in benefits, no increase in the size of the department, no money for new recruits. Normally, the chief would have reported this to the rank and file and that would have been the end of the matter, but not this time.

By the next meeting, the spirit of the CPOA had changed noticeably. Officers began openly questioning both the role of the association and its lack of clout. For the first time, pay and benefits were debated in detail; the issues of our inability to attract good recruits and the outdated equipment with which we were being forced to function were raised openly. Finally, my suggestion that the association ought to go public with our demands was put to a vote.

It passed overwhelmingly.

No one seemed more surprised or satisfied than the rank-and-file officers. For several hours we debated the new contract and what we should and could do about it. It was the first real discussion of our terms of employment in the history of the Police Officers Association, and it was at times heated and at others raucous. Finally, after several gallons of beer had been consumed, we came to an agreement on both our cause and our course of action. If the city council would not negotiate with us in good faith, we would go over their heads to the public.

Only one question remained: Who would be the spokesman for the association? Who would formally break the code of silence?

Joe Banovic was a ten-year veteran who had no wish to become a martyr, and neither the vice president nor any of the board members was willing to set the precedent. There was a long silence, and then Officer Dallas Elvis pointed at me. "Let Rick take it," he said.

Banovic asked if I was willing to speak for the department. Everyone was staring at me. I had been on the force only eighteen months; that meant that I would have little credibility, but it also meant that I was just naive enough not to realize what I was getting into. I told them I would accept. So, in 1970, I became the public face of the Compton Police Department.

I attended the next city council meeting, at which the new contract was to be considered. The small, austere council chamber was nearly empty, as usual. There was a handful of community activists, residents waiting to vent their peeves about speed bumps and sewers, and even one or two homeless folks who had wandered in out of the autumn chill. The discussion, everyone expected, would be little more than a formality: The contract would be ratified exactly as it had been proposed to us. When the time came for comments from interested parties, I rose to speak. Mayor Dollarhide seemed mildly surprised. He asked me to identify myself for the record.

"I'm Officer John Baker," I replied.

Burton Wills, the city manager, wanted to know whom I represented.

"I am speaking on behalf of the Compton Police Officers Association," I said. There was a momentary silence in the chamber. An association representative had never appeared before the city council before. The mayor asked for my statement.

I told the council that the terms offered to us by the city were unacceptable. Neither the pay increase nor the benefits package, which was to remain unchanged, nor the allocation of personnel and equipment reflected the wants and needs of the department.

Burt Wills scowled at me. "Do you realize," he asked, "that the contract has already been vetted by the chief of police?"

I told him I knew that it had, and that the rank-and-file members of the association had voted to reject it.

There was open disbelief in the room. Mayor Dollarhide appeared not to understand what I was saying. "You *voted*?" he said. "When did this vote take place?"

"At our last meeting," I informed him. Wills demanded what the vote had been. I answered that it had been unanimous.

Again there was stunned silence. Even the homeless spectators were listening.

Mayor Dollarhide leaned into his microphone. "Are you telling us, Officer Baker, that the police department refuses to accept the contract terms?" he asked with forced amiability.

"We do, sir," I stated. "And we demand the right to bargain collectively for new terms."

Dollarhide peered straight at me. "Or else, what?" he asked. He was a very light-complected man, his Creole heritage evident in his pale blue eyes. Those eyes stared straight at me with frigid spite. He was daring me to take the next step. Of course, it was not a personal matter between him and me; I was there to voice the will of the association.

"Or else," I answered, "we will take immediate action."

The council members sat back in their leather chairs and glanced at one another. They had no idea what to do, how to respond. At last, the mayor asked what I meant by "immediate action."

It was then that I used an expression that had not been heard in the United States since 1919, an expression that would forever change the face of Compton police politics. "There may be a case of the blue flu," I said.

We did not have the right to strike, even if our association had been an actual labor union. We risked our lives every day to protect the people of Compton, and the last thing we wanted to do was put them at risk. However, conditions were at such an extreme, both on the streets and within city government, that we felt we had no choice.

Mayor Dollarhide seemed outraged, as if the threat were directed at him as a personal affront, but it was Burt Wills who spoke first. "You're not telling us that the police department will refuse to work," he said. He was not a combative man by nature, and his question came more in the form of a plea than of a demand.

"If the city will not negotiate with us, yes," I replied.

Mayor Dollarhide sat fuming, pointedly saying nothing.

"Officer Baker," Wills went on, "what will happen to the city if you go on a sick-out?"

I told him that the detectives and sergeants would continue to report for duty, as well as the rookies who were not yet covered by the contract. "But the rank-and-file officers will stand by their decision," I concluded.

Mayor Dollarhide spat, "You wouldn't dare do that to this city!"

I turned to address him directly. "It's the city that we're thinking about, sir. If we can't recruit new officers or keep the ones we have, if the criminals have better weapons and equipment than we do, if the morale of the department falls apart, it will do more harm to the city than any labor action will. We're acting in the long-term interest of the city, and not just in our own interest."

Burt Wills seemed nonplused. "You're not serious."

"Yes, sir, we are."

Mayor Dollarhide leaned into his mike again. "You're bluffing," he said.

I turned to face him again. "No, Mr. Mayor," I answered, "I assure you we are not."

Following that meeting, the city council held a closed session in which they deliberated the question of the police contract. At Mayor Dollarhide's urging, they decided not to capitulate to association pressure but to insist that the rank and file accept the contract as offered. In return, we held our own closed meeting and voted unanimously to approve a work stoppage.

The next morning, the P.M. shift led the action by calling in sick. When other officers were contacted to replace them, they also reported that they were too ill to work. The blue flu had swept through the ranks of the CPD. The die was cast.

As agreed, the detectives and the rookies continued to work. An emergency was declared, in which only the most serious calls were responded to, and for several days the Compton police force was reduced to a handful of officers on each shift. The criminals, of course, were aware of this, and they acted quickly to take advantage it. Within hours, calls of burglary, assault, car theft, and drug dealing began to mount. Those of us who were on strike watched the situation growing toward crisis, and though it broke our hearts to see the city suffer, we knew we were at a crossroads in the history of the department. We remained unified.

Meanwhile, the local press was swarming over the story of the strike. As the department spokesman, I was inundated with requests for interviews, and I did as many as I could, speaking to the press and appearing on television several times. "Our job is to serve the people of Compton," I said, "and we do that as best we can. But we have families, we have children, we have futures, and we put our lives on the line. We are entitled to fair pay, decent benefits, and the full support of city government. And we have run out of options for getting them."

One L.A. reporter in particular, George Putnam of *Channel 11 News,* played up the story in vivid terms. "What if you called the police," he declared into the camera, "and they did not come? Well, that's the situation here in Compton."

Reports of the blue flu spread quickly throughout California and across the nation. No urban police force had refused to work in over fifty years. In the city's own terms we were not a union, and technically we were not on strike since all of us had taken sick leave. City officials applied to the state courts to secure an injunction to force us back to work, and they fired one officer chosen at random, Mike Bedley. We saw this for what it was: a crude attempt at intimidation. We immediately filed a protest with the personnel board, demanding that he be reinstated. He was, the following day.

Since we were forbidden to picket, we enlisted our wives to take our places. By this time, 1970, I had remarried. My wife Connie was a former bartender at the Golden Garter, the one who had been on duty the night Rutigliano had nearly killed Chickie for slapping his girlfriend. Since I was the front man for the association, Connie took on the role of strike captain, and she handled herself beautifully, organizing the picketers and dealing with the press. It did not hurt that she was a tall, stunning twenty-two-year-old blonde with a nuclear smile. She immediately became the favorite of the media, and her picture, hefting a sign demanding FAIR SHAKE FOR COPS! above her ample cleavage, appeared all over the state.

As the situation heated up, it became uglier. Someone called in a threat from a public phone that there was a bomb in City Hall. It was evacuated, and the scene was broadcast on television. Then Mayor Dollarhide held a press conference at which he insisted that the strike was racially motivated, directed against the first black administration in Compton's history. "If I was white," he declared, "this strike would not have happened!"

His statement caught statewide and national attention. Dollarhide had played the race card, trying to turn the black and Latino officers against the whites. To their credit, the minority cops did not buckle to his pressure, and the rank and file remained unanimous in its support for the association. Then, for the second time, a bomb threat was phoned in, and again City Hall had to be evacuated.

The pressure on me was mounting. While politicians made veiled threats that my career would be stopped dead, or that I would be fired or forced to resign, back channels from the city administration began to approach me, asking whether some kind of compromise could be reached. My response was that any offer made to the rank and file would have to be approved by them, but that in the meantime, our solidarity spoke for itself.

Meanwhile, I continued giving interviews to the press, something no Compton police officer had ever done before. In one, with a local TV reporter named Chuck Henry, I stated that crime in downtown Compton had gotten so bad that "no one would dare walk down Compton Boulevard between Willowbrook and Alameda after nine o'clock at night."

This remark provoked a great deal of controversy, with civic groups and black community leaders declaring that it was not true. Other spokesmen, mainly in the white community, backed up my statement. So heated did the argument become that Chuck Henry did a follow-up interview with me on Compton Boulevard one night around nine o'clock. He asked me whether I wanted to retract or modify my earlier assertion. Instead of doing so, I stated that "walking down Compton between Willowbrook and Alameda at night was like walking through the Gaza Strip." Knowing that this remark, too, was likely to spark protest, Henry walked over to a man, an ordinary citizen, who was sitting at a bus stop, and asked him whether he would walk down Compton Boulevard at night.

"No way," the man replied. "The officer is absolutely right. The way things are now, I'd never walk down this street after dark." With this report, public opinion, stirred by our action and the continuing picketing, began to turn in our direction.

In the face of growing public support for the strike, Mayor Dollarhide blasted us for being disloyal and for acting illegally. Again he declared that the association's action was racially motivated. The Compton Police Department was 60 percent white, he said, and never in its history, until a black administration took power, had it defied the city. Dollarhide hammered on this point. "The white officers are holding a gun to our heads!" he declared. "They are bleeding this city!"

The answer came from the wife of Officer Brent Nielsen. A few days before the blue flu, Nielsen had responded to a call of a robbery at the Safeway market, the same one into which the marines had fired during the Watts riot. When he entered the store, the thieves were waiting for him with shotguns. They fired point blank at his head, and only his helmet kept him from being killed. It took most of the buckshot, though a fistful struck him in the face. At the time of the strike Brent Nielsen was still in the hospital, fighting to save his eyesight. When Dollarhide declared that the white officers were bleeding the city, Nielsen's wife, interviewed on television, shot back, "My husband isn't bleeding the city; he's bled *for* the city!" The effect was powerful—public opinion, which had begun running in our favor, now turned into an overwhelming tide of support.

As the standoff continued, my status within the association grew. Before long, I was seen as not only the face of the police department but its backbone as well. I refused to submit to pressure from any direction, neither the mayor nor the city manager nor the civic associations that were clamoring for protection. I knew, as did the other officers, that we had reached a turning point in the relations between the police and the city. Either we took our stand now and prevailed, or we would forever be at the mercy of whatever administration happened to be in power, dictating our terms of employment without the right of appeal. It was a defining moment in the ninety-year history of the department.

Meanwhile, the city pushed forward with its effort to get an injunction against the strike. The district court moved with unusual speed, the injunction was granted, and we were ordered back to work. As officers of the law, we could not defy a court order, and so we suspended the blue flu and returned to our jobs. However, that was not the end of the matter. Our wives' picketing continued, and the CPOA made it clear that the blue flu would strike again the next time the contract came up for renewal. We had a weapon, we told the city, and we intended to use it whenever it was necessary.

It was the prospect of repeated labor action, together with mounting popular support for our cause, that finally tipped the scales. Though Mayor Dollarhide continued to argue that the association had violated the law and must be broken, the city council, under pressure from the press and the public, decided to hold a special closed hearing on the subject of the new police contract. The question of whether we should have the right to treat with the city was debated hotly, and a vote was taken. The council decided narrowly to allow us to negotiate through a bona fide labor attorney.

The blue flu had worked—we had won.

Although the city council still referred to us as a charity, by asking the police to hire an attorney as our representative, it was, in effect, recognizing the association as an authentic labor union. To this point, none of the local police and sheriff's departments, including the LAPD and the LASO, had such a union—ours was the first—and it set a precedent that the others would soon follow. Our attorney quickly entered into contract negotiations, with the result that we were granted a 4 percent raise in pay, an increase in the city's contribution to our health insurance and pension plans, and a resolution of the long-standing problem of overtime work. In the past, though we were regularly called upon to work overtime, we had never received additional pay for it. Since the city claimed that it could not afford time-and-a-half pay for overtime, we worked out a compromise by which officers would accrue compensatory time for every hour of overtime worked: Instead of being paid for overtime, we accumulated the equivalent in added vacation time. To us, this was a satisfactory compromise, at least for the present.

Perhaps the most important victory which we achieved was the recognition of the Compton Police Officers Association as the representative of the rank and file of the department, an organization with real status and power in our relations with the city. Never again would we be at the mercy of the mayor and the city manager; from now on we would be able to bargain collectively for a fair and just wage, and for the benefits and resources we needed to do our job for the people of Compton.

There was another result of the strike as well, more subtle than our contract terms but, in my view, far more important. For the first time, police officers began to see themselves as a political force to be reckoned with. City hall could no longer afford to take us for granted; the Compton

Police Officers Association had become part of the political infrastructure of the city, and the officers knew it.

This change in consciousness was driven home to me by an incident that occurred a few days after the new contract was approved. I was on patrol on the east side when a young rookie named Steve Finch approached me. He was a tall, square-jawed former army lieutenant who had been on the force only three months.

He introduced himself and said, "I just wanted to meet you and shake your hand." He then told me how much my efforts as the association spokesman had inspired him, and how grateful he was for the victory we had won.

I thanked him, and there was an awkward silence; Compton cops were not used to expressing themselves this way. "Here," he said finally, and he handed me a cup of coffee.

In some ways, that simple gesture meant more to me than anything else the strike had achieved. It meant that the average cop on the street understood that he was now the equal of any politician in Compton. We now had a police association with real clout, led by a group of young, politically minded officers. We were no longer just a force on the streets—we had extended our influence to city hall as well.

The Service Center and the Devil's Disciples

The end of the strike marked a turning point for me. In my nearly two years on the force, I had been at the scenes of at least ten murders; I had personally arrested a murderer and two rapists, stopping two rapes in progress; I had caught a dozen burglars, broken up a score of vicious fights, and run up against militants and drug dealers, all of whom we had either arrested or neutralized. Yet I still had three more years on patrol before I would be eligible to take the examination for sergeant. I felt that my career needed a boost, something that would enable me to expand my field of operations and better utilize my education to make a difference to my city. The opportunity came more quickly than I expected.

Because drug use had become an epidemic in Compton, driving the rising crime rate, the city joined in a cooperative program with the county mental health authority to create a pilot program to treat drug addicts and to try to rehabilitate drug traffickers. Called the Community Service Center, it was to be staffed by a team of social workers, mental health professionals, community activists, and police officers. My name was put forward as one of five officers who were to join the staff. I was delighted at the prospect.

I had to take a written exam and make an appearance before the Service Center board, which was comprised of the head of the Southeast Mental Health clinic, a couple of psychiatric social workers, two community leaders, and the new city manager, Howard Edwards, who had saved me from a beating by the Farmers gang. Edwards asked me why I wanted to work at the center rather than stay on the street.

"I joined the police department to use my training in sociology to do some good for the city," I answered. "This is the best way for me to accomplish that." The board recommended unanimously that I be appointed.

When I reported to the Service Center headquarters on North Wilmington Avenue near Rosecrans, one of the first people I met was David Hutton. Hutton, whom I had faced down in Victory Park, and whom Rutigliano had driven over the wall with his baton, had been appointed to the center staff by the city council. Their thinking was that hiring Hutton to work in a city-run program might soften his radical outlook and make him a part of the establishment. I was skeptical. It seemed to me that Hutton's appointment was a sop that the liberal members of council were throwing to the radicals. But whatever the reason, I wanted the Service Center to succeed, so I determined to work with Hutton, so long as he was willing to work with me.

Besides myself, the officers assigned to the center were Bob Walker, Hourie Taylor, who had slapped his Black Panther brother at the football game, a former Naval Reserve and police academy colleague of mine, Percy Perrodin, all of whom were Compton natives, and a young black officer who had been recruited out of Alabama named Roland Ballard. Ballard had finished second in the Service Center examination process, and I soon became friends with him. He was not a tough, aggressive street cop; instead, he was more of an intellectual, with a sense of the importance of politics in police work as keen as my own. On only one occasion had I ever seen him lose his cool demeanor, and that was in the case of Richard Kowalski.

A blond-haired, blue-eyed sixteen-year-old, the son of a Polish immigrant father and a Mexican mother, Kowalski had been raised on the north side. His ambition early became to join the Largo 36 gang, but he was a slender, frail-looking boy who barely spoke Spanish. Nonetheless, he did everything he could to insinuate himself with the gang, hanging on the street with them, affecting their manners and dress, and painting 3-6 graffiti prolifically. It was while he was in the midst of spray-painting a wall that he was arrested.

He was taken to the station, booked for vandalism, and put by himself in a basement holding cell. Graffiti was a misdemeanor, so he was to be held overnight and released with a notice to appear in court, where he would be fined a few dollars and given a warning. Later that night, though, five Crips were arrested for attempted murder in a drive-by shooting, and they were put into the same cell as Kowalski. It was a stupid clerical error, which ought to have been corrected the first time the jailer made his fifteen-minute check. Unfortunately, the jailer decided to take the night off, and Richard Kowalski, the wannabe Largo, was left in a fifteen-by-fifteen-foot cell with five of the worst gangbangers in Compton.

When the shift changed next morning and the replacement jailer came on duty, he found Kowalski naked on the floor of the cell curled in a fetal position, trembling and numb with shock, his face a blur of bruises, blood oozing from his anus. The Crips had made him perform oral sex on them and then had taken turns raping and beating him.

I was called to the basement, and Roland Ballard came with me. When he saw what had happened, he exploded. "Get that kid to the hospital!" he shouted. Then he turned on the Crips. "You lousy sons of bitches!" he roared. "You've disgraced our race—disgraced our people! You're animals—you're nothing but a bunch of goddamn *niggers*!"

I was shocked at the outburst. Though we had been in a lot of tough situations together, I had never seen Roland so incensed. By nature he was a gentleman, a diplomat; now he seemed out of control. I grabbed his elbow.

"Hey, Roland," I said, "take it easy." He turned to me, his face contorted with rage. "I'll take care of it."

Roland looked at me a long moment, his whole body tense. Then he went limp, the rage draining out of him. "It should never have happened," he said.

Here I am in the Aliso Projects, Los Angeles *(first row, far left)*. *(Courtesy Sandy Sandoval)*

My St. Leo's school buddy Bernard James (left) and I in Watts, 1951.
(Courtesy Father P. Cannon)

I'm mugging for the camera with my first love, Judy Ward, 1965. *(Author's collection)*

I'm *(middle row, second from left)* out on field exercises with the 23rd Regiment, 4th Marine Division, 1967. *(Courtesy Private First Class R. Mackrowki)*

Marine Corps buddies, 1968: *(from left)* Gonzalo Torres, me, and Bob Savedra. *(Courtesy Private First Class R. Mackrowki)*

Graduation from the L.A. Sheriff's Academy, 1968: *(left to right)* Lieutenant Jaeger, City Clerk Lionel Cade, Sheriff Pitchess (L.A. County), Officer Willie Mosley, me, Mayor Douglas Dollarhide, Councilman Wilson Buckner. *(Courtesy Compton Public Relations)*

Graduation day, with my mother, Elisa Oviedo Baker, and my father, John V. Baker. *(Courtesy Compton Police Officers Association)*

Detective Jimmy Pearson, who worked the case of the kidnapped mother and baby with me. *(Courtesy John Pranin)*

Detective Julio Hernandez, who discovered the high explosives under the Black Panther safe house in Fruit Town. *(Courtesy John Pranin)*

Officer Frank Brower, my training partner, with whom I busted Phil Lee, a major drug trafficker. *(Courtesy John Pranin)*

Sergeant Bob Stover, one of the leaders of the Dirty Dozen. *(Courtesy John Pranin)*

Detective John Soisson, my partner in two major homicide cases, succeeded me as president of the Police Association. Behind him is Detective Jerry Wortman. *(Courtesy John Pranin)*

Jackie Grant *(left)* and Betty Marlow *(right)*, two of the first female patrol officers in Compton PD history. *(Courtesy Jackie Grant and Betty Borowski)*

Sergeant John Pranin, section leader of the detective division, and my mentor. *(Courtesy John Pranin)*

Here I am as a detective in the juvenile division, 1976. *(Courtesy John Pranin)*

Detective Ed Kiernan, president of the International Conference of Police Associations. *(Courtesy New York Office of ICPA)*

Detective Joe Flores. He, City Manager Howard Bell, and I traveled to Mexico to find a wanted killer as well as the mother of a murdered baby. *(Courtesy John Pranin)*

I'm posing in front of the Compton City Hall with my wife, Connie, and daughter Michelle during the time of the Blue Flu, 1970. *(Courtesy Compton Police Officers Association)*

My daughter Tiffany is a fashion plate, modeling my riot helmet. *(Courtesy Elisa Baker)*

Chief Tom Cochée *(top row, fourth from left)* with plainclothes officers: His idealistic approach to police work nearly destroyed the morale of the department. *(Courtesy Bobby Orasco)*

Candy Donatelli accompanied me to Las Vegas for the mafia trial. *(Courtesy G. Donatelli)*

This is a publicity shot of me in the Police Olympics, 1976. *(Courtesy Tony Miranda)*

My wife, Connie, was a favorite of the media during the Blue Flu, 1970. *(Courtesy Compton Police Officers Association)*

Weight lifting became a religious ritual for me. *(Author's collection)*

I'm with Officer Steve Finch *(center)*, on his graduation from law school, and Officer "Flashlight" Joe Ferrell *(right)*, 1978. *(Courtesy Steve Finch)*

With my father *(second from left)*, my mother *(extreme right)*, daughter Tiffany *(seated)*, and community leaders *(from left to right)* Monsignor Dolon, County Supervisor Yvonne Burke, and Mayor Lionel Cade. *(Courtesy Compton Police Officers Association)*

I'm in the back lot of the Compton PD station with Dominic Rutigliano *(left)* and Detective Tom Barcalugi, 1978. *(Courtesy Steve Finch)*

Davey Arellanes saved me from being shot by the LAPD, 1980. *(Courtesy David Arellanes)*

Dominic Rutigliano's *(center front)* second graduation from the police academy, 1980. *(Courtesy Dominic Rutigliano)*

Weapons seized in a sweep of Bloods and Crips, 1986. *(Courtesy Tim Brennan and Robert Ladd)*

Crips in custody. *(Courtesy Tim Brennan and Robert Ladd)*

Bloods in the "hood." *(Courtesy Tim Brennan and Robert Ladd)*

A Blood's baby with a red "do rag" is sucking on a cigarette. His father had this photo in his pocket when he was busted for narcotics. *(Courtesy Tim Brennan and Robert Ladd)*

Frank Leroy "Casper" Ervin. His drug business helped bankroll the Lueders Park Bloods. *(Courtesy Compton PD)*

East side Blood enforcer Kenny "Jughead" Escoe. *(Courtesy Compton PD)*

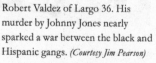

"China Dog" (Marques Nunn) kingpin of the east side Bloods. *(Courtesy Compton PD)*

Robert Valdez of Largo 36. His murder by Johnny Jones nearly sparked a war between the black and Hispanic gangs. *(Courtesy Jim Pearson)*

I give a "thumbs up," then, as a new sergeant, I'm ready to lead my first task force, 1980. *(Courtesy Compton Police Officers Association)*

Dominic Rutigliano and Officer Sydney Moore after their bust of a mobile PCP unit. The angel dust had a street value over $500,000. *(Courtesy Dominic Rutigliano)*

I received the state assembly's commendation for apprehending three Santana Blocc killers. *(Courtesy Assemblyman Frank Vicencia)*

Jane Dickinson Robbins *(center)* presents me *(right)* with a commendation by the city council. She was a direct descendant of the founder of Compton. My father is to her left; behind her is Mayor Walter Tucker Sr. *(Courtesy Compton Public Relations Department)*

Sgt. Rick Baker getting ready to go in the field. *(Compton Police Officers Association)*

Mike Markey *(second from left)* was a member of my gang task force. Barry Lobel *(far right)* was my partner when I found the severed head in the toilet. *(Compton Police Officers Association)*

Terri Lenee Peake, the *Penthouse* centerfold, whose ride-along with me ended our engagement, 1982. *(Courtesy Terri Lenee Peake)*

Playboy centerfold model Kara Styler, my fiancée at the time of my conflict with the Riverside D.A. *(Courtesy Kara Styler)*

The Dirty Dozen reunion, 1999. *(Courtesy Frank Brower)*

Retired CPD officers, 2001: *(from left)* me, Tony Ruiz, Tom Barclay, Julio Hernandez, Joe Flores, Davey Arellanes, and Dominic Rutigliano. *(Courtesy Shannon Evans)*

"I know, man, I know. Now, come on. Let's get some lunch." I led him upstairs, out of the jail.

Later, I made good on my promise. I went back down to the holding cell and slapped the five Crips around. They confessed to the torture and rape; all were convicted.

The Kowalski family sued the city and won a quarter of a million dollars in damages—but the damage done to Richard Kowalski's soul could never be healed.

Those of us who were assigned to the Community Service Center were given training in psychology, drug rehabilitation, counseling, and basic emergency medical treatment. Our role was to work with addicts in conjunction with the center's civilian staff. Clients were encouraged to pour out to us their life stories, their histories of addiction, their contacts, and their criminal activities, as part of their rehabilitation.

Because of this, we were strictly forbidden to relay any information we received to the narcotics unit. For us cops, this ran counter to everything we had learned and practiced on the street. These addicts, who had decided to clean up their lives, could be a valuable source of information about dealers, their networks, and their sources. Nonetheless, I had to agree with the prohibition. Making use of their information would undermine whatever trust the participants might place in the staff, crippling the program. Addicts who came to us to turn their lives around had to know that they could confide in us without bringing retribution on themselves or their criminal associates still on the street, thereby placing their own lives in danger. So I suppressed my instincts as a cop for the sake of the Service Center's success. It was not long before my resolve would be tested.

It was at about this time that the two Allen brothers, the musclemen of the Pope-Williams syndicate, were released from prison, where they had served part of their seven-year sentences for the beating of Officer Vince Rupp. Far from learning a lesson, the Allens had sworn that as soon as they were out of prison, they would "get" a cop. They moved quickly to do so, before we even knew they had been released.

One night their mother called to report a disturbance in her home on Salinas Avenue, west of Central. The officer on duty in that district was Dave Hall, Rutigliano's former partner, the training officer who had sent me into the Slick Chick to test me. He responded to the call, found the house in darkness, walked up onto the porch, and knocked on the screen door. Mrs. Allen called to him to come in. As his backup pulled into the street, Hall went inside. It was a trap.

The moment he was through the door, all three Allen brothers threw a blanket over his head and began beating him with baseball bats. The first blow crushed Hall's knee, and he crumpled to the floor. The brothers continued pummeling him sadistically while their mother shrieked at them to beat him to death. Any other officer would have been killed right then and there, but Dave Hall was the giant of the force. Despite his smashed knee he managed to get to his feet, tore the blanket off his head, and began fighting back, taking on all three brothers at once.

By this time his backup had arrived, and, hearing the commotion inside the house, three officers came storming in. A frantic, full-scale fight broke out among the Allens and the cops. One of the Allens was thrown up against the breakfront and smashed the glass. Another was driven into the kitchen and beaten senseless on the table.

Seeing her boys getting whipped, Mrs. Allen joined in, scratching and clawing at the cops. Hall punched her in the face and broke her nose, which spumed blood. Then two of the cops picked her up and threw her headfirst through the plate glass window of the living room. She hit the porch and went plunging into the front yard. The cops were now beating the hell out of the Allens, using their batons and the brothers' baseball bats. By the time they were through, the Allens lay bloodied and broken on the floor.

Dave Hall was rushed to the hospital, and the brothers and their mother were arrested and charged with the attempted murder of a police officer. They were convicted, and all four were sentenced to long terms in the state penitentiary. That finally was the end of the Allens' reign of mayhem in Compton.

It was also the end of Dave Hall's career. His knee was so badly broken that no form of physical therapy could return him to the force. After months of painful efforts at rehabilitation, he finally accepted the inevitable and took permanent disability leave. The giant of the CPD, Rutigliano's partner, had become another victim of life on the streets in Compton.

As my work at the Service Center continued, I spent less time on the street because there was so much demand for drug counseling and rehab. When word spread that Compton was offering these services, addicts and hippies began to flock to the city, and the center was quickly overwhelmed. In the first month, we treated 109 cases. By the second month, that number had doubled, and it tripled in the third. Because of this we were able to help a lot of people to turn their lives around and get off the streets, but the prohibition on sharing information with my fellow cops still rankled.

One night, a motorcycle gang from Chicago, the Devil's Disciples, rolled into Compton on its way to a meet in Long Beach. Twenty-five to thirty bikers stopped at the Naples Liquor Store on Willowbrook Avenue, which was owned by Vito Pasquale's brother Joe, to stock up on six-packs. The store was in CV3 territory, and before the bikers could get back on their choppers, a dozen gangbangers jumped them. A wild, brutal fistfight backed by chains broke out, and for a while CV3 seemed to be getting the best of it—but the bikers had automatic weapons, and in minutes three CV3 boys lay bleeding in the street. Two of them later died.

After the shooting, the bikers scattered in all directions, knowing that the cops would converge on the scene and shut the city down. One group, however, half a dozen or so, stayed in Compton, hiding out at the house of a friend. There they planned to lie low until things calmed down. Soon they were out of cash, so they decided to send one of their girlfriends, a young, good-looking blonde named Penny Sanatucci, out to work. She took a job as a stripper at the Golden Garter.

This was, of course, the worst possible thing she could have done, since before very long most of the cops in Compton knew Penny. None of them was aware of her connection to the Disciples and the double murder, however. Since Penny was a drug addict, her new cop friends directed her to the Service Center for help. It was there that I met her, and, since there was no rule prohibiting it, I began dating her. Then one night when we were in bed together, I mentioned the shooting, and the fact that we had not been able to crack the case. The bikers were gone, and the CV3 were not talking. I told Penny that we believed the murder weapons had been semiautomatics of some kind.

"They were autos," she said. "MAC-10s."

The remark startled me, but though I questioned her about it, she refused to say anything else except that her former boyfriend had been in the Disciples. This was more than enough information for the detectives to begin investigating, but I was forbidden to reveal it to them. It was a real conflict for me: I had an important lead in a double homicide, and I could do nothing about it. Under normal circumstances, the detectives would have taken Penny into custody as a material witness and grilled from her the names of the shooters. We could then have tracked them down and arrested them. As it was, no leads ever developed, and the case was never solved.

The Service Center proved to be like a small town: Everybody knew everyone else's business. That was how I learned that David Hutton, who had been imposed on us by the city administration, was sleeping with one of the psychiatric social workers, a white woman named Jane. Hutton, who was now the leader of the Malcolm X Foundation, was attempting to use the center as a recruitment ground, and he had spread his gospel of black separatism and Black Nationalism to patients and staff alike. It was difficult for us police officers to work alongside him, let alone to listen to him inciting people to violence, but again, there was nothing we could do about it. Two other officers, however, did not feel the same constraints.

Hourie Taylor and his partner Percy Perrodin despised Hutton, who, they knew, had helped the shooters of Burt Weingarten to escape. Though both officers were black, they decided to take Hutton down. They began calling Jane's number in Redondo Beach at three and four in the morning. After the first few hang ups, Jane gave the phone to Hutton.

"Who the fuck is this?!" he shouted. Silence. "I'm David Hutton, and if you all know who I am, you better know to cut this shit out or you're gonna have the Malcolm X Foundation on your ass!"

Taylor and Perrodin taped the furious tirade and spread the tape among the Service Center's black employees. It worked: Like Hakim Jamal before him, Hutton was discredited by the fact that he was preaching black and sleeping white.

To this point, he and I had had a nodding acquaintance, an uneasy sort of truce. The next time I saw him, he just scowled at me in silence. He had been declawed.

Before long, the Service Center was being overwhelmed with addicts in search of resources. Some wanted counseling, others needed medical and psychiatric care, a few came for maintenance drugs, and the worst cases, the overdosers, had to have emergency attention. We had only six beds at the center, so we began referring people to the county's drug program and to private clinics as well. Still the flood continued, and we found ourselves becoming desperate for help. An offer came from the most unexpected direction.

The Black Panthers had a drug treatment program in Watts, and they approached the center with an offer to take our overflow. I, for one, was reluctant to accept, suspecting that it might be another attempt by the Panthers to establish themselves in Compton. However, the center's director, a psychiatric social worker named Dan Hemmer, felt he had no choice but to agree to a meeting to discuss a possible collaboration.

Six Panthers, led by a bearded militant named Arnett, came to the Service Center for the meeting. Five of the Panthers were men, but one, their secretary, was a young, attractive black woman. We all sat in a circle in the center's office, and I found myself opposite this woman, whose name was Virginia. The Panthers were uncharacteristically accommodating: no demands, no revolutionary rhetoric. They talked soberly and earnestly about the need to service the community. Dan Hemmer seemed impressed.

As the meeting droned on, Virginia and I made eye contact, and by the time we adjourned, she had given me her phone number. We met the next night in Watts, and by evening's end, we had found our way to a seedy place on 107th Street called the Mirror Motel, since it featured mirrors on the bedroom ceilings. Normally, no white man would have gone there, but as I had practically grown up in Watts, I felt completely at ease, and the fact that Virginia was young and shapely and seductive made it easier. That night marked the beginning of a brief and fiery affair.

Though Virginia and I were as discreet as possible, somehow the Panthers found out about our relationship, and they were incensed. That one of their own was sleeping with a Compton cop—a white cop who might be trying to infiltrate their organization—was a threat to which they felt they had to respond.

It was at about this time that Officer Barry Case was transferred to the Service Center. Case, who had served in the marines with me, was nicknamed Captain Marvel because he fancied himself something of a superhero. He had recently been involved in a notorious incident that took place at the McDonald's on Temple and Long Beach Boulevard. A pair of robbers, a young white couple who were obsessed with the movie *Bonnie and Clyde*, had attempted to rob the place at gunpoint, ordering all the customers to lie on the floor. They ranted and waved their pistols around, and for a few terrifying minutes it looked as if they might begin executing people. One of the employees managed to trip the alarm, and the place was quickly surrounded with Compton cops.

The girl was young and slight, but the man looked like a professional body builder, thick with muscle, probably high on steroids. When they saw that they were surrounded, they came out shooting, and a blazing gun battle erupted. Barry Case had been trying to work his way around to the back of the restaurant, but the two robbers spotted him, and both fired. Case dived for cover but managed to get off a couple of shots as he tumbled into the bushes. He had been on the target range when the call came in, and his gun was loaded with "wadcutters," or practice rounds, made for shooting at paper targets. Though Case fired wildly, the muscleman went down. When the girl saw this, she threw away her gun and surrendered.

Case and Officers Don Sullivan and Larry Merchant converged to arrest the man, and were shocked to find him dead. Though they examined his body, there was no mark of a bullet—no entrance wound and no blood. They could only think that the man must have died of a heart attack as a result of the gunfight. It was a mystery that persisted until the autopsy, when the doctor found one of Case's wadcutters embedded in the man's heart. His chest was so muscular that the round had simply disappeared into his bulk, which had sealed the entrance wound tight.

It was very rare that a Compton cop used lethal force—we normally settled matters with our saps or our fists. For this reason, any time an officer shot someone to death, it could not help but be traumatic. Case had fired in self-defense and in a desperate effort to get under cover. Nonetheless, the shooting troubled him deeply, and it was thought best to transfer him to the center until he could deal with its aftermath.

We had taken certain security precautions at the center since there were so many criminals in and out of the place. Among these, we assigned a cop to check out the building each evening before it opened and periodically during the night. We did this to make sure that no dealers were waiting to ambush our clients and that bodies were not dumped in the alleys. One night, Barry Case made a routine tour of the outside of the center and, hidden in the long grass beneath the electricity meter, spotted a metal tube. He carefully parted the weeds: It was a pipe bomb, packed with enough explosive to demolish the center and kill everyone in it.

We evacuated the building and called the bomb squad. The bomb was safely removed, but the near catastrophe sent shock waves through the center. Patients began disappearing, and some of the civilian staff quit. No one claimed responsibility for the bomb, but before fleeing Los Angeles for her life, Virginia told me that it had been planted in retaliation for our affair. Once again, I was compelled to keep the information to myself, and, indeed, it has remained my secret until this writing.

Shortly after the incident, the Panthers returned for a follow-up meeting. By now we knew that Arnett was an associate of Bunchy Carter, the former Slauson gang member who had formed the Southern California chapter of the Panthers, and who had been shot to death at UCLA in a fight with members of US. The two groups had disagreed over who should chair the Department of Afro-American Studies at the university, and had settled the academic dispute with guns.

I sat opposite the Panther delegation knowing full well that they had tried to kill me—and everyone else in the center—but I was unable to say anything. This time, the Panthers were not the accommodating altruists they had been before; instead, they began laying down demands in return for their assistance with our program. They wanted control of half our beds, access to the lists of our patients and personnel, and a permanent office for their own program inside Compton. In other words, they wanted to harass and intimidate, and to regain their foothold in the city.

It happened that Barry Case was off duty that night, and his place had been taken by Joe Tice, a black veteran cop whose nickname was Crater, because of his craggy, pockmarked face. I watched him stewing as the Panthers became more hostile and defiant, until finally he could take it no longer. "Who the hell do you think you are?" he demanded.

"We represent the people!" the Panther leader shot back.

"Bullshit!" Tice shouted. "You represent nobody but yourselves."

Dan Hemmer, a slight and fidgety man, tried to calm Crater down, but he was too heated.

Arnett spat back at him, "You ain't nothin' but an Uncle Tom, you white-assed motherfucker!" Incensed, Tice ordered the Panthers to get out. "Make me, pig!" Arnett challenged.

Tice stormed out of his chair and across the negotiating circle. He punched Arnett in the face, propelling him backward to the floor, and began kicking him. One kick caught Arnett in the side of the head, and he let out a sickening grunt, his skull fractured. By the time we pulled Tice off, the Panther lay unconscious and bleeding. His colleagues, who had made no attempt to save him, dragged him from the room, muttering that they would return. They never did. It was the last time the Black Panthers tried to infiltrate the Community Service Center.

Joe Tice's attack on Arnett was a vivid illustration of the kind of hostility that existed between the Panthers and us. Though parts of their program were legitimate, even admirable, such as their effort to keep black families together and to get an education for their children, their methods belied their ideals.

They were themselves a primary source of the drugs, the violence, and the disruption in the areas they organized, as they sought not just to secure their own position but to displace the existing social order as well. It was their aim to create their own government within the cities and drive out the establishment—but that establishment, as personified by the CPD, was made up of people of all races who were risking their lives day after day to protect the community. We were not the Panthers' enemy until they declared war on us, and from that moment, it had to be a fight to the death. Either the Panthers would drive us out of Compton, or we would drive them out. There was no room for compromise.

Despite such incidents as these, the center remained in operation, and we did our best to help those in the community who wanted to kick drugs and regain control over their lives. Because of this, we were beginning to earn the respect and trust of the neighborhood, which was essential to our mission.

All that was threatened one afternoon, however, when a large, middle-aged black woman with gray-streaked hair stormed into the center screaming in near-hysterical fury. She was accompanied by her entire family, her minister, several community activists, and a dozen people from her neighborhood. They had marched on the center as the nearest city-owned facility. One of the first people they met was me. I was wearing civilian clothes, as we all did at the center, so there was no sign that I was a cop. I asked her what had happened.

It seemed that earlier in the evening, the woman's sister had been arrested by two Compton police officers, who, she insisted, had brutalized her. She was a large woman with a powerful voice and an impressive presence. Her name was Florence Elwood. "They stopped her right on our street, and when she didn't kiss their butts, they beat her up and threw her into their car," she shouted. "Well, they picked on the wrong family this time!" She told me that she was the president of the block club, and that the entire neighborhood was going to march on City Hall and demand that the officers be punished. "We're gonna light this city up!" Mrs. Elwood screamed. "And if it don't light up, we're gonna burn it down!"

I urged her to calm herself and invited her to come into the center's office. She, her pastor, and one of the activists did so. There I spoke with her for over an hour, getting the details of the incident and assuring her that I would look into it personally. As we talked, I could see her fury softening to indignation and then to a resigned exhaustion.

"If your family's been done an injustice," I told her, "starting a riot isn't going to help—it'll just make matters worse. Other people will get hurt, and you don't want that. Let me look into it, please."

Mrs. Elwood seemed to trust me, or at least to believe that I was sincere, and at last she made me swear to her that I would get to the bottom of the beating of her sister. I promised her that I would, and that I would report back to her with the result. It was enough for her. She got up, thanked me, and took my hand. "You saved us all one hell of a lot of trouble, whoever you are."

I told her that my name was Rick Baker, and that I was a cop. She looked closely at me, evidently surprised by the news. Then she said, "You're a good man, Mr. Baker." She gave me her phone number and left, followed by the pastor, the activists, and the members of her block club.

I made good on my promise to Mrs. Elwood to investigate the incident. I read the report by the arresting officers, Joe Flores and Clarence Bowden, and I spoke to them privately. They told me that they had responded to a domestic violence call, and had found the woman's sister fighting with another young woman in what appeared to be a jealous rage. They had tried to break it up, but the woman had become hysterical, and she clawed and bit at the officers. They had no choice, Joe Flores said, but to subdue her. I asked what he meant by "subdue."

"You know," Bowden shrugged. "We wrestled her to the ground and put the cuffs on her."

I had dealt with dozens of domestic violence calls myself, and I knew that any Compton cop would have separated the parties, cooled the situation down, and sent them packing. It was simply not worth our time to make an arrest. Only when a suspect resisted and posed a threat to herself or to the officers did they take direct action. So, Joe Flores told me, they had had to get physical in order to restrain the woman.

"But it was just a woman," I replied.

"Damn, Rick," Joe Flores said, "you weren't there. The bitch was 250 pounds and totally out of control. And besides, we had had one hell of a night—a couple of stabbings, shots fired, a homicide. We didn't have time to mess around with her. We took her down and hooked her up."

I knew and trusted both Joe Flores and Clarence Bowden. Bowden had gone through the academy with me, and it was Flores who had stood back-to-back with me when we faced down the mob in Victory Park. If they had acted with unnecessary force, they would have told me.

I called Mrs. Elwood and asked her to come back to the Service Center. We sat down together, and I explained what I had learned; though I went so far as to admit that the officers may have overreacted, I tried to explain the kinds of stress they were under. Mrs. Elwood seemed satisfied—she knew her sister, and she knew what she was capable of when she was provoked. She thanked me again and left. There would be no demonstration at City Hall. There would be no riot. The matter was closed.

Sometime later, I was given a commendation by the chief of police for having averted what could have been an ugly civil disturbance. It was my first accolade, and one of only two given at the Service Center. Ironically, the other was received by David Hutton.

He, too, was confronted by a group of angry civilians threatening a riot over an allegation of police brutality. Instead of inciting them, Hutton followed my example, calmed them down, and convinced them to go home. He then filed a complaint with the city council, demanding an investigation. In response, they gave him a commendation identical to mine. It appeared that the administration's hope of including Hutton as part of the establishment had worked, though I could not help but feel that his change of heart had been encouraged by the publication of the news of his affair with Jane.

Hutton and I had carefully avoided each other at the Service Center, but the next time I saw him, I made a point of congratulating him. He glared at me with vengeful eyes. I could see that he wanted to tell me to go fuck myself, but I had pointed a cocked .357 Magnum at his face only a few months before, and he knew that he dare not mouth off to me. He grunted, but said nothing.

Rapunzel, the Election,
and the Pastry Chef

It was the 1970s, the Age of Aquarius, hippies, and free love. Those of us who worked at the Service Center were allowed to wear our hair long and dress according to the fashion of the times. It was thought that in this way our clients could better identify with us. I did not argue. I let my hair grow and developed a bushy, curvaceous black mustache, which was the source of no end of ribbing at the station. There were pointed references to Pancho Villa and *Viva Zapata!* I liked it, though, and many of the patients, who were stoned-to-the-bone hippies, told me that I was cool.

One in particular, named Stuart, the first black hippie I had ever met, attached himself to me. He was cross-addicted to LSD, cocaine, and booze, and his chief boast was that he was a buddy of the members of the cast of *Hair*, which was playing at the Aquarius Theater in Hollywood. We had long talks about his plans to travel the world in search of enlightenment and new ways of getting high. In fact, he did find his way to Afghanistan, Pakistan, India, and Bangladesh. I met him again fifteen years later when he was arrested for possession and being under the influence. His quest for enlightenment had led him back to Compton city jail.

I had volunteered for the Service Center to try to do some good, but also in order to learn. I had seen a great deal of human suffering and the degradations and frailties to which human nature is prone, and I wanted to be able to do something to help. Indeed, I did learn a lot about dealing with broken, sensitive, borderline people. One of the deepest and most poignant lessons was taught to me by a girl named Susie Gee.

Susie was a fairylike love child who wafted in one night wearing spangled sandals and a thrift-store granny gown, looking for help or warmth or simply out of loneliness. She was a heroin addict, one of a steady stream of white hippies who found their way into Compton from the surrounding communities or from L.A., because the center staff had acquired the reputation of asking no questions and accepting anyone who came. In short, we were cool.

Susie had translucent white skin, delicate freckled features, and the longest hair I had ever seen. It cascaded down her back to her ankles in a flood of red-gold, making her seem like Rapunzel locked in her tower pining for help. There was a coy vulnerability about her, and a kind of purity that, after three years on the streets of Compton, I found refreshing. She seemed drawn to me, asking to see me especially every time she came into the center in search of someone to talk to—and we did talk, usually late at night, and often about her family, which had disowned her when she took up the hippie lifestyle and drifted into drugs. At nineteen, she was a lost, lonely child who came very quickly to depend on me. In some ways she reminded me of the nymphlike cop groupies who had haunted the nights on Long Beach Boulevard when I was a rookie.

It was a time of free love, when sex was as much a part of interaction as talk and laughter. So it was not long before Susie and I were seeing each other outside the center. I should not have done it, should not have taken advantage of her, but she was so different from Shondra Givens and Virginia and even my wife Connie, the former bartender, that I could not resist. Susie was like a presence from a dream, with a fey frailty that I found irresistible. For the first time in my life, a woman had seduced me not with her sensuality but with her innocence.

We saw each other every chance we got. I gave her money for food and urged her to go back home to her parents in Anaheim. Like Stuart, though, she was convinced that she was on a path to enlightenment.

"You're on a path, all right," I told her one dawn in the Big 5 motel in Lynwood, "but it doesn't lead to enlightenment."

She smiled a sleepy, girlish smile. "You won't let that happen to me," she purred. "You'll protect me."

The truth was that I did want to protect her; I wanted to get her off the drugs and back to earth, but she was a creature from a fairy tale, and confinement to earth was bound to kill her. It was clear to me that she was going to die if she went on, and also if she returned. There was nothing I could do for her, and I felt more and more guilty about using her for sex. So, helpless to save her, I told her that we could not see each other anymore. I abandoned her just as her parents had done.

I had not seen or heard from her in several days, and I was beginning to be worried about her. Then one night, after midnight, the phone in the center's office rang. It was Susie. "Rick," she said, her voice trembling, "I want to see you."

I told her I was on duty and could not leave.

"You have to come," she sobbed. "I'm all alone and I don't have anybody to talk to."

"I've got clients here that I have to deal with," I said.

"You don't understand, Rick. I'm so fucked up and I've got no one. Rick . . ."

I was impatient and wanted to get her off the line. "What?"

She was weeping now. "I need you."

There were half a dozen addicts in the center that night, desperate, sweating, wild-eyed, clamoring for my attention. I told Susie that she would have to wait.

"I can't wait, Rick, I'm all alone and unhappy and there's nobody in the world who cares but you. I have to see you now."

I told her that I had to hang up. Her voice thinned to a wailing screech. "Don't hang up on me!" she pleaded. "You can't hang up on me. Everybody's always shutting me off, like I'm dirty or stupid or nuts! You can't do that to me!"

"Susie," I said as evenly as I could, "other people need me."

"But they don't love you, Rick. I love you."

Her voice was distant and pathetic, like the cry of an exhausted swimmer who is drowning. "I've got to go," I told her, and I started to hang up.

"Rick!" I heard her shout. "Rick, are you there?" I answered that I was. "Rick," she went on much more calmly than before, "I'm in a phone booth at Compton and Central, and if you don't come get me, I'm gonna cut my wrists. I swear it, Rick, I've got a knife and if you don't come, I'm gonna kill myself."

I had heard such threats a dozen times at the center, and I knew they were always the last clutching cry for attention of wounded, taunting children. We had been trained to deal with this juvenile ploy, the ultimate form of manipulation. "You're not going to do any such thing," I replied as calmly as I could.

"I will!" Susie insisted. "I'm gonna do it right here in the phone booth!"

"Susie, cut it out," I snapped. "Come in tomorrow night and we'll talk."

"No! We gotta talk now. You come here or I'll kill myself!"

I lost my temper. She was a sulking child just trying to control me. "Susie," I said, "if you want to kill yourself, I can't stop you. But I know you won't do it."

"I will. I swear!"

"You won't. Now if you need a place to sleep, come here."

There was a sudden silence, and then I heard her body hit the floor of the booth. I yelled her name into the phone. In a few moments, a woman was on the line. "There's a girl here," she yelped, "and she just cut her wrists!"

I called for an ambulance, jumped into my car, and drove to Compton and Central. A small crowd had gathered around the phone booth. Inside, crumpled on the crusted metal floor, Susie lay like a dozing child, wrapped in a diaphanous gown. Blood streamed in silky ribbons from her wrists, which were crossed at her side. There was something horribly touching about her. I felt guilt, sorrow, and anger all at once.

I watched as the paramedics tied her arms off to stop the bleeding, the tracks of needles at her elbows dotting her pale skin like livid flea bites. They hefted her onto a gurney, and as they wheeled her past me, I saw her eyes flit open. She looked at me and smiled; it was the placid, self-satisfied smile of a child who has defied a parent even at the cost of punishment.

I hoped that Susie would not be taken to County, but to a private hospital where she would receive the treatment she so badly needed. Though I made enquiries about her, I never saw or heard from her again.

It was a hard and painful lesson for me, learned nearly at the cost of an unfortunate girl's life. It was one thing to be Rosecrans Rick, a young and aggressive cop surrounded by groupies and strippers; it was another to steamroll into the life of a brittle human being, insensitive to her aching need for someone to care. I had used her and then abandoned her, and that was a betrayal her delicate psyche could not bear. Her attempt at suicide was not a plea for attention; it was the logical outcome of her quest to find herself in the course of destroying herself—a quest that had led her to me, and to my callousness.

I swore that never again would I become emotionally involved with anyone who depended on me for help. It made me a better cop, I think now, but I am not sure it made me a better human being. In the words of T. S. Eliot, Susie Gee had taught me "to care and not to care."

As I broadened my career by working at the Service Center, I also expanded my role in the Police Officers Association. When Joe Banovic announced that he was not going to seek another term as president, several officers urged me to run. Though I had taken the leading role in the blue flu and was regarded as the association's spokesman, it was not at all clear that I could win. By this time, though the detectives were still overwhelmingly white, the rank and file of the department was 40 percent black and 10 percent Latino. The black officers decided to make an attempt to take control of the association, putting up Hourie Taylor as their candidate.

It was assumed that Taylor would carry the entire black contingent, and if he succeeded in getting half the Latino officers and the small percentage of the détente whites who felt they could promote their agenda by electing a black president, he would have a majority. Hourie Taylor was a friend of mine—we had been in a lot of scrapes together, and I liked and respected him. Even so, I decided to run against him, not to prevent his election but to pursue my goal of serving my city as well as I could. I believed that I was the person best suited to grow the political power of the association, and to negotiate new contracts in a tough and aggressive manner. For, as good a cop as Hourie Taylor was, I felt that he lacked political sensibility and the killer instinct needed when it came to dealing with the city council.

By my calculations, in order to win I would have to carry 80 to 85 percent of the white officers, all of the Latinos, and a few blacks as well. My strategy was thus the mirror image of Taylor's. The lines of the contest between us were clearly drawn. I knew that a few black officers would vote for me because of the blue flu, and because they believed I was better qualified to promote the association. I had to win more than just a handful, though, and to do this, I needed black running mates. I asked Officer John Smith to be my vice president, and my Service Center colleague Roland Ballard to run with me for the board. My goal was not only to win; it was to have a leadership that reflected the makeup of the force.

Working with Roland at the center, I had learned to admire his intelligence, his tact, and his sharp political sense. He was not the kind of cop with whom you would want to walk into Sonny's Pool Hall, but he had shown that he could handle city hall and the touchy business of community relations. Roland was a good cop, but he was an even better politician.

As we moved deeper into the seventies, the exodus of whites from Compton was nearly complete. The city was now 95 percent black, with a small Latino population and a tiny remnant of die-hard whites. The fact that the demographics of the police department did not reflect this reality further sharpened the divisions among the officers. The white apartheid group became more polarized, as did the black militant faction, with the moderates and the Latinos caught in a tug of war between them.

We were all on our guard in the matter of language, for example. The casual use of racial epithets, which had been common, began to disappear, and everyone was careful about what he said in the locker room, on the street, and over the radio. Some of the more colorful slurs became taboo. This was, of course, a good thing, but it was a difficult transition for some of the older officers, to whom such expressions were simply part of the jargon of police work. Even the simple matter of ordering coffee at a diner became sensitive. Formerly, a cop's coffee came as either "east side" or "west side." East side was coffee with cream; west side was black. Such references, which had been automatic, now had to stop.

In any other department this kind of racial tension would have been debilitating, but Compton was a special case. We were under such tremendous pressure from the army of criminals, gangbangers, and militants that we were compelled to bond closely just to survive. So, despite the differences among us, the one thing we had in common was the fact that we all wore a blue uniform. Gangbangers did not care about demographics; murderers and rapists did not know the backgrounds of the cops who broke down their doors; bullets did not distinguish color. In the end we were all cops, and, as Jack Kennedy had reminded us, we were all mortal.

This truth was illustrated in dramatic fashion when Officer John James, one of the leaders of the black militant faction, responded to a call of shots fired at the Patio Bar at Magnolia and Tamarind. The Patio was a notorious dive that was the hangout of killers and dope dealers, and so the call came as no surprise. James pulled up outside, but before he could even get out of his unit, he was met with a blizzard of bullets.

Three men with guns came storming out of the bar, shooting and taking up positions around the police car, while two more fired from inside. James put in a frantic 999 call for immediate backup as he took cover behind his car. The first to respond were two white officers who, just two days before, had been tagged by the FBI in a surveillance of the American Nazi Party headquarters in El Monte, where they had attended a meeting. Though they had been patrolling on the far side of town, they raced to the Patio with lights swirling and siren blaring, blowing through red lights and stop signs, and beating every other car to the scene.

The white cops rolled to a stop across Magnolia Street, jumped out of their unit with shotguns and pistols, and opened fire on the five men, who still had James pinned behind his car. For ten minutes the shootout on Magnolia raged back and forth, both cars riddled with bullets, the front of the Patio pocked and shattered like the Alamo. When more units appeared, the men finally put down their guns and surrendered.

That night when John James was changing into civvies in the locker room, he was still high from what was already being called the shootout at the O. K. Corral. "God damn it!" he roared to everyone in the room, "I was never so glad to see a white man as I was when them two honkeys rolled up to save my ass!"

It was a spontaneous acknowledgment that the leaders of the anti-black faction in the department had risked their lives to save that of the leading black militant. They had done it without thinking, without hesitation, for the simple reason that they were all Compton cops.

My six-month duty at the Service Center was coming to a close, and I had to consider once again what direction my career would take. One day, as I was checking in, I glanced at the bulletin board in the patrolmen's assembly room and saw that there was an opening in the juvenile division. It was just the sort of assignment I was looking for. It would mean an opportunity to work with kids, and in Compton that meant working with gang-bangers like Sylvester Scott, Lorenzo Betton, and A. C. Moses. It was also a promotion to detective rank with a raise in pay and access to that unbreachable inner sanctum, the second floor. Beyond that, it was a chance to work with Sergeant Arturo Camarillo, a former Compton High football star who had grown up on the north side, and whom I had long admired.

I scored first among half a dozen candidates in the written exam, and I did well in the oral interview. When the results were posted, I was at the top of the list: I would be moving up to juvenile.

Because of the rise of the gangs, juvie had become one of the largest and most important divisions in the Compton PD. We had our own cubicles upstairs with a secretary, drove our own unmarked cars, and were allowed to wear suits instead of uniforms. Our duties took us into the most violent neighborhoods in the city, but also to the juvenile halls, courts, and police headquarters in surrounding communities for training and consultation. My world as a cop was expanding.

As I started my career in juvie, I was actively campaigning for Police Officers Association president. I made a point of talking one-on-one with every officer on patrol, explaining to them what I intended to do with the association. My plan, in general terms, was to build our power to the point where we would be recognized not just by the city administration but beyond the city as well. To this point, the CPOA had been accepted as a de facto member of the state and national associations of police departments, but we had never really participated in their activities and had virtually no profile or prestige. I intended to change all that. I wanted cops all over California and the United States to give us the respect to which we were entitled. I wanted the Compton Police Officers Association to be as impactful a political force as we were a police force.

The election proved to be the closest in the history of the association. Hourie Taylor won almost all of the black officers' votes and 15 percent of the whites'. I took the remaining 85 percent, as well as all the Latino votes and nearly 10 percent of the blacks'. I won with a razor-thin majority. I was now president of the Compton Police Officers Association.

From the outset, I realized that mine was an extremely delicate position. The association had received a big boost from the success of the blue flu, but the city council was beginning to regard that as a fluke—a onetime victory. They had to be convinced that the association was here to stay, that we could and would continue to be a unified political force in the city. To do that, we would have to reorganize, and that meant, first of all, that we had to strengthen our treasury.

To this point, the treasury had existed primarily to buy liquor, throw parties, and run food and toy drives. My goal was to make it the source of organizational power. The officers' dues, which would have to be increased, would be used to promote their political interests as well as their social ones. Raising the dues was not a popular move—policemen's salaries were scarcely enough to allow them to pay their mortgages and put their kids through school. Nevertheless, I managed to convince them that, with a little extra sacrifice, we could achieve future gains in pay, benefits, and conditions. To their credit, the rank and file understood and agreed.

Our treasurer was Sergeant Robert Watson, a member of one of the last remaining Mormon families in Compton. He was a records officer who did not work the streets, but he was a brilliant money manager, and under his guidance, our treasury began quickly to grow. For the first time, the association would have not only the unity necessary to implement its agenda but the financial resources as well. This included a strike fund, the very existence of which put the city administration on notice that we had to be taken seriously.

Howard Edwards, the former cop, was now city manager, which meant that we had, potentially, one ally in city government. On the other hand, Mayor Dollarhide and the three black members of the city council had never forgiven us for defying them with the flu, and they made it clear that they intended to fight the association at every step. As time went on, Dollarhide became more and more implacable in his relations with the police department, playing the race card at every opportunity.

The situation was complicated by the fact that the chief, W. K. Ingram, was white, a holdover from the previous administration. Dollarhide was simply waiting for him to retire so that he could appoint his own chief. Ingram was thus nothing but a lame duck, with no real power or influence, unable to ignore the association, but unwilling, for the sake of his pension, to challenge Dollarhide's administration. This put the association in a very difficult position, and I knew that I would have to choose my battles carefully.

With my position as CPOA president and my new job in juvenile, my life was taking a different turn. All of my time was being consumed by these two roles, and that left precious little to devote to my marriage. In addition, as a juvie officer, I was spending my duty hours working in the gang strongholds, with all the risks and dangers that entailed. While I actually enjoyed the adrenaline rush of working gang duty full-time, the stress was more than my wife could bear.

Connie had been loyal and faithful to me, even managing to overlook my Rosecrans Rick escapades. She had backed me on the strike, leading the wives' picketing of City Hall, and had made me proud in her handling of the press and the pressure. Now, though, the strain of being a Compton cop's wife was overwhelming her, and she began to urge me to consider a transfer to another city.

It was a real possibility. Connie's father was a retired air force colonel who had been involved in the supersecret activities at Area 51 in New Mexico. He was highly regarded in the military and had influential friends in state government. Connie told me that her father had arranged for me to be transferred to the Redondo Beach Police Department anytime I chose, and she begged me to take advantage of the opportunity. In her mind, it was the key to saving our marriage. Redondo Beach was an upscale seaside community known for surfing, volleyball, and a low crime rate. It was a place where Connie knew we could settle down, buy a house, and raise a family without the lethal threat of my work on the streets every night.

It was tempting. I loved Connie, and I wanted to please her. However, I could not forget Rutigliano's description of his ride-along in Huntington Beach, and the way he had laughed derisively when he spoke of the "chicken shit" kind of police work it involved. I could no more take a job like that than he could, and, also, how could I abandon my work as Police Officers Association president? I could not be what Connie needed me to be and also be who I knew I had to be. I could not be married to her and to my job at the same time.

I chose my job. At the time, it seemed to me to be the only choice I could make. In the years since, I have often questioned my decision. Connie was a good and beautiful wife, and I had planned to make my future with her. Yet I simply could not live the kind of life she craved—an ordinary life, secure and predictable. I was addicted to the challenge and the risks of police work in Compton. I wanted more of them; I wanted to move up in the department so that I could make the kind of difference that only a Compton cop could make—a difference involving not only people's safety and lives but the future of the entire city, my city. So, for the very reasons that had induced me to join the police force, I now chose to remain with it at the cost of my marriage. When I announced that my decision was final, we agreed to divorce.

It was the practice of the CPD to keep two detectives on duty at all times, one in the adult division and one in juvenile, and for the first few months, I worked the 5:00 P.M. to midnight shift. On one of my first nights in juvie, a young white woman wandered into the station, frightened and disoriented. The very fact that an attractive white girl was walking the streets of Compton near midnight was unusual, but the story she told was tragically bizarre.

Because she kept wailing, "My baby . . . you gotta help my baby!" she was sent upstairs to see me. It took me a few minutes before I was able to calm her to the point where she could answer my questions.

"What happened to your baby?" I asked.

"They took her, they've got her!" she panted. I asked her who. "Holland and Garrett," she replied.

I knew Larry Holland and Nathaniel Garrett; they were small-time drug dealers and pimps who lived on the west side. I asked the woman her name. "Linda," she said.

Her story was this:

A few months before, she had come into Compton searching for the father of her two-year-old girl. He was a young Latino named Johnny whom she had met in Lincoln Heights. She had tried to raise the child by herself, but her parents had refused to help, and in desperation she decided to find Johnny and plead with him for support. She knew roughly where he lived, so she went to the neighborhood and began asking people if they knew where he was. That was when she ran into Holland and Garrett.

They told her they knew Johnny, and they could lead her to him. To make sure that Johnny understood how important the situation was, they said, she should go home and bring the child back with her. She did so the next day. Holland and Garrett took Linda and her baby to Holland's sister's house. They convinced her to leave the baby with the sister while they went to look for Johnny—but they never did.

Instead, they took Linda to Garrett's house, where they told her that if she did not do as they said, she would never see her baby again. They had guns, and they threatened that both she and her child would die. She was terrified and asked what they wanted from her.

"You gonna work for us, bitch," Garrett told her. "We gonna put you on the street."

For six months after that Garrett and Holland forced Linda to work for them as a prostitute. They knew that a young, attractive white girl would be in demand in East Compton. They took Polaroid pictures of her stark naked and showed them around local bars like the Fire Pit, the Copy Cat, and the Patio. While one of the men waited in the car with Linda, the other went inside. "We got this woman in the car," he would say, "and if you wanna have sex with her, we'll take you to the motel around the corner."

In this way they had sold Linda over and over, keeping her silent with threats and the occasional visit with her child. It was an ongoing nightmare in which she had been locked in the basement of Garrett's house, taken out at night to be prostituted, and allowed only a precious hour every few days to be with her baby.

At first, she told me, she had screamed and fought, but they beat her and refused to let her see her child. She realized that if she were ever going to escape, she would have to convince Garrett and Holland that she could be trusted, and so for weeks she had done everything they asked, including having sex with them, without protest.

Finally, that weekend, when she was on her period and could not work, she persuaded the two men to let her to go out to the drugstore. For the first time in six months, she left the house on her own. She walked to the Thrifty drugstore, and when she was sure they had not followed her, she came straight to the police station.

It was a sad and horrifying story, and as Linda sat at my desk, desolate and weeping, I ran over the situation in my mind. If we arrested Garrett and Holland, they would claim that the girl had been working for them willingly, and that the sister was merely taking care of the baby while she did so. At the most we could get the two of them for pandering. I wanted them for kidnapping, blackmail, and threatening to kill Linda and her child. To do that, we needed more than just her word.

Time was running out. Garrett and Holland would already be wondering where Linda was. I called over Officer Jimmy Pearson, the detective who was working the adult division that night. He was a big, young former sheriff's deputy whom I had trained when he joined the CPD. I quickly explained the situation to him.

"So what do you wanna do?" he asked.

"We have to put a wire on her and get these guys on tape admitting to what they've done. Otherwise they're gonna claim it was consensual."

Pearson agreed. I turned again to Linda. "You have to go back," I told her.

She looked at me in utter disbelief. "You don't know what I had to do to get out of there," she said.

It was a horrible thing to ask this young woman, but I felt I had no choice. "I want to bust these guys and put them away," I told her, "so you and your baby won't have to worry about them ever again."

She looked at me, her mind working. "What do you want me to do?" she asked at last.

"Go back to Holland's house like nothing happened. You're on your period, so we've got a few days. They won't do anything to you, and if something goes wrong, we'll be watching."

"If they know I talked to you, they'll kill my baby," she said.

I tried to reassure her, but I feared she was right. "What's your baby's name?" I asked her.

"Elena."

"You've got to do this for Elena's sake."

She looked at me a long, desolate moment. It was the hardest decision she had ever had to make, but she agreed.

I drove Linda back to the east side, where Holland and Garrett lived in the Santa Fe Apartments complex. I was surprised: The area was one of the better neighborhoods in Compton, and the building, in a gated community, was upscale. On the way over, Linda and I arranged to keep in contact. She was to call me every day whenever she had a chance, and we would meet as often as she could at the Santa Fe Plaza shopping center, when she would go to out to buy groceries and cigarettes.

I stopped the unmarked car across the street from the entrance to the complex. Linda sat rigid and anxious in the seat next to me. "I'm not gonna let anything happen to you," I told her. "You did the right thing coming to us."

She looked at me, the fear in her eyes clouded with tears. "I don't want to go back in there," she said in a thin voice.

I touched her hand. "We're gonna get these guys."

She stared at me a long moment—her life and the life of her baby were in my hands. Then she got out of the car. I watched her walk through the gate and disappear in among the whitewashed buildings of the complex. She looked very small and alone.

Over the next two days, I kept in touch with Linda as we had agreed. She made hurried calls to me from pay phones, and we met in the Plaza twice. I was undercover, wearing baggy pants and a sweatshirt, unshaven, doing my best to look like a john trolling for sex. We did this in case Garrett and Holland were watching her; she could always claim that I had tried to pick her up.

Meanwhile, Jimmy Pearson and I were keeping the house under surveillance. We learned that the two men had made so much money from selling Linda that they had been able to move from their west side dive into the apartments. We went through their trash, and discovered also that they were making hefty bets on the horses at Hollywood Park with the proceeds from Linda's prostitution.

On the third day, I told Linda to make an excuse to leave the house and come back to the police station. When she did, Pearson and I taped a microphone and transmitter under her clothes, and together we drove her in an unmarked van back to the Santa Fe Apartments.

Before she got out of the car, she gave me a desperate look. "If they find out, they'll kill me," she said.

"If you get too scared and you need us to come in, just say you want to see Elena."

We waited until she had gone into the complex; then we drove to the end of the block, did a U-turn, and parked across the street. We switched on the little Fargo recorder, an old-fashioned reel-to-reel, and waited.

At first there was a lot of random noise and interference, and I was afraid we would have to move in quickly and make the bust. Then we heard Larry Holland's voice demanding where Linda had been. She gave him a story about Thrifty's being out of what she wanted, and having to go instead to the supermarket. Then she asked tearfully what was going to happen to her baby.

"I told you, bitch," Holland answered, "nothin's gonna happen as long as you behave."

"How much longer are you gonna pimp me out?"

"Till we make enough money off you," he said, laughing.

For a few more minutes she kept him and Garrett talking about what they had done to her and her baby. It was exactly what we needed, and I could not help but admire Linda for her intelligence and her courage. Then we heard one of them demand oral sex from her.

"I'll do it," Linda answered. "But after, I want to see my Elena."

It was the signal to go in. Pearson and I jumped out of the van and rushed the house. We broke down the door, guns drawn, and shouted for Holland and Garrett to get on the floor. They looked at us in shock for a moment, then dropped flat on their faces. We found guns and a stash of cash and drugs hidden in the house.

We drove Garrett and Holland back to the police station, and I sent Linda with another unit to Holland's sister's house to get her baby. Later, while we were processing the two men, the officers brought Linda in. She was clutching in her arms a dark-haired little girl with enormous, intelligent brown eyes. "Elena," she said to me. "We wanted to thank you."

Holland and Garrett were booked for kidnapping, false imprisonment, blackmail, assault, possession, pandering, and making threats of bodily harm. Though Holland was held, Garrett was released on his own recognizance, a turn of events that was as senseless as it was infuriating. I wanted him back in custody, so I went through his file and found an old warrant for drug possession. That night, Jimmy Pearson and I drove down to Long

Beach to rearrest Nathaniel Garrett. He was a pastry chef on the *Queen Mary*, which is permanently berthed as a hotel and restaurant in Long Beach Harbor. We walked up the gangplank to the ship and were greeted by a man in a naval officer's uniform.

"Welcome to the *Queen*," he said with a British accent. "How may I help you?"

"We're detectives from Compton," I replied, showing him my badge. "We're here to arrest a member of your crew."

He frowned. "May I ask why?"

"No," I answered. "Which way is it to the kitchen?"

He called for a steward—at least, a young man in a steward's uniform—and told him to guide us to the galley. "Please," the officer said as we started down the companionway, "we have a full house tonight. Whatever you have to do, do it as discreetly as possible."

We found Garrett in a white chef's outfit with a tall paper hat, arranging meringues on delicate gold-filigreed dishware. When he saw us coming down the rows of stainless counters, he knew why we were there. He did not resist. We hooked him up in full view of the kitchen staff, and instead of taking him out the back as the steward asked, we marched him right through the dining room, while the waiters and diners gaped at us.

When Garrett and Holland came up for trial in Superior Court, which at that time was housed in the Brunswig Building near Olvera Street in L.A., I went down to testify, and to play the tape we had made with Linda. She was present, too, and I listened to her tearful testimony, once again impressed by her courage and strength.

Garrett and Holland were convicted and sentenced to twenty-five years in prison; the sister was found guilty of aiding and abetting a kidnapping and got five years. That night, after the trial was over, I took Linda out for dinner to celebrate her victory. With the nightmare behind her, she looked relieved, almost happy. I asked how Elena was doing.

"She's fine," Linda said. "It's gonna take a while, but we'll both be fine."

She smiled, and I realized how attractive she was. She had reddish brown hair, and the same large, expressive eyes as her daughter. I was separated by this time and getting a divorce, but I kept thinking about Susie from the Service Center. I paid the bill, drove Linda home to Lincoln Heights, and said good-bye. I never saw her again.

A few weeks later, I received a letter from a sergeant in the LAPD. He wrote to thank me for what I had done for Linda "and my granddaughter." Linda had not told me she was the daughter of a cop. He admitted that he had made some bad mistakes, but he wanted me to know that they had reconciled, and that he and his wife were helping to care for Elena.

I put that letter in a file together with my Service Center commendation, a handwritten note from Florence Elwood, and other letters of thanks from citizens I had helped. I decided that I would keep a record of the difference I was making in the lives of the people of my city. It was, after all, the reason I had become a cop in the first place.

Miami and the Siege
of City Hall

Early 1972 saw a watershed development in the history of the Compton Police Officers Association. As a result of the national publicity garnered by the blue flu, the International Conference of Police Associations contacted me. In fact, the director, Ed Kiernan, a retired New York City policeman who had worked the famous French Connection cases, flew to Los Angeles to meet with the board, and to invite me to attend their annual convention in Miami, Florida.

It was the first time that this powerful group, which was based in Washington, D.C., and represented over 150,000 police officers throughout the United States, Canada, and the Bahamas, had taken any notice of the Compton Police Department. It was exactly the kind of opportunity I had been looking for when I ran for president, and I accepted the invitation immediately. The ICPA convention would give our department a national platform for the first time in its history. When I arrived in Miami, I was met at the airport by Kiernan and his codirector, Robert Gordon. They asked me to deliver the convention's keynote address. This was much more than I could have hoped for.

The ICPA put me up at the Playboy Club, which was in itself a heady experience. All weekend I was surrounded not only by some of the most famous and notorious cops in America but by gorgeous, half-naked hostesses as well. It was the kind of experience, with all expenses paid, of which Rosecrans Rick had only ever dreamed. Still, the highlight for me was the opening night, when I delivered my speech.

The three-day convention was headquartered in the hotel's main ballroom, which was crowded with cops, lawyers, and politicians. Ed Kiernan rose to introduce me.

"I now have the honor to present," he began, "the president of the Compton, California, Police Officers Association, the leader of the blue flu, Officer Rick Baker."

The entire ballroom burst into applause as I made my way to the podium.

I had not expected anything like this. It was a proud and humbling moment. Here I was, the representative of a 130-man force, being applauded by cops from New York and Chicago, Detroit and Houston, Los Angeles and Philadelphia, Montreal, Toronto, and Vancouver, and touted as a kind of hero. Of course, I knew the applause was not for me—it was for cops like Carl Crosby, Dominic Rutigliano, Dave Hall, Joe Flores, Vince Rupp, Julio Hernandez, John Sutton, Dave Shepherd, and Burt Weingarten, who risked their lives every day in the guerrilla war we were fighting house-to-house in the streets of Compton.

I stood at the podium taking in the scene, hardly knowing what to think. Less than five years before, I had been a raw recruit struggling to establish himself; now I was speaking for all the officers of Compton, past and present. When the applause subsided, I tried my best to express what it meant not only to be a cop, but to be a cop in what had recently been labeled America's most dangerous city. I knew I was speaking for my fellow officers; I knew I had to represent them well.

"I'm a cop," I began hesitantly, "but more than that, I'm a Compton cop."

I had barely finished the sentence when the entire audience began applauding again. It was a long while before I was able to continue, but when

I did, it was to lay out our reasons for calling the blue flu, and the trials and accomplishments that we had experienced.

"What the politicians don't seem to understand," I told the delegates, "is that cops are people, too. We have families, we have careers, we have lives, and we have dreams, but most of all, we have pride. Pride in who we are and in what we do. And we do it not for ourselves, but for the people we serve. I truly believe that those people know this, and are grateful for it. But the politicians sometimes forget, and when they do, God damn it, we have a duty to remind them."

Again the room burst into applause.

I went on to explain that this was why we in Compton had called the first police labor action since the turn of the twentieth century, and I promised that we would do it again every time our city officials failed to negotiate with us in good faith. "Because our sworn duty is to protect the people of our communities—it's what we live for, and too often, it's what we die for. And we'll go on living and dying for it. But we in the Compton PD are damned if we'll do it for cut-rate wages, and benefits that the humblest of the people whose lives we protect would not accept. Because we are not politicians who come and go at the whim of the voters—we are the ones who have to be there in the middle of the night when the phone rings."

Now the audience was on its feet. I had more to say, but, as I watched them cheering and stamping, I realized I had said it all. The president of the Compton Police Officers Association had expressed what every cop in America was feeling: We wanted the support of our city halls, the official respect that what we did every day deserved, the fair shake that my wife Connie had demanded on the hand-lettered sign she had carried on national TV.

After the speech I was mobbed by officers from every city, clamoring to congratulate me and shake my hand. Later, when the convention had adjourned for the night, I was invited up to the hospitality suite by the members of the New York delegation, who were the official hosts.

When I got to the suite, I found it laced with some of the most gorgeous, accommodating young women I had ever seen. The New York detectives had hired the highest-class hookers in Miami to be our escorts for the night. It was like some fantasy of a *Godfather* party, complete with veteran NYPD detectives who had put away some of America's most notorious mobsters. As I talked with Ed Kiernan and Bob Gordon about Compton's role in the ICPA, one beautiful blonde or brunette after another draped herself on my lap or theirs.

As last Kiernan said, "Rick, I'd like you to become vice president of our Western States chapter." With the alcohol, the girls, and the flattery, I was nearly speechless, but I managed to accept nonetheless.

"Great," Kiernan said. "Now there's somebody I'd like you to meet."

He gestured across the room to a dapper man in a thousand-dollar suit, with salt-and-pepper hair. The man excused himself from his conversation and made his way toward us.

"Rick Baker," Kiernan said with a broad grin, "this is Jim van Norman." We shook hands. Kiernan went on, "Jim is the ICPA attorney."

He had the confident air of a man used to money and power. He seemed immune to the charms of the beautiful call girls, polite to them but clearly not impressed. "I'm very glad to meet you," he told me. "I enjoyed your speech."

He gave me his business card, which had a Manhattan address. "If you ever get into trouble, don't hesitate to call," he said with a smile somewhere between ingratiating and sincere. As I shook hands with him again I decided that, while I did not entirely trust him, he could be a valuable ally in the future.

Later I learned that James van Norman had been a standout student at the Yale Law School, and shortly after graduation he had won a major victory for a prominent New York Mafia boss. That had launched his career as a high-profile attorney who specialized in representing some of the most powerful and affluent personalities on the East Coast. He occupied that gray area of the law in which a number of household-name lawyers have made their reputations and fortunes—as advocates for millionaires whose money had come from varied but overlapping sources.

It was impossible to resist the appeal of the NYPD girls, and so, after a night of what can only be called debauchery, I attended the two remaining days of the convention. While there, I made contacts that, I felt, would help me to build the CPOA into a truly effective and powerful force for change, which had been my campaign pledge to the other officers. By the time I left Miami, my view of the role of the association had transformed—I now had a vision of us as not only an equal partner in Compton politics but perhaps the dominant force in the future.

When I got back home it was with a new sense of the mission of the CPOA. I knew that white flight had taken a terrible toll on Compton, both socially and economically. It had been not only a white flight but a green flight as well. The result was that the resources of the city had been depleted, which, among other things, meant that we could not expect massive increases in pay and benefits; rather, our demands had to be tailored to the realities of the city. So, while I determined to be an aggressive union leader, I had to take into consideration the needs of the community. For after all, as I had said in Miami, it was the community and not ourselves that we had sworn to serve. My firebrand labor instincts were thus tempered with an awareness of the challenges that faced my city.

Nonetheless, I pushed the agenda of the police department to its limit. I felt that in order to do this effectively, I had a responsibility to make myself aware of the economic developments in the city. I therefore insisted on attending every city council session, every planning commission hearing, every high-level development meeting that might affect the standing of the Compton police, either in person or through the eyes of my vice president, John Smith, or board member Roland Ballard. In this, Roland especially proved to be an invaluable ally. He had the command presence of a veteran cop combined with the acumen of a natural-born politician. He quickly became my right hand, and I trusted his judgment and relied on his advice implicitly.

One of the developments that we watched closely was the future of an open tract of land that stretched on either side of the 91 Freeway all the way west to the City of Carson. Like Dominguez Hills before it, this tract possessed inherent value as one of the largest open parcels in southern Los Angeles County, and developers, aware of the rising crime rate in Compton, were not slow to exploit the fact that it could be had cheaply.

In fact, before long, the commercial real estate giant Cabot, Cabot & Forbes was negotiating with the city to acquire the land.

As soon as I got wind of this deal, I insisted on attending the meetings between the developers and the city manager, Howard Edwards. Their plans were impressive: CC&F intended to bring into the area such multinational corporations as Xerox, Sanyo, Ralph's Grocery, and Craig Electronics, all of which were eager to take advantage of the depressed real estate values in Compton.

I saw this as a potential boon that would bolster not only police services but fire, urban renewal, parks and recreation, social services, and schools as well. I was therefore surprised to learn that the city council had cut a deal with CC&F by which any corporations they brought into the tract would pay no taxes for the first three years. It was a distressing prospect, but, I understood, it was necessary as an inducement to the corporations to accept the risks inherent in creating businesses in Compton.

Speaking for the CPOA when the matter came up for a vote before the city council, I did not object. We would reap the benefits, perhaps not immediately, but surely somewhere down the line. For now the important thing was that the Police Officers Association had been included in the negotiations and consulted before the vote was taken.

At the same time, there was another important development: federal revenue sharing. Touted as a prelude to the windfall expected from the end of the war in Vietnam, the Nixon administration's revenue-sharing program meant that the federal government would return a large portion of tax dollars to state, county, and municipal authorities in an effort to bring vital economic decisions closer to the local level. In theory, the poorest and neediest cities would benefit the most, and Compton was certainly one of these.

I could only imagine what would happen as federal money began pouring into the city government. Our city council, which for years had been penniless beggars for government funds, stood to realize a sudden influx of tax revenues estimated at sixty million dollars. Overnight, Mayor Dollarhide and his cronies were going to be transformed into tycoons with access to the national treasury.

In all of this it was vital that the police take an active role, but we were still saddled with a lame duck chief whose primary interest seemed to be protecting his retirement. Because of this, I formed a committee to conduct a search for an attorney to represent the CPOA in its dealings with the city. For this tricky task we chose an experienced black lawyer named Bob Edelen. Edelen was a dynamic and well-respected attorney whose portly frame and voluminous "natural" Afro gave him the appearance of a modern Frederick Douglass. He was outspoken and articulate, and he quickly set about trying to implement the association's agenda.

Almost immediately, however, he ran into a roadblock. The head of the city's personnel board was a fiery former civil rights activist named Lester Caldwell. Caldwell had been an associate of Dr. Martin Luther King Jr. and had participated in the Montgomery bus boycott and the march to Selma. As chief of personnel, Caldwell wielded a great deal of power, and, unfortunately, he hated Bob Edelen. This was so, I think, because Bob had made a successful career as an attorney, while Caldwell had failed the bar exam more than half a dozen times. Caldwell was, therefore, jealous of Edelen, and to me he appeared determined to thwart every one of Edelen's efforts on our behalf.

It was a frustrating and potentially delicate situation for the association. We were getting nothing done, but we dared not fire Edelen since he was an influential and popular figure who had the backing of the black officers. However, I knew that I had to replace him, and do it in a way that would not offend the blacks in the department or in the wider community.

I formed a committee chaired by John Soisson to look into the question of the effectiveness of the association's legal efforts, and I was careful to make this committee representative of the racial makeup of the department. We all agreed that, though Edelen was a skilled lawyer and an aggressive advocate, the conflict with Caldwell had rendered him impotent. I asked the committee to institute a search for a replacement, and, to their credit, they recommended a white lawyer from Santa Monica, a labor specialist named Steve Solomon. Solomon was known as a fierce and effective advocate for police rights, and, in fact, he did an excellent job for us.

The replacement of Edelen, a popular black from Compton, with Solomon, a white outsider to the city, was an object lesson to me in navigating the shoals of local politics. In order to be successful you simply could not run roughshod over racial considerations. Compton was a black city, and as a white official in Compton, I had to make every move with that reality in mind.

A sign that the status of the CPOA was growing was the fact that politicians from outside the city began seeking us out for endorsements, knowing that we were backed by the ICPA. Vincent Bugliosi, who had become famous as the prosecutor of the Manson family, was running for district attorney in Los Angeles, and he asked to see me and Roland Ballard at the Jack Tarr Hotel in San Francisco. He came straight to the point: He badly wanted and needed the backing of the Compton Police Officers Association. I questioned him at some length about his views on police-government relations and his plans for law enforcement in Los Angeles, and by the end of our hour-long meeting, I was able to shake his hand and promise him our public support. Similarly, the candidate for County Board of Supervisors in our district came to us for an endorsement, and before long, virtually every law-and-order politician in Compton and the surrounding cities coveted our support.

Our influence did not stop at the state and local level. Senator Ted Kennedy was sponsoring a bill in Congress that would require cities to engage in binding arbitration with police departments, and through the ICPA he contacted me to ask that I come to Washington to testify on behalf of the bill. I was far too busy to make the trip, so I sent Roland Ballard and an ambitious young white officer named Terry Ebert to represent the association. I did this very deliberately, since I wanted the rank and file to know that the perks, such as this high-profile trip to D.C., would not go to my racial cronies, as was increasingly the case with the mayor's office and city council.

All of this meant one thing, however: The Compton Police Officers Association was now a force to be reckoned with. No one in local politics could ignore us, and even on the state, national, and international level, our importance was being acknowledged. I was extremely proud of what the CPOA had been able to accomplish in the few short years since the blue flu had shaken the city and seized the country's attention. The CPD was no longer an outpost of order in a wilderness of violence: We had achieved my goal of being as effective in politics as we were in the streets. In the months and years to come, there would be many opportunities to test the limits of that power, contributing both to the good of the department and to its demise.

At this time my life was pretty evenly divided between my political work with the CPOA and my duties as a juvenile detective. Though I devoted as much time as I could to the association, I still had to deal with the reality in the streets. One aspect of that reality was the ongoing tension between the black and the Latino gangs of North Compton. While white flight had transformed most of the city, the small Latino population remained steadfast. The Latinos stayed in their homes, and, since they were surrounded by black neighborhoods with their growing black gangs, they defended their turf jealously. Though they were far outnumbered, the Latino gangs like the 1-5-5 and the Largo 36 were much older and better armed and organized than the black gangs.

By the late sixties, Sylvester Scott, the little kid with whom I had played football, was in high school. Among his friends were four boys named Larry Watts, Lorenzo Betton, Vincent Owens, and A. C. Moses, and together they formed a gang headquartered on Piru Street. Known as the Pirus, this gang, under Scott's leadership, evolved into the Bloods, who adopted the color red to distinguish themselves from the Crips.

The Pirus' turf was close to that of the 1-5-5, so they acquired their style and behavior from the Latinos. These included drive-by shootings, gang attire and language, and the use of finger signs, called "snapping," to show gang affiliation. Two hands forming the letter C meant you belonged to the Crips, three fingers pointing downward with thumb and forefinger curled formed a P for Piru, and one finger and two open palms signified the 1-5-5.

In addition, the black gangs adopted a practice from the Latinos that traced back to the interaction of the early European settlers and Native Americans. Called "slipping," it involved sneaking up on an enemy gang member in such a way that you could easily kill him. Instead, you announced, "I caught you slipping, man!" in much the same way as American Indians "counted coup."

The most obvious sign of gang presence was graffiti, or tagging, another practice that the blacks borrowed from the Latinos. Graffiti is a gang's way of communicating. It signifies their power and presence, marks their turf, and is used to send messages to members and warnings to outsiders. Upside-down graffiti is a challenge or a put-down of opponents, plans for fights are posted publically, and threatened hits are announced in the visual dialects of the gangs. Often a gang's tag, such as CV3, would be followed by the letters *C/S,* for *con safos.* This meant "fuck you double" to anyone defacing the tag.

Knowing how to understand these verbal and graphic languages was essential to police work in Compton, and because we had grown up with the people who created the gangs, it was almost a second language to us.

By the early 1970s, Sylvester Scott's Bloods had expanded from Piru Street to Lime Street on the east side (the turf of the Lime Hood gang), and south as far as Lueders Park. In all, there were some fifteen sets of Bloods in Compton. In response, Crips sets sprang up along the southern edge of the Bloods' turf below 166th Street. They called themselves the NBC, or Neighborhood Blocc Crips, and they were affiliated with the Crips of South Central L.A. Over the next twenty years, the wars between the Bloods and the NBC accounted for several hundred murders and thousands of shootings.

In 1970 there was a foreshadowing of the violence that was bound to occur between the Latino and the black gangs. In one area of the Nestor Tract, the acquisition of which had brought so many Latino gangbangers into Compton, black families had taken advantage of the exodus of whites to buy up some eight hundred houses on the north side of Compton Boulevard. This brought them to the edge of the Latino Corridor, and the old, established gangs whose turf it was. In response, black gangs began to form to defend their neighborhoods, and Compton Boulevard at Rosecrans became a no-man's-land between them.

The CPD had been careful to keep the black and Latino gangs separated, and for two years there had been relative peace in the area. We knew that this situation could not last: The interracial hostility and the gangs' aggressive territorialism were bound to erupt again.

Bunche Junior High School, on the north side of Compton, had long been predominantly Hispanic. In contrast, Whaley Junior High, on the far east of the city near the Long Beach Freeway, had gone from 90 percent white to 90 percent black, with a small minority of Latinos. As the black gangs formed and solidified, they felt they had to show the Hispanics that they were now in charge. Whaley was thus a tinderbox for racial tensions.

There were fights every week as the new black gangs attempted to assert their control while the Latinos, whose gangs were firmly entrenched, refused to back down. In one of these fights, a black kid named Johnny Jones, a recent immigrant from Mississippi, called out a Largo 36 member, Robert Valdez. The two sixteen-year-old boys met in the middle of the school playground and started a fistfight. While the other kids looked on, the fight became more and more vicious, with neither boy able to gain an advantage. Normally they would have fought each other to exhaustion or declared a draw, but suddenly Jones pulled a knife and stabbed Valdez in the chest. The Latino boy staggered some twenty or thirty feet to the sidewalk and collapsed.

The stabbing was the trigger for a brawl between the Latino students and the blacks. Within minutes, members of Largo 36 and blacks from the neighborhood began piling into the playground, and a dozen fistfights were swirling across the schoolyard and spilling onto the street. The Latinos were outnumbered some twenty to one, but they knew that if they did not make their stand there and then, they would be run out of the school.

Among the Largo bangers who raced to the scene were the Calloway brothers, two black members of the gang, who were called by the Chicanos Crow 1 and Crow 2. They were completely "Chicano-fied." They spoke Spanish, had Hispanic girlfriends, and did the popular Latino dances better than the Latinos. When they arrived, the other blacks assumed they would join them in the fight against the Latinos. Instead, the Calloways attacked the blacks, brutally beating several of them to the ground and kicking them unconscious.

Two Compton police units rolled to the scene, and the fight quickly broke up—but Robert Valdez lay dead on the sidewalk. Since he was a juvenile, his murder was assigned to me.

I drove up to North Compton that same day and picked up Crow 1 and Crow 2. They told me that they did not know who the killer was, but that I should talk to a black kid named Victor Gordon. I found Gordon on the east side and shook him down, and he gave up Johnny Jones. I then drove to Jones's house.

Jones was there, with his mother and sister. He was a muscular, dark-complected kid who vehemently denied everything. I could tell from his nervous, distracted manner that he was lying. I searched the house while Detective Bob Paige watched Jones, and found a bloody knife hidden under his bed. I took it and Jones to the police station.

Jones was not the kind of hardened gangbanger I was used to in Compton. His family had moved to the city only two years before, and he still had the raw, unsophisticated manner of a Mississippi country boy. Illiterate, barely educated, he had a chip on his shoulder the size of a plowshare. Most Compton bangers would have defied me, or shut up altogether, schooled as they were in the ways of police work. Not Johnny Jones. He pridefully admitted that he had started the fight and that he had stabbed Valdez. I brought in a stenographer to take down his confession, which he gave with sullen arrogance in his thick Mississippi drawl. When I told him that Valdez was dead, he made a show of indifference. "So what?" he said.

He displayed absolutely no remorse; indeed, he seemed nearly gleeful to learn that he had killed Valdez, speaking with a smug smile of the look of surprise on the Latino boy's face when he had driven the knife into his chest. I could see that Jones was a sociopath, perhaps a psychopath; a febrile mixture of inferiority—the residue of his upbringing in the South—and the grandiose self-image into which it had warped during his brief life. I asked him why he had stabbed Valdez.

"'Cause I was the one," he drawled.

"The one to what?"

"The one to prove to the *eses* that we're in charge now. These homeys 'round here don't know how to do it; I know how to do it." I asked him how. His eyes shone manically. "You got to kill 'em," he said. "It's the only way. You kill enough of them, they respect you."

That was why he had escalated the violence from a fistfight to a murder. It had been premeditated; the original fight had been nothing but an excuse to kill. I could not help but wonder if that lethal rage had been the cause of his family's move from Mississippi. I arrested Johnny Jones for murder in the first degree.

Meanwhile, I received word that the Largo gang was planning retaliation. They intended, the next day, to drive by Whaley Junior High and shoot any blacks who stood outside. There would be three cars, and each would carry two bangers with automatic weapons. I knew it was no idle threat. It had been the Largo gang that had ambushed the Watts rioters in 1965 and prevented them from entering Compton. They were a murderous and fearless bunch, and they were heavily armed. It would be nothing short of a massacre.

As soon as I heard this, I drove up to the north side and sought out the Largo leaders. They were righteous and furious, and made no attempt to deny that they had plans to deal with the blacks at Whaley. I knew these kids, had known most of them since childhood, and I felt they trusted me even though I was a cop. I told them that retaliating would only lead to more violence, more killings like that of Robert Valdez. "You do them," I said, "they're only gonna come back and do you. Then you've got a war on your hands—not just with them, but with us. And how many of you are gonna die?"

They heard me out in silence.

Finally I said, "If I can get Johnny Jones for murder one, would you be satisfied?"

They said yes, and I promised them I would.

A few days later, I went to juvenile court in Eastlake for Jones's arraignment. I was confident that, with his confession and the statements I had gotten from other kids at the scene, I could keep my promise to the Largos, and thereby avoid a war. However, when I saw who the judge assigned to the case was, my heart sank. It was Wendell Harkin, the judge who had handled my divorce from Connie the previous year. Connie had appeared in court looking alluring and pristine. Her blond hair was perfectly coiffed, and she wore a dress that showed off her long, shapely legs. It was clear to me that Judge Harkin took a liking to her immediately, and an equal disliking to me.

When it came time for my statement, the judge had listened impatiently, frequently interrupting me. His overt favoritism began to grate on my nerves. Then, when I had finished, he denied every one of my requests and imposed the harshest possible terms on me. I was to pay alimony for a time equal to the length of our marriage, and, in addition, I was to compensate Connie for her lost wages.

I could not contain myself any longer. I got to my feet. "I supported her the whole time we were married!" I shouted. "And she didn't lose any wages—she was still tending bar at the Garter!"

"Sit down, Mr. Baker," the judge grunted.

"Yeah, sure, I'll sit down—if you stop looking at her legs!"

Judge Harkin's face reddened. "One more word out of you, and I'll jail you for contempt."

I was going to let him know what I thought of him and his contempt, but my lawyer, Bob Edelen, the former CPOA attorney, grabbed my sleeve and dragged me back into my chair. There was nothing I could do. As far as I was concerned, Harkin had behaved with blatant prejudice and in a completely unprofessional manner, but he was the judge.

Now he was in the middle of a potential gang war in North Compton.

At Jones's arraignment, Judge Harkin continued true to form. Knowing that I was the detective in charge of the case, he had made a deal with the prosecutor that Jones be tried not for first-degree murder but on a charge of assault with a deadly weapon. What sense that made, in view of the fact that the victim was dead, escaped me, and I told him so.

"Mr. Jones is a minor," the judge snapped at me. "Only sixteen years old."

"He's a stone-cold killer," I shot back, "and if we don't put him away, it will send a signal to the Latino community that Robert Valdez's life isn't worth anything. And that is going to start more violence."

Judge Harkin peered at me with a snide smile. "Are you a social worker, Officer Baker?" he asked.

It was an ironic question, since I had originally wanted to be one. "No, Judge," I said, "but if we don't put Johnny Jones away for life, he'll kill again."

"Oh," Judge Harkin replied, "so I see that you're a psychic as well."

He remanded Jones on a charge of assault. I took my dudgeon to the prosecutor, demanding that he find a new venue for the trial.

"Can't," he said as he hurried out of the courtroom. "It's a done deal."

"You've got a goddamned body!" I shouted. "That's murder, not assault!"

"Don't worry," he replied, "Jones is a juvenile; he'll get the same sentence as he would for murder one."

"That's not the point," I fumed. "I promised the Latinos that he'd go down for murder."

The prosecutor shrugged. "Well, that's your problem now, isn't it," he said as he ran to his next hearing.

Actually it wasn't just my problem; it threatened to be a much bigger one.

When word reached the Latino community, there was an immediate uproar. A group of activists started a petition demanding that Jones be tried for murder, and when I met with them to discuss the matter, they told me that they were going to march on City Hall to protest the judge's decision.

"We're not leaving until we get justice!" one of them declared. "We'll besiege the damn place all winter if we have to!"

I knew what this would mean: Hundreds of Latinos would gather at City Hall, where they would be met by hundreds of blacks, and we would have a race riot on our hands. That, in turn, would trigger all-out war between the black and the Latino gangs. I knew that the city council could, and would, do nothing about the Valdez case, beholden as it was to the black voters. Once again, I felt that Compton was on the verge of anarchy.

There was not much time, and so, the day after the arraignment, I called Judge Marvin Greenberg, the presiding judge of the juvenile court, and explained my fears to him. I told him to expect trouble not only at Compton City Hall but at the court in Eastlake as well.

"I've had word that they plan to picket your office," I told him. It was true, but only half the truth. Before calling Greenberg, I had suggested to the activists that they ought to include the juvenile court building in their protest. Greenberg got the message; the last thing he wanted was a mob of angry Latinos shouting and waving signs outside his office. He promised to speak to Judge Harkin and call me back.

Meanwhile, tensions in North Compton were rising. Already, fights were breaking out again between the black and the Latino gangs, and the Latino leaders were holding rallies to whip up sentiment for the protests. We had to assign extra cars to the area, and to keep the entire force on alert in case of trouble.

The next morning, Judge Greenberg called me at my office. "I'm an old lawyer," he said, "and so I know better than to talk over the phone. Come down to the courthouse."

In his office he told me that he had decided Judge Harkin had made "an error in judgment" in his arraignment of Jones, and that the case would be assigned to a different judge. I suggested that it be given to a different prosecutor as well. Judge Greenberg agreed. Then he peered at me. "Judge Harkin doesn't like you very much, does he?"

"I think he likes my ex-wife more," I answered.

That seemed to confirm what he had already heard. "I'm going to move the trial to Norwalk," he said.

I thanked him, and took this information back to the Latino leaders.

"Jones will be tried for murder," I told them. "He'll get a fair trial in a different court." They were skeptical. "Look," I went on, speaking now in Spanish, "I'm a Latino just like you, and I'm not going to bullshit you. I can't promise Jones will be convicted, but you will get justice. Now I'm asking you: Call off the march; don't make this any worse for our brothers and sisters. Let me handle it."

Grudgingly, they agreed—there would be no protests until they saw the outcome of the trial. I also went to the leaders of Largo 36 and asked for their promise to do nothing until the trial was over. They, too, agreed to trust me.

Johnny Jones was convicted of first-degree murder and, as a juvenile, was sentenced to five years in the California Youth Authority facility at Preston. The verdict seemed to satisfy both sides, but I remained uneasy. Jones would be free again by the time he was twenty-one, and if he returned to Compton, it would be with an even bigger grudge against Latinos. In fact, my concern was proved right.

After serving five years, Johnny Jones was released, and within weeks he had stabbed to death a middle-aged Latino woman in her home on Mulberry Street. It was what today would be called a hate crime. This time, he was put away for good. Of course, by then it was too late for Robert Valdez and the Latino woman. There was at least one consolation: Compton itself had escaped becoming a victim of Johnny Jones's psychopathic rage.

Douglas Dollarhide's Chief, Doris Davis's Balls, and Politics, Compton Style

For many years, the Los Angeles County Sheriff's Office had been trying to gain a foothold in Compton. Sheriff Pitchess had openly courted Compton politicians, promising them that the sheriffs could police the city far more cheaply than the CPD. Their goal was nothing less than the dissolution of the Compton Police Department and its replacement by the LASO. The tactic had worked in other cities, but Compton's white administrations had always resisted it. Now we learned through friends in city hall that Mayor Dollarhide was having informal discussions with the sheriff's office about the future of policing Compton. This meant that, potentially, the very existence of the Compton Police Department was at risk.

We in the CPOA intended to have something to say about that.

By this time, 1973, the association was by far the strongest and richest union in the city. Our treasury and influence far exceeded those of the fire department, the teachers union, and even the chamber of commerce. We were collecting fifteen dollars a month in dues from each of our 125 officers, and that money was being used to promote the agenda of the department. (In an ironic twist, because the city insisted on calling us a social and charitable organization, our revenue was tax exempt.) We were a political force, and the Dollarhide administration knew it. So when the mayor and two members of the city council came up for reelection, the battle lines were drawn.

We knew that if Dollarhide and his antipolice backers on the council won another term, we would have a fight all the way to the next contract renewal. The only way to avoid that was to defeat them and replace them with pro-police candidates. The result was that, for the first time in Compton's history, the police department actively supported candidates for city council. We selected Hillard Hamm and Russell Woolfolk. Hamm was the editor of the *Metropolitan Gazette,* a local black newspaper, and Woolfolk was a real estate developer with a shady reputation. What mattered to us, though, was that both were strongly pro-police, and we began campaigning for them. Mayor Dollarhide was incensed that we should take a position opposing him and his handpicked councilmen, and he moved quickly to punish us.

Both Roland Ballard and I were working as detectives, and Dollarhide told his city manager, Howard Edwards, to order Chief Ingram to demote us. Ingram, who had only a few more months to serve until his retirement, had no choice but to agree. He called us into his office and informed us that we were going back on patrol. We demanded to know why.

"You need to be more closely supervised," he said, "because you're engaging in too much political activism." He did not even make an effort at an excuse—the move was politically motivated.

Besides the blatant effort to silence the CPOA, this was a blow to us professionally. We had worked hard to achieve detective status, and the regular hours, the extra pay and benefits, and the step up the ladder were important to us. Besides, a demotion on our records could be used to deny us future promotion.

Ingram had no objective reason for demoting us, and we let the community know it through Hillard Hamm's *Gazette* and my old friend Ray Watkins, who was the editor of the *Compton Bulletin*. Ray had been one of the bail bondsmen to whom I had referred business in my early years on the force, and now he repaid me by running an editorial supporting us against the administration's action. "Their sole intention is to improve conditions for police officers and serve the city," Watkins wrote, "and for this, Mayor Dollarhide has decided to punish them. Could it be because he fears Rick Baker and Roland Ballard and the Police Association they lead?"

Dollarhide remained adamant, and Edwards backed him up. However, word of our demotion had reached ICPA headquarters in Washington, and in addition to issuing a formal protest, Ed Kiernan asked James van Norman to fly out to Compton to represent us at the personnel board hearing. The prospect of a high-powered New York lawyer bringing the clout of the ICPA into the matter raised the stakes considerably. It was beginning to look as if the attempt to punish Roland and me for our political activities might become a national scandal.

Chief Ingram was now feeling pressure from the press, the CPOA, and the ICPA, and this was much more trouble than he had bargained for when he had meekly succumbed to the mayor's dictate. It was clear that he was looking for a way out, so I decided to offer him a compromise. Ballard and I were getting seventy-five dollars a month more than we had received on patrol, and we told Ingram that we would accept a transfer back to the Community Service Center with the proviso that we remain at detectives' pay.

Caught between the mayor and the Police Officers Association, Ingram was forced to accept the compromise. Dollarhide was furious. He and his cronies had lost the first round in their political battle with the association, but they were by no means through.

As Ingram's term drew to a close, the city council instructed the personnel board to begin a search for a new chief. Not surprisingly, the CPOA was not consulted. One obvious candidate for the post was Captain Manny Correa, a twenty-five-year veteran of the CPD. (The department's first Latino to achieve the rank of commander, he would eventually serve twice as acting chief.) He was also, in my estimation, the best qualified person for the job. Then again, that was not the way that Compton politics worked.

Earlier in the year, Howard Edwards had attended a conference of the League of California Cities held in the Bay Area. While there, he met a former L.A. sheriff's deputy who was a professor of social studies at Merritt College in Oakland. His name was Thomas Cochée.

Married at sixteen, Cochée, who was black, had worked his way up from poverty through the ranks of the LASO to become a sergeant. He was serving on the force at the time of the Watts riots, and the experience left him with very definite ideas about the causes of crime, and the means for combating it.

Crime, in his view, was essentially a socioeconomic phenomenon, with roots in racism, inequality of opportunity, and the low self-esteem and anger they engendered. Police work, he believed, should be directed toward the causes of crime and not just at the results. He talked a great deal about "sensitivity" among police officers, and about the need to reeducate rather than incarcerate members of youth gangs. Cochée was elegant and articulate, a large, well-dressed man with a carefully groomed mustache, who had a powerful public presence.

Howard Edwards was impressed. Off the record, and with no authority to do so, he promised Cochée the job as chief of police.

When Edwards got back to Compton, he informed the city council that Cochée was his choice. Though there were three other candidates, including Manny Correa, Edwards's decision made Cochée's appointment a foregone conclusion. Mayor Dollarhide announced Cochée's nomination with complacent glee. His own handpicked chief, whose idea of police work ran directly counter to our Compton Style of policing, would be running the department. The city council approved him unanimously. Tom Cochée thus became the first black police chief in California history.

Having a black chief in a city that was 95 percent black with a police force that was 40 percent black made good sense, and the decision was immediately popular with the black officers on the force. We knew nothing about Cochée, who was a complete outsider, but we decided to reserve judgment.

We did, however, resent the fact that the CPOA had not been consulted on the appointment, and that Dollarhide and Edwards had railroaded it through council. There was nothing we could do about the chief's appointment, but there was definitely something we could do about the mayor and city council.

In keeping with long-standing tradition, CPOA meetings were usually held at the Golden Garter over pitchers of beer and under the smoky gazes of the strippers. Vito Pasquale often sat in on these meetings, and one night, while we were discussing how to proceed with Dollarhide, Vito offered his opinion that only money could beat him.

"We can't contribute to a political campaign," I answered. "It's against the law."

"Maybe you can't," Vito said, "but I can." I asked him what he meant. "We gotta get rid of this son of a bitch. You find somebody you want to run against Dollarhide, and I'll bankroll the campaign." I asked Vito if he had that kind of money. "Me . . . and some other businessmen who want Dollarhide out," he answered. "You just find us a candidate with balls."

I knew who we wanted.

Doris Davis, the city clerk, had supported us through the blue flu and consistently beyond. She was probably the best friend the association had on the council, and as a woman and a black, she would be a credible candidate against Dollarhide. Vito agreed, and he gave me an envelope containing $2,500 in cash. "If she goes for it, give this to her," he said. "Tell her it's just the start. But one thing I ask: If she gets in, there'll be no more topless licenses granted in Compton."

I knew Mrs. Davis pretty well, and so one night I called her and told her that Roland Ballard and I would like to speak with her. She asked what it was about.

"I'm sorry, Mrs. Davis," I said, "but I can't discuss it over the phone."

It was late at night when we arrived at her house on Palmer Street, having taken care to be sure that we were not followed. We met in her parlor over cups of coffee. She was a tall, slender, hard-driving woman in her thirties who, eight years before, had defeated a white man to become the first black female city official in Compton's history.

I told her that if she ran for mayor, she would have the full support of the Compton Police Officers Association. For a moment, she seemed surprised, but then she said, "Don't think I haven't considered running. But it's going to cost money."

I leaned over the coffee table. "You'll have money," I said, and I put Vito's envelope on the table.

She picked it up and glanced inside. She frowned and looked at Ballard and me closely. "I couldn't take police money," she said firmly. I told her that I knew that. "Where did this come from, then?" she asked.

"A group of Compton businessmen who want to see a change."

"There'll be more," Ballard added.

Mrs. Davis sat back on her sofa. She had a quick mind, and I could practically see it working. "And these contributions would be legitimate?"

"Entirely legitimate," Ballard assured her. "Though some of the donors may want to remain anonymous."

Mrs. Davis asked us for a day to think it over. I told her to take as much time as she needed. "I know my own mind," she answered with a sly smile. "But sometimes it helps to convince my husband that what I want to do was his idea."

We shook hands, and I told her that I would wait to hear from her.

The following weekend, Doris Davis announced that she was a candidate for mayor of Compton.

At that point, the gloves came off. Douglas Dollarhide knew that he could beat any white man or woman for mayor, and he felt that no male black candidate could challenge him seriously. A black woman entering the race blindsided him, though, and from the start, she challenged Dollarhide on the issue about which he was most sensitive: the police.

"It was this administration's callous attitude toward our men in uniform that provoked the blue flu," she declared at her press conference. "If Mayor Dollarhide had any sense of how important our police force is to this community, he would have sat down with them and talked, instead of calling them racists who were trying to bleed the city white."

That same night, I met with Vito Pasquale at the Garter. "You asked for a candidate with balls," I said, "and you've got one. Except that she's a woman."

Vito laughed. "That woman's got more balls than Dollarhide ever had."

Over the next few days, Vito tapped his associates in the business community of Compton for hard cash. Thousands of dollars poured into Doris Davis's campaign headquarters, some of which I delivered personally.

Money was not the only weapon we had. Roland Ballard had a friend named Earl A. Carson, a black community activist who owned a printing press, and together they began publishing an underground newspaper called the *Communicator*, which attacked Mayor Dollarhide and his two cronies on the council using information provided from inside the administration. Some of this information was being provided by an unlikely source.

Jim Carrington was one of the first black officers hired in Compton. He had a reputation as a good street cop, but also for having a chip on his shoulder. His anger was directed equally at everyone, from the police administration to the city government. As the senior black officer, Lieutenant Carrington, whose nickname was Candy Man, was close to the Dollarhide administration, and he began feeding Roland Ballard information that appeared in *Communicator* articles, some of which Carrington wrote anonymously. Carrington's articles were incendiary. In them he lambasted the mayor and city council for incompetence and corruption, calling them "smiling minstrels" with "Cadillac pockets and Volkswagen brains," slurs no white member of the CPOA would have dared use.

The mayor hit back, enraged. He accused the association of a conspiracy to unseat him, a charge that, while technically true, he was unable to prove. Aside from our statement of support for Doris Davis, there was nothing to connect the CPOA to her campaign, which continued to outspend Dollarhide's.

While all this was going on, I was working in the detective division. One morning an alarm went off in the station signaling a robbery at the Capitol National Bank at 100 East Compton Boulevard. I was on duty with Flashlight Joe Ferrell, one of the so-called bourgeois blacks in the department. The son of a wealthy family of undertakers, he wore Botany 500 suits and custom-made shoes and drove to work in a new Mercedes. He lived in a condo on Peacock Ridge on the Palos Verdes Peninsula overlooking the Pacific. Joe did not have to work at all, but, like so many of us, he thrived on the thrill and danger of Compton.

The Capitol Bank was less than half a mile from the station, so Joe Ferrell and I jumped into a "dick unit," an unmarked detectives' car, and raced up Compton Boulevard.

In the bank lobby, we found customers standing dazed or sitting on the floor hugging each other and crying. Under one of the tellers' cages, an elderly man lay in a cape-sized pool of blood. He was dead, shot in the chest with a load of buck that had ripped him open. He was a frail man, probably in his seventies, and the shotgun blast had blown him up against the counter, where he lay with his face to the wall and one arm twisted behind him. His hand still clutched a deposit slip.

Other units were arriving, so Joe Ferrell and I ran back to our car and began cruising the area north of the bank, the direction one of the employees had indicated the three robbers took.

Up by Wilson Park, less than a mile from the bank, I spotted two men hurrying along the sidewalk. They were wearing three-quarter-length coats, even though it was a warm autumn day, and they seemed agitated and nervous. I pulled up behind them. They turned and saw Ferrell and me getting out of the car, panicked, and took off.

We chased them into a side street, but as they reached the end, Officer Corny Adkins's unit screeched to a stop, blocking their escape. They were trapped, and they knew it. The two men turned toward us as we approached. They had a shotgun and a pistol, but I could see in their eyes that they would not use them. They were beaten, like rottweilers who know they are whipped, and so I did not pull my gun. Instead, Ferrell and I jumped them and wrestled them to the ground. I put my man in a choke hold with one arm and pulled the sawed-off out of his hands. Ferrell also had his man down, and he took the ugly black .32 automatic from him. We dragged the two back to our car, threw them across the hood, and cuffed them.

Meanwhile, Officer Griff Chase had gone in search of the third robber. Neighbors told Chase that a man in a long coat had run down the alley behind the bank and jumped several fences into the residential area nearby. Chase followed, going through one yard after another, until he spotted a young black man sitting on the back porch of a house. He was trying to appear casual, gnawing at a fig. Chase approached him and asked who he was.

"This is my house, man. I'm just sittin' out here havin' a fig."

Chase told him to stand up. As he rose, he began reaching under his coat. Chase lunged at him, knocked him to the porch, and wrestled a shotgun from him.

Within ten minutes of the murder, we had captured all three robbers without firing a shot or even drawing our guns.

The robbers were James Bowen and two brothers named Joshua and Melvin Lloyd. It was the Lloyd brothers whom Ferrell and I had captured. They confessed to the murder of the elderly man and told us what had happened.

They had entered the bank, pulled out their guns, and ordered everyone to lie on the floor. They were nervous, shaking and shouting as the terrified patrons got down. One of them, the old man, froze. When Joshua Lloyd pointed his shotgun at him and screamed at him to drop, the man was too petrified to move. So Lloyd fired at him, the blast ripping into his chest and sending him sprawling across the floor. They grabbed as much money as they could and ran from the bank. Outside they split up, the Lloyds going in one direction and Bowen in another.

Because it was a bank robbery, the FBI sent two agents to the station to make copies of our reports. To them it was a question of bureaucratic routine: interview the cops and the suspects and get statistics for their files. Before they left, however, one of the agents stopped to talk with me.

"How come you didn't just kill them?" he asked matter-of-factly.

"What do you mean?" I said.

"They'd committed a cold-blooded murder; they were armed. If it was LAPD or LASO, they'd have just shot them on the spot."

I told the agent that wasn't the way we operated in Compton. He shrugged and left.

The next day there was a front-page story about the robbery in the

L.A. Times. FBI AGENTS CAPTURE BANK KILLERS, it proclaimed. In one of the closing paragraphs it mentioned that Compton PD had assisted in the arrests. That, I learned, was the way the FBI operated.

The race for mayor was heating up, and Tom Cochée was settling in.

Chief Cochée, who had been out of police work for over five years, made it clear from the first day that he intended to change the face of the CPD. "From now on," he informed us, "all patrol units will be integrated; white officers will partner with either a black or a Hispanic. No two white officers will be allowed to work together."

This mandate was the worst thing Cochée could have done, for it broke up partnerships that in some cases had endured for years. Nearly everyone was infuriated with the order, and instead of promoting better relations among officers, it had exactly the opposite effect. Forced to work together whether they liked it or not, many officers felt greater resentment against those of other races. Cochée's "salt and pepper" policy only served to further polarize the department.

He did not improve matters by insisting that all patrol officers become "more sensitive" to the thinking of criminals. Gang members were deprived and misunderstood youths, he told us, and we were to treat them as such. We were to be cordial to them but not to fraternize with them. No negotiating or excessive force would be tolerated.

Finally, Cochée announced that he was going to create a "freedom wall," on which gang members would be invited to voice their frustrations and their hopes in graffiti. We were to encourage them to use it. In other words, we were being asked to convince Sylvester Scott and Jake Guerina and Debo to put down their guns, come together, and express themselves in art.

Marquette University in Milwaukee was conducting a series of studies of inner-city conditions and crime rates and the effectiveness of police forces. The CPOA badly wanted the researchers to come to Compton. Though the study was free, funded by a federal grant, Cochée and the city council refused to authorize it. We suspected that their refusal was due to the fact that the researchers would conclude that the chief's office and the council were largely responsible for the problems we faced.

In response, the CPOA paid to have thirty-foot by forty-foot billboards erected at the main northern and southern entrances to the city declaring that crime in Compton was getting out of control, and we needed Marquette to analyze the causes and make recommendations. Cochée and the council took this as a slap: a vote of no confidence by their own police force in their willingness to promote public safety. The dispute between the CPOA and the chief had thus become public.

To say that we, the line officers, were mystified by the new chief's approach would be an understatement: We were in a state of shock. Every day we worked the streets of what had become the most crime-ridden city in America, struggling with inadequate resources and little official support, just to keep it this side of anarchy. Now our new chief was telling us that we had to sensitize ourselves to the criminal mentality and attack crime at its socioeconomic roots. In the middle of a shooting war, our chief was ordering us to stop fighting and reflect on its causes. It was madness, a complete disregard for the daily reality we faced. Compliance might very well mean the deaths of officers and the destruction of the department.

We could not fight the crooks and the chief and city hall all at the same time, and so we increased our efforts to change the administration. In a very real sense, we understood that our lives might depend upon it.

By backing a black candidate, we had cut into Dollarhide's base, but it was not enough. We had to go after the mayor directly. Dollarhide, however, was a careful and clever man who guarded his image as California's first black mayor jealously. He seemed untouchable. Until Roland Ballard found the photo.

It was a candid snapshot taken on one of the mayor's many junkets. In it he was shown on a yacht in Florida with a gorgeous blonde on either arm. He was smiling broadly, and the girls were suitably adoring. It was the exact opposite of the staid, straitlaced image of the black role model Dollarhide liked to project.

The next issue of the *Communicator* featured the photo on its front page with the caption "He can pass for white when he wants to." The picture circulated quickly, and the effect was instantaneous. Some people in the city raced to the mayor's defense, but many others were dismayed. This was not the Douglas Dollarhide for whom they had voted four years before, with his platform of black pride and black preeminence. Though he had built a new city hall and a community center, and had managed to lure some businesses back to Compton with the promise of tax breaks, he still presided over one of the poorest cities in California, and one of the most violent in the nation. If people were looking for a reason to elect a new mayor, they found it in the photo.

In 1973, Douglas Dollarhide was defeated for a second term, and Doris Davis became the first black woman to be elected mayor of a large city in the United States. Hillard Hamm and Russell Woolfolk were also elected, and so the Compton Police Officers Association had some new friends in city government.

The question now was what to do about the chief of police.

Instead of adjusting to the realities of Compton, Tom Cochée was becoming more adamant about his personal views of law enforcement even though morale in the department was plummeting. To make things worse, he began handing out suspensions to officers who violated his prohibition on excessive force. This meant that some of the most aggressive patrolmen were being taken off the streets, sometimes for a few days, sometimes for two weeks at a time.

One such case involved two officers—one of Cochée's salt-and-pepper teams—who responded to a call of a stabbing on the west side. It was a domestic violence incident: Two men with knives were fighting over a "Brook." (This referred to women who lived on Willowbrook Avenue, who had the reputation of being the ugliest in Compton.) When the unit arrived, one man fled, but the officers disarmed the other. While they were walking him to the unit, a call came in of shots fired at a house around the corner. Knowing that there would be hell to pay if they put the man in the backseat and he was shot in the second incident, the officers quickly decided to handcuff the stabber to the chain-link fence in front of the Brook's house.

They jumped back into their car, drove around the block, and found themselves in the middle of an ugly domestic violence situation in which the wife was cranking rounds from a revolver at her husband, who was hiding inside the house. They swarmed the woman, disarmed her, and hooked her up. As they did, a third call came on the radio. "Report of a man cuffed to a chain-link fence," the dispatcher said. "Claims he is being beaten and stripped."

The officers threw the woman into the patrol car and raced back around the block. It was true. The man they had cuffed to the fence was naked and bleeding. In the few minutes it had taken the cops to disarm the woman and arrest her, neighborhood thugs had assaulted the handcuffed man and taken all of his clothes. The officers found him hanging half conscious from the cuffs, wearing only his socks. Instead of being commended for stopping two attempted murders within a few minutes, the officers were suspended for having cuffed a suspect to a fence, thereby exposing him to danger.

It was not surprising, then, that resentment against the chief was growing among the rank and file. Many officers griped openly about Cochée's policies, and some stopped talking to him completely. A few, like Frank Brower, Julio Hernandez, and John Sutton, left the department for other cities. With Rutigliano gone, and John Soisson and me moving to detectives, the Dirty Dozen had effectively been dismantled.

One of those who left in frustration was Jim Carrington, the senior black lieutenant who had helped us unseat Mayor Dollarhide. Disgusted with the new chief's attitude, Carrington accepted a job in the Irvine Police Department in Orange County. His defection was seen by many in the department as a betrayal, but it proved beyond doubt that the reaction against the new chief had nothing to do with race.

As our authority was undermined, crime, which was already spiraling out of control, accelerated. By 1975, the situation in the streets had become so dire that the NAACP petitioned President Gerald Ford to declare the City of Compton a disaster area. To all this, the chief remained blithely oblivious. Even as the city slid toward chaos, Cochée stated that it was his goal to make Compton "the safest city in America" within ten years. It was clear to us that Tom Cochée was living in an academic fool's paradise. Asked at a press conference whether he believed that the term "law and order" had racial overtones, Cochée answered that it did. Adopting his most professorial tone, he added, "The people who are committing the crimes are victims of a much larger system that is ripping us all off."

Cochée's implication was clear: It was the American system, and not the criminals in the streets, that was to blame. Tom Cochée was beginning to sound more like Hakim Jamal than the leader of the CPD.

The Police Officers Association could not stand by and watch the situation deteriorate. Once again, I found myself in a delicate position. We had just removed the city's first black mayor, and now we were faced with the prospect of moving against its first black chief of police. While it was evident from our discussions that the CPOA was overwhelmingly opposed to Cochée, I knew that the board was split along racial lines. The two white members and I favored getting rid of the chief, while the two black members opposed it. My hands were tied: Because of the split, the association could not move officially against Tom Cochée as we had done against Douglas Dollarhide.

Meanwhile, Mayor Davis was viewing events with increasing alarm. She had run and been elected on a pro-police platform, and now she saw the department being torn apart by her predecessor's chief. It was almost as if Dollarhide had deliberately inflicted Cochée on us as punishment for the blue flu. His continuing presence and his polarizing effect on the department were threatening to undermine Mayor Davis's credibility. She knew she had to act, and act boldly—and she did.

Howard Edwards was Tom Cochée's main supporter in city government, so Mayor Davis fired him. The move sent shock waves through City Hall and the police department. Those of us who opposed Cochée saw it as a brave and brilliant move, but the black officers who supported him were outraged. In response, they did something equally assertive: They split the Police Officers Association.

Led by militants, the black officers announced that they were forming their own union, to be called the Guardians. The two most radical officers, John James (who had been involved in the Patio Bar shootout), and Cornelius Adkins, were elected president and vice president. John Soisson was now CPOA president, and though he and I tried to stop it, though we argued and cajoled and bargained with them, James and Adkins remained defiant. The "white-Chicano dominated" CPOA had failed to represent the interests of the black minority, they declared, and so they were creating their own alternative.

James and Adkins expected that the entire black contingent of the department would join the Guardians, but, though the bourgeois and militants did defect, the jocks remained with the CPOA. There was one curious and unexpected development, however—a white officer, Terry Ebert, whom I had sent to testify in Washington, chose to join the Guardians. His defection was a carefully calculated political maneuver, and it would be many years before its meaning would become clear.

After all the efforts and sacrifices expended to build up the CPOA, despite its successes and its growing political power within the city, the militant black offers were determined to go their own way. When contract time came around again, there would be two competing unions bargaining with the city, two conflicting agendas, two contradictory voices speaking for the rank and file, when what was needed above all was unity. The city council could, and would, play us off against each other, and it was the officers on the streets who would pay the price—and we would have Tom Cochée to thank for it.

Citing the dissension the chief had caused in the department, Mayor Davis's new city manager, Daniel Lim, called on him to resign. He refused. In his own way, Tom Cochée was setting a precedent: No police chief had ever refused a direct order from the city manager. Instead, Cochée challenged Lim to try to fire him, counting on the fact that Dan Lim, as an Asian American, had no constituency in the city. It was a subtle new version of the race card.

Meanwhile, with little support from the city council and none from the chief, police morale plummeted to a dangerously low level. We could not be sure from one day to the next what to expect. Just the act of going to work became a chore for many of us.

One night during this period, my partner and I were dressing for patrol in sullen silence. Then, as I watched, he sat on the bench in the locker room, took out his .357 Magnum, and put the barrel in his mouth. A chill went through me. I approached him cautiously. "What are you doing?" I asked.

Without even looking up he answered, "Getting ready for tonight."

This was one of the most courageous and committed officers in the department. Seeing him in this condition, I made up my mind: Something had to be done about Tom Cochée. For the good of the department and of the city, he had to go, and go quickly. Still, how could we remove him in such a way that the white and Latino officers would not be branded as racists, and the black officers would not be further alienated? It was the trickiest question the CPOA leadership had yet faced.

The answer soon suggested itself.

Captain John Start, Dominic Rutigliano's old mentor, had been offered the post as chief of police in Porterville, in Tulare County. When any officer left, it was customary to throw him a going-away party at the Golden Garter, and Vito Pasquale readily agreed to close the place to the public. We invited the entire association, as well as the members of the Guardians, though we knew it was unlikely they would attend. The guest of honor was to be Tom Cochée. This was unusual, since the chief, not being a member of the CPOA, never attended such affairs. Even so, we insisted that he come, and we invited the members of city council as well.

That night about eighty officers and their friends gathered at the Garter, where there was the usual complement of topless barmaids and strippers. Among them was a new face. She was an Asian woman called Tiger Lily, once a well-known dancer on the burlesque circuit who had fallen on hard times. It was Rutigliano who found her, living in a trailer park in San Bernardino. She had become a forlorn figure, aged, overweight, but still fiery, and badly in need of quick cash. Rutigliano hired her for the night. Lily put on her makeup and her most outrageous dress, and Rut drove her to the Garter on his Harley.

Vito had pulled out all the stops: The Garter was blazing with light and music, and the liquor flowed freely. As we expected, the Guardians righteously boycotted the party, but to our surprise, one member of the city council showed up, Jane Dickinson Robbins. She was a direct descendent of the city's founder, the Rev. Griffith Dickinson Compton, and a close friend of my mother. When Rutigliano walked in with Tiger Lily on his arm, the place erupted into cheers.

Rut was as boisterous as always, but to me he seemed hollowed. I could not discern in him the old abrasive brassiness that had made him such a formidable presence on the street, and such a volatile friend in private. He had lost weight, his hair and mustache had grown thinner, and the intimidating look in his eyes was dulled. He was still Rut, though, and he quickly dominated the proceedings.

Tiger Lily was another matter. I could see that she had once been exotic, even beautiful, but now she looked like a gaudy, painted curio lamp rescued from an attic. Carmine lipstick, heavy mascara, and a pall of face powder could not conceal the toll the years had taken. She did not smile, she grinned desperately with square crowned teeth, artifacts of her former stage glory, and the long mesh sleeves that circled her arms and laced between her fingers could not conceal the violet needle tracks.

I took Rutigliano aside. "Couldn't you do any better than that?" I whispered.

He smiled smugly. "Just try to keep your hands off her."

There was no danger of that, I thought. As the evening wore on, though, I began to understand what he meant. The more Lily drank, the more seductive she became. The old stage presence returned, there was a heat that emanated from her, and she moved her body and rolled her eyes suggestively. She was like an aging panther freed from its cage after years of neglect, slowly rediscovering its stealthy danger. Tiger Lily was a bubbling hot spring of sexuality; in her prime, she must have been a force of nature.

By the time Tom Cochée appeared, the party was rollicking. Everyone was drunk, and we welcomed the chief like an old friend. He seemed genuinely appreciative as we toasted him and John Start, filling his glass the instant he drained it. Before long, the chief was as drunk as the rest of us. That was when Tiger Lily made her move.

Cochée was at the bar, loud and massive in a designer suit, and Lily wafted up to him like a Chinese kite borne on a thermal breeze. She mounted the stool next to him and put a hand on his shoulder. Within minutes she had woven her spell, and Chief Cochée disappeared with her out the side door.

Lily led him to the motel around the corner, which was the habitual haunt of the Garter girls, but this time, there was a difference. The room to which she took the chief was wired with microphones, and in a night-stand was concealed the same obsolete Fargo recorder I had used on Holland and Garrett. For the next hour, everything that happened in that cheap motel room, every drunken word and guttural grunt, was taped, and in the morning Rutigliano collected the reel.

In the meantime, the leaders of the Guardians, unaware that Cochée had attended the party, filed a complaint with the city manager, accusing the white officers of behaving like thugs and hooligans. Because of the black officers' complaint, Cochée was summoned to appear before the city council. As he was standing outside the council chamber waiting to testify, a CPOA board member approached him.

"Chief," he said, "can I have a private word with you?"

Cochée walked down the hall with him. "What is it?" he asked.

"There's something I want you to hear," the officer replied. He took from his pocket a miniature tape recorder and switched it on. Through the tinny speaker came the sounds of panting and groaning passion.

Cochée froze. He stared at the officer a long moment as the tape played. "Turn it off," he muttered. Then he asked through tight lips, "What do you want?"

"I'll tell you what we *don't* want," the officer replied. "We don't want to have to go in there and play this tape before the city council."

Cochée glared at him. "Just how badly do you people hate me?"

"Bad enough to want to send you back to college," came the reply.

Before the first councilman could ask the chief to respond to the black officers' accusation about the party at the Garter, Tom Cochée said that he had an announcement to make. He drew himself up with dignity.

"In recent months," he began, "it has become clear to me that there are important differences between my approach to police work and the traditions of the department. And while I continue to believe that the key to successful policing is understanding the socioeconomic conditions that motivate crime, I have come to the conclusion that the CPD is not yet ready to implement that approach."

There was a long pause as the council members waited, bewildered, for him to go on.

"For this reason," Cochée resumed deliberately, "I have decided that it is in the best interests of the city that I resign as chief of police."

There was an immediate uproar in the room. The black council members pleaded with him to reconsider, but Cochée was steadfast. He said that he had thought the matter over carefully, and that his decision was final. He insisted that they initiate a search for his successor.

Within a year, we had gotten rid of the city's first black mayor, its first black city manager, and its first black chief of police, not because they were black, but because they were endangering the lives of citizens and police officers. Dollarhide had refused us the material and support we needed to do our jobs; Howard Edwards had imposed on us a daydreaming and divisive chief; and that chief had reduced the morale of the department to ashes. It made no difference to us what race they were: We had to protect our lives and the lives of the people of Compton. To do that, we had to have the support of the chief, the city manager, and the mayor. If we could not get that support any other way, we would take the responsibility for changing the administration on ourselves.

It was a new era in the history of our city: We had invented politics, Compton Style.

Tarzan, a Severed Head, and the Shack

During his exile from the department, I had remained in touch with Dominic Rutigliano. The news was not good.

In the wake of his resignation, and the department's refusal to provide him with a letter of recommendation, Rut had been unable to find a job as a cop. He had lost his home, and then, even more tragically, his wife had left him, taking their children with her. After that he had worked at day labor. For a time, he hammered at the foundations of houses that had to be moved because of urban redevelopment, and when that work ran out, he was forced to take odd jobs to survive. With no place to live, no family, and no income, he was reduced to living in the streets, his Harley his only possession. He told me that at one time he was so hard up that he had to drive his hog into gas stations and try to siphon the drops from the pumps, with the bike chained to his leg so that no one would steal it. The best cop I had ever known was prohibited from doing the thing he did better than anyone else—police work.

Dollarhide and Cochée were gone. I remained in detectives and was assigned to the burglary-specific detail. The detective bureau was divided into two sections: crimes against persons and crimes against property. Art Thomas was the bureau captain, and Sergeant John Pranin, an extraordinarily skilled and effective cop, was my section leader.

Captain Thomas, who had trained at FBI headquarters in Washington, D.C., was an efficient, old-school administrator. I liked and admired him, though I did have reservations about his practice, gleaned from the FBI, of bugging the patrol officers' locker room to keep tabs on their informal conversations. He kept the recording equipment in a sealed room on the second floor. One of my duties was to collect and replace the reels of tape.

John Pranin was the Carl Crosby of detectives, a legend within the ranks of the department. In 1962 he had made his bones by solving the famous "Unseen Murderer" case. A prowler was preying on elderly white women, breaking into their homes late at night, and robbing and murdering them in their beds. Pranin had taken the lead in the case and caught the serial killer, which earned him statewide attention. He became my mentor, teaching me the investigation and interrogation techniques he had developed over twenty years as a detective. Later, this knowledge would help me solve many high-profile cases. Together, Thomas and Pranin turned the detective bureau into the elite unit of the CPD, and I spent twelve of my eighteen years in the department working with them.

One afternoon, I was driving down Long Beach Boulevard in an unmarked car when a call came over the radio of an armed robbery at a nearby Bank of America. The suspect was described as a white male in his late twenties, so I pulled over the first white man I spotted on the street. Call it racial profiling if you will, but the sight of a white man on Long Beach Boulevard in Compton was itself suspicious. The moment I got out of the car, the man took off. I chased him for several blocks and tackled him on the fly, sending us both crashing to the sidewalk.

"Hey, man, what the fuck?" he grunted.

I knelt on his back and twisted his arm up behind him. When I patted him down, I found the cash from the bank and a black plastic comb.

"Is this what you used to hold up the bank?" I asked him.

"Yeah, man," he panted. "I'm scared of guns."

Around the same time, Officer Griff Chase was pursuing a robbery suspect. A young, popular cop who had joined the force the year before me, it was Griff who had caught the fig-eating Capitol Bank robber on the back porch. He was known as the comedian of the department, an intelligent, personable cop who could make anybody laugh no matter how badly the day had gone. We all relied on Griff for a joke or a wry comment that would dispel the atmosphere of gloom in the locker room, or over the radio. More than once, Griff's spontaneous humor had defused a potentially dangerous situation in the streets.

The robber raced for several blocks and then jumped a chain-link fence at a junior high school with Griff Chase right on his heels. He ran up a fire escape to the roof of one of the buildings, dashed across it, and leaped onto the building adjacent.

Griff followed him, but when he tried to jump between the two buildings, he missed his footing and fell, landing in a drainage ditch and wrenching his back. The robber, seeing that Chase was lying helpless on the ground in pain, ran back to him. It turned out that the man had known Chase from prior contact. Instead of fleeing, the robber took Chase's radio and called the police station. "There's a cop here who was chasing me," he said. "He fell into a ditch, and I think he hurt himself. You'd better send backup."

The dispatcher asked for the address, and the robber gave it to him. "Stay with the officer until help arrives," the dispatcher said.

"Sorry," he replied, "but I can't do that," and he took off.

That was the way things went down in Compton in those days: We knew the crooks and they knew us, and there was a kind of mutual respect between us.

Unfortunately, that was not the end of the story.

Griff Chase had injured his back so severely that he was unable to return to duty. He tried physical therapy without success, and then psychological counseling for his increasing depression. What compounded his dilemma was the fact that he was the heir of heroes: His grandfather was Admiral Jehu Chase, a World War I legend for whom the destroyer USS *Chase* had been named. The *Chase* itself became a naval legend, fighting off kamikaze planes at Okinawa in World War II, and making it back to port with damage that would have sunk another ship. With such a heritage to live up to, Griff Chase had tried to vindicate himself in the streets of Compton. No longer able to do that, he turned to drinking, and soon became an alcoholic. His wife left him, and he spiraled into a whirlpool of drunken despair. At last, living alone in Harbor City, Griff Chase put in a call to the LAPD of a man with a gun.

When the officers arrived, Chase walked out onto the front porch of his empty house in nothing but boxer shorts, carrying a revolver. He had been known as the best shot in the Compton PD—he could hit any target at any distance without even thinking. He could have killed the L.A. cops easily if he had wanted to. On this occasion, though, he stood with the gun dangling at his side. In a few minutes, half a dozen units had responded to the scene, and Griff was surrounded by twelve or fifteen cops.

"Put down the gun!" they ordered through a bullhorn as they crouched behind the doors of their cars. Instead, Griff raised the pistol to his head. "Put it down!" they repeated.

He lowered the gun. "Drop it on the porch and walk toward us," the voice commanded.

A second time, Griff Chase pointed the pistol at his head.

"Put down the gun!" the L.A. cop bellowed. Again Griff lowered it.

One of the officers came out cautiously from behind his unit. "Drop the gun and walk toward me," he commanded.

This time, instead of pointing the gun at his head, Griff Chase raised it to his waist. The result was instantaneous. A dozen LAPD cops opened fire on him at once, striking him twenty or thirty times, blasting his body apart.

Griff Chase, the bright young CPD officer who could make anybody laugh no matter how bad a night he had had, was dead. He had very deliberately committed suicide by cop.

When I heard of this, I could not help but feel that, had the incident occurred in Compton, Griff Chase would still have been alive. Unlike LAPD, Compton cops did not respond with their guns first—Tom Cochée notwithstanding, we used them only as a last, desperate resort. In Griff's case, we would have talked to him or rushed him, knocked him over the head, and disarmed him. For the truth was that we in the Compton PD could have shot and killed suspects every other night—addicts, gangbangers, career criminals—and no one would have questioned it. We knew the people we were dealing with, though, and we knew the danger to our citizens, and almost any Compton cop would have risked his life before he would have used lethal force when fists, or truncheons, or a joke like those of Griff Chase, would have defused the situation and saved lives—the bad guys' or our own. That was what made us special, that was what made us proud—that was what made us Compton cops. And that was what broke Griff Chase's heart when he knew he could no longer serve.

As it was, the shooting turned out to be a tragic irony. The officer who had approached Chase from behind the LAPD car was named Waugh. He was the son of Don Waugh, a veteran Compton police detective. Griff Chase had attended the boy's graduation from the police academy, and had been photographed with the young smiling rookie on that occasion. Yet it was Don Waugh's son who fired the first shot at Griff Chase. The rest was just a meaningless, frantic fusillade.

In the mid-1970s, an epidemic erupted in Compton—PCP. Known on the street as angel dust, PCP was synthesized in the 1950s for use as an anesthetic, but its monstrous side effects, including manic behavior, paranoia, hallucinations, violence, and suicidal rage, made it impossible to control. Horror stories of PCP abuse became urban legends, but these did nothing to curb its popularity on the street.

Most of the PCP in Compton came from a supplier named Jack Hill, who bought it from manufacturers in Australia and distributed it through a warehouse in Malibu. Hill would later be murdered in the Rodeway Inn in Compton, lured there by two black hookers who had been hired by the Mafia. The moment they left the room, a pair of mob hit men entered and shot Hill, who was still in bed, over twenty times. John Soisson and Ramon Allen handled the case and quickly arrested six suspects.

PCP rapidly rivaled cocaine as the addicts' drug of choice, and by 1975 it could be bought on nearly every block in the city.

Angel dust introduced new dangers not only to the users but to the police as well. A suspect high on dust had bursts of psychotic violence, superhuman strength, and complete disregard for his own safety. In one case, Rutigliano responded to a call of a man down, to find a duster whose hands had been mutilated, reduced to raw meat. High on angel dust, he had bet his friends that he could stop the spinning fan of a '56 Chevy with his bare hands. On another occasion, a duster had taken a chain saw to his own neck, nearly severing his head. Criminals we had known for years and who would normally have surrendered after a chase or a fistfight became homicidal psychopaths, immune to beatings or even to chemical sprays.

Eventually, we developed a swarming technique to take down dusters involving five officers and a rope-mesh net. Four officers surrounded the duster and threw the net over him while the other officer jumped him and beat him into submission. On one occasion, Bernie Brown and I were confronted by a six-foot-three-inch duster who was manically out of control. I sprayed him with foam from our fire extinguisher; then Bernie and I tackled him before other officers threw the net over him. The next morning, the incident, which had been witnessed by a reporter, made the front page of the *Long Beach Independent* newspaper. The story commended us for putting ourselves at risk to take the man down without using lethal force.

Invariably, when we dragged a duster out of the net, his fingers were bent grotesquely backward, dislocated from the struggle to free himself. It was a horrible way to have to deal with a human being, but the drug gave us no choice.

There were so many dusters on the street that we ran out of handcuffs and had to improvise. On one occasion an officer made a bust near a telephone repair truck. Having no cuffs left, he asked the repairman if he could borrow one of his plastic cable ties, and he put it on the duster's wrists. Though now it is common practice, this was, as far as I know, the first time that plastic ties were used as cuffs by police.

One of the biggest PCP dealers in Compton was a lifelong criminal called Odell Willis. Willis had brick red hair and wore glasses, giving him a resemblance to Malcolm X. He was a scrawny, high-strung hustler who never went anywhere without a squad of lookouts and a personal body-guard whose street name was Dirty Larry. Dirty Larry was a hulking, ugly thug whose tiny head surmounted an enormous physique that made him a terror on the west side. He had a thick neck adorned with a six-inch scar across his jugular, the souvenir of a Folsom Prison fight with a Latino gang member. Despite our determination to take Odell down, between Dirty Larry and his lookouts, he carried on his trade in PCP unmolested for months.

Two narcotics cops in particular had targeted Odell Willis: Bobby Baker and Myron Davis. Though they were patrolmen, they specialized in busting crack and dust pushers and had made many sensational arrests. The longer Willis evaded them, the more determined they became to nail him, but he always seemed to be one step ahead. Finally, one night, Baker and Davis decided that they had had enough.

From surveillance on Odell, they knew that he usually slept until nightfall, when he would go out with Dirty Larry to make his rounds. Lookouts preceded him, scoping out the street corners where he met his distributors, often teenagers, who ran the drugs into the neighborhoods for him. Baker and Davis knew that Odell worked one west side inter-section in particular nearly every night, and so, before dusk, they staked it out.

A towering sycamore tree grew in a vacant lot overlooking the corner. As night fell, Baker, who was short and wiry, had Davis hoist him onto the lower branches. Baker then scrambled halfway up the tree and hid his small frame among the foliage. Davis, in an unmarked car, kept watch from the end of the street.

For three hours, Bobby Baker squatted among the sycamore branches until Willis's lookouts made their appearance. Davis crouched down under the dash of his car. The lookouts checked the intersection carefully and then signaled to Dirty Larry, who waited by Willis's Buick. While Larry stood watch, Odell Willis, in fur-trimmed fedora and shades, strolled to the intersection and set up shop. Eighteen feet above him, Bobby Baker looked on from his perch in the tree.

When the first of Willis's runners, a kid no more than fifteen, jogged up to Willis, Baker was ready. The instant that Willis handed his goods to the kid, Bobby leaped from the tree and landed directly on top of him. Willis grunted to the ground, stunned at the aerial attack. While his runner disappeared, Willis began screaming for Larry to help. At that moment, Myron Davis jumped out of his car with his gun drawn. Dirty Larry threw one look at him and took off, lumbering down a side alley.

Bobby Baker twisted Willis's arms behind him and cuffed his wrists. Willis craned his neck to look at the diminutive man kneeling on his back. "Who the fuck are you?" he demanded.

Bobby grinned. "Don't you know, Odell? I'm Tarzan."

In the wake of Tom Cochée's sudden resignation, his deputy, Bob Walker, became acting chief, and the search for Cochée's replacement began. Once again the CPOA favored choosing a chief from within the department, but the city council had other ideas. They appointed a search committee comprised of people from outside Compton, and, in September 1976, they announced that their leading candidate for the job was an L.A. captain named Joseph Rouzan. Rouzan, who was black, was the head of LAPD's Equal Opportunity Commission, which was tasked with bringing more minority recruits into the department. He had commanded the 77th Division and had a good reputation as an administrator. We knew nothing about his attitudes toward police work, or his service on the street.

Once again, Captain Manny Correa, who remained our choice for chief, had been passed over for an outsider. This, together with the fact that the search committee had not included a single Latino, touched off an emotional protest that introduced a new theme into Compton politics; namely, that the black leadership of the city was practicing its own form of racial discrimination, aimed at Latinos. It was an idea that was to take hold and deepen as the years went on.

The interim city manager was Howard Bell. Dan Lim had taken a better-paying job in Orange County, and Bell was hired to replace him until a new city manager could be found. He was a former deputy in the Sheriff's Reserve in Tucson, Arizona, who combined administrative ability with some knowledge of police work. We liked Bell, but, as we had done with Tom Cochée, we anticipated Joe Rouzan's hiring with reserved judgment.

One part of Tom Cochée's legacy was already in place, however. Two women had been hired as patrol officers.

Lowerstean Lewis was the first female in history to ride in uniform as a Compton cop. She was a tough, determined woman who stood up to all the harassment and rejection directed at her by veteran officers, many of whom refused to partner with her. In response, she developed a reputation for being heavy-handed. She took no nonsense from anyone, and used her nightstick more often and more brutally than many of her male counterparts.

In 1981, she moved to the juvenile division, where I supervised her. I gave her high marks for her ability to work with gang members and young criminals. Lowerstean served as a patrol officer for seven years before suffering a nervous breakdown. She paved the way for the women who followed her, refusing to quit no matter how tough things got, both on the streets and in the locker room.

Betty Marlow, a former Compton court clerk, was born and raised on the east side. At five feet two and a half inches, she was one-half inch too short to qualify for the force. In the weeks before her physical, she hung from doorways, and consulted a chiropractor who used a "stretching machine" to boost her height to five-three. She passed the physical and was sent to the LASO Academy.

The fact that Betty was a Compton native made her transition to patrol easier than Lowerstean Lewis's had been. She partnered with several officers on the A.M. shift and acquired a reputation as an efficient and reliable street cop. In 1978 she achieved the distinction of being the first female to work the P.M. shift, and the first to ride solo. Together with another female officer, Debbie Bivens, she arrested Dexter Fuqua, one of the notorious Fuqua brothers, a fact that earned the respect of the male officers.

Betty moved into the detective division in 1982, where she worked under my supervision. She made national headlines when she used ana-tomically correct dolls to interview a retarded rape victim. The informa-tion she gathered resulted in the rapist's conviction, the first time this technique had been accepted as evidence in court.

Lowerstean Lewis, Betty Marlow, and Jackie Grant, the third woman hired, were known as Charlie's Angels. Jackie was a tall, statuesque blonde who had graduated first in her class. She was partnered with veteran offi-cer Richard Spicer, and quickly earned her own place on the P.M. shift. She became the first female officer to ride with another woman, Evelyn Iams, who, in turn, became the first woman to reach the rank of sergeant. She later became a lieutenant.

The fifth woman to be hired was Serette Mitchell, a former Roller Derby jammer for the Texas Outlaws. Serette was Rutigliano with lipstick. Though small and wiry, she was as tough as any male cop. She worked with me on the P.M. shift, and once, in a fight with two gangbangers, she knocked out her man before I could knock out mine. Whereas many vet-erans had not wanted to ride with Lowerstean Lewis or Betty Marlow because they thought them unreliable, some cops refused to partner with Serette Mitchell on the grounds that she was too aggressive.

All these women met with a great deal of resistance in their early years on the force, ranging from snubbing to practical jokes to the crudest forms of sexual harassment. Even so, all of them survived to become good cops and, in the process, to open the road for the others who would follow them.

In 1975 my second daughter, Tiffany, was born. Her mother, Shannon, was a dancer I met at the King Henry VIII club at 135th and Crenshaw Boulevard in Gardena. Tiffany was my princess, a beautiful, fairylike little girl who was the antidote to the reality I dealt with every day in the streets of Compton. She was delicate and pure, clever and charming, and, as little girls do, she moved into my heart and set up her giggling pastel flag. Though my relationship with Shannon survived only a year, I remained friends with her, even after she married and she and Tiffany moved to

Oregon. Tiffany represented one of my few remaining and tenuous links to innocence. As long as that crystalline creature could exist in this world, I felt, hope was not entirely beyond reach.

Meanwhile, I was assigned to a special gang unit, which meant that I was again in plainclothes, working out of the station. One night a woman called in, her voice terrified, in tears. She told me in Spanish that her estranged husband had recently been released from prison, and that he had come to her apartment and kidnapped their four-year-old daughter.

"He says if I don't go back with him and be his woman, I'll never see my baby again," she wailed. "I don't want nothing to do with José, he's a psycho, a crazy *pinche cabrón!*"

I took her address and drove to the apartment. She was a tiny Latina in her early twenties, living in a one-room flat on Alondra Boulevard. The place was nearly bare of furniture, though there were pictures of the Sacred Heart and candles before a shrine to the Virgin of Guadalupe. Her name, she said, was Isabel.

"He's not alone," she told me. "He's with another man, a black man, Vinny. They were in prison together. José said he'd do anything he had to do if I don't go back with him. He's crazy, Officer, he'll kill the baby!"

Her husband was living in a rooming house in East L.A. near Broadway. I knew that there was an arcade off Broadway between 5th and 6th streets, which, though it was a public place, was closed in on three sides. I told her to call her husband and tell him to meet her in the arcade the following day, and to bring the child.

Her eyes narrowed. "You gotta be careful," she said. "He's got a gun, and he says he's not going back to prison, that he'll die first. And Vinny says the same thing."

That night I huddled with Officers Reggie Wright and Dave Arellanes and planned a strategy. Reggie would dress as an MTA bus driver, Arellanes would be in plainclothes, and I would pose as a homeless man. Reggie and I would go into the arcade while Davey stood guard outside. Since the bust would take place in Los Angeles, I called the LAPD and alerted them to what we were doing.

The next afternoon Arellanes drove us down to Broadway and

dropped Reggie and me off. We walked separately to the arcade, he in his bus driver's uniform, and me in the filthiest rags I could find. The arcade was a foul-smelling, derelict cave lined with shops and an old movie theater, the Globe, once the gem of Broadway. Now it was thick with the stench of urine and littered with trash, a flop for the homeless and drug addicts.

I spotted José at once. He was sitting on a bench halfway down the arcade. Next to him was a small, frightened-looking little boy. Vinny was nowhere to be seen. Reggie Wright walked to the entrance of the arcade, sat down on a bench, and pulled a sandwich out of a brown paper bag. I staggered in, looking for a place to sleep off my drunk. I got as far as the bench and collapsed in a streak of Spanish curses. José was looking for Isabel to appear, and he took no notice of either of us.

The plan was to tackle José and get the kid away from him before he knew what was happening. I crawled over to the wall behind the bench where he sat with the child and pulled myself up. There was still no sign of Vinny, but we could not wait any longer. If Vinny was standing outside the arcade as a lookout, Arellanes would have to take care of him.

I gave Reggie the signal. He moved slowly down the arcade to where José waited and sat down on the bench beside him. I jumped up, grabbed José from behind, and put a choke hold on him. While he struggled and gagged, Reggie scooped up the kid.

I quickly patted José down. He was carrying a snub-nosed .38 in his pocket. I hoisted him up and turned him over to Reggie, who cuffed him, and I picked up the kid. By now the addicts and drunks in the arcade were watching, and people had begun to gather on the sidewalk outside. I knew we had to get out of there fast, so I carried the child in one arm while I kept my gun out in case Vinny was waiting.

When we emerged from the arcade onto Broadway, the street was busy with pedestrians, who stopped suddenly to watch. Reggie was shoving José forward, gripping the cuffs in one hand, his pistol in the other. Arellanes was parked around the corner, so I started with the kid up the sidewalk, shouting in Spanish that we were cops.

At that moment, an LAPD squad car came screeching around the corner and pulled to a stop across the street. Two cops jumped out brandishing shotguns. Reggie Wright had a gun to José's head, and I was carrying a four-year-old with my gun at my side. The L.A. cops took in the scene and pointed their shotguns at us, yelling, "Drop the weapons and get down!"

Neither of us could get to our badges. For an instant I was terrified that the L.A. cops would open up on us. So I spun around against a building and shielded the kid with my body while I shouted to them that we were police.

"Drop the damn weapons or we'll shoot!" they yelled again.

At that moment, Davey Arellanes came racing around the corner bellowing at them to hold their fire. For a fraught moment, the L.A. cops seemed not to know what to do.

"We're cops, we're cops!" he shouted, waving his badge at them. Finally they put up their guns. I slumped against the brick wall. I had been sure that they were going to fire—that was the practice in LAPD: shoot first and ask questions later. I was sweating and out of breath. I glanced over at Reggie, who still held José at gunpoint.

"I guess nobody told them," he said.

It was true. Though I had given LAPD the time and place of our operation, word of it had not reached the units in the area. As Reggie put José into the car, I tried to calm the child, who was shaking and confused.

One of the LAPD officers walked up to me. "Man, we're sorry," he said. "We didn't know." I asked him if he would have shot me. "Nah," he drawled, "I was afraid I'd hit the kid." Then he added. "Until you turned your back."

I had come within a split second of being blown away by another police officer. Given all that I had been through in Compton, it would have been an ironic end—shot dead on an L.A. street with a kidnap victim in my arms, and all because of a bureaucratic screwup. I promised myself that never again would I carry out a bust in another city unless I knew for a fact that the officers on patrol were aware of what I was doing. It was a lesson I had learned nearly at the cost of my life, and perhaps that of a child as well.

Later, at the station, I asked Davey Arellanes what he would have done if the L.A. officers had shot us. Without blinking he replied, "Then I'd have shot two LAPD cops."

The answer surprised me. "You would?"

"Damn straight," he said. "You think I'd let them kill two Compton cops?"

In the CPD, loyalty was absolute.

By the mid-1970s, murder was a way of life in Compton. Drugs or jealousy, marital disputes or money, anger, depression, fear, or just beans cooked the wrong way—all were potential causes of killing. Life was cheap in Compton in those days; for some, murder was a way of resolving disagreements, releasing lifetimes of rage, establishing one's street creds, or just collateral damage to another, lesser crime. Whatever the cause, the one constant of murder in Compton was that we in the police had to clean up the mess, clear up the mystery, and catch the criminals.

This is a fact, I think, which too few citizens reflect on. It is the police who have to deal with the dregs of human behavior, and though many people have mixed feelings about the police, and some even resent them, it is the cops they call when humanity goes badly wrong. In Compton, that meant as badly wrong as humanity can go. Police work in Compton was like war—dark and brutal, drenched with continual danger, and flecked with unexpected heroism. There were many cases of citizens and even crooks who helped us in times of peril—as Jesse Sida had done in the Laundromat shootout, or the robber who stopped to call in Griff Chase's injuries. Like war, police work in Compton brought out the best and the worst in people. As in war, too, often we had thrust into our lives, which were as precious to us as anyone's, acts of unspeakable brutality.

One stifling July night I was working detectives with Barry Lobel, a tall, scholarly Jewish cop whom I had trained, when a call came in of strange noises in a vacant house on Washington Avenue on the extreme east side. We drove to the address and found the neighbors who had put in the call, waiting curious and concerned on the sidewalk. There was a

FOR SALE sign on the tiny brown patch of lawn, and they told us that no one had lived in the house for months.

I walked up onto the stoop and found the front door ajar. While Barry went around the back, I called in, "Police!" No one answered. I pushed it open with my foot and shined my flashlight inside. "Police," I yelled again. Again there was silence. I moved into the house.

The place was in darkness, and the first thing I saw in the beam of my light was the crimson streaks on the wall. They were smeared chest high, like the frantic finger painting of demonic children. I ran the light over them. PIG, one declared, BLACK POWER, and BLUE EYED DEVIL. There was a smell I recognized at once—the iron-cold odor of blood, and the sweet, sickening reek of incipient decay.

Barry Lobel came in from the kitchen, and I switched on the lights. The walls were streaming with blotched blood, the finger tracks in the livid epithets clearly visible. On the floor in the middle of the parlor lay a corpse. It was spread-eagled on its back, big, blue-limbed, beginning to bloat—and headless. Thick pools of black, congealing blood soaked from the gaping throat, smeared into slick slurries by footprints around the walls where the words had been scrawled.

"Where's the head?" Lobel said to me.

One of the blood trails led toward the bathroom. I told Barry to wait by the body. I took out my .357, edged open the bathroom door, reached in, and turned on the light. "Police," I said, then pushed it open.

In the green fluorescent glow from the mirror and tiles, I could see that the toilet was streaked with dried blood like a crusted spaghetti sauce pot. The seat was propped open slightly. I moved to it and used the muzzle of my gun to lift the lid.

A severed head stared back at me with empty eyes from a bowl of clotted slime.

We called in the SI unit and waited in the living room till they arrived. "Panthers or Muslims," the crime scene photographer remarked to me.

I knew it was not so. In fact, I was pretty sure that no black criminal had done this. In my experience, black murders tended to be quick and spontaneous. The killing was done in an alley or a park, and the killers were gone long before the corpse was cold. This had taken time—a lot of time. The man had not been killed in the house but had been brought here, probably after he was dead. The murderers had taken the time to remove the head—the wounds showed that it had been done crudely with a knife, which had taken even more time—and then they had used the victim's blood to paint the walls. The fact that the slogans were clichés of black rage was, to my mind, another indication that this had been done by whites, who had tried to make it look like a racial crime.

There was nothing in the victim's pockets except a matchbook. It was from a club in Lynwood called Annie Wannie's, a strip joint I knew well. I drove back to the station with Lobel, who made out the initial report of the crime, and went home. I got no sleep that night. The eyes of the head in the toilet were gaping at me every time I closed mine.

The next night, after my shift, I drove over to Lynwood, to Annie Wannie's. It was on Imperial Highway near the 710 Freeway. I knew some of the girls there and asked if any of them had seen a big white guy in the place within the past few nights. One of them, a short, huge-breasted stripper named Adrienne, admitted that she had. She seemed nervous and reluctant to talk, so I invited her to meet me for drinks after her shift. It was nearly 2:00 A.M. when she came out of the club and got into my car. I drove her to Ford Park in Bell Gardens, where we parked and talked and drank, and made out. I said nothing about the murder or the missing man.

Things were progressing, so I folded back the seats. After the sex and several more drinks, Adrienne was relaxed enough to talk. She told me that a white guy had come into the club a couple of nights before, flush with cash. He had been gambling in a casino in Gardena—a high roller, he was—and had scored big. His name, she said, was John Bolla. He had been in before and was sweet on her.

Bolla had waited until Adrienne came on to do her number, then began spreading the money around, throwing twenties onto the stage, showing off a bulky wad of bills.

"You couldn't help but notice," Adrienne slurred, her eyes sleepy. "I mean, the guy was crazy drunk and the money was just fallin' outta his pants."

It would have been a stupid thing to have done in any public place, but Annie Wannie's was a biker bar, a hangout for the Heathens and the Hessians. In his drunken effort to impress the big-busted stripper, John Bolla had been setting himself up to be mugged.

Adrienne was dating a biker named Donny, and he told her to get Bolla into the alley out back. She sat in Bolla's lap, nuzzled him with her enormous breasts, and whispered that she would meet him in the alley for sex in fifteen minutes. He said he couldn't wait. Then, as Adrienne walked to the ladies' room, she told Donny that their high roller was on the hook.

When Bolla staggered into the alley in search of sex, it wasn't Adrienne's big breasts that were waiting for him, but Donny and two of his biker buddies.

"What happened?" I asked.

She choked up and began to sob. "They jacked the guy up, but he tried to fight, and one of them hit him, and Donny kicked him in the head a coupla times . . ."

She broke down, so I wrapped my arms around her and told her that it was all right, that she could go on telling me.

"Well," she sniffled, "the guy was dead, and they didn't know what to do with him. So they put him in Donny's car and drove over to Compton, you know, 'cause Compton's full of dead bodies. And they found this house that was empty, and they put him in there. When Donny got home, he was all covered with blood. So I said, 'Well, if you just kicked the guy, what's all the blood?' And he told me he didn't wanna talk about it. He was real upset."

I asked if she knew what they had done in the house. She said she did not, and she had been too scared to ask Donny, seeing what a state he was in. Still, what had happened was now clear: Donny and his pals had cut off Bolla's head and stuffed it in the toilet, then painted the racist slogans on the walls to make it look like a black-on-white killing.

"Where's Donny now?" I asked.

"I dunno." Adrienne looked at me with big, bloodshot eyes. "What're you gonna do?"

I held her closer. "I'm just gonna talk to him," I answered.

She said he would be at Annie's the next night.

Lobel and I arrested Donny for murder, and he agreed to give up his pals in exchange for a plea deal. Adrienne had been an accessory, but I managed to keep her out of it. She had not been guilty; she had just been stupid. The fact that she had had sex with a cop the night after her boyfriend killed a man proved that, and stupidity, even though it can be dangerous, is not a crime. Before the trial started, she left town. Donny and his pals were convicted of second-degree murder. I never saw Adrienne again.

Compton cops had to develop defense mechanisms to deal with the stresses and dangers of the job. The most common of these was alcohol, and alcoholism among cops was an ongoing problem. A few—not many— turned to drugs. They were everywhere in Compton, in every kind and amount, and they were readily available in the evidence lockers in the basement of police headquarters. Some, like Griff Chase, descended into despair and suicide.

In my case, it was sex. I used sex as a narcotic, a way of anesthetizing myself against the knowledge that there was no end to the work that was consuming my life, work that at any time might kill me. The intimacy of sex, the sudden, searing contact with another human being, no matter how brief or how impersonal, was reassurance that I was not alone, not cut off, and that humanity, close and naked, was still open to me.

The irony, of course, was that using sex as a crutch made true intimacy impossible. The more I came to depend on sex as a way of protecting myself against the reality I was dealing with every day, the more I came to regret the loss of Kitty and Connie and my daughters, and Judy Ward. I was beginning to understand that, though I thrived on confronting the violence of Compton, my psyche was becoming another of its victims.

This all began to come home to me on a trip up north. As part of the burglary detail, I was invited to take part in a seminar for crime-specific units in Carmel. Usually I shunned such events: They were boring, and there was always too much to do at home. However, since this one was in

Carmel, one of the loveliest spots on the California coast, I decided to attend. Six of us drove up the interminable strip of I-5 in our unmarked cars, before turning west to Highway 1, the curving, scenic stretch along the Pacific.

Before leaving, we learned that one of our colleagues, Bobby Erlanger, who had quit the force two years before, was living near Carmel. He was a big, fresh-faced kid from the Bay Area who had worked the streets for four years and then disappeared. Jimmy Pearson and I checked into our hotel in Carmel and went looking for him. We were told that he was working in a restaurant called Nepenthe overlooking the beach at Big Sur, so Jimmy and I drove up to see him.

The manager of Nepenthe confirmed that Erlanger worked for him part-time, and that he lived in a shack on the beach not far from the restaurant. We trudged down through the dunes and scrub and spotted the place on a spit of land in a cove. A tiny frame structure, it looked like it had been hand-built and could not have withstood a decent windstorm or heavy waves. It was painted electric blue and turquoise, and the door, a piece of unfinished plywood, was decorated with garish psychedelic swirls. I knocked, and Bobby Erlanger opened the door.

I scarcely recognized him. Instead of the bulky cop from Compton, clean-shaven and garrulous, he was now a tall, sinewy hippie with stringy hair down past his shoulders and a beard that tangled to the middle of his bony, naked chest. He had the half-vacant look of a stoner, his eyes dulled and drained by too much pot and hash. When he saw us, though, he broke into a big, yellow-stained grin. "Hey, Rick, hey, Jimmy, come on in!"

The one-room shack was a caricature of the hippie lifestyle. There was a waterbed in the middle of the floor that took up almost the entire space. Bead curtains closed off the toilet and sink, and there were tie-dyed sheets over the windows. An enormous bong sat in a kind of shrine in a corner, with Indian flake-fringed pillows heaped around it. The cushions were the only place to sit, and so, as Bobby folded his bare legs into the corner, we sat down with him. He asked what brought us up to "the Sur." As we told him about the conference, he picked up the bong and sucked at the mouthpiece, smoke and water burbling in the cylinder. On one side of him was a stash of pot, and on the other, bricks of hash.

"Cool, man, that's cool," he nodded. He asked about the cops he had known, and we filled him in. The whole time I was peering at him, trying to remember the young recruit I had helped to train when he came on the force in 1971. That was during the period of the Panthers, the Muslims, and the Malcolm X Foundation, and the rise of the gangs—some of the worst times we had had to face. Bobby Erlanger had lived through it with a stolidity and a humor that had helped keep us all sane.

As we talked, the plywood door was pulled open, and a girl walked in. She was lithe and pretty, dressed in cutoffs and a diaphanous dashiki, her tawny hair trailing to her waist. She could not have been more than seventeen.

"This is my woman, Shell," Erlanger said. "You know, 'Shell,' like you find on the beach." She smiled vaguely at us. "Shell, babe, these are some guys I used to work with in Compton."

"Oh, cops, yeah. Bobby used to be a cop." She seemed embarrassed by the admission. She knelt on the waterbed, which shifted under her girlish bare knees, and then stretched herself out on her stomach. She made no effort to conceal her breasts, which hung pendulous over the edge.

"Rick and Jimmy and me, we were catching up on old times," Bobby went on. "It was a real bad scene in those days, wasn't it, guys? I try to tell Shell what a bad scene it was, but she don't want to hear about it, do you, babe?"

Shell grunted in affirmation. It was clear that Bobby's former life was off-limits in the shack, but he appeared glad of the chance to talk with us about it. He passed the bong back and forth with Shell as we spoke. Then she closed her eyes, her thin frame lolling on the waterbed like a child being rocked to sleep. In a few moments, she was.

"She does that, man," Bobby said, tilting the bong toward Shell. "She just goes out. Don't take any notice." He straightened himself and took a last, long pull, filling the little room with smoke. "Come on, we'll go outside."

We walked along the beach as far as the stony, pine-fringed point. The surf slid tranquilly along the sand and ran with a soothing plash against the rocks. It was as restful and picturesque a place as I had ever seen, so far removed from the chaotic streets of Compton that it might have been in another world. This was the world that Bobby Erlanger had chosen to withdraw to, after four years of mayhem and violence. As we walked and chatted, I began to understand why, ceasing to be surprised at the transformation that had come over him.

"You're happy here?" I asked as we sat down on the black basalt of the breakwater.

He looked out at the ocean and nodded. "Yeah."

"You ever think about Compton—those days?"

Again he nodded, more heavily. "All the time, Rick. Every night when I go to sleep, and even more when I can't. This . . ." He leaned back and stretched himself. "This is my healing. You know? From all that."

"She's pretty," I said. "Shell."

Bobby grinned at me. "Still Rosecrans Rick, huh?"

"She's not of age, is she?"

"That's why I'm with her," Bobby answered. He lowered his eyes, reflecting. "Those skanks in Compton, that pussy that used to hang on Long Beach, the strippers at the Garter . . . Shell is the opposite of that. She's part of the healing. She's pure." He turned to me, and for the first time I saw the old, fresh look in his eyes. "That's why I love her, man," he said.

We walked back to the shack and hung out for a little while longer, sitting cross-legged on the cushions, Bobby draining and refilling the bong. Shell snored softly, sleeping as earnestly as only a little girl can. Then, as Jimmy and I got up to go, Bobby said, "There's something I want to show you guys."

He moved to the little bamboo shelf that tilted precariously on the wall. It was crowded with tiny blue and green bottles culled from the beach. Among them was a photograph, half hidden by the colored trinkets. Bobby took it down and turned it toward us. It was his graduation photo from the police academy. In it he stood tall and smiling in his blue uniform and high-peaked hat, the eagle and crest shining. Alongside him were four other cadets who had graduated with him that day.

"You see," he said. "I never forgot who I was." Then he broke into a small, sad smile, a shadow of the one in the picture. "But I'm tryin', man," he added. "I'm tryin'."

By the time we left Bobby's shack, the sun was setting. As I made my way up the dunes to Nepenthe, I looked back. The ocean was glowing gold and peaceful, the shack nestled against the dunes, looking for all the world like a cast-off glass bottle half buried in the sand. This was his healing, Bobby had said, and he had asked me if I knew what he meant.

I supposed I did know . . . and I supposed that one day, if I survived, I, too, would need a healing.

Lueders Park, the Olympics, and Mexico

By the late 1970s, the population of Compton had reached over ninety thousand. Conceived as an agricultural community for a few hundred families, Compton had become one of the most congested urban areas in the nation. The average population density of the United States is about seventy-five people per square mile, and that of Los Angeles County, some twenty-three hundred per square mile. But though the population of Compton had steadily increased, its area had not. By 1975, there were over ten thousand people per square mile in the city, and too many of them were poor, or drug addicted, or alcoholics; too many were undereducated, unemployed, angry; too many were hopeless.

At a time when American urban centers were beginning to lose population, Compton's was increasing. People ought to have fled the city, but they could not. They were like the dwellers of New Orleans's Lower Ninth Ward during hurricane Katrina: They could not get out no matter how bad things got. Forced by poverty and circumstance to remain, the people of Compton had to ride out the storm as best they could.

The result was a crime rate unparalleled in the nation. At any given time, fully 10 percent of Compton's population was either in the justice system or in jail—but while the criminal element grew and became more desperate and more violent, the number of policemen remained unchanged.

Compton was a city of nine square miles, with ten thousand criminals and 130 cops.

When Joe Rouzan took over as chief, we waited anxiously to learn what his approach would be. His first official act gave us an answer: He asked us to remove the billboards we had posted requesting the Marquette study. "We don't need any outside help," he told us. "We can handle the situation ourselves."

It was exactly what we wanted to hear. Joe Rouzan seemed to understand the reality we faced on the streets and was willing to back us up. He was a chief we could work with, and it mattered to us not at all what color he was or where he came from or what his background was. He was a cop's chief—he got it. Almost at once, morale began to improve.

There was a little park on East Rosecrans Avenue called Lueders, one of the few grassy areas in the neighborhood. A fixture in this park, as much as the trees and the drinking fountain, was an old man named Mac. Mac was a World War I veteran, a doughboy who had served in the trenches, and who walked every day from his house on Long Beach Boulevard two blocks away to feed the pigeons.

I had seen Mac in Lueders Park since I was a letter carrier for the post office. He was not a street person; he was always neatly dressed and groomed, and, though he walked with a cane, his bearing reflected the fact that he had been in the military. What had first struck me about him was his shoes—they were the old high-buttoned kind, such as men had worn at the turn of the century. I had never seen such shoes, and for some reason, the fact that old Mac still wore them had endeared him to me.

He was a harmless gentleman in his eighties who had never entirely recovered from the carnage in France sixty years before. On one occasion I had stopped my patrol car in the park to talk with him. It was raining, and I wanted to make sure he was all right. He was far from all right—he was in the grip of a wrenching flashback. He stared through me with watery blue eyes, the rain pouring down, and began muttering, "When they tell you to go over the top, you gotta go over the top."

I asked him what he meant. His eyes found mine, and he shouted, desperate and terrified, "When they say go over the top, it don't matter who you are! You gotta go over the top!"

I put him in the car and drove him back to his one-bedroom shingle house. "You stay inside now, Mac," I said as I walked him to the door. He grasped my shirtfront; the melancholy in his dripping face was inexpressible. "We went over the top," he said, "but a lot of us didn't come back."

Mac was a prisoner not only of the past but of Compton as well. Too old and too poor to move, he found himself the last white person in the neighborhood. It made no difference to him. He had his pigeons to feed and his demons to subdue, and he did both every afternoon in Lueders Park.

One day in the summer of 1978, Mac was making his way to feed his pigeons when he was stopped by three bangers from the Bloods. They must have known him, and they must have known he had nothing of value, but that did not deter them. They roughed him up and demanded money, and when he became too addled to answer, one of them punched him in the mouth.

The blow was so powerful that it drove Mac's dentures back into his throat, and he began choking. Rather than help him or even just leave him alone, the gangbangers knocked him to the ground and began kicking him. Savagely, brutally, they beat the old man, who was gasping for breath, his gullet clogged with his broken teeth.

That was when a car rolled around the corner. It was an off-duty CPD officer, Galen Chapman. He was a local boy who knew old Mac and made a point of driving by the park to check on him on his way to work. When he saw what was happening, he pulled out his gun and jumped from the car, shouting for the bangers to get down on the ground. They took off, and Chapman chased them.

Two got away, but he caught the third, tackled him at full speed, and drove him headfirst to the pavement. He hooked the gangster up, dragged him to his car, and called for an ambulance. Old Mac was writhing in suf-focating agony on the sidewalk, his skull fractured, blood and mucus frothing from his mouth with every futile gasp. Chapman tried CPR, but Mac was dead by the time the ambulance arrived. What the Germans had not been able to do in the Argonne in 1918, three young punks had ac-complished sixty years later within a stone's throw of Lueders Park.

Galen Chapman brought the Blood into the station. I was one of the detectives on duty, and the homicide was assigned to me. When Chapman told me what had happened, I was beyond furious. This was so uncalled for, so gratuitous, even for Compton; Mac was an eighty-year-old man who threatened no one and could not defend himself. Killing him was worse than callous, it was animalistic.

I went down to the basement holding cell to collect the banger. The jailer took off the cuffs and turned him over to me. He was tall and thin, no more than eighteen, and wore a red sweatsuit and red sneakers. I took him by an elbow and marched him upstairs to an interview room. Barry Lobel was working that day, and he asked me if I wanted him to witness the ques-tioning.

"No," I answered. "You'd better stay out of it."

When I sat the kid down in the wooden chair, he turned his back to me. There was nothing else in the room but a narrow desk.

"What's your name?" I began. He did not answer. "I can find out in an hour, so you might as well tell me."

He looked at me defiantly, affecting fearlessness. "Anthony," he grunted.

"Anthony what?"

"Toles." His chin was thrust out and his eyes were hard. Though he was a Blood, I did not know him. He had to be a "junior flip," a new recruit.

"The guy you jacked up, he's dead." For an instant, I saw fear in his face, but he buried it just as quickly. "Why'd you do it?"

"He called me nigger," he spat.

"Bullshit. What did you do it for? To show you have guts? Does it take guts to beat an old man to death?"

He glared at me in arrogant silence. The truth of his situation was be-ginning to seep in, but as a Blood he knew how he was expected to act.

"You and your buddies, you murdered an eighty-year-old man. That doesn't take guts—that's a cowardly thing to do."

"I told you," he snapped. "He called me nigger."

I leaned closer to him. "You're gonna give up your two buddies. You're gonna tell me their names."

"Fuck you—" I slapped him hard across his ear. He grabbed at the table to keep from falling. "Hey, fuck that—" This time I hit him with my fist in the chest. The wind grunted out of him, and he struggled to breathe. "You can't do that, man!" he gasped.

"You cocksucking motherfucker!" I yelled. I gave him two more body shots that drove him off the chair. I was out of control, and I knew it. "You're gonna tell me who the other two were!"

Toles was writhing on the floor pinned beneath me, trying to protect his ribs against the beating. "I wanna talk to a lawyer—" he whimpered.

"You're gonna talk to *me,* you son of a bitch!" I flipped him over, wrapped my arm around his neck, and wrenched his head back. "You're gonna tell me or I'm gonna choke you to death. I'm gonna make your eyes pop out of your head. I'm gonna give you what you gave that old man." He was wheezing, his fingers tearing at my arm. "You're gonna know what it feels like to choke to death, to feel yourself dying and there's nothing you can do about it." I tightened my grip on his throat. "You give up your friends or you're gonna die right here, motherfucker. You understand me? I'm gonna kill you, right here and now. Are you gonna give them up?"

He began nodding furiously, as much as the choke hold would allow. I let go of him and stood up. Toles staggered to his feet and collapsed, gagging, onto the desk.

"What's their names?"

He was clawing at his Adam's apple. "I . . . can't . . . talk . . ."

"You better fuckin' start talking," I said and slapped him across the back of the skull. His forehead smacked against the desk.

"Okay . . . okay . . ." he gasped. There were tears in his eyes, and his whole body was shaking. "Daryl Savage . . . Sterling Lewis . . ."

I knew both of them, OGs, veteran Bloods and shooters. Lewis especially was a dangerous character. It was Lewis who had given up Debo; when I took down Debo to prevent a resumption of the gang war, he told me that Sterling Lewis had murdered a Crip from the Front Hood and that the Crips had put out a contract on him. Debo had been assigned to find him and kill him.

Savage and Lewis had evidently taken Toles out looking for someone to murder, so that he could make his bones. Old Mac had been a quick and easy target. I grabbed Toles by the back of his shirt and dragged him to his feet. "I'm not done with you, asshole," I told him, and I took him back to the cells.

I drove to Daryl Savage's house first. His mother answered the door. I identified myself and asked if I could talk to her son.

Savage was in a back bedroom. "What you want?" he snarled at me. I told him he was under arrest.

"What for?" his mother demanded.

"Murder."

"Bullshit!" Savage said.

I ordered him to get on his feet. He refused. I pulled out my gun and shoved the muzzle under his chin. "Get the fuck up!"

While his mother screamed and protested, I pushed him against the wall, patted him down, and cuffed him. She was still howling as I marched her son to the car.

By the time I went after Sterling Lewis, the street telegraph had alerted him, and he had disappeared. His relatives were not talking, but one of my informants told me that he had a girlfriend named Pearleen in the neighborhood. Barry Lobel and I drove to her house.

Pearleen was sixteen or seventeen years old, and pregnant. As the woman of a Blood, she knew what she was supposed to do, but when I told her that Lewis had murdered an old man, I could see that she was scared. Still, she remained silent. I asked Lobel to wait in the doorway while I took Pearleen into a bedroom in the back.

"You know where Sterling is," I began. "Tell me." She pouted at me defiantly. "You tell me, or I'm gonna tear your fuckin' wig off."

"I ain't tell you shit," she spat.

The Bloods had trained her to deal with threats; this was not the way to get to her. I pointed at her bulging belly. "Is that his baby?"

"Yeah," she said.

"I'll tell you what I'm gonna do," I went on evenly. "When that baby is born, I'm gonna have it taken away from you. They're gonna take it away and they're gonna put it up for adoption."

She looked at me in disbelief. "You can't do that."

"I can. I can do it, Pearleen. You're an accessory to a murder. They're gonna put you in jail, and they're gonna take your baby and give it away, and you'll never see it again."

She was beginning to tremble, fighting tears. "I can't tell you where he is," she moaned. "They'll kill me if I do!"

There was no need to bully or shout; she was breaking down. "I know where he lives," I told her. "He lives off Central near 136th. I grew up four blocks from there. I know the neighborhood, I know the people. It's only a matter of time—a little time—till I find him."

She dropped onto the bed and began to cry. I leaned down and spoke nearly in a whisper. "And when I do, Pearleen, when I find your man, I'm gonna shoot him."

"No, no," she sobbed.

"I'm gonna shoot him as soon as I see him," I went on, "and I'm gonna write it up that the Crips killed him, and nobody will ever question it. They put a contract on him for the dead Crip."

"He'll get away."

"He won't get away, Pearleen. He'll get caught."

Her eyes flared through the tears for an instant. "Then they'll put him in prison. He'll be safe there!"

I shook my head slowly. "Debo's in prison," I told her, "and you know that Debo's the one that got the contract." She did know it, and the fact that *I* knew it stunned her. "I can see to it that Sterling goes to the same prison. And then what do you think Debo will do?"

She was trembling now, her whole body shivering with fear. "Sterling will be dead, Pearleen," I went on calmly. "One way or the other, the daddy of your baby will be stone-cold dead, and you'll be in jail, and your baby will be sent someplace where you'll never see it again."

She collapsed on the bed, her nose running mucus on the worn flannel sheet. I leaned closer and said more gently: "But if he turns himself in, I'll make sure he gets a fair shake. And that he doesn't go to the same jail as Debo. I promise you that."

"Okay," she sobbed, "okay! I can't tell you where Sterling's at, but I can talk to him . . . I can tell him to turn himself in." She glared at me furiously. "But not to you!" she snarled. "Not you."

I straightened and stepped away from her. "All right," I told her. "You talk to Sterling and you tell him to come in. Or everything I told you will happen is gonna happen, exactly like I said." She was crying uncontrollably now, sticky strings stretching from her nose and mouth. "You understand me, Pearleen? You believe me?"

"Yeah," she moaned. "Yeah . . . I believe you."

I left her weeping on the bed and walked out of the house with Barry Lobel. He had heard the whole thing.

"You think she'll do it?" he asked.

"She'll do it."

"And he'll come in?"

"He will."

He shook his head. "That was some fucking interview," he remarked as we got into the car.

"They're like POWs, these bangers and their bitches," I told him. "They're trained to resist interrogation. You gotta find something to break them with. And when you find it, you gotta use it. A mother, a brother, a baby, whatever it is, once you find it, you have to use it."

Three days later, Sterling Lewis walked into the office of the *Los Angeles Sentinel* newspaper and asked to speak to a reporter. When the receptionist inquired with a smile what it was about he replied, "They want me for killin' some old guy."

He gave his story slowly and hesitantly to the reporter, who asked him why he had not gone to the police.

"They're lookin' for me," he said. "I don't wanna turn myself in to the Compton cops. They're gonna kill me."

"Nobody's going to hurt you," the reporter assured him. "I'll make sure of that."

Lewis shook his head. "You don't understand, man. This one cop, he said he'd shoot me on sight, make it look like a retaliation. My girlfriend told me he said it." He was scared—terrified, in fact. He asked the reporter to take him to the sheriff's substation in L.A.

Sterling Lewis was in custody within an hour. He, Daryl Savage, and Anthony Toles were all charged with murder.

That Saturday I attended Mac's funeral. He was buried at the military cemetery in Westwood with the honors due a combat veteran. Galen Chapman and a few other Compton cops were there. No one else.

The three Bloods were tried and convicted of murder in the first degree and sentenced to life in prison. It was the end of old Mac's story, which had begun six decades before in the trenches of the Western Front. I always thought of him when I drove past Lueders Park, where there was no one left to feed the pigeons.

I had boxed since grade school. It was not only a vital skill in police work where we regularly tangled with drunks and addicts and thugs; for me it was also a release of the tension and aggression I accumulated on the street. Pounding a heavy bag or sharpening my reflexes on the speed bag was like unloading a pistol cocked and pointed at my head. I was also working out regularly in the basement gym at the station, and the farther I got into it, the more important to me my workouts became.

I worked out every day that I could, and on my days off, twice a day. I pushed myself harder and farther, tuning my diet to my workouts, filling my system with the protein it craved, challenging myself and the metal with a single-minded devotion. I set goals, modest at first, then more ambitious, and as I met them and exceeded them, I set more distant ones. Weight training became for me a kind of religion.

I "did the stacks," lifting all the weight on the machines, and then I hung free weights over them and went heavier. For me, lifting was a battle and a joy—a battle against myself, and a joy in knowing I had won, I had beaten the metal, I had mastered myself. Lifting was a discipline that, like spiritual exercise, demanded utter concentration, controlled breathing, and unflagging devotion. Every set was like an incantation, every rep was like a musical note in a Gregorian chant; my workouts became a sort of prayer—my god was a god of iron.

I was not the only one, of course. Most of the patrol officers were into lifting, and some even tried their hand at competitive bodybuilding, though I never toyed with the idea. For me, weight training was a necessity of life; a way to keep myself in shape, mentally and physically, and to up the odds of survival in a fight. Small guys, skinny guys, guys who could not impose their presence on the street, were more at risk than those of us who bulked up. So, like most religious people, we gave our bodies, minds, and souls to our devotions in the hope of salvation—not in the next life, but in this one.

Every four years, the police departments throughout California held an Olympics, and the rivalry among them was intense. Bagging a medal at the Police Olympics was a boasting point, and winning the overall games carried with it a prestige that was coveted by every department in the state. The 1976 Police Olympics were held in San Jose, and departments from all of the major cities in California competed. Compton sent a team of sixteen officers, one of the smallest of all, but when the games were over, we had placed second in total medal count, beating teams from San Diego, San Francisco, Sacramento, and San Jose, and being bested only by LAPD, a force of over nine thousand officers, whose three teams were ten times the size of ours.

We dominated the boxing competition, winning medals in three of the eight divisions. I fought in the 175-pound class, and my first opponent was a former Diamond and Golden Gloves champion named Marcello Hernando. He had a reputation as the best fighter in the LAPD, and while I prepared for our bout in the basement of the San Jose Arena, I was as nervous as I had been my first night on patrol.

The old San Jose Arena was a classic cracker box of a ring, its balconies piled atop one another almost vertically. It was so small and resonant that, as I sat having my hands taped, I could hear bodies hitting the canvas above, and the roars of the crowd reverberating. I felt like a gladiator in the catacombs of the Coliseum. Then an old black pug with a heavy limp stuck his head in at the door. "Five minutes!" he called.

As my trainer, Johnny Heaton, snugged up my gloves, I wondered, *What have I gotten myself into?*

When I jogged into the arena, the tiny Compton contingent exiled to the top tier went nuts. They were so vocal and so pumped that all I could think was *If I lose this fight, I'm mud.*

Hernando was already in the ring, and the sight of him was not reassuring. He was a thickset Latino whose face was a rugged map of his history as an amateur champ. As I loosened up in my corner, my second, Officer Stone Jackson, took off the HUB CITY robe I had to share with all the other Compton boxers. Jackson was a massive hulk of a man whose size was belied by his equally formidable stutter.

"This g-g-g-g-g-uy ain't n-n-n-n-n-othin'," he told me.

"Then you fight him," I said.

Early in the first round, Hernando and I measured each other carefully. I got in a few good shots, which made me think that he was not as tough as his reputation implied. He seemed confused by my southpaw style, and I began to loosen up a little, challenging him to come at me. He did. As I leaned in for a jab, Hernando launched a right hand that must have started at the Boys' Club in Boyle Heights. It caught me square on the temple, and suddenly there was a symphony of strings in my head.

I managed to stay on my feet and cover up, but as I backed away, he came after me again. I hit the ropes and there was no place left to go, so I opened up with three or four jabs, more in desperation than defense. One caught Hernando on the chin and staggered him. He fell off away from me, and instinctively I went after him, driving him all the way across the ring with combinations. The LAPD crowd was stunned to silence, and the Compton boys were on their feet screaming.

I knew that I had him. In the next round, I hit him pretty much at will. By the middle of the third, I was toying with him. I did the "Ali shuffle," and late in the round I windmilled my right arm like Kid Gavilan and nailed him with a bolo punch that put him on his backside. I won the fight by unanimous decision.

All the fighters I faced were LAPD, and I put them away efficiently. The night before the final bout, the other guys took me to the Jabberwocky Room atop the Le Baron Hotel to celebrate my certain gold medal. Afterward, I had a marathon sex session with my girlfriend of the time, Brooklyn Patty, who came up to watch me become immortalized.

In the gold medal bout I faced yet another LAPD fighter, Shane Pappas. A big, muscular Greek, Pappas was the middleweight champion of the department and a former gold medal winner. He was my toughest opponent yet, but I was confident, and I handled him pretty easily through the first two rounds. Then, late in the third, my nightlong celebration suddenly caught up with me. I ran out of gas, and my legs began to buckle. Pappas, who knew he was losing the fight, saw it as his last chance and attacked me with everything he had left.

He was swinging wildly, trying desperately to connect, but I parried him and kept my distance. Then, after a couple of quick jabs that stopped my rubbery legs in their tracks, he threw a roundhouse right that caught me on the nose.

"Six!" I heard the referee intone.

What happened to one to five? went through my head.

I realized I was on the canvas, flat on my back, blood clogging my nose and running down my throat. The ref, an old fighter named Pappy Gall, was counting me out as Shane Pappas smacked his gloves in anticipation of victory. Somehow I dragged myself to my feet, just beating the count, and fell back toward my corner. Stone Jackson was shouting at me, "Sevent-t-t-teen seconds l-l-l-left—you w-w-w-w-won the f-f-f-fight—just t-t-t-t-tie him up!"

With the cotton wool in my skull and Stone's heavy stutter, I could not make out what he was saying. I leaned over to try to catch it, and the blood began pouring from my nose onto the canvas. Under the rules of the Olympics, if either man is bleeding uncontrollably, regardless of the scoring, the ref has to stop the fight. Pappy Gall took one look at the puddle forming at my feet and began waving his arms. The fight was over. Shane Pappas won the gold medal, and I, the bronze.

One morning shortly after I returned from the Police Olympics, Howard Bell, who was the interim city manager while the council searched for Dan Lim's replacement, came to see me.

"I hear you've got an unsolved murder on your books," he remarked. I answered that we had plenty. "Yeah, but this one's special," he said. "Alfonso Toledo."

Alfonso Toledo was a construction worker who lived on the north side. He was married to a fiery pro-police activist named Lorraine Cervantes. Lorraine, who was half black and half Hispanic, never missed an opportunity to harangue the city council about its history of corruption, and its lack of support for the police. Early one morning, in the 200 block of West Reeve Street, Alfonso Toledo, after a night of drinking, shot another man to death in a petty dispute over a gambling debt. Within hours, he had fled the country.

"He's in Mexico," I told Howard.

"I know. We want you to go down there and get him."

It was a suggestion so bizarre as to be comical, but Howard Bell was not joking.

"There's a hundred murderers running around the streets," I replied. "Why should I go to Mexico to arrest one?"

It was a rhetorical question, but Howard had an answer for it. "The city council wants you to."

All of a sudden, it became clear. Lorraine Cervantes was a thorn in the council's side; arresting her husband would embarrass her. It was a political maneuver in classic Compton Style. I told Howard that I was far too busy to go to Mexico.

"I'm coming with you," the city manager said, "and so is Joe Flores."

I knew that Flores was working an extremely sensitive case, which also involved Mexico. Some weeks before, four illegal immigrants had been driving down West Poplar Street when they were hijacked by a pair of black men with guns. Bob Livingston and Rhone Watson (who was known as Scope because of a drooping eye), preyed on illegals, because they knew they were easy targets.

They came up on either side of the car and pointed their guns at the men in the front. On the backseat were two young women, Esther Chavez, and her girlhood friend Gloria Gonzales, who was eight and a half months pregnant. When the men refused to get out, Livingston and Watson opened fire. The bullets shattered the windows. Neither man was hit, and they threw open the doors and raced away from the scene. On the backseat, however, Gloria Gonzales gasped and doubled over. She had been shot in the stomach. When the police arrived, they found her in shock, her swollen belly leaking blood and fluid, cradled in the arms of Esther Chavez.

Surgeons were able to save Gloria Gonzales's life, but not the baby's. I had seen the autopsy photographs: It was a pathetic, huddled figure, fully developed, with fingers and toes, but its tiny chest had been blasted away. It had died of a gunshot wound before it had even been born, one of the youngest victims of Compton violence. Prosecutors, arguing that the child was a viable human being, asked for and got a murder charge against Livingston and Watson.

The case was scheduled to go to trial, but as soon as Gloria Gonzales was well enough, she and Esther Chavez fled back to Mexico. Both the victim and the government's chief witness were out of reach. In addition to kidnapping Alfonso Toledo, Joe Flores and I were being tasked with finding Gloria and Esther and convincing them to come back to testify. Though the Toledo kidnapping was essentially a political ploy, finding the women was not. I agreed to go.

The city council, which was always complaining that it was strapped for funds, nonetheless allocated the money for our trip. In addition to airfare and expenses, they had given Howard Bell two thousand dollars in cash for what was described as incidentals. We assumed that the money was to be used for *la mordida,* "the bite," which was slang for bribes. Mexican police officials from top to bottom were as corrupt as any in the world, but nothing could be done in Mexico without their help, and that could not be secured without *la mordida.*

The bribes would help to cover the fact that what we were doing was completely illegal. It would have been as if Mexican police slipped into the United States and kidnapped one of our citizens. Howard Bell implied that if we were arrested, the city would deny any knowledge of our trip. My response was that Howard's presence would make that difficult, and I suggested strongly that he not accompany us. Howard had been a reserve deputy in Tucson, though, and he fancied himself something of a cop. He insisted on going.

In addition to the cash, Flores and I took our weapons and half a dozen boxes of .38 caliber ammunition. I had heard that police in Mexico were always short of bullets, which the government allocated carefully. No Mexican police officer carried more than one or two rounds at a time, a deliberate policy aimed at preventing an armed revolt by the police.

We had been told by informants that Alfonso Toledo was living in the state of Jalisco in the west-central part of the country. Howard Bell, Joe Flores, and I flew down to Guadalajara, where we contacted the local police chief, Alfredo Castellanos-Mendoza, who went by the impressive title of *Procuraduria General de Justicia*. The *procuraduria* told us that for a consideration he could provide us with a guide, transportation, and an introduction to the chief of police in the town of Autlán de Navarro, where Toldeo was believed to be hiding. We gave him $350 in cash and three boxes of cartridges, which seemed to satisfy him.

The next day a scrawny, ferretlike Mexican in unwashed fatigues showed up at our hotel. His name was Basilio, a state policeman assigned by the chief as our guide. He told us that he would drive us the 120 kilometers to Autlán, saying that it would take three to four hours. I assumed this was due to the condition of the roads until I saw his vehicle. It was a World War II surplus jeep that looked like it had been through the Battle of the Bulge. It was scarcely capable of thirty miles per hour.

Basilio bustled around stuffing our bags into every open orifice in the tiny, rusting jeep. I sat in front, Howard and Joe settled into the back, and we bounced off.

I had never been to Mexico, though my parents' families had emigrated from there. Guadalajara had been a cultural shock for me, crowded, noisy, dirty, and disorganized, but nothing could have prepared me for Autlán. The twisting, half-paved roads led through jungle that became denser the farther we drove into the interior. It was like traveling back in time, or into the heart of darkness. We passed roadside towns that were little more than hovels, tilting tin-roofed shacks where children played in dirty rain-filled ditches and old people sat idly smoking. Poor as Compton was, it was paradise compared to this, and I understood why these people risked their lives to get to what they called Alta California.

Autlán was a good-sized town, though as impoverished as the rest of the district. Basilio pulled up outside police headquarters, and we climbed out of the jeep, sore from hours of jostling on the springless seats. He took us inside to meet the chief of police.

"He is Commander Archivaldo Diaz-Baez, but you must call him 'El Jefe,'" he cautioned solemnly. "You must never say anything but 'El Jefe,' and you must show him great respect."

El Jefe was straight out of a B-movie cast. He was tall, portly, and unshaven, and he wore a lengthy Fu Manchu mustache that snaked down past his grimy folds of chin. His uniform was like something from a comic opera: a drum major's jacket festooned with braid, English riding pants, and knee-high black jackboots laced up the front that reminded me of photographs I had seen of World War I cavalrymen. He greeted us expansively, declaring that he had spoken with the chief in Guadalajara and understood perfectly our mission.

"You have come for the assassin Toledo," he said with a conspiratorial nod. We assured him we would be as discreet as possible. "Discretion, yes!" he rumbled. "In such matters, discretion is everything," and he stroked significantly at his mustache. I could scarcely believe what I was seeing.

Joe Flores reached into his backpack and took out a box of cartridges and a roll of bills. El Jefe seized them with fat fingers, quickly counted the money, and offered us a drink. "Tequila," he declared. I had had tequila often before but never like this. It was powerful and bitter, and by the third glass my head was swimming.

"Toledo lives near the village of El Grullo," the chief informed us.

"One of my men will go with you and guide you there, but you must tell no one what you are doing." He pointed at Flores and me. "When you get to El Grullo, you will not speak. Your accent is the black Spanish of the Alta California. And you, *el negro*," he said to Howard Bell, "you must stay in the hotel here. In El Grullo, there would be too much suspicion."

"We must get Toledo out of the country," I said, "and we have other persons to locate."

El Jefe nodded knowingly. "Once you have Toldeo, we will put him in a *federales* jail. But we can hold him for only three days before we must file a habeas corpus." He grinned with grimy teeth. "We are after all a nation of laws."

I asked, "What if it takes more than three days?"

"The solution is a simple one. There are twenty-six such jails in the state. We will move Toledo from one to another for as long as you require." He drained his tequila. "But, of course, you must pay the *federales* in each jail you bring him to."

We thanked him for his hospitality and started out. He walked us to the door, weaving drunkenly. "Whatever you do," he said to us with a pudgy raised finger, "tell no one that you are *policía*. There are guerrillas in that part of the country, *23 septiembre,* and so far they have killed twenty-five of my men. If they learn who you are, they will cut your throats."

I now understood the absence of police and of uniforms.

We left Howard Bell in the town's only motel, a dank and aromatic place, and set off for El Grullo. Our local guide was another threadbare state policeman, a lean, swarthy Indian named Francisco. He and Basilio were old friends. Both were from Guadalajara, and they had joined the state police together. Francisco wore a bandolier of bullets over one slim shoulder and a short-snouted P90 submachine gun on the other. Before we started, Basilio took an identical P90 from under his seat, unfolded it, and slung it across his back. "From here," he said solemnly, "*23 septiembre.*"

Francisco climbed into the front seat next to him; Joe Flores and I endured the jostling of the rock-hard back bench. I had brought my .357, and Joe Flores, his .41 Magnum. We put them in our belts beneath our shirts.

A few miles out of Autlán, we turned off the paved road onto a dirt track. This we followed for some miles through the jungle until Francisco pointed to an even smaller and more rugged mud trail. After sliding and jouncing along it for over an hour, we came to a village half buried in the undergrowth.

"El Grullo," Francisco triumphantly announced.

It was as isolated and pathetic a place as I had ever seen. The plaza was nothing more than a sunbaked sandy clearing among the few run-down buildings. There was a cantina and some derelict houses, tin roofed, most of sun-dried mud brick. Steam was rising from the surrounding vegetation, the sun blazing off the corrugated roofs. When our jeep rolled to a stop, it seemed that most of the town, with nothing better to do, came out to gape at us.

We piled out, sweaty and splattered with mud, and followed Basilio into the cantina. Francisco remained outside to guard the jeep. The bar was a slouching whitewashed room with half a dozen tables and chairs. We ordered beers, and while we drank, three diminutive men materialized from out of the jungle. They were not much more than five feet tall, naked except for ragged shorts, their skin baked brown, their hair hanging in filthy tangles to their shoulders. They made their way across the square toward us. They were barefoot, and I could not imagine how they stood the sizzling sand. For a moment I thought they were wearing yellowed flip-flops, but as they approached I saw that their feet bore an inch or more of calluses. Each had a bow and arrow slung over a shoulder and carried a pair of fussing chickens tied with a length of twine.

"Indians," Basilio said. "They come to trade their chickens for drink and tobacco."

Francisco spoke to them curtly in their dialect, which sounded nothing like Spanish, and they turned away. To me they seemed like a vision from the Stone Age, with their sun-browned bodies, their bows, and their scrawny, sinewy limbs.

We ordered more beers, and Basilio chatted with the bartender, a tall, lanky, balding man with thick forearms. At last I heard him ask about Alfonso Toledo. The bartender stopped short and peered at us. "You know him?" he asked.

Basilio replied that he was Alfonso's cousin, and that his family in Los Angeles had sent him money. He motioned to Joe Flores, who took some bills from his pocket. The bartender eyed them hungrily. Flores put a twenty on the table. "If you can tell us where Alfonso is," Basilio said, "you can keep the change."

The bartender scooped up the money and leaned closer. Faces were staring in at us through the empty window frames. "He was staying out on the road to Ayuquila," he whispered. "A shack with a Madonna painted on the door."

"Is he still there?" Basilio asked. The bartender nodded. "How far?"

"Half an hour. Just follow the road."

We got back into the jeep and rolled out of the village. The road beyond El Grullo was even narrower, and so overgrown with jungle that we had to duck our heads to avoid the branches and tangled vines. There were huge iguanas hanging from the trees, and beyond the edge of town a hand-painted sign nailed to a tree warned PELIGROSO TIGRES.

"Tigers?" I said to Francisco.

"Jaguars," he explained. "But don't worry—they not gonna bother you if they not hungry."

We followed the road to a sandy clearing in the jungle in which three or four tin-roofed shacks slanted on either side. The first had a faded image of the Madonna of Guadalupe painted on the plywood door. We pulled off into the underbrush. It was sunset, but there were no lights inside the shack.

I took out my .357. "I'll go in the front," I said. "Francisco, you back me up. Joe, take the back with Basilio."

We waited a moment until Flores and Basilio had disappeared behind the hut. Then I crossed the road and kicked in the flimsy door. When my boot hit it, it snapped in two like a piece of balsa wood. As soon as Flores heard the sound, he broke in through the back. We faced each other across a tiny, darkened room, guns drawn.

The place was empty.

Toledo had been there; that was clear. We found some clothes, and receipts for money transfers addressed to him. There was no indication that he had been in the shack recently, though. The bed had not been slept in, the cooking pots were cold, and already the ants, beetles, and lizards were beginning to swarm over the place. Joe Flores and I put away our guns and walked outside.

"Gone," I said to Basilio. "And before today."

Francisco nodded. "*Sí, claro,*" he muttered. I asked him what he meant. "He was alerted."

"By who?"

He looked at me as if the answer were obvious. "El Jefe. You paid *la mordida* to find him; Toledo paid *la mordida* to escape. That's two bites for El Jefe."

I felt myself growing angry. "Did you know this before we came here?"

Francisco shrugged his bony shoulders, over which the P90 and bullets hung like the Indians' chickens. "I know El Jefe," he said.

"Then why didn't you tell us? Why did you let us come all the way to this godforsaken place?"

Francisco smiled. "I told you, the *tigres* don't bother you unless they're hungry. El Jefe, he's always hungry."

We drove back into El Grullo in silence. I watched the submachine guns jouncing on the state policemen's backs and wondered what their rules of engagement were. Given the isolation and corruption of the place, I did not doubt that the jungle all around the little villages was littered with bodies. Whether they were victims of bandits, guerrillas, or the police probably did not make much difference.

Then I thought about Compton. There were the gangs, the radicals, the drug dealers, and the crooks, and all of them were armed. They lived in a kind of wilderness, too, in which corruption hung like giant lizards from the trees, and where each distinct 'hood, each turf, was like a village sunk in a jungle prowled by *tigres*.

Hakim Jamal had said that we were nothing but a gang of thugs in blue, that we defended our turf like the Slausons defended theirs. "What's the difference?" he had sneered.

I had not given Jamal an answer then, but I knew what it was—every cop knew it. The difference was a line that separated us from the criminals, one he could not see. We did not live for *la mordida,* and we did not prey on the people who depended on us. We carried weapons, but we used them only when given no choice, and sometimes not even then. Nearly every cop in Compton had been shot at more than once, and many had been shot. The blue that made us visible also made us vulnerable. In either case, it set us apart, marking us as the good guys.

By this time, Hakim Jamal was dead, killed in a drug deal in Boston. I, too, might well be killed in a drug deal, but if I were, it would be because I was trying to prevent it, not profit from it. That was the difference: We were on the right side of the law; the crooks were on the other. Though the line was sometimes razor thin, sometimes blurred, it was there to protect the innocent, and we were there to defend it.

It was dark by the time we got back to El Grullo. We were dirty and hungry, and so we stopped again at the cantina. A mariachi band was playing, and the place was full.

The bartender greeted us with a smirk. "Did you find your cousin?" he asked. He already knew the answer. He offered to buy us each a beer.

The four of us sat at the bar. At every table were one or two women, garishly made up, their blouses pulled down to show their breasts. They were prostitutes, and each one was fatter and homelier than the next. Except one. She was young, and though she was what the bangers called "thick," or heavyset, she had a bright, open face and fine white teeth behind her scarlet lipstick.

The band thrummed and honked through a few raucous tunes while the whores danced and drank with the locals. We ate a supper of beans and rice, and a kind of fish stew called caldillo. Basilio and Francisco took advantage of our expense account to get roaring drunk. They banged on the table in time to the tunes and flirted clumsily with the women, who became more alluring as the night went on. Meanwhile, I was engaged in a serious bout of eye-mating with the young one.

At last, the mariachis packed up their instruments to leave. Basilio staggered to his feet. "Hey!" he shouted. "Where do you think you're going?"

The lead guitarist explained that their set was over.

"Stay!" Basilio bellowed. The musicians said they would like to, but they had to get home to their wives and children. "Fuck them!" Basilio retorted. "We have two American guests here, and they want to dance."

I tugged at his sleeve and told him to let the musicians go.

"No! We want to show our hospitality. Play!"

The musicians apologized with nervous smiles and started toward the door. Basilio cut them off. When the lead guitarist again asked to be allowed to leave, Basilio shrugged the P90 from his back and shoved the truncated snout under the man's chin. "You're not going anywhere, understand?" he grunted.

The guitarist was terrified. He knew that any local cop was capable of killing him, but a drunken one was sure to. He nodded stiffly and took the band back into the bar. As they began playing again, things relaxed. The women got up to dance, and Basilio and Francisco joined them. A bulbous whore in a red wig grabbed Joe Flores by both arms and dragged him to his feet. "I feel like Alfonso Toledo," he said as she hauled him onto the dance floor.

The young woman walked over to my table. "You are *norteamericano*?" she asked. I told her that I was. "Do you like to dance?"

"Con tigo, sí," I replied.

She smiled, and we moved onto the floor. Her eyes were enormously brown, and she swayed her wide hips and small breasts like branches in the wind. When she danced close to me, she smelled of lemons and peppers. Her ample body was warm. "I like to go with you," she whispered to me. I asked her her name. "Maria."

"My hotel is in Autlán," I said.

She edged her face away. "I like to go with you to America."

I thought of the life she must have in El Grullo, the poverty, the hunger, the hours with filthy men on naked mattresses, and, melted by the tequila I had drunk, my heart went out to her. "Come with me to Autlán," I said.

"And then to America?"

"Autlán first."

She smiled and nuzzled back against me, and we danced to the jangling music.

When Basilio finally let the musicians go, I bundled Maria into the jeep between me and Joe Flores. Francisco was still relatively sober, so we hefted the half-conscious Basilio into the front, and Francisco drove. Back in Autlán, I led Maria up to the room we were to share with Howard Bell. He was still awake.

"Did you get him?" he asked anxiously.

We explained what had happened. He slumped onto the bed, then glanced at Maria, who waited by the door. "What's this?"

"I'm taking her back to America," I answered.

Bell's eyes bulged. "What?!"

"He made her a promise," Joe Flores said with a grin.

The Compton city manager looked at me, then at her. "Oh," he grunted.

I got a separate room and spent the night with Maria. She was wild, nearly vicious, using her nails and her white teeth. As I wrestled beneath her, I could not help but remember the sign pinned to the tree: PELIGROSO TIGRES. I had found my jaguar, or she had found me. She wanted to be sure that I would keep my promise.

In the morning, early, I watched Maria dress. Her clothes had been carefully folded on the little rattan chair; I knew they were the best she owned. "When will you take me to America?" she asked as she tugged her blouse down. I felt drained, and guilty.

"I can't this time," I answered. She stopped and fired an accusing look at me. I added quickly, "But I'll come back for you."

"You said," she pouted.

"I'll come back," I told her. I was beginning to feel angry that I had put myself in this position.

"You will not."

"I will."

She looked at me closely. There was more than scrutiny in her eyes, there was suspicion, and shreds of betrayal. "Do you swear on the Mother of God?" she demanded. I told her that I did, solemnly. She peered at me a moment longer. "All right," she decided.

I walked with her outside, where Basilio was nodding in the front seat of the jeep, his skinny frame slumped over the steering wheel. "We're taking Maria home," I told him.

He looked at her dully. "Back there—no way." I said that I was responsible for her and wanted to be sure she got home safely. "Let her walk," he grunted.

"Get in the jeep," I told Maria. "We're going."

Basilio fumed and grumbled all the way back to El Grullo. Maria sat in the back alone. She scarcely spoke to me, and when I turned to look at her, she regarded me with mournful mistrust. We dropped her at the cantina. I kissed her and said good-bye.

"You made a promise," she said.

"I know."

She looked at me a moment longer, then turned and walked across the little sandy square, her hips swaying smugly.

"They always want what they can't have," Basilio said. I turned to look at him. "Women," he added. "They live on dreams."

We started back up the road toward Autlán. It was 6:00 A.M. and already the jungle was sweating. As we made the turn onto the broken pavement, Basilio slowed, then stopped, the idling engine rasping. I glanced at him, and he nodded toward the roadway up ahead.

Five or six figures in dirty fatigues were emerging from the vegetation. They were scrawny and barefoot, and they carried automatic weapons. *"23 septiembre,"* Basilio said. "We better go back."

"No," I answered. I took out my .357. "Drive."

He threw a glance at me, then shoved the spindly gearshift forward. As the jeep picked up speed, he slipped the submachine gun off his back. The guerrillas were splitting up, taking positions on either side of the road. As we approached them, I began firing to the left and right, and Basilio sprayed the roadside with auto fire. The guerrillas fired back wildly, then scattered, disappearing into the jungle as the jeep chugged past. I do not know if we hit any of them, but we did not slow down again until we got to Autlán.

I could not tell Howard Bell what had happened. The *federales* might hear about the gunfight and come looking for us. Howard had been nervous from the time we arrived in Mexico. I was sure that if he knew about the gunfight, he would panic and insist on leaving, and we still had to find Gloria Gonzales and Esther Chavez.

He and Joe Flores were waiting in the lobby cantina.

"You take her home?" Howard asked me. I said that I had. "How did it go?"

"No problem."

He looked at me sidelong. "Are you coming back for her?" he asked with an ironical smile.

"Maybe," I said.

We had learned from relatives that Gloria Gonzales and Esther Chavez were living in Colima, about fifty miles southeast of Autlán. There were no roads that led directly there, and we were forced to make a wide detour around the rugged volcanic terrain that lay between the two towns. By the time we pulled into Colima it was already evening. It lay high on the slopes of a volcano and had the reputation of being the cleanest town in Mexico. After Autlán and El Grullo, it was a pleasant surprise. We checked into the Ceballos Hotel on the *zócalo*, the main square, and began inquiring discreetly after the two women. In less than an hour we had located an aunt of Esther Chavez, and we went to see her.

She was terrified. Clearly, she had been living in dread of the moment we walked into her little tourist boutique. She was a woman past middle age, very pale and slender. She trembled as we identified ourselves and asked to speak with her niece and Gloria Gonzales.

"You cannot take them," the aunt said. "They will never go back."

"We didn't come to take them," Joe Flores explained. "We came only to talk with them. Can you arrange that? In some public place, where Esther and Gloria will feel safe."

Joe's tone seemed to calm her. She agreed to speak with her niece.

The next morning, the aunt came to our hotel. "Esther and Gloria will meet you at the café of the hotel at noon," she told us. "But I and Gloria's grandmother will also be there."

"We understand," Joe Flores said, "and we thank you."

It was the busiest time in the picturesque public square. Cars sped around the gray brick plaza at lethal speed, honking and swerving as pedestrians rushed to and from lunch. The café was under the arches of the ornate hotel, its tables and green umbrellas facing the cathedral, which was topped by a gleaming amber dome. At the center of the square was a fairy-tale-like gazebo where a band played *ranchera* music, which I recognized from my childhood.

When Flores and I arrived just before noon, they were waiting for us. The aunt sat on one side of the two young women, and on the other was a formidable old matron in black upon black lace, *la abuela*. Gloria Gonzales was in her midtwenties, as was her friend Esther Chavez. They were attractive women, small and neatly dressed, and very frightened looking. We sat down at the table opposite them as the aunt twisted distractedly at her napkin and the grandmother eyed us with undisguised disdain.

"We represent the district attorney of Compton," Joe Flores began, addressing himself to Gloria. "He needs you to come back to testify at the trial of the men who shot you."

She shook her head like a willful schoolgirl.

Esther answered for her. "She cannot."

Joe smiled in reply. "We want you to testify as well."

"No!" Esther said.

"We will provide you with the airplane tickets and money and a hotel," Joe went on mildly. "We will meet you at the airport and remain with you until it is time for you to leave."

Gloria Gonzales looked at him closely. "The men who killed my baby, they will go to jail?"

"Only if you testify, and Esther testifies."

"And if they do not?" the aunt asked.

"Then the men will go free."

There was a long silence. It was clear that Gloria was struggling within herself, the memory of the shooting and the lost child tormenting her. At last she said, "If we go back, what of *la migra*?"

"You will have no difficulty with Immigration," Joe answered. "The district attorney has arranged for special visas for you."

Gloria looked at her friend. They had been together in the car; they had shared the nightmare and the loss. Now they did not know what to do, or whether they could believe us or the people we spoke for. We had failed to protect them then; how could they trust us now?

"Gloria," I said at last, "I participated in the investigation of the crime. I saw the photographs . . ." I hesitated as she peered at me, uncertain what I meant.

"The photographs of your baby," I went on. "He was a beautiful boy . . . a strong boy. He would have been a healthy child." There were tears in her eyes, and in Esther's. "The district attorney will prosecute the men for murder, because your baby was a human being, a person, just as if he had been born. It will be an important trial; it will change the law. If we can convict these men of the murder of your unborn baby, other women's babies will be safer."

She was listening to me with a tortured expression of grief coupled with an understanding of the importance of what I was saying. She thought a long moment as the band played in the wedding-cake gazebo across the square and the bells of the cathedral chimed.

Esther took her friend's hand. Both were crying. "Gloria," she said, "what do you want to do?"

"What about you?" Gloria responded.

"I will do whatever you decide."

Gloria looked between Flores and me a moment, then turned to her grandmother. *"Abuela,"* she implored, "what shall I do?"

The grandmother adjusted the black lace mantilla around her shoulders. "You must go," she stated.

Gloria looked at her a long moment and then nodded.

We gave her our business cards and a letter from the DA's office outlining in English and Spanish the arrangements that would be made for the two of them. In turn, they gave us their addresses and numbers at which they and their relatives could be contacted. It was all we needed.

When we got up to go, we thanked them and assured them that everything would be well. I then turned to the *abuela* and thanked her. She declined to take my hand, wrapping hers instead in her mantilla. "My great-grandchild is dead," she replied stonily, "and my granddaughter nearly died. See that nothing happens this time."

Gloria took her arm, and they, Esther, and her aunt crossed the broad square toward the gazebo, where the band still played the folksongs of my childhood.

To celebrate our success, Basilio suggested that we spend the afternoon at Barra de la Navidad, Christmas Beach. We loaded a case of Bohemian beer into the back of the jeep and drove down to the coast.

The beach was broad and tranquil, with soft, russet sand, and coy waves swishing seductively to the shore. The cove was fringed with misted rock formations, and, anchored in the bay, a blue and white fishing boat nodded on the swell, its nets webbed over the side from spidery booms. Basilio shrugged off his sweat-stained fatigues, waded into the surf, and swam out to it, while Howard Bell, Joe Flores, Francisco, and I stripped down and sprawled out on the warm sand.

In ten minutes, Basilio was back. He had brought with him mesh bags swarming with live shrimp, which we roasted on a fire pit scooped in the sand. When I tasted the first one, I had to close my eyes in sheer satisfaction. The shrimp exploded in my mouth like ripe grapes, flooding my senses with rich voluptuousness. After a dozen or more of them, and a few bottles of the creamy beer, I was at peace. I lay on the sand, lulled by the music of the surf, and realizing for the first time since I arrived in Mexico that this was a beautiful place.

I had sensed it in the jungles around El Grullo, and in the volcanic slopes that spined in verdant ridges toward Colima, and in the passion of Maria, and in the invisible threat of jaguars. This was the country my people had come from. My great-grandfather and his French army had not been able to subdue it, but neither had the corrupt police officials we had dealt with, nor the ragged bandits we had fired at. No one would ever be able to conquer Mexico, I reflected as I lay upon the near-deserted beach, sated with shrimp and beer. It was a force of nature, seductive and dangerous and raw, and beyond anyone's ability to grasp—only to marvel at and be mystified by. Mexico, I realized, was a mystery in my blood.

It was time to go home. As Basilio drove us back to Guadalajara airport, I finally told Joe Flores and Howard Bell about the shootout on the road from El Grullo. As I had expected, Bell was furious.

"What? What?!" he sputtered. "Why didn't you tell me?"

"Because I knew you'd want to leave."

"God damn you, Baker, you're damn right I would!"

Joe Flores interrupted. "Then we'd have missed the women."

"City council doesn't give a shit about the women!" Bell shouted.

"But I do," Flores countered. "Rick did the right thing."

There was nothing Bell could do now. He slumped in the backseat. "We've got to get out of this fucking country," he fumed, "before the *federales* catch up with us. God damn it to hell." He lapsed into sullen silence.

Basilio dropped us at the airport, and we gave him the last of our money. When we checked in at the counter, we were told that our flight to L.A. was delayed. Howard Bell began rumbling about being captured and spending the rest of his life in a Mexican prison. While Joe Flores tried to calm him down, I searched for a drinking fountain.

As I did, two cars pulled up outside the terminal, and six men in suits and sunglasses emerged. They walked in and fanned out across the lobby. As I bent over to take a drink, my coat rode up, exposing the gun in my waistband. One of the men saw it, and they started toward me. I saw them coming, and I hurried back to Flores and Bell. *"Federales,"* I said.

The men were converging on us. We grabbed our bags and darted out of the terminal.

"Where the fuck are we going?!" Howard Bell demanded.

There was only one plane on the tarmac, a bright yellow Hughes Airwest "banana."

"There," I said.

We made a dash for the plane as the *federales* spilled out of the terminal.

The ramp was pressed against the open door, and we raced up it two steps at a time. The stewardess greeted us uncertainly. I pulled out my badge. "I need to talk to the pilot," I told her.

She led me down the aisle past the few passengers to the cockpit. The pilot and copilot were going through their preflight checklist. I shoved my badge between them. "We're cops from Compton, and we have to get out of here right now," I said.

I could see the *federales* swarming toward the plane. The pilot saw them, too.

"No problem, bro," he answered. "Get in the back and sit down."

Bell, Flores, and I took our seats as the engines whirred to life. The *federales* were surrounding the plane, yelling at the pilot to stop. In a moment they were forced away by the exhaust. The pilot pivoted the little jet, taxied out to the runway, and took off. I sat back in my seat and exhaled deeply.

The stewardess was at my elbow. "Please buckle your seat belt," she said, smiling, "and welcome aboard, Officer."

Back in Compton, we were received as heroes. Though we had not captured Alfonso Toledo, we had secured the appearance of Gloria Gonzales and Esther Chavez, and the prosecutors were delighted. They hoped to make legal history: the first conviction for murder in the killing of a fetus.

When I saw John Soisson at the station the next day, he seemed genuinely surprised. "When we heard what you were doing," he said, "nobody expected you to come back."

Two days later, Joe Flores and I met Gloria Gonzales and Esther Chavez at LAX and drove them to their hotel. The following morning, they testified in the trial of Bob Livingston and Scope Watson. They were on the stand all day, while we sat with them in the courtroom. Both women told the story of the shooting calmly, in Spanish, which was translated for the jury. I was proud of them, and as Flores and I took them back to LAX, I told them so. "You were very courageous."

Gloria Gonzales smiled sadly. "You were right," she said. "I had to do it for my baby."

Livingston and Watson were found guilty of first-degree murder for the death of the baby, and attempted murder in the shooting of the mother. They were sentenced to twenty-five years on each charge. They were also convicted of robbery and kidnapping. They would spend the rest of their lives in prison. It was a satisfying conclusion to a tragic story, but the story did not end there.

Three months after the trial, I received a tip that Alfonso Toledo was in Compton. He had come back, my informant said, to see his three kids. He was saying at a friend's place, and he planned to slip in and out of the city within forty-eight hours.

I was on detective duty alone that morning. Everyone else was either on calls or in court. So I checked out my dick car and drove to the address the informant had given me, on 133rd Street off Grandee. The house appeared to be empty. I tried the front door; it was unlocked. I slipped inside.

There was no one home. I searched the place, checking each room until I came to the back bedroom. The closet door was ajar. I took out my gun and pushed it open with my foot. There among the hanging clothes was Alfonso Toledo, cowering like a not very bright child playing hide-and-seek. I ordered him to get out.

He was not armed, and I hooked him up and marched him outside. "I missed you in El Grullo," I told him in Spanish as I put him into the car. He looked at me uncomprehending. "The little hut with the Madonna on the door? El Jefe told you I was coming."

He stared at me. "That was you?"

"It was me," I answered. "Thanks for coming back."

He was sentenced to twenty-five years in prison, of which he served eight. When he was released, he returned to Compton, to his wife and kids, and also to his construction job. He was no killer—he had simply been caught in the cauldron of violence that was Compton in those days. We never had any contact with him again.

There was one final note. A few weeks after the trial of Livingston and Watson, I received a letter postmarked Colima. It was just a few words, written in a florid hand in Spanish, thanking Joe Flores and me for what we had done. It was from *la abuela*.

The Councilman's Dilemma, the Back Door, and the Giant

The Nation of Islam had long been a presence in Compton. In the late seventies, the Muslims opened a mosque on Long Beach Boulevard opposite the Golden Garter. Whether they were unaware of the Garter's reputation or they chose the spot deliberately I do not know. However, it was not long before they were calling the police department on a regular basis to complain about the goings-on at the Garter.

The complaints fell usually under the rubric of disturbing the peace: loud noise, drunkenness, rowdy women in the parking lot. We were obliged to respond, at least to the extent of sending a patrol car to park outside the Garter for a few minutes. The responding officer, having spoken to Vito, would then cross the street to assuage the Muslims.

Of course, since the Garter enjoyed the special protection of the CPD, nothing was done. Finally, the Muslims organized a picket line around the club and circulated a petition demanding that it be shut down. When this failed, they took their grievance to the city council. One of their most vocal supporters on the council was Lester Caldwell, the former Alabama civil rights worker who had forced us to fire the CPOA's first attorney.

Caldwell took up the Muslims' cause, denouncing the Garter as a menace to the morals of the community.

A few weeks later, I was patrol sergeant when we received yet another call from the mosque, this time reporting a man exposing himself in the Garter's parking lot. I got into my patrol car and drove over to Long Beach Boulevard. Indeed, it was true. There was a middle-aged black man lying half unconscious in a corner of the lot, his fly gaping open, his member exposed, and his trousers soaked with urine. When I got him to his feet, I realized who it was: Lester Caldwell.

Vito told me that Caldwell was a frequent customer, and that he often had too much to drink. On this occasion, he had staggered outside to take a leak and had passed out in the process. I put him in the backseat of my car and drove him to the station. The watch commander that night was Mardrue Bunton, a senior lieutenant. When I half carried Caldwell inside, he asked me what I had.

"A city councilman," I answered.

Bunton peered closely at the man. "Holy shit," he muttered. He was an easygoing commander who liked to run a calm watch, avoiding paperwork and administrative hassles. For him, this was a nightmare. "What do you wanna do with him, Rick?" he asked.

I told him that there was no point in arresting and booking Caldwell, that more could be achieved by filing the paperwork and burying it. So I filled out a five-by-eight card, making a record of the incident, sobered Lester Caldwell up, and drove him home. The next morning, the Muslims called demanding to know what had been done about the naked man at the Garter. I asked if I could come over to discuss the matter.

At the mosque, I met with Ali Hassan and explained that the man had been taken briefly into custody and then released. The Muslims wanted more—they insisted that they would go to the city council and file a formal complaint.

"You don't want to do that," I replied.

"Why not?" Hassan wanted to know.

"The man I picked up," I began carefully, "he's a fairly prominent black city official." That stopped him. "And I thought it was best just to let the matter drop. You know, to spare him the embarrassment."

The Muslims got the hint and backed off. I complimented them on their program of community pride and public morals, bought some bean pies for the station, picked up a copy of *Muhammad Speaks,* and left. After that, Lester Caldwell never again raised the matter of the Garter's morals in the city council.

In the fall of 1980, the local congressman, Mervyn Dymally, asked me, as the former president of the CPOA, to represent him on the regional selection committee for the United States military academies. Every congressman has the authority to nominate young constituents for full scholarships to the army, navy, air force, and merchant marine academies, and the fact that Dymally chose me as his proxy was both an honor and an index of the importance of the Police Officers Association. I was happy to accept.

I drove to Leuzinger High School in Lawndale, near the L.A. airport, and, together with two other civic leaders, interviewed a large number of student hopefuls from around the county. Each had a 4.0 GPA, with many academic and community service honors. They were an impressive group of boys and girls, and I enjoyed both meeting them and hearing their stories, some of which involved overcoming great obstacles. It was a pleasure to know that I was helping them realize their dream of higher education and service to the nation.

It was also sobering to realize how different a world they inhabited from the gangbangers of Compton. They had much in common, but the differences that separated them were differences of life and death.

All had faced trials and setbacks; all had received raw deals of one kind or another. Some had transformed them into sources of strength, others into excuses for violence and murder. The futures of children are balanced on a knife's edge of character and choice, and perhaps a little luck. With proper parenting, or good guidance, or moral role models, any child, no matter how unfair his circumstances, can succeed, and excel, and live a life of accomplishment and dignity. Without these, what will become of him? Every day on the streets of Compton I saw that the answer, too often, is a dizzying descent through mayhem to a lifetime wasted in prison, or to an early death.

One of my duties as a detective was to speak periodically at schools and to community service groups as part of the department's public safety and PR campaigns. Though some officers regarded this work as a waste of time, I took it seriously. To my mind, citizens had to know that we were on their side. Young people had to be persuaded to stay clear of gangs, and old people needed reassurance that we were there to protect them.

Almost all of the people I talked to at these community meetings were black, but that made no difference. For the truth of the matter was that we in Compton protected the lives and property of more black people per officer than any other police force in the nation. In all my years in the department, I never encountered a situation in which an officer failed to risk his safety or even his life for a citizen because of the color of his or her skin. As human beings, we were not blind to color, but as police officers, we had to be.

On one occasion, I was invited to address a group at a senior citizens center at Wilson Park. I was to advise them on ways in which they could avoid being mugged or robbed by the thugs who were saturating the city, and making it impossible for the elderly to leave their homes at night. Some fifty people were in attendance. I was about halfway through my presentation when the center's director, a social worker named Stuart, interrupted and called me aside. It was clear from his demeanor that the matter was urgent. So as not to alarm the elderly audience, I announced a fifteen-minute break. I followed Stuart into the hallway and asked him what the problem was.

"There's something going on outside," he told me. "It looks like a robbery."

He led me to the center's office, one wall of which had a big bay window overlooking the park. Among the trees across the street were three young black men in trench coats standing over a black teenager, who lay terrified on the ground. As I watched, one of the men slid a rifle from under his trench coat and pressed the muzzle to the kid's head.

There was no time to get to the front door. At any moment, the man with the rifle could put a bullet into the kid's brain. I pulled out my gun. It was a .45 caliber Colt Mark IV automatic, not the .357 I always carried. I had not wanted to frighten the seniors by packing a cannon, so I had opted for the smaller pistol. I raised the gun and took careful aim. As I did, the secretary in the office screamed and ducked underneath her desk.

I hesitated. I could not know whether the rifle was real, a BB gun, or a toy. Also, I would be shooting through a plate glass window, which might deflect the shot, missing the man with the rifle, or even hitting the teenager.

In the next second there was a muted explosion, and I saw the kid's head shatter in a spray of blood. I told Stuart to call the station and an ambulance, and I dashed out the door as fast as I could. By the time I reached the park, the three men were fleeing the scene. I ran to the kid, and, though I could see that he was still breathing, there was a hole in his forehead from which blood was spurting straight up in the air and spattering over his face.

I had to make a decision—whether to stay with the kid, do CPR, and try to stop the bleeding, or go after the killers. My instincts told me that it was too late for the kid, so I left him for the ambulance and chased after the three men.

They had ducked down Rose Avenue off the park, which ended in an alley that ran behind a church. I dashed into the alleyway, my gun out in front of me. They were gone. The only person back there was the minister, who was standing on a ladder, painting the window frames of the church. I asked him if he had seen three black males in trench coats run past.

"No," he said. "No, I haven't . . ." As he did so, though, he motioned with his eyes toward a fire escape behind me.

I turned and saw the three men huddled on the top landing. The shooter was pointing the rifle right down at me. He had me cold. I had seen these three kill a kid five minutes before, and now the murder weapon was aimed at me. The only cover was a clutch of trash cans, and for an instant I considered making a dive for them. There was also the minister to consider, though; they might shoot him or try to take him hostage.

So I did the only thing left to me, what the marines had trained me to do—I let out a guttural yell and I charged them.

All the way up the twisting flights of iron stairs I continued screaming at the top of my lungs, waving my gun. When the men saw me coming, they panicked. They were passing the rifle back and forth, yelling, "You shoot him! You shoot him!"

I reached the top flight and threw myself on them. I grabbed the rifle and flung it down the fire escape, and since I had no other weapon, I bashed at their heads with my .45. Blood began to gush, and they clawed at one another trying to get away. I kept pistol-whipping them until they lay quiet on the metal grating. I put cuffs on one, stood on the second's back, and aimed my pistol at the third. In the distance, I could hear sirens.

As the units rolled into Rose Avenue, I marched the three men down the fire escape to the alley, where I picked up the rifle, which was loaded and cocked. The reverend still stood on his ladder, having witnessed the whole thing. When I nodded my thanks to him, he just stared back, numb, the bushy paintbrush still clutched in his hand.

The shooter was Harvey Hartsfield, a member of the Santana Blocc Crips. His street name was Sag, because of his oversized, baggy pants. Though he was still a juvenile, he had already been involved in several shootings. The other two were Crips nicknamed Tank and Cranberry. I handed them over to the patrolmen.

As I was making out my report back at the station, the deputy chief, Roger Moulton, whom Chief Rouzan had brought over from LAPD, approached me.

"I heard about what you did," he said, and he put out his hand. Then he asked me, "Why didn't you just shoot them?"

It was the second time I had been asked that question. Both times, it was an outsider to Compton who had asked it. I gave him the same answer I had given the FBI agent after the Capitol Bank robbery. "It's not the way we do things."

Moulton shook his head. "You'd just seen them commit a murder. They could easily have shot you. Why didn't you kill them?"

I put the unfinished report aside and turned to him. "I didn't have to," I replied. Moulton looked at me, puzzled. "When I was running up those steps, I could see the fear in their eyes. And when I got on top of them, I knew they were beaten. All they wanted was to get away. You don't kill an animal when it's trying to run away from you. You don't have to."

The truth of the matter was that, given the number of violent situations we faced, including shots fired, man with a gun, armed robbery, attempted murder, and murder in the first degree, there were dozens of situations in which we could have—and other departments would have—used lethal force. Compton cops had a different mentality. We faced so much violence, and dealt with so many killers and would-be killers, that we had developed a sixth sense about when to use a gun and when not to. In almost every case, we chose not to.

A study by UCLA showed that a Compton police officer was eleven times more likely to be a victim of violence than any other officer in the state. Yet in the 112-year history of the department, we lost only two officers to violence, both in the same incident on the same day.

Whenever I read of cases in which police officers have shot an armed suspect ten, twenty, or thirty times, I have to shake my head. It is likely that a Compton cop would have defused the situation without lethal force, and would either have taken the suspect into custody to face trial or dealt with him personally on the spot.

In the Wilson Park shooting, I had done my job, as I and all Compton officers did it every day, with no expectation of reward, or even of recognition. So I was surprised when, a few days later, I was notified that I was to receive a special commendation from the state assembly. Our representative, Frank Vicencia, sent me a plaque on behalf of the legislature recognizing my action in capturing three killers single-handedly.

In the meantime, my mother had heard what had happened, and she mentioned it to her friend Councilwoman Jane Robbins, the descendant of Compton's founder who had attended John Start's (and Tom Cochée's) going-away party at the Garter. Jane Robbins invited me to a meeting of the city council as a special guest, and there the new mayor, Walter Tucker, presented me with a plaque honoring me for heroism.

It was an irony upon an irony. Through the CPOA I had helped defeat Douglas Dollarhide, and we had also replaced two members of the council, which had never previously singled out a police officer for tribute. In addition to that, the idea for the occasion had come from the member who had attended the party at which Chief Cochée had been lured to his resignation. I accepted the plaque as graciously as I could, being careful to point out that any Compton cop would have acted exactly as I had.

"My only regret," I added, "was that I was unable to prevent Andre Avery's death."

In my final report of the crime, I had learned something about the victim—the terrified teenager whom I had seen murdered that day in the park. He was a Compton kid, born and raised, and, like me, he was an amateur boxer who belonged to the same Boys' Club I had. By all accounts, he was a model kid; mannerly, well behaved, a good student. The one fact I learned that I wished I had not known was why he had been murdered.

He was walking home through the park from a friend's house, where he and several other boys met every weekend to play board games. The Crips had heard he had a lot of money, and when they stopped him and demanded it, he reached into his pocket and pulled out a thick wad. They grabbed it, then threw it furiously on the ground. And they shot Andre Avery to death.

It was Monopoly money.

Because Compton cops dealt with so much crime and so many criminals, we developed a special relationship with the judiciary. We often settled cases on the street, either with humor, negotiation, fists, or clubs, both to save us time and to spare the judicial system, which would have collapsed under the sheer weight of the rising tide of criminality. Even when cases reached the court system, we sometimes felt it was necessary to intervene to make sure that the worst of the worst did not escape the justice they deserved. We called this our "back door policy."

Linda Yarborough was a young woman who lived on the east side in one of the last remaining white enclaves. She was eight and a half months pregnant, and she made the mistake of walking into the west side after dark. A local thug grabbed her off the street and took her to a nearby garage to rape her. She resisted so violently, screaming and yelling, that the thug beat her into submission. He dragged her to a corner of the garage and shoved her facedown over a workbench, but her belly was so big that he could not get into her. In a frustrated rage, he beat her again and forced her to straddle two chairs, bending her swollen stomach between them.

A CPD unit was working the neighborhood, and as it cruised past the garage, the officer, Brent Nielsen, heard Linda Yarborough's sobs and yelps. He broke in the door and caught the rapist in the midst of his grotesque assault. Nielsen clubbed the thug, hooked him up, and called for an ambulance. Linda lay bloated and bleeding on the grimy floor.

The case was assigned to me for investigation. I knew the rapist, a lifelong criminal who had been involved in other assaults, always against helpless victims such as children and old people. Attacking a near-term pregnant woman was exactly the kind of bestial behavior his twisted mind craved. Though the circumstances were clear-cut, the case was by no means ironclad.

The thug's lawyer was already preparing a defense on the grounds that his client had been struck by the officer, that he had not been read his rights, that his confession had been coerced, and that the woman had had no business walking in the west side neighborhood at night. The suggestion would be that the rapist was, in some sense, a victim, both of the woman and of the cops.

The judge in the case was Jimmy Mansfield, my old classmate from Compton College. It was Jimmy whom I had tried to help in his painful transition from the East Coast, even taking him with us to dance clubs in Hollywood. I had singled him out, despite his social awkwardness, as a bright and ambitious kid, and, in fact, he had gone to law school, worked for a prestigious L.A. firm, and been appointed to the municipal court bench.

I called him at the courthouse one evening and invited him to meet me at King's Restaurant in Long Beach. Over dinner, we rehashed old times at Compton College and talked about the people we knew and what had become of them. Some were lawyers and doctors, some had become famous athletes, and a few, like me, had gone into law enforcement.

"You got the best of it," Jimmy said, laughing.

"Or the worst," I replied. "Take this case of the rape of the pregnant woman."

Jimmy frowned at me. "You know I can't discuss that."

"Yeah, I know," I replied. "I know that you can't discuss the fact that this scumbag has made a career of attacking and raping helpless people. That he preys on old women and kids, and even a woman who's three weeks away from giving birth."

He regarded me dispassionately and went on with his dinner, saying nothing.

"I know you can't discuss the fact that he beat this woman, nearly broke her arm," I went on. "That he forced her to straddle two chairs, which might have driven her into labor, and that when our guy caught him, he had his dick so far up inside her, he could have ruptured her womb and caused her to lose the baby and bleed to death."

"No," said Jimmy, "I can't discuss that."

I sipped at my wine. "And I know I can't discuss with you the fact that I am as sure that he'll prey on some other innocent person, maybe somebody's daughter or grandmother, if he's let off, as I am that this is a pretty good Napa Valley merlot."

"No, you can't," Jimmy said, daubing at the corners of his mouth with his napkin. "Because that would prejudice me; it would contaminate my mind."

"And we wouldn't want that," I agreed. "Just like we wouldn't want his lawyer contaminating your mind with the idea that this eight-months-pregnant woman somehow deserved what she got."

Jimmy straightened in his chair. "I have to listen to both sides, Rick, the defense and the DA."

"And you have to listen to Charles Dickens, too: 'If the law permits this, the law is an ass.'"

Jimmy regarded me with a wry smile. "You're not suggesting that I'm an ass, are you, Rick?"

"No, Judge," I answered, "but you sure were one hell of a pathetic dancer."

Jimmy Mansfield smiled.

When the case came up for trial, Judge Mansfield denied every one of the defense motions to dismiss on the grounds of police misconduct. When his lawyer tried to put the raped woman on trial, the judge vehemently refused to allow it. "It is a not a crime to go walking in your own city," he snapped. "And if it ever is, we will all be in danger."

The jury found the man guilty both of rape and of assault. Judge Mansfield sentenced him to the maximum for both crimes. I never discussed the case with him again. However, some weeks later I learned that Linda Yarborough had had her baby, a big, healthy boy.

There was another case in which I used the Compton back door policy, and that involved the death of a suspect while in police custody.

Jonathan Wilson was a gentle giant, a six-foot-five-inch 240-pound retarded man whom many of us in the department had known since he was a boy. He lived with his mother and his teenaged sister, who was pregnant, and though he often kidded and joked about breaking people's heads with his enormous strength, he had never harmed anyone we knew of.

Then he got into PCP. On angel dust, Jonathan Wilson became every cop's nightmare. He was massive and powerful, and with the drug in his system, his strength was magnified tenfold. However, he remained a six-year-old mentally, so it was impossible to reason with him. PCP had turned Jonathan Wilson into a nuclear bomb.

One night, the Wilsons' neighbors put in a call of a violent disturbance at the house. There was shouting and the sounds of furniture being thrown and the screams of women. Two officers responded, Reuben Chavira and Jasper Jackson, and they found mayhem inside the house. Jonathan was cranked out of his feeble mind on dust. He had beaten his mother senseless and punched his pregnant sister in the stomach. Blood was pouring from between her legs as she lay half conscious on the kitchen floor. When Jonathan saw the cops, he let out a hoot-owl screech and darted into the bathroom, locking himself in. Chavira called for an ambulance and backup, and he and Jackson began battering at the door.

Inside, they could hear Jonathan howling, and the sound of metal rending and water gushing. As they continued beating at the door, water began pouring out from under it. When they broke in, Jonathan was standing mad-eyed in the bathtub, holding the toilet up over his head. Water was geysering from the broken pipe, soaking him and them. He had ripped the toilet out of the floor, and he threw it at the officers as they rushed at him.

By now, three backups had arrived, and they barreled into the bathroom. Water was still spraying from the floor, and Jonathan was tossing Chavira and Jackson up against the sink and into the bathtub. He turned on the other three officers, and, though they grappled at him all together, he threw them off as if they were dolls.

Finally, Jackson managed to trip Jonathan, and he toppled to the flooded floor. On instinct, Reuben Chavira jammed his boot against Jonathan's throat and held him choking until the other officers could cuff and truss him. They tied his ankles to his shackled wrists, and together the soaking officers lifted him and carried him out of the house.

By the time they got Jonathan into the backseat of the unit, his breathing was strained. Chavira and Jackson drove as quickly as they could to a hospital, and, though the ER team worked over him frantically, Jonathan Wilson, the gentle giant, died within minutes, asphyxiated by a broken windpipe. When Chavira and Jackson were told the news, they nearly cried.

The case was assigned to me for formal investigation. I knew the officers involved, and I knew Jonathan Wilson and the ferocious and devastating effect that his PCP addiction had had on him. It had been a terrible tragedy, a confluence of human frailty in a massive frame and the drug culture of Compton, that did not leave even the feebleminded at peace. It was as if Lenny in *Of Mice and Men* had met Faust's Mephistopheles.

I hoped the matter would end with that, but it did not. Lawyers mobbed the Wilsons, and before long the family had filed a multimillion-dollar wrongful death lawsuit against the city. Jonathan Wilson had died while in police custody, the attorneys were trumpeting, though they did not mention the fact that he had beaten his own mother and pregnant sister into unconsciousness.

An inquest was scheduled at which the cause of death and the results of the autopsy would be announced. Our local pathologist told me in advance that his tests had revealed no evidence of PCP in Jonathan's blood. I knew that in the absence of such evidence it was likely that the city would negotiate a settlement with the Wilsons' attorneys, and that Chavira and Jackson would be held responsible for the death. That, in turn, might mean suspension, a trial, and even jail time for the officers who had tried so desperately to take him into custody without using their guns.

I spoke to Inspector Gil Sandoval, who was in charge of detectives. He was another of the LAPD brass who had been brought over by Rouzan, and I knew that he had connections in the L.A. County coroner's office.

"I need to talk to them before the inquest," I told Sandoval.

"That's highly irregular," he responded.

"This whole damn thing is irregular," I answered, "and it could get a lot more irregular unless we do something."

A few days later, on the eve of the inquest, Inspector Sandoval and I had lunch at Taix Restaurant on Sunset Boulevard in Los Angles with the commissioner in charge of the case for the coroner's office. I laid out the entire investigation as I understood it: that Jonathan Wilson had been high on PCP, that Chavira, Jackson, and the other officers had done their best to restrain him, and that he had died as a result of the struggle in their effort to take him into custody. We all knew Jonathan, I told him, and the tragic irony was that, in their attempt to save his life, the officers had inadvertently brought about his death.

The commissioner heard me out in silence. "Don't say anything," he said at last. I asked him what he meant. "At the inquest, all of you take the Fifth. Decline to testify until this whole mess can be sorted out."

The next day, the Wilsons gave heartbreaking testimony about how Jonathan had meant no harm, how the officers had ganged up on him, and how they had hog-tied him and carried him out of the house. When the coroner called Chavira and Jackson, they invoked their Fifth Amendment right. Unable to budge them, the coroner called me.

"Detective Baker," he asked when I had been sworn in, "what do you know about this incident?"

"I respectfully decline to answer the question on the grounds that it may tend to incriminate me," I answered.

"Do you intend to answer that way to every question?" he said.

"Yes, sir," I responded.

The coroner had no choice but to suspend the hearing.

Meanwhile, I had been looking for some way to prove that Jonathan Wilson had been under the influence of PCP. The L.A. coroner's report had been inconclusive, but I learned that a lab in Orange County had developed a neurological test for the presence of toxic chemicals that was ten times more sensitive than that used by the L.A. office. During the suspension, I took custody of Jonathan's brain and drove it down to Fullerton. While the lawyers wrangled over the inquest and negotiated with the city council for a settlement, I waited for the lab results. In a few days, they came.

Jonathan Wilson's brain showed definite signs of the presence of PCP.

I took the evidence to the L.A. coroner, and he showed it to the Wilsons' attorneys, who abandoned their case. Jonathan Wilson's brain, which had rendered him a helpless child before the PCP, had exonerated our officers. The gentle giant had been a victim not of police brutality but of the brutality of the dope dealers who had not scrupled to sell their poison even to the most innocent of our citizens.

A few weeks later, I received a call at the station from an unexpected source. It was Linda Yarborough. "I just wanted to let you know," she said, "that I named my baby Rick, after you." I told her that I was flattered. "So," she continued in a coquettish voice, "can we get together sometime? You know, maybe have dinner?"

The image of Susie from the Service Center flashed through my mind. "No thanks," I told her. "I don't think so."

There was a long silence on the phone. Then Linda said, "Are you sure, honey?"

"Yes," I told her. "I'm absolutely sure."

A Gun to My Head, Casinos,
and Mulberry Street

Someone wrote that policemen are soldiers working alone, and armies are policemen working in unison. In small cities with low crime rates, police are peacekeepers, negotiators, mediators between government and citizens. In the big cities, they are like an army sent into the field to maintain order. In most cases, they do not live in the neighborhoods they patrol, and often they do not even live in the cities where they work. Compton was different. Most of us had been born or raised in the city, some still lived there, and all of us had strong ties to it.

Compton was not our assignment, it was our element. We all knew each other, and we knew the criminals. That put us in a unique situation: We were protecting our friends and neighbors, and in many cases arresting their sons and daughters. We were close to the criminal element not by choice but by destiny.

If the Compton Police Department was an army, it was an urban guerrilla army. There were no battlefields in Compton; the entire city was one, and ours was a house-to-house fight in which every kind of weapon was used. Whether it was the broad expanse of Compton Boulevard or the constricted alleys of Fruit Town, we had to be ready to go into combat at any moment.

At its usual strength, the CPD counted 130 officers. There were three shifts each day, with forty officers per shift. Of these, a quarter were at the station doing administrative work, and so, at any given time, no more than thirty police officers worked the streets. In a city of nine square miles, this allowed three cops per square mile, as opposed to fifteen per square mile in Los Angeles. And with some ten thousand crooks, addicts, and gangbangers, this meant one cop per thirty-three hundred criminals. Such things as Miranda warnings, prolonged negotiations, warrants, probable cause, and the time and paperwork of arrests for minor offenses were luxuries we could not afford.

Had we not been a homegrown force, had we not known the city and its criminals intimately, had we not been willing to bend the rules and use whatever means were necessary, we would have been overwhelmed, and Compton would have dissolved into anarchy. As it was, we kept the lid on, and we kept ourselves alive.

In the history of the CPD, only three officers died in the line of duty. One, Dess Phipps, was killed in a freak automobile accident. The other two, Kevin Burrell and Jimmy MacDonald, were the only officers who died from criminal violence. Burrell was a veteran cop, a giant like Dave Hall at six foot five and three hundred pounds. MacDonald was a youngster who had been on the police reserve for only eighteen months. He had been offered a job with a department in Northern California and was to have left Compton the following day.

In 1993, they pulled over a speeding car in what they thought was a routine traffic stop. What they did not know was that the driver was Regis Thomas, one of the Bloods' most notorious Bounty Hunters, who had recently been released on a charge of attempted murder, the only witness to the shooting having been gunned down on the eve of the trial. Thomas was not from Compton; he was an L.A. banger who haunted Nickerson Gardens on Imperial Highway, Los Angeles's most deadly housing project.

As Burrell and MacDonald walked up on Thomas's car, Thomas jumped out and began shooting. Both men were hit several times. They went down, and Thomas coolly walked over to each and put a bullet in his head.

I have often thought that if Thomas had been a Compton criminal, Kevin Burrell and Jimmy MacDonald would be alive today.

In 1975, I came close to a situation like this, but I survived.

Craig Electronics, one of the companies in the industrial tract along the 91 Freeway, reported the theft of an entire shipment of citizens band radios. Shortly after the theft, Joe Ferrell, Johnny Garrett, and I arrested a small-time drug dealer nicknamed Birdhead for possession of five balloons of heroin. Birdhead, whose handle came from the fact that drugs had so scrambled his brain he scarcely knew who he was, offered me a deal.

"You let me go, Rick," he stammered, "and I'll give you a big, big bust." I asked him how big. "Them radios that got stolen over at Craig's," he said. I asked who had taken them. Birdhead lowered his voice, his eyes searching for imaginary snitches. "Jerry Cofer. But you can't tell nobody I told you 'cause Cofer's a bad dude, man; he'll kill me."

I knew Jerry Cofer. He was a tough, mean professional thief who worked not only Compton but the surrounding cities as well. I had arrested him once for possession of stolen property. I asked Birdhead if he knew where Cofer was keeping the radios. He said he would take us there.

Ferrell, Garrett, and I put Birdhead into the back of our dick unit and drove to the address, an apartment building on Elizabeth Street on the east side. We told Birdhead to stay on the floor of the car while we checked out the building.

"What if he's in there, man?" Birdhead said, panicking. I told him that if we caught Cofer, he was to jump out of the car and disappear.

While Ferrell and Garrett watched the front of the building, I went around the back. Birdhead had said that Cofer was living on the third floor, so I climbed the fire escape and peered in through the window. Though it was dusk, and the light was fading, I could see that the tiny apartment was packed with boxes labeled CRAIG. There must have been thirty or forty of them, still unopened, stacked from floor to ceiling.

At that point, I should have left Ferrell and Garrett to guard the place while I went back to the station, filled out a report, and called a judge for a search warrant, but if Cofer was out arranging the sale of the radios, I might not have much time. I checked the back door, which was locked, took out my pocket knife, and jimmied it open.

It was getting dark now, and the apartment seemed empty. I made my way through the labyrinth of boxes, having to squeeze sideways among them to get to the hallway that led to the front door. I was going to bring in Ferrell and Garrett and call for a truck to pick up the radios—but as I moved down the darkened hallway, a door at the end suddenly swung open and a pucker of cold steel was shoved against my forehead.

"I got you, you motherfucker!" a voice hissed from the darkness. I froze. There was a bulking Magnum revolver pressed to my head.

I could not see the man who held it, but I had my own gun out, and I pointed it at his stomach. "No, motherfucker," I said. "I got you."

There was a breathless moment while neither of us moved.

"Put it down or I'll blow your fucking guts out," I said.

"Rick?" the voice answered. "Is that you?"

"Yeah, Jerry, it's me."

"Oh, shit, man." Cofer stepped back and threw his revolver on the floor. "I thought you was a burglar," he said.

I switched the hall light on. Jerry Cofer was stark naked.

"I was asleep," he explained. "Shit, Rick, if I'd known it was you . . . Excuse me, man, I'da never shot *you*."

"Yeah," I said. "I appreciate that, but I don't believe it."

He seemed genuinely contrite. "No, man, it's true. I got nothin' against you. Forgive me, man."

By this time Ferrell and Garrett had come in through the back door with their guns drawn. They found me in the hallway with a buck-naked Jerry Cofer, surrounded by boxes of stolen radios. Ferrell asked if everything was all right.

"Yeah," I answered. "My buddy Jerry and I were just talking."

The truth was that I was shaking. When I picked up Cofer's gun, I saw that it was loaded and cocked. If he had so much as twitched, he would have blown my brains out right there in that dingy hallway. Only the fact that I knew him, and that he recognized my voice, had saved my life. Once again, I had come within a hairsbreadth of death.

We hooked Cofer up and called for a truck to collect the evidence. Ferrell and Garrett stayed in the apartment while I walked Cofer down to the car. Birdhead had fled, so Jerry and I were alone. Instead of putting him in the car, I took the cuffs off. He looked at me, uncomprehending.

"I'm turning you loose," I told him.

"What for?"

"For not killing me, that's what for," I said.

Cofer nodded at me slowly. I had had no search warrant, so I knew that it was unlikely that I could get a conviction if the case went to trial. The search and seizure had been completely illegal. I also knew that Jerry Cofer would put the word out that Rick Baker had done him a solid.

He shook his head. "You know, man," he said, "you cost me a shitload of money."

"What the fuck?" I answered. "I just gave you a pass."

Cofer smiled. "I was gonna sell them radios to the Muslims. They were gonna pay me fifty grand for them." These were the same Muslims who had been so irate about the girls at the Golden Garter.

We returned the radios to the Craig Corporation and reported that no one had been in the apartment when we had found them. Jerry Cofer had gotten away free, which burned me—even though I knew that my life would be a little bit safer as a result.

Joe Rouzan had established a good reputation as chief. Unlike Tom Cochée, he did his best to back us up, and in general, relations between him and the Police Officers Association were cordial. When my term as president of the CPOA expired, Roland Ballard was elected to replace me. I remained, however, as a member of the board. During the Rouzan regime, we continued to push our political agenda, and were able to negotiate several good contracts. This was despite the fact that Chief Rouzan had brought over from LAPD half a dozen lieutenants, who filled the upper echelons of the department; he was careful to appease middle management and to keep the rank and file happy. For several years we enjoyed a period of labor peace. Then two things happened to change all that.

For years, ever since the white flight, Compton had been strapped for cash, and the police department, like every other city service, suffered from the fact. In 1977, however, there was a development that could have altered the city's financial fortunes forever.

Legalized gambling was spreading throughout the country, from Atlantic City to the Indian reservations of the Southwest. The neighboring city of Gardena had legalized gambling, and the casino owners there proposed building a casino in the industrial tract on South Wilmington Avenue. Given Compton's central location between L.A. and Long Beach, and the site's easy access to the 91 and 110 freeways, it promised to be a lucrative venture. Gambling could mean millions of dollars in revenue, an influx of new businesses, and an opening to the outside world that might rejuvenate both Compton's economy and its spirit. Gambling's advocates touted it as the salvation of the city; its opponents denounced it as a pending disaster.

All at once, the question of legalized gambling became the hottest issue for discussion on the streets, in the newspapers, and before the city council. Some people grasped at it as a lifesaver thrown to our drowning city; others viewed it with alarm, citing the possibility for government corruption and organized crime. As far as I was concerned, corruption and crime were so much a part of Compton's character that a bit more would scarcely be noticed.

Compton's leaders began choosing up sides in the gambling debate. The political wrangling for favors, kickbacks, and special consideration grew more and more intense, and soon the question of gambling's benefit to the city was submerged beneath a tide of avarice and self-interest. Everyone in any position of power wanted a piece of the proposed gambling windfall, just as everyone had scrambled for the federal revenue-sharing money five years before. Fortunes were to be made, and once again, it was the city that stood to be the loser.

Joe Rouzan had kept himself carefully aloof from the furious debate that was swirling around legalized gambling, but as police chief he would have the primary responsibility for guaranteeing the safety of the casino, and for managing the inevitable criminal activity that it would bring. So everyone was anxious to hear his views.

Prior to the Rouzan administration, the Compton PD had had a tiny intelligence division, but Rouzan had beefed it up and entrusted it to my old partner, Joe Flores, who had gone with me to Mexico. The chief asked Joe Flores to research the question of legalized gambling and prepare a recommendation, which he would present to the city council. Joe thus suddenly found himself one of the most important people in Compton, potentially holding the key to its financial future.

He had no idea what to suggest, so he went to the bunco division of the Los Angeles County Sheriff's Office for advice. LASO had had a good deal of experience with legalized gambling throughout the county, and they told Flores that it was a terrible idea. It would mean organized crime, traffic congestion, union corruption, and an increase in assaults, extortion, robberies, and prostitution.

Joe Flores took their views back to Chief Rouzan, who reported them to the city council. That, together with protests from the ministers of Compton's twenty-five black churches, who feared that gambling would dry up their financial base, tilted the balance. After months of greedy wrangling and impassioned debate, the council voted against the casino. There would be no legalized gambling in Compton.

The loss of this potential revenue stream was compounded in 1978 with the passage of Proposition 13. Called a taxpayer revolt, Prop 13 severely limited the state's ability to tax real estate and made it more difficult for the legislature to impose new taxes. Municipalities across the state responded with deep cuts in spending, and with hysterical doomsday warnings. Compton was no exception, and one of the first groups to feel the crunch was the CPD. We had twelve recruits going through the sheriff's academy, young cops who were desperately needed on the street. When Prop 13 passed, Joe Rouzan announced that the twelve recruits would be put on hold. The CPOA was furious.

At that time, I was still on the board, and John Soisson was president.

We protested the chief's decision in the strongest possible terms, taking out ads in the local papers and going before the city council to demand that the recruits be hired. Rouzan was adamant, insisting that the city did not have enough money.

In response, we pointed out that when he took office, Chief Rouzan had brought with him from LAPD six captains and lieutenants, who were accountable only to him. These six had not taken the civil service exam when they transferred, and had been named inspectors, at salaries higher than those of comparable Compton lieutenants, in addition to their pensions from LAPD.

We argued that six full-time inspectors for a department of 130 cops were far too many—a top-heavy bureaucracy that was eating up the department's shrinking funds. We demanded that Rouzan get rid of four of them, which would free enough money to pay for the recruits. Again the chief refused: Like King Lear, he was determined to keep his retinue, no matter how unnecessary or excessive.

The CPOA decided to take legal action against the chief. Our lawyer, Steve Solomon, went to district court to secure an injunction to prevent the suspension of the twelve recruits. In his brief, he argued that the training of the recruits constituted a contract the city could not breach, and that hiring them was an urgent matter of public safety. The city's attorneys countered that the passage of Prop 13 was forcing a radical reallocation of government resources, and until its constitutionality could be determined by the Supreme Court, all spending had to be taken under review. It was a complex and controversial legal conflict that might affect the future of tax policy in the state, and so the judge simply stepped away from it. He declined to act on our injunction until the Prop 13 question could be resolved. Rouzan would keep his retainers; we would get no new cops.

There was one bright moment in this legal and financial mess, however. The CPOA's treasurer, Sergeant Robert Watson, had for years skillfully managed the association's funds. Watson was one of the last remaining Mormons in Compton, and he had devoted his life to the city and to the department. Though he was still a few years away from his pension, he took early retirement, asking that his salary be used to cover the cost of two or three of the recruits. It was a selfless act reflective of the spirit of the CPD.

The financial crisis in Compton encouraged the L.A. County Sheriff's Office to renew its effort to take over policing of the city. Sheriff Pitchess argued that the LASO could patrol Compton at a savings of millions of dollars, and he backed up the claim with figures from other municipalities. Mayor Davis had consistently refused Pitchess's overtures. However when she was named as an unindicted co-conspirator in a real estate scandal involving the old J.C. Penney building, she dropped out of the race for reelection. It came as no surprise that Russell Woolfolk, whom we had endorsed despite his shady reputation, was behind the scandal. He was indicted, but not alone—he had also involved our other supporter on the council, Hillard Hamm. Both men were convicted and sent to prison. In one swoop, we had lost our three leading advocates in city government.

Doris Davis was succeeded by Lionel Cade, a quiet, reserved World War II combat veteran and former certified public accountant. His audit of city finances revealed a two-million-dollar deficit, and for a time we were concerned that he might accept Pitchess's offer to take over Compton. Instead, Cade, like Davis before him, turned the sheriff down. Though only 130 strong, he declared, the CPD had maintained order despite being outnumbered and outgunned by the criminals. "We don't need the LASO," Cade stated. "Compton has its own police force, and it's a good one."

Sheriff Pitchess responded with the familiar charge that the CPD was "too close to the criminals." How else, he argued, could we keep control in a city that had been identified in a national survey as the most dangerous under 100,000 population in America? Actually, he was correct: If we had not known the criminal element so well, had not had the network of informants we developed, had not devised our own form of police work, we never could have succeeded.

The fact was that we were succeeding because we knew what the sheriff's office could never know, used methods they would not dare to employ, did every day what they would never dare to do. We went into the worst neighborhoods, sought the gangbangers out where they lived, and made it clear that we, and not they, controlled the streets—and we had rarely asked the LASO, or any other outside agency, for help. Mayor Cade understood this, and his expression of confidence came as welcome news.

The sheriffs would not police Compton; the CPD would continue to exist.

At the end of 1977, I transferred from the burglary-specific detail to homicide. It was another step up the ladder to sergeant, and the fact that I had already worked a dozen homicides made it a natural one for me.

I found murder fascinating. It is life taking life, and so it is, in effect, life canceling itself out. Murder is a tragic contradiction: You have to be alive to take life, yet, by taking a life, you undermine the value of your own life. John Donne said that every man's death diminishes us; but murder does more than that—it threatens life itself. If one man can find a motive to kill another, then no one is safe, because there is no logic that can defend life. Murder is not only the death of humans, it is the death of reason. Furthermore, because God alone creates life, murder is an assault on God. It is sacrilege, the unholiest of crimes, which, as St. Thomas Aquinas said, makes every other crime possible. For if life is not sacred, then nothing is.

Life in Compton was far from sacred. Anything, I learned, could be a motive for murder, from the most impassioned rage and jealousy to the most trivial dispute or possession. In my second homicide, the cowed little man, Willie, had shot his wife to death because she had not cooked his beans the way he liked. In Compton, life was, literally, not worth a hill of beans.

The homicide squad consisted of six detectives under the command of Sergeant Harold Fuske. Fuske was a longtime veteran, regarded as a policeman's sergeant. If there was a homicide in the middle of the night, Harold could be counted on to show up with coffee and supervise the crime scene personally. He was not a big man, but he was a good cop and an extremely popular commander.

Once, when he was a patrol sergeant, he was approached on the street by an enormous thug named Herman Perkins, who asked him for a pen. As Fuske reached into his pocket, Perkins coldcocked him—slugged him square on the jaw, knocking him unconscious. At that moment, Officers Clarence Bowden and Percy Perrodin drove by. They jumped out of their unit and approached Perkins. Perkins attacked them, and in the wild fight that ensued he received injuries so severe that it took two cotton turbans to close the fractures on his skull. Both men had served under Fuske, and both idolized him.

Harold Fuske was one of the reasons I transferred to homicide; I wanted to learn from him, and, if and when I made sergeant, I was determined to be like him.

The other members of the homicide team were Joe Ferrell, Brent Nielsen, Tom Barkley, John Soisson, and Barry Lobel. While other small cities in the county averaged two or three homicides a year, we had fifty or sixty, and in 1978, our team solved 100 percent of them. It was a proud record, if based on a dubious distinction.

One of my first calls as a homicide detective occurred on Christmas Eve. My phone rang at 3:00 A.M.; it was Harold Fuske. There had been a killing on Mulberry Street, he said, and he asked me to meet him at the address.

As innocuous as it sounds, Mulberry Street, in the northeast corner, was one of the most dangerous streets in Compton. Nearly every night there were reports of drug deals and shots fired there. The 3:00 A.M. wake-up call came as no surprise.

By the time I reached Mulberry Street, the body had been removed, and the SI team was finishing up. It had been raining, and the reflection of parti-colored Christmas lights glimmered dully in the sidewalk sheen.

I asked Fuske who the victim was. "Not a clue," he responded. He told me that it was a young Latino who had been stabbed multiple times. I could see that it had been a particularly brutal killing; there was blood splashed all over the sidewalk and trickling into the gutter.

"When the paramedics got here, the kid was still alive," Fuske went on. "They asked him who stabbed him, and he refused to say. He was dead before they got him to the hospital." Fuske told me that the case was mine. "Oh, and merry Christmas, Rick."

The next morning, Christmas Day, I drove down to the L.A. coroner's office to look at the body. There was always the possibility that I knew the victim. When they pulled the sheet back, I could see just how vicious the attack had been. The boy, who could not have been more than twenty, had been stabbed repeatedly in the chest and stomach. The corpse was drained of blood, and the stab wounds looked like the work of an inept butcher, the edges jagged, some of the cuts crisscrossing on the gelid flesh. Though the face was blue and shrunken, there was something familiar about it. Whoever he was, there would be no Christmas for him, or for me either.

I called my former supervisor in burglary, Art Camarillo, and asked him to meet me at the morgue for the autopsy the following day. Art had been born and raised on the north side, and I hoped he might recognize the boy.

When he saw the body, he frowned. "That's Luli," he said.

The victim, Arthur Gonzalez, whom everyone called Luli, was the youngest son of a family that was so close to Sergeant Camarillo's that Arthur had been named after him. His parents were popular local merchants, owners of a grocery store on Willowbrook Avenue. The Gonzalez children had all gone to St. Anthony's High School, where many of them had been star athletes. Luli's older brother, Remi, had been a classmate of mine; that was why the boy's face had seemed familiar. The Gonzalez family lived in the same neighborhood as the Camarillos and the Pasquale family, and both Art and Vito Pasquale had watched Luli grow up. They had also watched him become a drug addict, a wannabe gangbanger who hung out with the CV3 on Mulberry Street.

When I stopped at the Garter a few nights later, Vito had already heard the news. "Remi's one of my best friends," he told me. "He's all broke up about it." I said that I was handling the case. "I'm glad," Vito nodded. "Rick, you got to find out what happened. You got to find out who killed Luli."

From the condition of the body I did not believe it had been a gang killing. Bangers stabbed once or twice, then fled the area. This boy had been annihilated—his murder had taken time. It was not the result of a turf dispute or a "junior flip" making his bones; it had been personal— there was passion behind it.

I began working my informants on the north side, but I found a strange reluctance to talk about Luli's murder. It was as if the subject had been declared taboo. At last, one of my contacts grudgingly said, "Go talk to Lois Wilmer." I knew her. She was a seventeen-year-old Creole girl, a kind of celebrity on the north side for her exotic beauty.

When I turned up at her door two days after Christmas, she seemed nervous. "What you want, Officer Baker?" she asked. I told her that I just wanted to talk. "About what?" She was becoming more anxious by the second. She was clearly covering something.

"You drink coffee?" I asked. She said she did. "Let's go get some coffee."

The fact that I was not going to question her in her parents' house or take her to the station seemed to calm her. I drove her down Rosecrans to a diner, and we sat and talked. I asked her how her Christmas had been.

She turned suddenly morose. "Lousy," she said. She was beautiful in the way that so many Creole girls are, with honey-colored skin, luxuriant brown hair, and green eyes.

"Did something happen?" I asked.

She looked up at me. There was an anxious appeal in her eyes. "Are you a nice man?" she asked. I told her I hoped I was. She nodded. "Yeah, I think you're a nice man."

"You can talk to me, Lois," I said. "Did something bad happen over Christmas?"

"Are you gonna be nice to me if I tell you?" She was frightened, fighting tears. "I mean, you ain't gonna hurt me or nothing? You'll take care of me, Officer Baker?"

"Call me Rick."

"'Cause I need somebody to take care of me," she went on, tears running down her face. She was scared and lonely, this lovely girl with emerald eyes, begging for someone to understand the burden she was bearing.

I had often encountered this before: People who have guilty secrets are desperate to share them with someone, just to relieve the strain. The worse the secret, the more desperate the need to share.

I handed her a paper napkin. "Tell me what happened."

Lois dabbed at her cheeks. "It's my brother . . ." she sobbed. "My brother Frank . . ."

I knew Frank Wilmer; he was a fair-skinned boy of nineteen, exotic-looking like his sister, with light brown curly hair and delicate features. "What did Frank do?"

"He got beat up. Christmas Eve." She began crying. "He killed somebody, Rick." She broke down, and it was a few minutes before I was able to calm her sufficiently to tell me what Frank had confided in her.

Luli Gonzalez and two gangbangers had come to the Wilmers' house late on Christmas Eve. Luli and Frank were friends, and Luli knew that Frank was gay. He took Frank outside to meet the other two, who told him they wanted a Christmas present. When Frank asked what it was, Luli said, "They wanna get their dicks sucked."

Frank was horrified and refused, and the bangers began to threaten him. When he tried to run back into the house, they grabbed him and pounded him savagely with their fists while Luli looked on. At last Frank was able to break away, and he staggered inside.

Lois wanted to take him to the hospital, but he was furious, crying hysterically, and shouting that he was going to "get the motherfuckers." He went to the kitchen, snatched up a carving knife, and stormed back outside while Lois begged him to stop. When he came back a few minutes later, he was panting and covered with blood.

"I said, 'Frank, what'd you do?'" Lois pattered out. She was headlong into the story now and could not stop. "He didn't say nothing, but there was this look in his eyes, I mean, I never seen anybody look like that. Like he was crazy, like he was sad and crazy and all broke up inside." She stopped, finally, exhausted.

I patted her hands, which were clenched on the Formica tabletop, clutching the paper napkin. She looked at me, eyes drained. "Did I do the right thing, Rick? Telling you, I mean?"

I assured her she had, and I asked where Frank was now.

Her green eyes grew large. "What are you gonna do?"

"Just like I'm doing with you," I answered. "I'm gonna talk to him."

"You ain't gonna hurt him, are you, Rick? 'Cause he's real confused, y'know. He's a confused person."

"No, Lois. I promise I won't hurt him."

She thought a moment. "He went away," she said, "but he'll be back tomorrow."

When Frank returned to his parents' house next morning, I was waiting for him. I identified myself.

He frowned. "What do you want?"

"Luli Gonzales was killed Christmas Eve," I said. "Do you know anything about it?" He started to cry. "Why did you do it?" I asked.

He continued sobbing, his narrow chest heaving. I cuffed him and walked him to my car.

At the station, I sat across from Frank at the little wooden table of the interview room as he told me the story.

Luli came to his house, as Lois had said, to visit for Christmas. Frank went outside with him, but when he saw the bangers, he stopped.

"He told me they were his friends," Frank said in a voice scarcely more than a whisper, "but I knew they were bad news. I told Frank I was going back inside, but the other two wouldn't let me. They were giggling, and they said that Luli had promised to get them a Christmas present. I was the present."

"You were the present?"

His voice tightened. "Luli promised I'd suck their dicks. He told them I'd do it."

For an instant, I thought I saw in his eyes the emotion his sister had described—anger and hurt, and something else I could not identify.

"I told them I wouldn't do it," he went on. Suddenly his temper flared. "I told them to go fuck themselves! That was when they started beating on me. And Luli, he didn't do nothing. He didn't help me . . ." He trailed off, exhausted, his voice choking.

I realized that the other part of his emotion was betrayal—a deep, crushing sense that he had been betrayed by his friend.

"What happened next?" I asked.

Frank sniffled back tears. "I went in the house, and I got a knife. I wanted to cut their hearts out! But when I went back outside, the only one that was left was Luli. He told me how sorry he was, that he didn't mean for it to happen. I said, 'You told them I'd suck them off as a Christmas present?!' He said they promised to get him into the Tres . . ." He trailed off again, beginning to cry.

"Why did you stab him, Frank?"

He bent double and rested his head on the table. He was so quiet and so still that, for a moment, I thought he had fallen asleep. "He was my friend," he said at last. "He was more than my friend . . . I thought he loved me." He was crying uncontrollably now.

I leaned over and put a hand on his shoulder. "That's all right," I said, not knowing what else to say.

Frank raised his head and looked at me, his face wet with tears. "What are they gonna do to me?"

I told him he would be charged with murder, but since he had been beaten, it would not be in the first degree.

He nodded wearily. "I'm sorry about Luli," he said. "I'm sorry for what I did."

Then something occurred to me. "When he was in the ambulance," I told Frank, "when they asked him who stabbed him, he refused to say. He wouldn't tell them. He tried to protect you, right up till he died."

Frank looked at me a long moment, wiping at his eyes. "Thank you," he said.

With all the risks of living in Compton in those days, perhaps the greatest was being gay. Just the suspicion of it was enough to make life hell. Falling in love made it impossible. From the moment that Frank and Luli trusted each other with their secret, they were doomed. Like the tragic love stories of antiquity, like Romeo and Juliet and Tristan and Isolde,

Frank's and Luli's tale could have ended in only one way—in death. As it did.

I had learned from my first homicide—the man with the car aerial in his chest—that it was dangerous to become emotionally involved in murder. A murder shakes your sense of your own security, perhaps due to the dark truths that it lays bare about human nature. I think that a homicide investigator has to approach his job as a surgeon does: You are going to see inside the human condition, see the viscera and the vulnerabilities you yourself contain, work at the very edges of humanity, and handle with your own hands that which makes us human, that which is concealed from everyone else. For that reason, you must remain objective. You cannot allow your emotions to become victims of the crime. Otherwise, you will either lose your sanity, or you will lose your humanity.

I had been a homicide detective for a little over a year and had handled or worked on over thirty murders. Statistically, this is eight or ten times more than the average cop deals with in his career. I had seen murders committed with every imaginable kind of weapon, and for every unimaginable kind of motive:

A seventy-eight-year-old woman strangled with her own nylons in the bedroom of her home, her face covered with a mirror so she could watch herself die; an old man shot to death in a grocery store simply because he had referred to another man as a "blood" relative; a housepainter who beat his partner to death with a bucket full of stucco because he had accidentally knocked him off a ladder; and a young woman stabbed in the heart with a barbecue fork because she had eaten a piece of fried chicken before the cook had tasted it.

For the most part, I succeeded in maintaining a professional distance from such callous, even casual, taking of life, but there was one case in which I could not.

Cal Washburn was a Compton police officer who had been on patrol for three years. He had moved to Compton from Texas with his best friend, Daryl Simms, who became a security officer for the Compton School

District. Washburn and Simms had a reputation as heavy drinkers, and when they got drunk, they played a game called Wyatt Earp. They would put their service revolvers in their waistbands, count to three, and draw, to see who was faster.

Washburn was dating a girl named Arleen Wilson, who lived in a town house on Tucker Street off North Long Beach Boulevard. One night, Washburn, Daryl, and Arleen went out drinking. By the time they got back to Arleen's place, the two men were boisterously drunk. Arleen made collard greens, mashed potatoes, and corn for them. They had some more to drink, and after dinner Daryl announced that he was in love with Arleen. The friends argued, and as the argument became uglier and more heated, Arleen went upstairs and locked herself in a bedroom.

Meanwhile, the argument was escalating toward a fight. Both Washburn and Simms were carrying their guns, and, drunk as he was, Washburn had the presence of mind to tell Simms that they should lock the guns in a drawer in the first-floor bedroom so that there would be no shooting. The men did so, went back to the parlor, and began whaling on each other with their fists. Upstairs, Arleen could hear the living room being torn apart as the two friends fought. Then everything fell silent.

Washburn had beaten Daryl unconscious. As Daryl lay on the floor, his face bloody, Washburn went to the back bedroom and retrieved his gun, leaving the drawer unlocked. He put the gun into the waistband of his trousers and sat down on an ottoman in front of the TV. When Daryl came to, he dragged himself to the bedroom, got his gun, and staggered back down the hallway to the living room.

"Cal, you fucker!" Daryl yelled. Washburn looked up. His friend was standing in the doorway, his gun protruding from his waistband. "We gonna play Wyatt Earp. But this time for real."

Washburn told him to put the gun away. Daryl slid it out and began waving it around. "I'm gonna fuckin' kill you, man," he slurred. His face was swollen and smeared with blood.

"Put it down, Daryl," Washburn told him. Instead, Daryl raised the gun. "Don't point that thing at me," Washburn warned. "You do and I'm gonna have to shoot you."

"You ain't fast enough," Daryl said, and he raised the barrel to his waist. As he did, Washburn reached into his belt, drew out his gun, and fired. He was drunk and Daryl was weaving; he did not even aim—but the bullet struck Daryl in the heart. He dropped to the floor dead.

Washburn was still sitting on the ottoman, the gun trailing a tendril of smoke in his hand, as Arleen came running down the stairs. When she saw Daryl, she stopped, and then she screamed. Neighbors called the police at the sound of the shot and the screaming.

Officer Al Preston responded, and when he saw that the suspect was Cal Washburn, he called me at home. It was after midnight.

I drove straight to the station, where Washburn was being held in an interview room downstairs. I asked Al Preston if he had cuffed him.

"No," he said. "I didn't know what to do."

It was a problem we were all going to have to face: As far as I knew, no Compton police officer had ever been a suspect in a murder.

Washburn was still very drunk, practically incoherent, so I went across the hall to the break room and made a pot of coffee.

Whenever a police officer kills someone it is a complex situation; but when he is a suspect in a murder, the problem is compounded. As a fellow Compton cop, Cal Washburn was a brother to me. I scarcely knew him and had never worked with him, but he wore a blue uniform, and I knew that he would give his life for me, as I would for him. Now I had to interrogate him in the killing of his best friend.

For the next hour, I poured cup after cup of black coffee into him. I was not going to question him while he was still drunk—whatever he told me, whatever went into the record, he would have to say when he was in full possession of his faculties. I asked John Soisson to witness the interview. It would be the most difficult I had ever conducted, and I wanted to make sure that it was seen as having been fair and complete.

When I judged that Washburn was sober enough, I took him upstairs to the interview room in the detectives' offices. I did this for two reasons: Unlike the rooms downstairs, the detectives' interview room was wired for sound, and it had a two-way mirror, which meant that Soisson could watch the interview from outside. When I knew that Soisson was ready, and that the tape was rolling, I recited Cal Washburn his rights and started.

The first story he told me was nonsense. He claimed that he and Daryl had gotten drunk and Daryl had shot himself by accident. He was distraught and still somewhat disoriented, and I did my best to calm him down.

"You have to tell me the truth this time, Cal," I said to him. "You know I'm gonna work with you, give you every break I can, but I need to know what really happened."

He broke down and began crying, and the story poured out. When he was finished, he moaned, "I didn't mean to shoot him."

"He was your friend," I said. "You'd played that game before."

"This was different, Rick. I thought he was gonna kill me. It was self-defense; I had to do it. But I never meant to kill him."

I glanced up at the mirror where I knew Soisson was watching. We had been at it for over an hour. I patted Washburn's shoulder and told him we were going to take a break.

He looked up at me with tears in his eyes. It was odd, I thought, how many times I had had to deal with men's tears. "You're not gonna put me in the cells, are you, Rick?" he asked.

"No . . . You can stay here."

I walked outside. John Soisson was waiting with Gil Sandoval, the inspector in charge of detectives. It was now nearly 4:00 A.M., and he had driven down from his home in El Monte. "It wasn't premeditated," I said. "They were both drunk, and the other guy did pull first."

"Manslaughter," Soisson said.

Sandoval agreed. "Second degree at most."

"I'm not even sure we can get manslaughter," I said. "I'll file involuntary manslaughter."

It was, I felt, the fairest way to go. Washburn had been reckless, but he had shown restraint in locking the guns away. On the other hand, it had been stupid for him to retrieve his gun while he was still drunk, leaving the bedroom drawer unlocked. Daryl Simms had provoked the shooting by pointing his gun at Washburn, who believed his life was in danger. Washburn clearly had not intended to kill him.

A man *was* dead, though, and Washburn *had* killed him. The fact that the bullet had hit Daryl Simms in the heart had been a tragic accident. Unlike the shooting at the Paradise Liquor Store, this could not be hushed up. Cal Washburn had been off duty; Simms's family would demand an investigation and a trial. Someone had to pay for the death.

Later that morning, I attended the autopsy on Daryl Simms. His death was officially ruled a homicide, the result of a single bullet wound to the heart. When his stomach was opened, it still contained the greens, corn, and potatoes Arleen Wilson had made for him and his friend. I filed my report with Don Carlson, the Compton DA, with the recommendation that Cal Washburn be charged with involuntary manslaughter.

When I got back to the station, Deputy Chief Roger Moulton was waiting for me. I explained to him briefly what had happened, and what Washburn had told me.

"Did you Mirandize him?" was Moulton's first question. I assured him I had. Moulton thought a long moment. "This is no good," he said.

"What do you mean, 'No good'?" I asked.

"A Compton cop, a suspect in a murder, being investigated by other Compton cops."

"We've got his story," I said. "It's pretty clear what happened. Everything's on tape, and Soisson witnessed it."

Moulton shook his head. "If there's no murder charge, it's going to stink of cover-up."

"You'd never make a murder charge stick. We can get IM."

"We can't do this," Moulton said.

"I've already filed with Carlson," I responded, feeling myself growing angry.

Moulton cut me off. "Chief Rouzan wants this case out of Compton." He called Gil Sandoval over. "You're taking over this investigation," he told him. I started to protest, but Moulton ignored me. "And you're getting it out of the department."

"Where?" Sandoval asked.

"Take it to the L.A. district attorney."

I was fuming now. "This is a Compton crime," I said, "and it should be handled in Compton. We've done everything by the book; there's no need to go outside."

"It's going to cause a shit storm," Moulton snapped. "Rouzan doesn't want it in his backyard. We're filing in L.A."

There was nothing I could do. The next day, Inspector Sandoval referred the Washburn case to the DA's office in Los Angeles.

There, it took a bizarre turn. Instead of charging Cal Washburn with manslaughter, the DA filed murder charges *against Arleen Wilson*. His investigation concluded that a second shot had been fired—by Wilson—and it was that one that had struck Daryl Simms. She had killed him in a lover's triangle, the DA contended, and Washburn had tried to cover for her.

The entire case was a sham: There was no evidence of a second shot, and Washburn had already confessed to the shooting on tape. Nevertheless, the DA ignored our investigation and pushed on with his own theory.

The case went to trial and was summarily thrown out. No charges were ever filed against Cal Washburn, who was given the option of resigning from the CPD rather than being fired. He did so, and, in another ironic twist, he was hired for the same job that his friend Daryl Simms had held—Compton School District security guard.

When the case was taken from me and referred to Los Angeles, my fear had been that Washburn would be tried for murder, but I had not counted on the hierarchy's desire to avoid a scandal. By filing against Arleen Wilson, the DA and the chief's office virtually guaranteed that Cal Washburn would never be charged with murder. He had then been allowed to resign—after having killed a man—the same option that was offered to Dominic Rutigliano over a bogus stolen horse trailer.

It made no sense, but it was, after all, Compton. I had tried to see to it that justice was done in the case, but I was overruled by higher authority. I had hoped to spare Cal Washburn being tried for murder, but Daryl Simms was dead because of Washburn's irresponsible actions, and Washburn could not be allowed to go free. Yet I also knew what happened to cops who went to prison, and I could only imagine the fate of a Compton cop behind bars. The jails were full of gangbangers whom we had sent there; if they had gotten their hands on one of our own, I do not think he would have lasted long.

More than any other homicide I had handled, this one drained me, and made me rethink my whole approach to justice. A man was dead, and that fact demanded justice. On the other hand, if Cal Washburn had gone to prison, he, too, would in all likelihood have been murdered, and the punishment for involuntary manslaughter is not death. Perhaps in some sense, I reflected, justice *was* done in this case after all. One life had been taken, but another had been saved. The scales had been balanced, but it was just as well that Justice was blind.

I had brought with me into police work a concept of justice instilled in me by my religious education. Justice was healing; justice meant restoring the equilibrium upset by wrongdoing. When justice was achieved, those who suffered had the satisfaction of knowing that the guilty would be punished, and their suffering would be vindicated. It was an idea defined by the desire for order, and reinforced by the hope and expectation of righteousness.

Justice as I encountered it on the streets of Compton was more complex, and far less clear. Like love, it was embedded in the human heart and at the whim of human foibles. Justice was neither fixed nor equal. In our society, I came to understand, the rich, the famous, the privileged, the beautiful received one form of justice. Those who were humbler and more sparsely endowed were subjected to another.

For the same crime, a person of status might be merely reprimanded, or avoid justice altogether, or even be lauded by the media, whereas a gangbanger or an addict would be shunted off to prison. In my own work, justice proved a fluid commodity—it was what we said it was in an alley or a parking lot; it was a talking to or a whooping; it was what we needed it to be in order to do our jobs. Justice, I concluded, was nothing but a noun—a flowery noun that judges and poets and professors used. To us, though, justice was more often than not a sap glove in the face or a baton across the buttocks, or a sense that we had done our best after a long night of abuse and inhumanity and murder.

In the canons of the law schools and in the writings of philosophers, justice was an ideal. It meant "giving to each man his own," a reflection of the divine will that the universe make sense, and that all people know that goodness ultimately prevails. On the streets of Compton, justice was what we made it. It had to be—we had no time or money or patience for anything more ornate. The burden of proof was on the bad guy; the burden of punishment was on us.

If, as Disraeli said, justice is truth in action, then Compton cops were just. More often than not we knew who the bad guys were and what they had done, and we dealt justice to them in proportion to their crimes. That proportion was key to the Compton Style of justice. When Ruben Verra stole a Hershey bar, Carl Crosby had given him a talking to, and then befriended him. When John Sutton caught the liquor store robber, he whipped him and returned the money. When the Allen brothers beat Vince Rupp nearly to death, they had been beaten nearly to death. We did such things in the certain knowledge that the perpetrators were guilty, and in the hope that they would be dissuaded from future wrongdoing.

It is true that we often took justice into our own hands, molding and shaping it according to our lights and the exigencies of our job. We did not think of ourselves as God; but that we had been entrusted as the enforcers of the right we never doubted, and we took that role with the seriousness of life and death.

It was a heavy responsibility; one that fueled us to our highest efforts on behalf of the people we served, and that ultimately proved too much for some of us to bear. When we acted, we always acted in the name of justice. Because justice was what we did for a living, every day and every night; it was what we trained for and worked for and risked our lives for. In the end, though we wore blue uniforms and gold badges, though we made ourselves seem bigger than life, and we honed command presence to an art, we remained human beings—cops and criminals alike.

Rut Returns, the *Sentinel,*
and the Stinkers

It had been seven years since Dominic Rutigliano had been forced to resign. In that time his fortunes had gone from bad to worse, but then, due to his passion for motorcycles, they suddenly improved.

Sonny Boden, who had made history by placing first in his class at the sheriff's academy, had resigned from the Compton Police Department over an incident involving a stolen Cadillac. He was accused of removing the tires from the car before it was impounded and putting them on his own Caddy. Like Rut, Sonny had left the force under a cloud, and like him, he was an ardent Harley-Davidson fan.

In the late seventies, Sonny Boden and a biker named Glenn Nesbitt, called Nez, invented a rubber primary chain for Harleys, and, since they controlled the patent, they began to make a fortune. Knowing Rutigliano's status among the motorcycle clubs in California, Sonny hired him to help market the chains, and Rut began to make money. I was happy for him; his life seemed to be turning around. Still, in our talks, he made it clear that there was something missing. He wanted to be a cop again. At my urging, he applied to the department for reinstatement.

I suggested to him that I might be able to get him a job as a police reserve. That would mean that he could ride along with regular Compton officers, essentially as a volunteer, since reserves were paid one dollar a year. Rut jumped at the chance.

The question was how to get Rut into the reserve while he was still officially banned from the department. His application would have to be approved by the city's personnel board, and that was what provided the opening. For the most powerful member of the board was Lester Caldwell, the councilman whom I had found drunk and exposed in the parking lot of the Golden Garter.

I called his office and requested a meeting. When Caldwell asked what it was about, I told him that the matter was confidential. The next day we sat down and talked. I explained what I wanted: that Dominic Rutigliano be allowed to join the police reserve. Caldwell frowned and muttered that it would be difficult. I did not mention the Garter incident, but I did say that there was some old paperwork in the files that I had buried, and that could be made to disappear forever. He gave me a long glance and promised to see what he could do.

Lester Caldwell personally pushed Rut's request through the personnel board, which unanimously approved it. After seven years in exile, Dominic Rutigliano would again be allowed to wear a Compton PD uniform and ride in a patrol car. Though he had no power of arrest, and could serve only a few hours a month, he was a cop again. He was thrilled. In the weeks following, I watched his spirit revive, and with it the spirit of the patrol units, as he brought his old bravado and his supreme confidence back into the locker room and onto the streets.

By 1977, the CPOA also had undergone ups and downs. We had called the blue flu, negotiated new contracts, joined the ICPA, and gained political power. The split with the Guardians, however, remained a sore point. My fear that they would compromise our bargaining position with the city had not been realized for the simple reason that the Guardians never achieved any real status. Unable to organize the entire black contingent of the force, they had remained a majority of a minority. At no time did they represent more than 25 percent of the rank and file.

With such a small base, the Guardians had not been able to build a treasury, and therefore could not generate the benefits and perquisites the CPOA offered. The fact that the Guardians lacked political clout, and that the dissention they represented was an unnecessary blow to the unity and morale of the department, seemed to offer an opportunity for reconciliation.

Unlike Tom Cochée, Joe Rouzan would sit down in a bar and talk with us over drinks. So one evening I asked him for a meeting. I told him that it was time for the split to be resolved, and for the Guardians to return to the CPOA. He agreed. Their original grievance, involving the controversy over Cochée, had long been moot, and a number of their members were disgruntled because of their lack of influence and benefits. He promised to talk to them and try to heal the rift.

That was not all I wanted to discuss with the chief. I told him that we should bring back Dominic Rutigliano. Rouzan answered that he did not know who Rutigliano was.

"He's the best cop I ever worked with," I said, "and he got blackballed out of the department. He wants to come back, and we need him."

The chief said he would look into the case and get back to me.

Near the corner of Santa Fe Avenue and Pine Street on the east side was a halfway house for gang members who had been released from prison. It was run by a well-meaning county social worker named Bob Simmons. The neighborhood was one of the quietest in Compton, a residential area with trim houses, a church and a playground, and small local businesses. At any given time, Simmons had five or six parolees living at his ranch-style house, which we called the Ponderosa after the homestead in the TV series *Bonanza*. Simmons ran a good program, and we rarely had trouble with his residents.

Late in 1978, however, there was a series of shootings in the area, in which Lueders Park Bloods were being targeted. Our sources were as baffled as we. There was no word of an incursion into LP turf, and no new set had sprung up, but clearly *something* had happened. Roland Ballard and

I decided to look into it, and my suspicions soon were focused on Bob Simmons's Ponderosa. One morning, Ballard and I drove down to Santa Fe and Pine.

The ranch house backed onto the Oak Avenue Playground across from the Northside Church of Christ. It seemed a peaceful enough place. We walked across the newly mowed lawn to the front door and rang the bell. Bob Simmons answered.

He knew us, and he smiled as we shook hands. I asked if we could talk for a minute. He invited us into the living room.

"Who have you got on board?" I began. He listed three or four names I recognized. "Anybody else?" I went on. "Anybody new?"

He hesitated. "Why are you asking?"

He was not normally uncooperative with the police, so his response surprised me. I told him about the shootings and asked again whether he had taken in any new parolees.

"There is one new guy . . ." he began reluctantly. I asked who it was. "Stanley Williams," he replied.

Stanley "Tookie" Williams was one of the most notorious OGs, original gangsters, of all. In 1971, he and Raymond Washington had created the Crips in South L.A. in an effort to eliminate all the other gangs, and establish a super-gang controlled by themselves. In the seven years since, the West Side Crips had grown into the most violent set in Los Angles, responsible for hundreds of shootings and dozens of murders. Tookie Williams was known for his immense, muscular body and his demonic stare. With a reputation for ruthlessness, he was a killing machine, as dangerous for his dark temper as he was for his intelligence.

The previous August, his partner, Raymond Washington, had been murdered in a gang shootout, and Tookie had been arrested. Released on parole, he was now living at the Ponderosa. That, then, was what had changed in the area.

I told Bob Simmons that I wanted to talk to Tookie.

"You just want to send him back to prison," he said.

"I want the shootings to stop," I responded. "This is a decent neighborhood."

Simmons bristled. "Tookie Williams deserves the same as anybody else here: the chance to turn his life around."

"Where is he, Bob?"

"At work," Simmons snapped. "He's got a job."

When I asked him where, he refused to say. Two days later another Blood was shot. I was sure I knew what Tookie Williams's job was.

One afternoon I asked Bernard Brown to drive me to Santa Fe and Pine. It was Brown I had taken with me to Water Way when I spoke to Sylvester Scott. I explained the situation to him, and told him that I was going to hijack Tookie Williams. Bernard frowned. "He's one mean son of a bitch," he said.

We cruised the neighborhood around the Ponderosa until we spotted him. He was even bigger than I had been told. His chest was a wheelbarrow bulging with muscles barely contained by his denim shirt; his arms were thicker than my legs. He wore an enormous Afro and a Mephistophelean goatee, and he walked with the arrogant assurance of a man who feared no one and nothing. Brown and I glanced at each other; then he pulled our dick car over to the curb.

I leaned out the window. "Tookie," I said. He frowned. That ominous gaze would have bent iron. I showed him my badge. "Get in."

He growled, "What you want?"

"I want you to get in the fucking car."

He hesitated for a moment, calculating his options. Then he opened the door and squeezed his bulk into the backseat. Bernard pulled away from the curb. Williams said nothing, but I could feel his eyes on me as we drove to the railroad tracks on Alameda. At last he grumbled, "Where you takin' me?"

I turned toward him. "A lot of Bloods are getting shot in the neighborhood," I said.

"So?"

"So we need to talk about that."

Bernard pulled across the tracks and into the parking lot of an abandoned iron processing mill and stopped. This time we both turned toward Williams.

"You listen to me, motherfucker," I began. "You don't bring your shit down here from Watts into my city. You understand?"

The Crips founder seemed vaguely amused. "I don't know what the fuck you talkin' about," he said, and he looked out the window at the gray wall of the plant.

I exploded in a calculated show of temper. "You're gonna get your black ass outta Compton, you hear me!" I shouted. "'Cause if I see your ugly face in my town tomorrow, I'm gonna shoot your brains out! You understand?"

He was looking at me now, not with the lethal scowl, but with an expression of surprise. "What the fuck you doin' man?" he said.

"I'm telling you what's gonna happen to your sorry ass tomorrow if I catch you anywhere in Compton. I see you and you're gonna be one dead motherfucker, and I'm gonna say that Pit Bull or China Dog did it."

Bernard Brown added, "And if he don't get you, I will."

Tookie looked back and forth between us. He could see that we meant it.

"Do you understand now?" I said.

He nodded his mammoth head. "Yeah."

"Then get outta my car. And get the fuck outta my town," I told him.

He opened the door and stepped out into the empty, crumbling parking lot. Bernard put the car in gear and whipped it around him, spraying him with gray dust.

We drove in silence for a few moments; then Bernard remarked, "That was one big motherfucker. How come you didn't whoop his ass?"

"I didn't want to make him mad," I said.

We both broke up, a nervous, relieved laughter.

"Shit. Can you imagine fighting that dude inside a car?"

"He'da probably taken both of us."

"And the car," Brown said.

The next day, Tookie Williams left the Ponderosa without a word to Bob Simmons. He never returned.

Three months later, Williams shot a twenty-six-year-old store clerk in the back twice with a 12-gauge shotgun, boasting to his friends that he had killed the man "because he was white and I'm killing all white people." The following month, he broke into the office of a motel in Los Angeles and shot to death a seventy-six-year-old Korean man, his sixty-three-year-old wife, and their forty-three-year-old daughter.

He was arrested, tried, and convicted of the murders and spent twenty-six years on death row. While in prison, he claimed to have reformed, and he wrote a series of children's books intended to dissuade kids from joining gangs. A campaign was mounted in left-wing circles to have his death sentence commuted, but his execution was scheduled for December 13, 2005.

An *L.A. Times* staff writer, Louis Sahagun, called me for a comment the day before Williams's execution. I told him that I agreed with the decision to execute him. "His gang, the Crips, has been responsible for fifty times more murders than the Mafia," I said. "Giving Tookie Williams a pass would be like electing John Gotti as mayor of New York."

The following day, Williams was executed by lethal injection at San Quentin State Prison, after having been nominated for the Nobel Peace Prize.

Meanwhile, the latest municipal election in Compton had produced one surprise. Wilson Buckner, who represented the Fourth District on the east side and was the last white member of the city council, was defeated by Floyd James. James had grown up three blocks from me, at 134th and Parmelee, and we had been lifelong friends. He was pro-police, which meant that, having lost Hillard Hamm and Russell Woolfolk, we had at least one advocate on council.

It also meant that the mayor, the city manager, and the entire city council were now black. This was perhaps inevitable in a city that was 95 percent black, but it effectively excluded the remaining 5 percent Latino population. When Manny Correa had been passed over for chief of police, we had seen the first incipient claims by Latino residents of discrimination. Now the festering suspicions of reverse racism bubbled to the surface.

In 1978, Compton saw a series of protests by Hispanic community groups. The incident that sparked them was the firing of the last nonblack city employee of any significance, Commissioner Robert Ochoa of the personnel board. When Ochoa was dismissed after only one term in office, Latino activists organized a march to city hall. There, some sixty to seventy-five protestors chanted and carried signs declaring THE OPPRESSED ARE NOW THE OPPRESSORS and EQUALITY FOR LATINOS IN THE CITY OF COMPTON. It was too little, too late. Blacks had organized and struggled for over twenty years to take political control; they were not about to share that control with a tiny minority of Latinos. This fact would have great significance for the future of the city.

In response, however, Mayor Cade issued a statement insisting that the Latino citizens of Compton were an important part of the community, and that their views would be fully heard. To placate them, he went so far as to attend the Cinco de Mayo celebration wearing a gaudy sombrero. With his diminutive frame and owlish glasses, he looked more like a cartoon character than a mayor.

Just as with the black officers, there were divisions within the tiny ranks of the Latino cops. A few, like myself, Frank Villigas, Reuben Chavira, and Art Camarillo, had grown up in the black areas of Compton, and we had adopted more of a black culture than a Latino one. In fact, most spoke no Spanish, and a few were married to black women. In contrast, the Latino officers recruited from East Los Angeles and Monterey Park were heavily imbued with Hispanic culture, and they tended to regard us as inferiors.

There was a similar divide among the white officers in the department. Those who had been born and raised in Compton knew the city and its criminals, and were, because of that, effective cops. They understood the lore and language of the city, and knew instinctively how to relate to its residents and deal with its criminals. White officers who had been recruited from Los Angeles and Orange County, however, had to master Compton's culture, and learn a new attitude toward police work. Some never did, and they soon left for other departments. Among the ones who remained, like Jimmy Pearson and Brent Nielsen, both of whom I trained, were some of the best cops in Compton.

After Roland Ballard's term as CPOA president, John Soisson was elected and Ballard became vice president. I continued to serve on the board. Ballard and I had been through several wars together, and we had always made a good team. When Mayor Dollarhide had tried to demote us, the ICPA attorney, James van Norman, had come to Compton to represent us at the personnel board hearing, and his very presence had been enough to move the city administration to a settlement. Now James van Norman appeared in Compton again.

He had had an acrimonious falling-out with the ICPA leadership and had resigned as the association's legal counsel. He then went into business with a man named David Zukor who ran a magazine in Boston called the *Sentinel*. The *Sentinel* was dedicated to publicizing the activities of police departments back east, and van Norman and Zukor came to Compton to solicit our support for a West Coast edition. The idea was to use the status of the CPOA to persuade other departments to join them in their effort to raise advertising money for the magazine. A portion of the revenue would go to the Police Officers Association.

Shortly before they arrived, I received a letter from ICPA president Ed Kiernan warning me that Zukor and van Norman had been cited for soliciting the citizens of East Orange, New Jersey, for donations in violation of a local law. In effect, Kiernan claimed, they had attempted to extort money from a black community. I looked into the matter and discovered that the *Sentinel* had, indeed, solicited support from the people of East Orange, but van Norman and Zukor had done so without realizing that the municipal code prohibited police associations from private fundraising. I concluded that Ed Kiernan's letter was simply an attempt to retaliate against van Norman by sabotaging his efforts on the West Coast.

Jim van Norman had backed us up in our fight against Mayor Dollarhide, so I was inclined to support him. Roland Ballard, however, felt that loyalty to the ICPA precluded this. For the first time, we found ourselves on opposite sides of an issue. Aware that I could not offer van Norman and Zukor the association's support without Ballard's cooperation, since he was the leading black officer in the CPOA, I attempted a compromise.

I proposed that we send a delegation to Boston at the *Sentinel*'s expense to evaluate the magazine and investigate Kiernan's charge. For this I was careful to choose three black officers, Joe Ferrell, Chuck Windom, and Overton May, all of whom I knew would be impartial in their inquiries.

I also wanted to send Bob Edelen, the CPOA's first counsel, and the attorney who had handled my divorce, but when I tried to contact him, I learned that he was in Folsom Prison. The fact came as a complete shock to me. Edelen, who lived in the upscale Windsor Hills neighborhood of Los Angeles, discovered that his wife was having an affair. He lured her lover to his home, where he tortured and murdered him. He was convicted and sentenced to life without the possibility of parole, the latest victim of what we had come to call the Compton curse.

I sent Ferrell, Windom, and May to Boston, where the *Sentinel* publishers treated them like royalty. They were given full access to the magazine's offices, staff, and printing and warehouse facilities, and they were very impressed. They concluded, as I had, that the incident in East Orange was, at most, a tort, or misdemeanor, probably as a result of ignorance of the local code. By the time they returned, they were prepared to recommend that the CPOA endorse the *Sentinel*'s West Coast initiative. It was too late, though. Before the delegation had a chance to make its report, the proposal was voted down.

There was cause for the decision, of course. I myself had been inclined to mistrust James van Norman when I had first met him at the ICPA convention in Miami, but he had more than vindicated himself in my eyes by coming to Compton to represent Ballard and me before the personnel board. There was, too, the question of the tort charge against the magazine in New Jersey, which I considered to have been an oversight, rather than a crime. However, Ballard had political ambitions—he was planning to run for city council—and he wanted the support of the ICPA, so he had persuaded the board and much of the rank and file that van Norman and Zukor were not to be trusted. What was more, a group of black officers had spread a rumor that I was going to receive a kickback from the magazine, and Roland Ballard had not come to my defense.

The fact that Ballard had not backed me up was a blow to me. We had worked well and closely together, but now I saw him as allowing his personal ambitions to get in the way of the interest of the association. The *Sentinel* incident drove a wedge between us. The partnership that had rebuilt the Police Officers Association, staged the blue flu, and removed a mayor, a city manager, and a police chief was, sadly, at an end.

It was shortly after this that Roland Ballard announced his decision to run for council. In a curious oversight, the city charter allowed a police officer to serve on the council while remaining with the force, and Ballard intended to take advantage of this. Knowing that the law prohibited him from campaigning on police department time, Ballard took a week's vacation to prepare for his run.

By that time, Howard Bell had been replaced as acting city manager by Alan Parker. Though Parker was white, he had been chosen for the position because of his demonstrated ability in revitalizing municipal finances. Mayor Cade, himself an accountant, valued Parker's expertise, and overcame the implicit prejudice against hiring a white city official. Parker more than justified his confidence. He was a brilliant city manager who helped Mayor Cade close the two-million-dollar deficit he had inherited on taking office.

Parker quickly formed an alliance with Joe Rouzan, and when Roland Ballard announced that he was running for council, the two men saw him as a common threat. With Ballard on the city council, Rouzan and Parker would, in effect, be reporting to a man whom they considered to be their employee. Neither looked forward to the prospect of his election.

They responded with typical Compton Style politics. Pointing out that Ballard was receiving pay while on vacation, they cited him for violating the charter's prohibition against political activity on city time. Ballard was fined $630, the equivalent of his salary while on vacation, and suspended for two weeks. It was a cheap political maneuver aimed at damaging his candidacy, and Roland Ballard was furious. When he returned to work after the suspension, he began submitting court slips. These were forms we had to file to be reimbursed for time spent appearing in court, and Ballard filed them for exactly $630. He was, therefore, reimbursed for the amount of his lost wages.

The tactic, a result of justifiable anger, backfired. When Parker discovered that Ballard had not, in fact, appeared in court for the time billed, he charged him with embezzlement and fired him. I tried to marshal support for Roland within the association, but John Soisson pointed out that, in contrast to Rutigliano, Ballard had declared his guilt by filing the court slips. Given this, the association could not officially protest his firing. Though he was not prosecuted, both his political ambitions and his career as a police officer were over. Roland Ballard had become another victim of life in Compton.

One morning I received a call from a Lieutenant Snowden of the Seattle Police Department. What he told me presented me with the most poignant dilemma of my career.

My ex-wife Connie had married a man named Bob Miller. They had met in Las Vegas and had a whirlwind courtship, and she fell madly in love. Miller was a slick, shady character, a high roller who spread money around liberally, and who clearly had connections on the Strip. What Connie did not know, or had chosen not to know, was that Bob Miller was a contract hit man for the Mafia.

As I listened dumbfounded, Lieutenant Snowden told me that Connie's husband, together with his partner, a character nicknamed Sharp Stick, had murdered a pit boss in Vegas and buried his body in the desert, where it was dug up and half devoured by coyotes. Miller and Sharp Stick had then gone to Los Angeles, killed a Beverly Hills couple named Roth, and stolen over a hundred thousand dollars in jewelry from their home, which they brought back to Las Vegas and turned over to their boss. Miller and Sharp Stick had been arrested. Connie was in custody in Seattle, where she had gone to visit relatives, awaiting extradition to Nevada as a material witness.

The arrest caused a sensation in Vegas, where the case was being handled by the Las Vegas DA personally. Miller's defense was that at the time of the killings he had been with his wife, Connie. Connie was his only alibi, and the prosecution needed me to discredit her. They knew I was a prominent detective in Compton, and they were going to subpoena me to testify that Connie was the sort of wife who would do anything to protect her man. That, said Snowden, was why he was contacting me.

I knew that it was true: Connie was loyal above all. She had walked the picket line for me during the blue flu, had volunteered when I was working juvenile to come to the station and type up my reports, and had stuck with me through all of my Rosecrans Rick escapades. Of course she would swear that Miller had been with her; that was the kind of wife she was. Beyond that, I was sure that if she did not, she, too, would most likely disappear in the desert.

What the Nevada prosecutors were asking of me was nothing less than character assassination. I would have to get on the stand and swear that my ex-wife was probably lying to protect a murderer, and that might expose her to a charge of perjury. On the other hand, as a police officer I could not refuse to respond to a subpoena. I could take the Fifth, but that would just be a signal to the jury that I was doing exactly what Connie was doing: substituting loyalty for the truth.

There was another aspect of the case that I had to consider. By testifying, I was putting myself squarely in the middle of a Mafia murder. I had never had any dealings with the mob, nor did I wish to. I had no idea what the implications would be if I helped send one of their boys to prison, so I asked the only person I thought might know, Vito Pasquale.

Vito agreed it could be trouble, and he offered to make a few phone calls for me. I told him that I simply wanted to know exactly whose toes I would be stepping on. A few days later, after I had received the subpoena from the Nevada DA, he got back to me.

"Look, Rick, far as I can tell, you're in the clear on this," he told me. "These guys are hee-holes, contract killers with no blood ties. They're not even Italian. So don't sweat it."

I supposed that was reassuring, so when the DA's office offered to provide me with protection, I declined. All that I asked was that I be allowed to bring my own weapon, my .357, with me to Vegas. They agreed.

There was still the problem of labeling Connie a perjurer. I had not seen her in years, and the prospect of watching her face across a courtroom while I destroyed her credibility was heart-wrenching to me. I was sure she would cry, and, while I had dealt with the tears of many people, both guilty and innocent, I did not know how I would handle hers. I prepared to leave for Vegas with deeply mixed feelings.

I took with me my girlfriend of the time, Candy Donatelli, both because I needed someone to support me and because she was one of the toughest women I had ever met. If I did get into trouble, I knew I could count on Candy to be my backup. She was beautiful and gregarious, but she could handle herself in a fight, and she knew how to use a gun. She would be more valuable to me than any U.S. Marshal the court might have provided.

The DA's office had booked me a room at the Four Queens Casino Hotel in downtown Las Vegas, but Vito had suggested that I would be more comfortable at the Dunes. Before I left, he handed me an envelope. "There's a guy's name in there," he told me. "When you get to the Dunes, give it to the floor manager. He'll take care of you."

I did as Vito said, and the result was instantaneous. When the casino manager looked at the name in the envelope, he practically groveled. "Yes, Mr. Baker," he oozed, "we've been expecting you. Your suite is ready, sir." Then he lowered his voice dramatically. "If you'd like to check your firearm with us, I'll see that it is put in the safe and kept strictly under lock and key."

I thanked him, followed him to the back room of the casino, and watched as my gun was sealed in a safe deposit box. The floor manager ceremoniously handed me the key.

It was much later that I surmised that the name in Vito's envelope was Oscar Goodman. Goodman was a well-known attorney who had made his reputation defending organized crime figures such as Meyer Lansky, Nicky Scarfo, and Anthony "the Ant" Spilotro. In 1999, Oscar Goodman was elected mayor of Las Vegas, and, as of this writing, he is still the mayor.

Candy and I checked into a luxury penthouse suite, and I began to prepare for my testimony. She took the role of the prosecutor, asking me to comment on Connie's character.

"What am I supposed to say?" I responded.

"Just tell the truth, Detective Baker," she scowled. "Is your ex-wife's testimony credible?"

I shrugged. "She's an honest person, if that's what you mean."

"It is not what I mean!" Candy snapped. "Is she lying to protect her husband?"

"How would I know?" I answered.

Candy bored in on me like a DA. "Is she the kind of person who would do or say anything to shield someone she loved from harm?"

The answer was yes, and I knew it, but I could not bring myself to say so.

Candy would not let up. "Well, Detective Baker? If it was you on trial, would you expect Connie to lie for you?"

I sighed and sat back in the plush armchair. This was exactly what it would feel like on the stand.

"Remember, Detective Baker, you're a sworn officer of the law, and you're under oath in this courtroom!"

I nodded. "Yes," I said. "Yes, that's exactly what I would expect her to do."

Seeing how deeply moved I was, Candy dropped the DA demeanor and sat on my lap. "You still love her," she said, searching my eyes. "Don't you?"

"No," I answered, "but I don't want to see her get hurt."

She stroked my face. "You do what you have to do, sweetheart," she said. "Everything will be all right. I promise."

The next morning the state sent a car to drive me to court. The driver and his partner were U.S. Marshals, and both were ostentatiously armed. When Candy started to get into the car, one of the marshals told her she was not permitted to accompany me. She threw him a lethal glance. "The fuck I'm not," she said, and she got into the backseat.

All the way to the courthouse I was dreading seeing Connie, dreading what I would have to do. I had rehearsed in my mind over and over the statement I was prepared to give. I would deliver it, and that was all. I would say nothing about the case or Connie's role in it, even if it meant that I was cited for contempt.

The local district attorney was waiting for me outside the courtroom when Candy and I arrived. He held out a hand, smiling broadly. "Detective Baker," he said. "Good morning. Thank you for coming."

I resented the smile; it was not a good morning for me. "I'd just as soon not be here," I answered him. "Frankly, I don't want to testify."

"Well," he said with an even more expansive smile, "you won't have to. The trial's off."

Candy clapped her hands. "I told you everything'd be all right!" she exclaimed.

I was relieved but still puzzled. I asked the DA what had happened.

"When we told the defense that you would be testifying, they offered to cut a deal," he explained. "We won't get them for everything we wanted, but we've got them." This time he smiled in triumph. "Thanks for your help."

I congratulated him, took Candy's arm, and left the courthouse.

The department had given me three days' leave to attend the trial, so Candy and I had a mini vacation at the expense of the State of Nevada and courtesy of Oscar Goodman. We took in a show, blew a hundred bucks at the craps table, and relaxed in the hot tub in our hotel suite. Before we left, I retrieved my gun from the casino safe.

"I hope you had a pleasant stay," the floor manager purred.

I told him that I could not have asked for anything more. In fact, there *was* something else. I would have liked to see Connie, and to tell her what my testimony would have been. I would have said only that I knew her to be a good woman, and that I could always count on her while we were married, and that was all I planned to say. Because it was the truth.

I had never smoked. Even though all my friends in school and most of the cops I served with smoked, I had always avoided it. I hated the smell and the acrid taste, and the fact that smoking meant you could never enjoy the savor of food or fresh air. In my mind at least, smoking marked you as shortsighted, someone who did not respect his health and could not identify with his own future. After I became a homicide detective, though, I started smoking, because of the Stinkers.

Stinkers are corpses that are so foul that you cannot get rid of the stench of them. When you attend the autopsy, the smell clings to your clothes, cloys your flesh, lingers on the hairs in your nostrils, and nothing, no shower or soap, will get it out. When we were called to a murder scene, we always hoped for a fresh corpse, one that had only recently been killed, or had been dumped in the open on a frosty night. As bodies went, a fresh corpse, in which the decay had not begun, was a welcome sight; a Stinker was a waking nightmare.

In my career I worked on more than two hundred homicides, and many of them were Stinkers. Three in particular stand out in my mind.

In my rookie year, I was on patrol in District 3 when a call came over the radio of neighbors complaining about the smell from a garage on Santa Fe Avenue. I drove to the location and found another unit already on the scene; it was Officer Rex Council, a fifteen-year veteran. He was standing outside the garage, which was attached to a small frame house, waiting for me. He knew he had a Stinker, and he had no intention of going in first. Indeed, the odor of putrefaction was overwhelming.

I wrapped a handkerchief around my face and broke the lock on the garage. When I lifted the door, the stench nearly made me pass out. The garage was crammed with the usual junk, but on the floor near the back was a mangy rug rolled around a corpse. While Council watched at a safe distance, I knelt and tugged at the fringe. Out tumbled the most horrific thing I had ever seen: a woman's body, so thick with flies that it was vibrating. They were huge green monsters sated with flesh and blood, so swollen that they could not fly. Instead, they spilled off the body as it rolled onto its back with a swishing sound like pebbles in a surf.

Half the body had been eaten away by rats; the remains were barely recognizable as human, a grisly, pathetic mush of decaying flesh and skeleton. The odor forced me, gagging, from the garage. When I was able to catch my breath, I told Council what I had found.

He said, "I'll call the meat wagon."

"There's not much meat left," I croaked.

We were able to determine that the victim had been a prostitute from Los Angeles, a young black woman who had been beaten and raped, and then her throat was cut. Her abductors had evidently driven her into Compton, where they had dumped her body in the garage some ten days to two weeks previously.

It was my first Stinker, and while I watched the coroners take away the corpse, I felt as if my uniform had been saturated with slime, just as if I had run through some horrid sprinkler. I drove back to the police station, where everyone avoided me as I made my way to the locker room. I changed uniforms, balled the foul one up in a plastic bag, and took it to the cleaners. Even though they soaked it in carbon tetrachloride, they could not get rid of the smell. I had to go out and buy a new uniform at my own expense.

On another occasion, when I was working detectives, I received a call for assistance at the scene of an apparent homicide. It was the middle of August, the hottest time of year. I drove to a little bungalow in a court on the east side and found three patrolmen standing on the front lawn. I asked what they had, and they said there was the body of a woman inside the house.

"What's the cause of death?" I wanted to know.

One of them answered, "We're not sure. We haven't been inside yet."

To me this was totally unacceptable. Three patrolmen had been at the scene for at least fifteen minutes, and none of them had entered the house.

"Well, what the hell is the problem?" I demanded.

"When we got here no one answered," the patrolman explained. "I went around to the bedroom window and saw the body. The front door was locked, so I broke the window to try and open it—"

I was getting angry now. "So? Why didn't you go in?"

He gave me a sheepish look. "Because of the smell," he said.

He told me that when he broke the glass, the odor had hit him like a blast of radiation. He gagged and nearly vomited, and all three had withdrawn to the front lawn to wait for me.

I fumed and cursed and stalked up onto the porch. I had had to deal with Stinkers as a patrolman, and these three were taking a pass. Holding my handkerchief over my nose, I kicked the door in. The gush of odor was visible, a fetid cloud that drove me back to the sidewalk. "Holy Christ!" I gasped. "Get some towels and wet them down. And call the goddamned coroner!"

We wound our faces in the sodden towels, but no matter how we tried to force ourselves, we could not get inside the house. I could see the ankles of the corpse, its bare blue feet hanging off the bed, but I could not get to it. Finally we gave up and waited for the coroner's team. When they arrived, they, too, were unable to penetrate the fog of decay that was emanating from the bedroom. In desperation, I called the fire department and told them to dispatch a hazardous materials crew.

The firemen suited up in full protective gear with masks and oxygen tanks, and entered the little house as if it were a nuclear power plant in meltdown. They brought the body out in a zipper bag as the assembled crowd of neighbors retched at the smell that penetrated through the vinyl casing. It was not until the coroner's van's door had closed and the body had been taken away that any of us dared to enter the house.

There was no blood in the bedroom, no sign of a struggle, and no weapon. The firemen had told us that they had had to remove a silk scarf that was knotted around the woman's neck. I found it hanging from the bedpost. We identified her from the contents of her purse, and I began making inquiries. What I learned was a story almost as sordid as the odor of decay.

The woman was one of those odd, pathetic creatures who strike up romances with convicts. It seemed that she was involved with an inmate at Tehachapi State Prison, who, being in a work-release program, was allowed to come home on weekends. I went to Tehachapi to interview him, and he admitted that on his furloughs, he would meet the woman at her house for lengthy bouts of sex. When I told him that she had been strangled to death, he seemed genuinely surprised.

"She was alive when I left her," he insisted. I asked if he had any idea who had killed her. He thought a long moment and answered, "She musta done it herself."

I bristled. "Don't fuck with me! You were the last one with her before she died. She had a silk scarf tied around her neck. You tell me the truth, maybe I can work with you, try to get you a break. If it was rough sex—"

He cut me off. "Was the scarf tied around the bedpost?"

I thought a moment. "Yeah," I said. "Why?"

He shook his head sadly. "It was a thing she was into. Sometimes, if she didn't get enough sex, she'd tie a scarf around the bedpost and choke herself while she made herself come. She got a rush out of it, y'know? I used to warn her about it, but she said it got her off real strong. She musta done it after I left."

It was possible. There had been no struggle, and the convict had no history of violence; in fact, he was in work-release because he was in jail for petty crimes. He was a slight, mousy kind of man; it would have been difficult to believe he could murder anyone.

I wrote up my report and submitted it to DA Carlson. He looked at the evidence, the autopsy report, and the results of my investigation, and decided that the death was probably due to self-inflicted sexual asphyxiation.

It had been an act of frantic frustration by an obsessed and lonely woman. I could not help but feel that the squalid cloud that I had seen emanating from her bedroom might well have been the ghost of her despair.

The third case began with a call that a body had been recovered from the Compton Canal. This was the narrow concrete trench that separated Crip and Piru turf, running from Los Angeles down to the Port of Long Beach. At its deepest point it measured perhaps five feet, and it was here that the body had been submerged for nearly two weeks.

When I got to the location, I was horrified. The corpse was bloated to the point where it was hardly recognizable as a human being. It was naked, having burst through its clothes; the skin was ghastly gray, nearly translucent, so that it was impossible to tell whether the victim was black, white, or Latino.

We knew that it was male, since a portion of the penis remained, the rest having been eaten by the crawdads that inhabited the canal. The nose, lips, ears, fingers, and toes all had been gnawed away. He had evidently been a big man, over six feet tall, and it took both coroners and three patrolmen to hoist him onto the gurney. As they handled the corpse, it sloshed and bulged like a putrid beached walrus. To me it looked like some horrible inmate of hell from a Brueghel painting.

We had no medical examiner, so I drove the corpse to the morgue in Los Angeles, which had a room in the subbasement for bodies in an extreme state of decomposition. It was wheeled into a giant freezer that contained several other corpses, some decapitated, some missing limbs, all horribly decayed, all unclaimed.

The next morning I attended the autopsy to fill out what we called a schematic. This was an official report of the cause of death, which I might have to use at the trial of the killer. The corpse was wheeled in; it was frozen now, but still it sagged over the sides of the gurney. The pathologist slipped on his mask and surgical gloves, and stepped to the table with a scalpel in his hand. He nodded to a technician to start the tape machine that would make a record of his findings. I stood off to one side, taking notes.

"I'm ready to begin," the pathologist said through his gauze mask. "I am making the preliminary incision..." He leaned over and pressed down with the point of the scalpel.

The corpse exploded. It burst like a giant balloon with a bang and a horrid hissing sound as the gases of decay that had been building for weeks were suddenly released. With them came a jet stream of writhing, shimmering masses the size of thumbs—maggots propelled by the eruption.

They sprayed across the room, splattering against the walls and sticking to the light fixtures in the ceiling. As I stood there in shock, a dozen of them dropped onto my suit, still wriggling obscenely, bloated like the corpse whose internal organs they had devoured. Even worse was the smell, a gray-green putrid stench more acrid than the rot of eggs, more penetrating than the spray of a skunk.

I ran from the room, shivering in disgust. In the corridor I swiped and swatted at the maggots, which dropped to the tile floor with pustulant plops and began slithering away. A scene from *The African Queen* flashed through my mind, when Bogart surfaces from the river to find that he is covered with leeches. I raked my fingers through my hair, and more came away on my hands, and I flung them off with a violent shaking of my fingers.

It took me nearly an hour to calm down. In the men's room I stripped to my underwear to make sure than none of the filthy creatures remained in my clothes. I dressed again, but every few minutes I ran back to the mirror to check myself. I imagined I could feel them wriggling in the collar of my shirt or in my socks.

After the autopsy room had been cleaned, I returned to complete my schematic. As I watched the surgeon sort through the ruptured remains of the corpse, I had to keep reminding myself that this had been a human being once, a man with a history and hopes, with parents, perhaps a wife and children; a victim who, like any victim of crime, deserved my attention and demanded justice.

When it was done I went home, threw my clothes in the trash, and took shower after shower, but nothing could erase that stench, or the sight of that squirming geyser of maggots. For months afterward I had nightmares—there would be an explosion, a horrific odor, and I would wake up, sweating and scratching at myself, my skin alive with invisible, vile wriggling.

One night I lay there, alone and exhausted, and realizing that for all the defenses of detachment and sex I had built up, my psyche was slipping. In twelve years on the street I had seen the worst that human nature can become, had handled hundreds of murdered corpses, attended scores of autopsies, been shot at a dozen times, seen official corruption and incompetence, had friends become alcoholics and addicts, and commit suicide. I had watched a human being's body erupt before my eyes, covering me in maggots.

Was that, I wondered, the nature of us all, bloated with mortality, being eaten from inside by a swarming decay that would suddenly burst out and destroy us? I was no longer the idealistic sociology student who wanted to serve his community—that much was clear. How could I be? Humanity cannot endure such trauma and remain tender. What, then, was I becoming?

I remembered being called to the scene of a grisly murder, in which I found a young woman's body lying half out of the back of a van. The van was parked at the Compton Canal in a desolate spot near the 91 Freeway. The woman had been raped and shot and the van set on fire, though the position of the body indicated that she was still alive as it burned. Officer Jeff Nussman was on the scene when I arrived. It was a tragic and horrifying sight. The woman's body was charred and half consumed by the flames, and as I approached, it was still smoking. The stench of burning flesh was nauseating. Nussman asked me what I thought had happened, and I heard myself reply, "Worst case of suicide I've ever seen."

The joke had come spontaneously, unbidden, and I recalled the vapid lyrics of the song the Dozen had made up when the Maoist radical had blown himself to bits: *With a Tommy here and a Tommy there, a little bit of Tommy everywhere*... At the time it had seemed to me callous and cruel, a bleak humor that had infected those veterans who had taught me, and who were struggling against the odds to retain their sanity. Now, I realized, that bleakness was infecting me, and in my turn I was teaching it to others. I was drifting into what the philosophers call a dark night of the soul, tumbling slowly into space like an untethered astronaut.

I was irritable all the next day, impatient, short-tempered, a pain in the ass. There was only one possible antidote for it: When I got home that night, I called Oregon. I had to speak to Tiffany. She chattered on about school and her friends and the latest toys, and I felt myself relax. I was still connected to the Earth after all; there was still, no matter how tenuous, a light left in my soul.

Chief Rouzan was taking his time. I had heard nothing about Rutigliano's rehiring, and I knew that in the bureaucratic way of things, some impetus was needed.

When I was a junior at St. Anthony's prep, I had to make up a course, which meant going to summer school. Given my parents' address, I would normally have taken the course at Centennial High School, but because all the neighborhood thugs were there, they preferred that I take it at Compton

High. My friend Andy Salcido lived in the Compton High district, so that summer I used his address on Peach Street in Fruit Town, and I went there every few days to pick up mail from school.

Next door lived the Padilla family, whose youngest son, Santos, attached himself to me. I had a reputation as an athlete, and Santos idolized me. He was a bright if brassy six-year-old, with a wicked smile that spoke of mischief. I spent time with him, playing ball and watching cartoons, and when the summer ended, he sometimes came to my house to hang out with me.

As he grew up, Santos Padilla turned his mischievous streak to crime. He joined the Largo gang; though he never became a shooter, he did get into many fights at parties. Every time he was busted, he appealed to me for help, and I did what I could for him. I was a cop and he was a crook, but some part of him was still the little kid with the wicked smile who had idolized me.

One night when I was visiting with Andy on Peach Street, I called Santos and said we needed to talk. He came running over from his parents' house next door.

"Hey, Johnny, bro, what's up?" I told him I needed a favor. "Favor, man, yeah, sure. Anything."

I explained that I was trying to get an old friend reinstated on the police force, and it would help if I could give him a big bust. "I need you to turn me on to something hot," I said. "Something that'll get the suits' attention."

He asked, "Who is it?"

"Rutigliano."

Santos nodded solemnly. He knew Rut, and he said he understood. "Gimme a few days, okay, Johnny?" he offered.

I told him to take all the time he needed.

About three weeks later, Santos called me at the police station. "Listen, Johnny," he said, "there's a dude the sheriffs want real bad, over in Lynwood. Double murder, drive-by, you know. He's with the Paragons." They were a gang in the City of Paramount associated with the Largo.

"You know where he's hiding out?"

"Yeah, man, my buddy in the Paragons told me. But there's a problem." He lowered his voice. "This dude, the sheriffs are gonna kill him. He wants to surrender, but he knows they'll shoot him on sight. He needs somebody he can trust to turn himself in to."

"He can turn himself in to Rutigliano," I told him.

"All right, Johnny, but you make sure the sheriffs know that he's the only one. There can't be no sheriffs. Otherwise, they'll kill him."

I assured Santos that I would arrange it, and he gave me the address.

That night I called Rutigliano and told him what Santos Padilla had given me. "But you have to make the collar," I said. "He'll surrender to you, but only to you."

Rutigliano drove over to Lynwood, and the shooter surrendered to him. Rut brought him in to the station, where sheriff's deputies picked him up.

It did the trick. The next day, Joe Rouzan formally recommended to the personnel board that Dominic Rutigliano be rehired as a Compton police officer. The board agreed, but on the condition that Rut go through the sheriff's academy training program again. He would start out as a recruit, but he would get his job back.

When I told Rut that night at the Garter, I half expected that he would be indignant at the prospect of starting over with a bunch of new recruits. Instead, he broke into a broad grin. "It'll be a pleasure," he said.

There is a coda to this story. When Santos Padilla was seventeen years old, he was shot five times after a party in Long Beach. He survived, but when I asked him who had done it, he adhered to the gang code of silence and refused to say. I had expected as much, and I did not pressure him.

My sources told me that the shooter was Jake Guerina, the psycho hit man of the Setentas, or 7-0, gang. Jake had been responsible for a dozen shootings, including the murder of two Crips in L.A. County. There was an unwritten law in Compton that Latinos did not kill black bangers, and it had long helped keep peace between them. Jake Guerina had shown he was willing to violate this law, and I wanted to get him off the street before he killed a Blood or Crip in Compton and started an all-out war—but since the shooting of Santos Padilla had not taken place in Compton I had no jurisdiction, and the Long Beach PD ignored my information.

I was not going to let it go, however. I knew that Officer Steve Beckman was close to the Guerina brothers and used them as a source of information. Beckman was a blond-haired, blue-eyed white kid, but he had grown up on the north side, and he knew the Latino gangs and spoke Spanish fluently. I asked him to set a meet for me with Jake Guerina.

El Castillo Restaurant across Rosecrans from the old Compton Drive-In was a hangout for cops, since it served the best Mexican food in Compton. The parking lot in the back was ringed with thick juniper trees, which made it a very private place. It was there that I met with Jake. He came with his brother Frank, and I showed up with Beckman. They trusted him, and had insisted that he be present, since they knew about me and they knew my reputation.

"What does he want, man?" Jake asked Beckman in Spanish.

I answered for myself. "Santos Padilla is a friend of mine. You did him down in Long Beach."

Jake looked closely at me. "So what you want?" he asked.

"I wanna go fist city with you, motherfucker," I told him. "I'm gonna beat your ass like I own you."

He seemed startled. Beckman stepped between us. "Rick," he said, "you don't want to do this now."

I told him that I did, and I handed him my gun and badge. "Just me and you, Jake," I said. "Right here and now."

I could see that he was scared, and Beckman saw it, too.

"Look, Rick," Beckman said to me quietly, "Frank isn't gonna just stand by and watch you whip his brother. If you bust Jake's ass, I'm gonna have to knock out Frank, and that'll mean I lose them as sources. Let me talk to them."

I knew he was right. He had a relationship with the Guerinas, and they had provided him with valuable intelligence on rival gangs. I knew how I would feel if another cop shut down a critical source of mine to settle a private score.

I backed off. "Okay," I said, "but I want them out of Compton."

Beckman told Frank and Jake to get lost. They seemed eager to do so. Before they left, though, I told them, "Don't ever fuck up in front of me—either of you. 'Cause the first excuse you give me, I'm gonna kill you. I'm gonna shoot you in the fuckin' face, and I'm gonna put a throw-down in your hand. You understand me?"

They said they did, and they disappeared out of the parking lot.

The next day, Steve Beckman met with the Guerinas and made a deal. They had relatives in El Monte; they were to go there and stay out of trouble until I cooled down. I did not see or hear about either of them for the next six months.

When Santos Padilla recovered from his wounds, Rutigliano and I convinced him to join the army as a way of getting out of Compton and away from the gang culture. He completed boot camp with honors and was posted to Germany. There, he started experimenting with heroin. He was discharged, and by the time he got back to Compton, he was a hopeless addict.

One night, when I was the detective sergeant on duty, a couple of patrolmen filed a report of an addict found dead in the Glenmore Hotel. I glanced at the cover sheet. It was Santos Padilla.

The mischievous little kid from Peach Street had become a victim of Compton after all.

The Ballet, the Hypnotist, and the Task Force

In 1979, I was promoted to sergeant. I had been on the force now over ten years; I had worked the street, the juvenile division, burglary, the Service Center, and homicide, and I had received half a dozen commendations. This was the next big step up the ladder for me. I had never lost sight of my original reason for becoming a policeman; namely, to use my training in sociology to do some good for my city. In addition to meaning better pay and benefits, being a sergeant offered me more opportunities to accomplish that goal.

It also meant more of a leadership role for me. I had been a platoon sergeant in the marines, and as a CPD sergeant I would once again be able to command a squad of men. It was a role I relished: putting together teams to undertake hazardous operations, leading them personally, the first one through the door. It was the kind of excitement and satisfaction that I craved. I could not wait for my first chance to lead my own troops into battle.

It was not long in coming.

Since the Korean War, the marines had had a base in Compton, at 600

North Alameda. It was to this base that I had reported during the Watts riots, and from the roof of which the marines had fired into the Safeway store. By the early 1970s, however, the crime situation had become so dire that the marines decided to leave the city. There were simply too many gangs, not to mention the Panthers and the Muslims, and the base was a stockpile for rifles, ammunition, explosives, and machine guns. They could not risk a raid in which these weapons might fall into the hands of gangs or militants.

This fear was confirmed the following year when the National Guard armory, which was housed next to the former Marine Corps base, was raided. Half a dozen crates containing eighty M-14 rifles were stolen. These rifles, however, lacked selector switches, which toggle back and forth between auto and semiauto fire. Still, we knew it was only a matter of time before the thieves bought the switches and the M-14s became a devastating commodity on the black market. In the hands of gangbangers, the Muslims, or the Panthers, they could have tipped the balance against the CPD.

I pulled out all the stops in trying to identify the thieves. At last, an informant told me that the word was out that a guy named Black Ice was looking for selector switches. I knew who he was, and had had several encounters with him. His handle came from the fact that his skin was so black he had to use white ink to tattoo himself. In fact, the words BLACK ICE were emblazoned across his chest in ghostly letters.

He was a prolific thug who had been arrested for burglary, armed robbery, assault, and drug dealing. Every time the cops stopped him and asked him his name, he would answer, "Guess." This always earned him a clout across the skull, but the truth was that his name really was Guess—Jerry Guess.

He lived in Cocoa Street, and we were tipped that he had stashed the rifles in his house. Given how dangerous the weapons were, I organized a team to raid the place. Dominic Rutigliano was completing his academy training, and he was the first team member I chose.

It was a weird sensation—not just leading my first operation as a sergeant, but having Rut under my command. I nearly apologized to him for the fact, but he took it graciously. He was just glad to be going back into action.

On the day of the raid, Rut and I and three other officers pulled up outside the Cocoa Street house in an unmarked van. I knew that if we all swarmed the house, Guess might flee, or worse, if he had found the selector switches, use the M-14s on full auto.

The plan was for me to go in solo—as sergeant, that was my job. I would check the place out, then break in the front door and take Guess down while the others rushed in after me. I carried a shotgun and had an M-14 slung over my shoulder. I told Rut to sit tight and wait for my signal. While he and the others remained in the van, I walked carefully onto the porch. There was no sign of anyone inside.

I leaned back and kicked out with my boot, but instead of the jamb, I hit the upper panel. It shattered, and my foot went through. I was trapped. I could not get my foot out of the door, and I could not force it open. For a few horrible seconds, I did an impromptu ballet on the porch with one leg pinned above my waist while I hopped on the other. The idea that Black Ice had found the selector switches and at any instant I would be riddled with automatic fire raced through my head.

Behind me, Rut saw what was happening. "Shit!" he exclaimed. "His goddamn foot's stuck!" He and the others came barreling out of the van.

They pulled me loose and smashed in the door. We all piled into the living room and cleared the house. It was empty, and the only sign of the M-14s was some empty crates hidden in the backyard. Informants claimed that Guess had taken the rifles out of the city; later, they were recovered in a warehouse. As we feared, his plan had been to sell them to the Black Panthers.

We got the rifles back and returned them to the National Guard. It had been a major success, and, as usual, no official notice was taken of it. Rutigliano took notice, though. For days afterward, he entertained anyone who would listen with the story of my brief career in ballet, complete with delicate dance moves and Tchaikovsky music. All he needed was a tutu.

It was a fact of life in Compton in those days that police officers were rarely rewarded for their achievements, no matter how spectacular they were. When the Tiffany's store in Beverly Hills' Rodeo Drive was robbed of an estimated half-million dollars in diamonds, every cop in Southern California craved the credit for recovering them. The Beverly Hills PD put out a nationwide alert, and the hunt was on.

In Compton we did not take much notice of the theft, but one detective, Paul Herpin, the Mummy, decided to make some inquiries. He checked with his contacts on the west side, and he began to pick up word that the River brothers might have been involved.

We knew them well, three brothers who lived on Harlen Street off Central Avenue, and had been lifelong thieves. They had begun as children, stealing bicycles and hubcaps, and had advanced to breaking into candy shops and liquor stores. At the same time, of course, they had graduated from juvenile hall to state prison. Herpin could not imagine the Rivers attempting something as grandiose as a Tiffany heist, let alone pulling it off, but nonetheless, he drove to the house off Central to have a look.

The brothers were at home, and were clearly nervous when the Mummy showed up. He told them he was looking into the robbery, asking if they knew anything about it, and they grew even more anxious. At last, he announced he was going to have a look around. In the backyard he spotted a patch of newly turned earth. When he scraped at the soil with his fingers, it came away, revealing a shoebox buried six inches below. Inside were the Tiffany diamonds.

Herpin arrested the River brothers and delivered the jewels to the Beverly Hills police. He received no commendation nor even any press for his efforts. Instead, the BHPD announced that it had recovered the stolen gems after weeks of intensive investigation. They had had nothing to do with it; Paul Herpin had handed the diamonds over to them.

At around the same time, I was involved in a similar unheralded incident. I got a call for assistance from Officer Alfred Skiles, who had grown up in the notorious Nestor Tract, the 1-5-5's turf. Skiles, a Filipino who spoke fluent Spanish, had been recruited by the Fives but had resisted and, instead, had become a cop. Skiles had, he told me, a "situation."

He was at a house in Richland Farms where a demented woman was holding her children hostage on the front porch. She was brandishing a pair of knives, threatening to kill the children and to cut anyone who came near her. Skiles wanted me to back him up.

I understood why. Just a few days before, LAPD had faced a similar situation. They had stopped a homeless woman pushing a shopping cart, and when she pulled out a knife and moved toward them, they had shot her repeatedly, killing her. The shooting had caused an uproar: Community activists had staged protests, and a civil action had been filed against the police department. Now we had the same thing right in our own front yard.

I drove over to the house, where Skiles was still trying to talk the woman down. A crowd had gathered, and I moved them back. The woman was slovenly and disheveled; her eyes were wild—she was clearly out of her mind. She held a butcher knife in one hand and a carving knife in the other, and she was shrieking at the top of her voice that she was going to cut someone, kill someone. Three little kids were huddled on the porch, wailing hysterically.

There was a utility pole right outside the house, and I noticed a telephone repairman perched atop it, watching the scene unfold beneath him.

It was a textbook hostage situation, and any other police department would have called in the SWAT team and a negotiator, cordoned off the area, and surrounded the woman. We had neither the time nor the resources for such tactics. I told Skiles to keep the people back, and I marched up onto the porch.

"You get away from me!" the woman bellowed. "You get away or I'm gonna cut you!"

I walked right up to her and got in her face. "Drop those knives, woman," I snapped, "before I shoot your head off!" She stopped screaming and stared at me. "Don't make me kill you," I yelled at her. "I don't want to be a killer."

She did not know what to do; this was the last thing her addled mind had expected. She gaped at me with confusion clouding her eyes. Behind her, the kids were still bawling.

"You got children here," I went on, more quietly this time. "You're disturbed, and you can get a little bit of help. And then you can go back home and cook them some pork chops and be happy."

She was still staring at me; her face was twitching, but she was otherwise immobile. A moment passed. I could hear her breathing grow heavier, the dirty, tattered blouse over her loose breasts heaving. Then tears began to form in her eyes.

"Drop the knives," I said gently.

Her whole body seemed to go limp, and she let them fall from her hands. I thought she might collapse, so I moved to her and put an arm around her. She was nearly passed out. By this time other units had arrived, and as Skiles and the patrolmen secured the knives and hurried the children away, I helped the woman to the broken porch swing. She eased onto it heavily.

Up on the utility pole, the repairman applauded.

"I wasn't gonna hurt nobody," the woman sobbed. I told her that I knew that. She looked up at me, her eyes streaming. "I'm just so fucking unhappy," she stated simply, "and don't nobody give a shit . . ." She trailed off, put her hands to her face, and wept.

"I do," I told her. "I give a shit." There are people in this world who are so desperate, so desperately lonely and unhappy, that they will do anything to elicit some form of solicitude. She was one. I held her until the ambulance arrived.

The paramedics checked her vitals and strapped her onto a gurney. As they hefted her into the back, she kept her eyes on me. I was probably the first caring human contact she had had for a long time. She seemed sorry to let me go.

In late 1979, Chief Rouzan approached me with the idea of forming a special task force to deal with the gangs. I had already had experience in juvenile, but now I was to create my own team, and concentrate specifically on suppressing gang violence, which had escalated to the point where Mayor Cade had declared, "We are not going to allow anarchy in our streets." My new task force was to be the answer to this problem.

Rouzan had chosen me, among other reasons, because he knew that the task force would be controversial, and he needed a leader who was not himself controversial. I had by that time received a half dozen commendations. There had never been a complaint sustained against me—my record was clean—and in fact, in eleven years, there had only been two complaints lodged against me.

The first occurred in 1969 during my rookie year. A man by the name of William Brown Jr. claimed that while giving him a ticket for tailgating, I had hit him on the knee with the door of my patrol car, and then forced him to sit on the curb while I abused him verbally. The whole incident was witnessed by the reserve officer who was riding with me. I did stop Brown for tailgating—tailgating my patrol car—and was writing a ticket when he began badmouthing me. I ordered him out of his car and to the curb. While my reserve officer was opening his door to get out, he accidentally hit the man in the knee. The complaint was so transparently false that it went nowhere.

The second, which occurred five years later, was more serious. A Los Angeles man named Clarence Briles alleged that I had assaulted him, verbally abused him, and threatened to kill him, all in front of witnesses at the Golden Garter.

Briles was a well-known pimp who ran two Italian girls at the Garter. He was a gaudy customer who sported a bulbous Afro and wore fan-tip shades, gold and purple leisure suits, and platform heels. He was the archetype of the Hollywood street hustler of the seventies.

One night I was dropping off my girlfriend, Candy Donatelli, at the Garter just as Clarence Briles sashayed out, his opera cape swishing. I was about to pull away from the curb when I heard Briles yelling and swearing at Candy. "You white honkey bitch!" he was saying. "You leave my girls alone!"

He launched into a string of curses at Candy, and she was throwing them right back at him as I got out of the car. I told Briles to shut up and move on, and he turned on me. "Fuck off, motherfucker!" he shouted. "Get out my fuckin' face! She ain't nothin' but your whore—"

I slugged him in the jaw, and he staggered back against the wall. Again I warned him to leave, but he came right back at me, his ermine hat cockeyed atop his natural. "That's police brutality!" he screamed. "I'm gonna fry your ass for police brutality!"

I had had enough. I grabbed a handful of his fluorescent shirt and shoved him through the door into the Garter. I beat him all the way across the bar while Vito and a dozen customers watched, until he hit the soda machine by the bathroom. He fell in between it and the wall and I finished him off with a couple of shots to the head. He lay there, a limp, bloodied mass of garish silks and gold chains.

I stood over him, wild-eyed and raging. "If I ever see you in Compton again, you lousy piece of shit," I told him, "I'll kill you. You got that?!"

His head sagged in acknowledgement.

The following day, Clarence Briles filed a formal complaint against me for brutality and death threats. As I mentioned, we had no internal affairs division, so the investigation was handled by Sergeant Art Camarillo, who was also my supervisor. He asked me what had happened.

"I wasn't gonna stand there and watch some two-bit pimp hassle my girlfriend," I replied, "so I beat the shit out of him."

Camarillo nodded soberly. "You had reason to believe that he was going to assault her."

The truth was that I was worried that she would assault him, in which case he would have been worse off, but I did not argue.

Camarillo then interviewed Candy. "Did Rick use excessive force?" he asked.

She shrugged. "He did what he had to."

"Did you feel that you were in danger?"

"Me?" She laughed. "It was that punk-assed pimp that was in danger."

Camarillo frowned. "What do you mean?"

"I mean, if he'da touched me, I'da killed him."

Camarillo recorded the results of his investigation and sent the report upstairs. With all the heavy-duty crooks in Compton, I knew what the consequences would be if I allowed a cheap hustler like Clarence Briles to pressure me, so I put the word out on the street that if he appeared again in Compton, I was to be told immediately. Briles evidently learned of it, and two days later he called Sergeant Camarillo.

"I'm dropping the complaint," he said. Art asked him if he had been mistaken. "No. Everything I said is true. But I got business in Compton, and I can't be havin' that man as my enemy. So forget it."

Nothing more was heard from Briles, and he never showed his face in Compton again. My record remained clean.

Stone Jackson, who had been my second in the Police Olympics boxing matches, was everything a Compton cop had to be. Big, physical, smart, and fearless, he was one of those officers we hired after he had been cashiered by another department. The L.A. Sheriff's Office had let him go following an incident at their academy.

One of the courses all recruits have to take is stress training. They are put through every form of harassment and intimidation by professional drill instructors, whose job it is to prepare them for the most extreme situations they might have to face. Students are subjected to mental, physical, and emotional abuse, almost to the point of breaking them. Not surprisingly, the DIs sometimes go too far.

Stone Jackson had been a professional boxer in Pittsburgh, and he was not used to being pushed around. When one DI got in his face and tried to humiliate him in front of the other cadets by using racial and sexual insults, Jackson decided he had had enough. He challenged the instructor to fight him one-on-one out in back of the academy that night. Wisely, the DI declined, but Jackson, who was seven weeks into his training, was dismissed.

The Compton PD picked him up immediately. He was exactly the kind of officer we needed to deal with the street thugs we faced every day—one who could not be intimidated, and who would not back down. He proved us right, too, becoming one of the most effective cops in the city. However, as I have mentioned, he had a terrible stutter, which meant that he had to be doubly tough on the streets.

On one occasion he was working a major narcotics case, and he was detailed to bring the confiscated drugs from the storage locker in the basement of the station to the court, so as not to break the chain of evidence. It was a busy day, and Jackson, like the rest of us, was run all over the city. When he finally found time to drive to the courthouse, he realized he no longer had the drugs—and he had no idea where he had put them.

He came back to the station, where I was on duty. "R-r-r-rick," he said, "I d-d-d-don't know where they're a-a-a-at." Formidable as he was, he had the look of a schoolboy who forgot his homework.

"Try to remember," I said.

"I d-d-d-did, R-r-r-rick, b-b-b-but I c-c-c-can't."

I took Jackson to see Inspector Sandoval, who was in charge of detectives, and I explained the situation. Far from being upset, Sandoval seemed pleased. "I got it covered," he said.

What we did not know was that Gil Sandoval was a certified hypnotist. He told Jackson that he would put him into a hypnotic state and help him to remember what he had done with the drugs. Jackson was desperate, and he agreed.

I told Sandoval that I thought it was a waste of time. "It's all Hollywood bullshit," I said.

"Watch," Sandoval smirked. "Watch and learn."

He took Stone Jackson into the detectives' interview room, sat him down, and told him to relax. While I looked on, he put Jackson into a deep sleep, guiding him with caressing tones through his activities of the morning. When they came to the drugs he said, "Now you will remember where you put them."

Jackson furrowed his brow. "I left them . . . I left them in the trunk of my car in the parking lot," he said in a hollow voice.

Sandoval smiled at me. "You see?"

He brought Jackson back to consciousness again. We told him what he had said, and his face lighted up. "Yeah, that's right! I stashed them there while I took a couple of calls—" He stopped short.

"What's the matter?" I asked him.

He looked at me, mystified. "I'm not . . . I'm not stuttering anymore."

It was true. From that moment on, Stone Jackson's signature stutter was gone. It never returned.

In early 1980, I had a series of meetings with Chief Rouzan about the special task force. It was to be a maverick unit answerable only to watch commanders with the rank of captain or above, and with a mandate from the mayor to keep constant pressure on the gangs, using any means necessary. I told him I understood exactly what he was saying, and that I would put together a team to get the job done.

"Remember, Rick," he cautioned, "you can't break the law." Then he smiled. "But you can bend it into whatever shape you need to."

For me it was a dream assignment, the highest expression of my long-standing desire to use my skills to make a difference to my community. It was sociology in the streets, armed academia, theory made practice in the most effective way possible.

I chose my team carefully. I knew that I needed a mix of skills and personalities, cops who were smart, tough, and knew the gangs inside-out. The first one I picked was Reggie Wright. He had been born and raised in Imperial Court Gardens in South Central L.A., a critical asset. Imperial Court was at the apex of what we called the Golden Triangle, which also included Nickerson Gardens and Jordan Downs. These three projects were the most crime-infested in Los Angeles, and Reggie knew their gang cultures and personalities intimately. He was the department's leading expert on gangs, both black and Latino, and I knew his expertise would be invaluable. I also wanted him for political reasons: Reggie was a nephew of Joe Rouzan, and I thought that fact might be useful given the controversial nature of the task force's mandate.

Next I recruited Bobby Baker, the Tarzan who had dropped from the tree on top of Odell Willis. Bobby, who was white, was not one of the toughest cops in Compton, but in my view he was one of the smartest, and he was also the best writer in the department. I knew that the reports we would file would require some creative writing, and I counted on Bobby to take care of that.

I needed a Latino officer, so I chose Tony Miranda. Tony was a Compton boy from the 300 block of Cedar Street on the north side. He was as streetwise as they came, and had he not become a cop, he would have made an excellent street hustler. Tony had a wide and deep knowledge of

the Hispanic gangs, but I valued him especially for his close association
with the Samoans.

The Samoans had been the Mormons' answer to the Muslim occupation of Park Village. Rather than sell their properties, the Mormons im-
ported from their missions the biggest, most intimidating Samoans they
could find to take them over. Many of these young Samoans were three
hundred pounds or more, and their sheer size terrified Hakim Jamal's
radicals. Badly outnumbered by the black gangs, the Samoans soon
formed their own gang, which they called SOS, or Sons of Samoa. This
was the least known and least understood of Compton's gangs, but Samoan bangers like Carlton, Knuckles, and Beef knew and liked Tony
Miranda, which would prove useful whenever we needed information
about the black gangs with which the Samoans were perpetually at war.

I had a black gang expert, a white intellectual, and a Latino hustler.
Now I needed an Asian, and the choice was self-evident to me: Alfred
Skiles. It was Skiles whom I had backed up in the incident involving
the demented woman with the knives. He was a short, stocky Filipino
who had been raised in the Nestor Tract in the heart of 1-5-5- territory.
He knew the gang and its members, and he was one of the most fearless cops in Compton. If some crook required individual attention to
get his head straightened out, I turned to Al Skiles, and he never let me
down.

The odd man out on the team was Mike Markey, and my choice of him
was met with some skepticism. Mike was young and Irish, and he had
been raised in Thousand Oaks in Ventura County. His main drawback was
not his outsider status, however, but his driving. He had already totaled
three police cruisers, earning for himself the nickname of Crash. He was
so notorious that for the first two years on the force he was not allowed to
drive at all, but was required to ride in the passenger seat as a recording officer. I had watched him since his days at the academy, though, and I believed he possessed great potential.

This was the group I was to lead into the worst neighborhoods of
Compton in an effort to suppress a rising wave of crime and violence that
was being fueled by a new scourge in the streets—crack cocaine.

Crack had replaced powdered cocaine as the drug of choice in Compton. It was cheaper, which made it accessible in even the poorest neighborhoods, and it was much more potent. Crack delivers a high that is more intense and shorter-lived than powder, producing a euphoria that has been described as a full-body orgasm. The resulting crash is as devastating as the high is exhilarating. The most insidious aspect of crack is that the more you use, the more you crave, which throws the addict into a downward spiral of addiction that sooner or later must be financed through crime.

The appearance of crack in the streets of Compton had exactly the same effect on crime that it did on the body—it upped everything suddenly and exponentially, and brought in its wake a nightmare of violence and despair. How the epidemic started is a subject of intense historical debate, but I can say that, in the course of our war against crack, we discovered evidence that it was coming into Compton via a railroad that led through Manuel Noriega's Panama to the Colombian drug cartels and, ultimately, to the Contra war in Nicaragua. The legendary crack dealer Freeway Ricky Ross, for example, had direct ties to Contra leaders who supplied him with cocaine. By 1982, Ross was making *two to three million dollars a day* selling crack to the Bloods and Crips. Whether the CIA had anything to do with it, as many have speculated, I do not know.

Crack quickly became the main source of revenue for the gangs. The Bloods, the Crips, the Largo, the Tres, the 1-5-5, and the sets that either broke off from them or were affiliated with them were soon making fortunes. Money was pouring into the gang culture, crack was flooding the streets, and customers, many from outside Compton, were lining up to buy. With this windfall, the major gangs began to grow, and to spread beyond their original turfs. The Crips and Bloods established sets throughout California, and then across the nation, from the Midwest to the East Coast and into the South.

Unlimited money also meant unlimited arms. From the clasp knives and single-shot zip guns of the early 1970s, gang weaponry evolved to automatic weapons with armor-piercing ammunition, machine guns of all kinds, and even heavier arms such as grenade launchers. By 1980, records of arrests and interviews showed that there were some eight thousand black gang members in Compton, and over two thousand Latino and Samoan bangers as well. This meant there were more than ten thousand gang members in a city whose population had not reached a hundred thousand.

Gangs were no longer loose associations of street thugs protecting their turfs; they were now armies, heavily armed and well trained, with outposts all over the nation. It was these armies that my task force of six officers was to take on. We knew we could not defeat them, but we could harass and contain them, and play them off against one another. The old divide-and-conquer strategy was back.

Because the task force was so small, we had to identify the most important targets for our attacks. There were three of these.

The first was the Wilmington Arms complex at 700 West Laurel. This was an old self-contained enclave on the edge of White Island, the one into which the Samoans used to fire their weapons for sport. In the early days, the Wilmington Arms had been a tightly knit, exclusive community enclosed by an eight-foot iron fence, the entrance protected by security officers who manned a quaint little guard shack. Now, instead of keeping the thugs out, the fence kept them in. The security guards, from the firm of Land Johnson, were all winos, and they were so terrified of the gangs that infested the place that they never left their shack. Gang members used to sell crack through the fence on all sides of the Wilmington Arms, and every night carloads lined up to make their buys.

The second target was 152nd and Dwight. This dead-end street backed onto the Nestor Tract and was the 1-5-1 Bloods' chief marketplace for crack. The third was Willowbrook and Alondra, behind Margi's liquor store. There the four Sessions brothers dealt crack in the shadows of a giant eucalyptus tree that grew in the alley.

We hit all these locations on a regular basis, driving up on drug deals, busting heads, and arresting the pushers. Our goal was to put as big a dent in the gangs' business as possible, disrupting their ability to make money. It was economic warfare as much as police work, and we went about it systematically and aggressively.

For the first time in my career, I used my gun as a first resort; in fact, of the ten shootings in which I was involved as a policeman, six occurred on the task force raids, and only one of those was reported. It was dangerous and wearing work, but I loved it. Leading my team into hornets' nests like the Wilmington and the Dwight-'52 knowing that the brass would back me no matter what we did was exhilarating. We hit them hard and we hit them often; we varied our timetable and our tactics, and they never knew what to expect or when. Gradually, we began to have an impact.

For example, we hit Dwight-'52 so often that the 1-5-1 dealer, Charles Davis, was having trouble getting his supply. On one occasion, he sold baking soda to the Carbajal brothers, the killers from the 1-5-5. When the brothers snorted the powder, they became sick. Next day they went back to Dwight looking for Davis, and they demanded their money back. Davis refused.

There was a junior flip in 1-5-5 looking to make his bones, a homicidal lunatic named Joe Pores, whose handle was Little Hi-Fi to distinguish him from the 1-5-5 leader, Luis Lasoya. The Carbajals gave Pores a shotgun, and a mandate to make his bones by killing Charlie Davis. Joe Pores was thrilled. He drove to Davis's parents' house, got out of his car, and walked up to the front window, where he began blasting the place apart. Windows shattered, furniture was torn up, and the family inside was screaming as Pores circled the house reloading and firing manically.

Inside, Charlie Davis hid under his bed. When the firing stopped at last and he was sure the shooter had gone, he crawled into the bathroom, opened the tiny window, and eased his head out. Joe Pores was hiding in the bushes underneath. He stuck the snout of the shotgun under Davis's chin and blew his head off.

We arrested Joe Pores for the murder; he was booked, arraigned, and, over our objections, released on bail. A few weeks later, while awaiting trial, he attended a party in Long Beach given by members of the Longo gang. There was a fight, and then a shootout, and Joe Pores was shot to death. He was seventeen.

Another hot spot that we raided on a regular basis was Tragniew Park at 159th Street and Keene. There were tennis courts in Tragniew, and often, when we rolled up for a raid, I found two five- or six-year-old girls practicing intently under the critical eyes of their father. I knew there would be shooting when we hit the park, and so I always waited until the girls had finished before moving in. Years later I learned that the two little tennis players were the Williams sisters, Venus and Serena.

Some of the other hot spots we targeted were 131st and Wilmington, the crack market of the five Fuqua brothers, murderous Haitians from the Front Hood, and the parking lot of Nocker's Restaurant on El Segundo east of Central. Nocker's was the habitual watering hole of Lieutenant Mardrue Bunton, who would solemnly announce in his guttural basso that he was "going Code 7 at Nocka's." The parking lot behind the restaurant backed onto an industrial zone, which offered an easy route of escape, so it was there that the West Side Pirus set up shop.

One of the most notorious of Compton's PCP dealers operated at the corner of Saunders Street and Bradfield near Lueders Park. His street name was Squirt, not because he was small but because he was parsimonious, giving his buyers only "a squirt" of dust. His main distributor was Marcus Nunn, nicknamed China Dog because of his almond-shaped eyes, and he was backed up by a psychopathic thug named Jeffrey Wesson, whose handle, appropriately, was Pit Bull.

One afternoon, around four thirty, I was patrolling in the Lueders Park area. It was a rare occasion when I was in uniform and driving a unit. With me was Officer D. W. Smith, whose car had broken down. He had asked if he could ride with me to fill out the hour remaining on his shift. As we drove up Bradfield to Saunders, I saw a Volkswagen Bug in Lueders Park. There were four white boys in it.

Racial profiling, which is such a sensitive subject today, was a way of life with us. We knew all of the whites who remained in Compton either by sight or by the way they behaved on the streets—to us they were unmistakable. They kept to their own neighborhoods and appeared only at very prescribed times of the day. Identifying them became an instinct with us, whereas whites from outside of Compton were as conspicuous as sheep in Times Square.

There were only two reasons why white outsiders would be in Compton in those days: either they were lost, or they were buying drugs. If they were lost, we would escort them out of the city. If they were buying drugs, we would pull them over, pat them down, search their cars, and arrest them if we found drugs or a gun. When we took such cases to court and the defense attorney demanded to know our probable cause, we answered that we had stopped the suspects because they were white. That argument held up in the Compton courts in those days. The judges, all of them, accepted our racial profiling as a legitimate justification for a search leading to an arrest.

In this case, it was clear that the white boys had come to score PCP from Squirt, so I put the siren on, turned into the park, and drove across the grass right onto the playground where the car was parked. When Squirt, China Dog, and Pit Bull saw me get out of the unit, they put up their hands and spread-eagled against the wall along the edge of the playground. While Smith patted them down, I ordered the boys in the VW to get out of the car and onto the ground.

They panicked. The driver shoved the Bug into gear and spun his wheels, digging up the playground dirt. As it careened past me, I pulled out my gun and yelled at them to stop. When they did not, I fired a couple of shots after the Bug. D. W. seemed surprised and asked me what he should do.

"You see what I'm doing, don't you?" I snapped. "Crank off a few rounds at them."

He did, and then we both jumped into the unit.

It was rush hour, and we immediately hit traffic as we followed the VW. I asked Smith, "Did you see any guns in that car?"

"No," he answered.

"How 'bout drugs?" Again he said no.

Usually on drug raids I carried a throw-down gun, a cheap revolver that could be left at the scene of a shooting if need be. Since I was in uniform, though, I did not have my throw-down with me. "Damn!" I said. "There's gonna be a shitload of paperwork on this."

"What should we do?" Smith asked.

I thought quickly. By now the dispatcher had put out a call of shots fired, officer in pursuit. The VW was right in front of me, stalled in traffic, but I had no evidence to back up an arrest and no justification for the shooting. I knew that other units were rolling to assist me, so I put in a call that I had lost the vehicle in traffic, and canceled the pursuit. Later I filed a report stating that the VW had tried to run me down, and that I believed the occupants had a gun. No one was convinced, and I was given a written reprimand—a slap on the wrist. At least one thing had been achieved: The white boys had learned a lesson I was sure they would never forget. They would not be coming back to Compton to buy drugs, nor would their friends.

Meanwhile, the carnage over crack continued. With so much money on the line, even gang leaders were being targeted by would-be millionaires.

The Tate brothers, Kim and Ken, who were twins, had founded the Santana Blocc Crips on Santa Fe Avenue. They were prolific killers, cold, heartless reptiles who reminded me of a two-headed snake, as deadly a pair as one could imagine. There was a carnival in Compton held in the parking lot of the old, abandoned Sears building, a tawdry, gaudy affair with a neon Ferris wheel, sideshow rides, and kewpie doll booths. It was the first time there had been any activity at the site since white flight had closed the store down.

One night Kim Tate attended the carnival with half a dozen of his boys. In the crush of the crowd he became separated from them. That was when he spotted a beautiful black girl who caught his eye and flirted with him obscenely. He followed her through the labyrinth of gaudy attractions to the far side of the fair.

It was a honey trap. Tate did not know that that corner of the fair had been taken over by members of the Lime Hood and Lueders Park Bloods, deadly enemies of the Santana Blocc Crips. They were waiting for him. By the time he realized what had happened, it was too late.

Knowing that shots would attract too much attention, the Bloods had armed themselves with golf clubs. They closed in on Tate. He fought his way out and ran. The Bloods chased after him. When the crowd saw what was happening—one man being pursued by half a dozen others with clubs—they parted like the Red Sea.

One of the Bloods made a flying tackle as Tate reached the fence at the back of the parking lot. In a few moments, he was surrounded. The first Blood swung his club in a savage arc that caught Tate on the side of his head. He staggered under the blow and went down on his knees. Then the others took turns stepping up to him and ritualistically slamming their golf clubs into his collapsing body. They beat him to death. It was like something out of the Old Testament, or some pagan blood rite, carried out to the gaudy racket of the fair and with the most unlikely of weapons.

The homicide was assigned to John Soisson and me. The murder of a leader of one of the most notorious gangs in Compton was bound to be a complex and high-profile case, and I valued Soisson's knowledge of forensics. A former Arthur Murray dance instructor, he had, through hard work and patient study, made himself an expert in fingerprints, DNA evidence, and crime scene analysis.

One of the golf clubs had been dropped at the scene as the Bloods had fled the carnival. From the fingerprints we were able to identify one of the killers. A few days later, we learned that the man, Donald Hazelwood, was in the custody of the Manhattan Beach PD.

Shortly after the murder of Tate, Hazelwood and three other Bloods had driven to Manhattan Beach to rob a bar, forcing the patrons against the wall at gunpoint while they robbed them and cleaned out the register. They jumped into their car, but, unfamiliar with the city, they were soon lost. They were only a few miles from Compton, but their turf mentality was so strong that they had rarely ventured outside it, and now they had no idea where they were.

Though fleeing from the scene of an armed robbery, they stopped at a gas station to ask directions. To pass the boring hours late at night, the clerk had a police scanner in his cubicle, and when he saw them, he was immediately suspicious. He gave them directions back to Compton and called the MBPD. They chased the car down and arrested Hazelwood and his three accomplices.

John Soisson and I drove down to Manhattan Beach and picked up Hazelwood. We took him back to the station, where, after a harsh interrogation, he gave up the five other Bloods, telling us that the death blow had been delivered by James Cooper, whose street name was Porky. In a matter of minutes we had identified all six murderers, and within twenty-four hours they were in custody. We quickly put the word of the arrests on the street, hoping to prevent a retaliation. Unfortunately, it was already too late.

The following day, Donald MacQuillers, a member of the Lime Hood Bloods, was walking back to his home on Temple Street when a carload of Crips drove by. The word on the street was that Freddy Staves, known as Baby Gangster, pointed an automatic pistol out the window and shot him six times. MacQuillers was dead before his body hit the pavement. When I heard about the killing, I knew that the target had not been random— MacQuillers had been carefully and deliberately chosen. For Donald MacQuillers and his brother Ronald, like the Tate brothers, were twins.

One afternoon while I was upstairs in the detective division filing paperwork, I heard a commotion from the parking lot below. It was laughter, and it was growing by the second. I hurried downstairs to see what had happened.

Officers Johnny Garrett and Rich Daniels were leading a suspect to the basement holding cell, and when I pushed through the raucous crowd of cops surrounding them, I could not at first understand what I was seeing. The suspect, a young black man, was covered from head to chest in yellow foam, and there was smoke rising from his Afro, the top of which had been cleft into a smoldering V. He was humiliated and furious, cursing nonstop as Garrett and Daniels shoved him into the cell.

What had happened was this:

They had responded to a call of DTP, disturbing the peace, in Richland Farms on the east side. They found the young man, whose street name was Kraz-e, involved in a screaming match with two others with whom he had been gambling. The other men fled, but Garrett and Daniels tackled Kraz-e and cuffed him. He wore a goatee and an ample, mushroom-shaped Afro, and as soon as they busted him, he began cursing at them in the vilest language. They threw him into the cage in the back of their unit, and all the way to the station he ran his mouth, calling them every name he could invent.

Johnny Garrett was chain-smoking, and after ten minutes of this scabrous rant, he had had enough. "Just shut the fuck up!" he yelled, and he flipped his cigarette butt at him over the seat.

The burning butt landed in Kraz-e's hair, which, saturated with Afro Sheen, caught on fire. He started yelping, but because his hands were cuffed behind his back, he could do nothing. When Garrett and Daniels looked back, sulfurous flames were shooting from the top of the man's head as his Afro sizzled down toward his skull.

"Do something, motherfuckers!" he was screaming. "I'm on fuckin' fire!"

"Oh, shit," Daniels muttered, and he pulled the unit to the curb.

By now the Afro was fully engulfed and Kraz-e was screeching hysterically. Garrett jumped out of the car, ran to the trunk, and took out a fire extinguisher. He yanked open the back door, pointed the extinguisher at the man's head, and pulled the trigger.

In seconds, Kraz-e was doused with bright yellow fire retardant. He was coughing and gagging, but the flames in his hair had been put out. Above the yellow crust of his face and shoulders, his Afro smoldered and smoked, the whole center section of it having been burned away.

When they took him to court for his preliminary hearing, he was still coated in foam. As soon as he saw the judge, he began cursing again, claiming the cops had tried to burn him alive. The judge tried to calm him down, but the man turned his rage on him, swearing at the top of his voice. The judge ordered him sent back to the cells just as he was—looking for all the world like a furious, foul-mouthed bumblebee.

This was not Johnny Garrett's only smoking mishap, however. Once when he and Ron Malachi, the one-legged sergeant, were working narcotics, they set up a sting on a major cocaine supplier. Posing as a dealer, Malachi arranged to meet the supplier and drive with him to the safe house where he kept his product. The plan was for Johnny Garrett to hide in the trunk of the car and, when the deal went down, jump out and make the arrest.

Because the pushers knew all of our unmarked cars, we bought junked cars from a local lot each month for use in narco operations. Malachi checked one of these out of the pool—an aging, battered Buick sedan with a big trunk. On the day of the sting, Garrett climbed into the trunk, and Malachi drove to pick up the supplier.

The drug dealer was no amateur. Instead of leading Malachi directly to his safe house, he made him take a complex, circuitous route through the city. Inside the trunk, Johnny Garrett was becoming desperate for a smoke. When he could take it no longer, he reached into his jacket, took out a cigarette, and lit up.

The dealer led Malachi around town for nearly half an hour. In that time, Garrett had smoked half a pack of cigarettes. The trunk was filling up with smoke, and Garrett was trying desperately not to cough. Then his jacket caught on fire.

As the old Buick rumbled through Fruit Town, Garrett pitched from side to side and swatted at the jacket as best he could in the confines of the trunk. It was smoldering, and the smoke was getting thicker. He tried to open the lid, but the lock was jammed. At last, he began kicking frantically at it.

Up front, Malachi and the drug dealer could hear the pounding in the trunk, and when they turned, they saw smoke pouring out of it. Malachi pulled over, ran to the back, and opened the lid. Out tumbled Johnny Garrett in a cloud of smoke, swearing and choking. He stripped off his jacket, flung it to the ground, and stomped the fire out.

The drug dealer looked on mystified.

"What the fuck took you so long?!" Garrett yelled at Malachi.

"The guy wanted to make sure we weren't followed."

At last, the dealer realized what was happening, and he took off. Garrett and Malachi watched him disappear down the street.

"That's great!" Garrett yelled in disgust as he snagged up his jacket. "That's just fucking great! We lose the collar, the guy's made both of us, my jacket's got a hole burned in it, and I nearly died of asphyxiation!"

Ron Malachi looked at him sternly. "You know, Johnny," he said in his most solemn tone, "you really gotta quit smoking."

Among the officers with whom I had attended the police academy was Percy Perrodin, who had grown up on Central Avenue at 166th Street. He was an excellent cop and we had often worked together. 166th and Central was the turf of the NBC—the Neighborhood Blocc Crips—and Percy told me that the gang was harassing his younger brother Eric, who was in high school. Eric was a slight, studious kid who did well in school and had his sights set on college and a career in public service. Precisely because of his ambition and his love of books, the bangers had targeted him, and they were making his life hell. Percy asked me to use my contacts in the gang to help.

I drove over to Central Avenue and found the NBC leaders, Lance Singleton, Johnny Taylor, and the Robinson brothers. They were sitting on the stoop at Singleton's house. I got out of the dick unit and called them over. They pretended not to hear me. I was in no mood for foolishness.

"Get your asses over here!" I yelled at them.

They ambled across the lawn. "What you want?" Singleton snorted. "We ain't doin' nothin'."

"You're hassling Eric Perrodin," I snapped.

"So?"

"He's the brother of a cop. If you got any sense at all, you'll lay off him."

Lance Singleton smirked. "We ain't do nothin' to that pussy." The others laughed.

I got right in his face. "If I hear you fucked with him again, I'm gonna kick up on your asses, all of you. You get me? There's not gonna be any other answer if you mess with that kid again—just a straight-up ass kicking. You understand?"

Singleton grunted that he did.

"You other assholes—you got my message?"

They all nodded.

"Good. 'Cause I don't wanna have to come back down here and repeat it."

I turned and got back in the car.

From that day Eric Perrodin had no more trouble with the NBC. He graduated from high school, went to Cal State University, and joined the police force. I supervised him and gave him his first field evaluation, which was outstanding. While serving, he attended Loyola Law School, and the later became a district attorney in Los Angeles. In 2001, Eric Perrodin was elected mayor of Compton, and he remains mayor as of this writing.

Boot Hill, the Chief's Mother, and Jack in the Box

The Grandee Apartments were located near the corner of Grandee Street and Alondra, and the building was a stronghold of the Crips. This set called themselves the Grandee Crips, and, difficult as it may be to believe, every apartment in the building was inhabited by gang members, either active, associated, or affiliated. It was a kind of fortress of gang activity, a Bastille of the Crips.

Our task force invaded this building every ten days or two weeks, and each time, we found a body, either severely beaten or dead. The bodies were dumped in a section of the building that the gang had named Boot Hill, after the legendary graveyard in Tombstone, Arizona. Nine times out of ten, the victims were Bloods.

The Grandee Apartments were so notorious that the Bloods used them in their initiation process. Any junior flip who wanted to be accepted as a full-fledged member of his set could make his bones by running the gauntlet of the Grandee. His homeys would drop him at the front door late at night, and he would have to race to the top, then make his way down the hallways, usually at Olympic speed, and out the back door alive.

One of the targets of the task force was a Santana Blocc Crip nicknamed Jackoff Sleepy, a handle that fit his personality. Sleepy was particularly notorious in that he preyed on drunken Mexican illegals. He would wait for them to tank up on Tecate at a local bar, then ambush them in alleys, club them over the head, steal their money, and shoot them. We could never catch him, but his method was always the same, and we watched his body count increasing.

He attacked the illegals because they were easy targets. They did not carry guns, and they had no family or friends who would retaliate for them. The situation became so bad that some community activists marched to the police station to ask for help. It was Rutigliano to whom they spoke. His advice was curt and to the point. "Buy some guns and arm yourselves," he told them.

There was also another reason Jackoff Sleepy targeted Mexicans: He had a vendetta against them. Some years before, he and his brother were in Lueders Park when they were confronted by Latino gang members. The Latinos demanded money, and when Sleepy and his brother refused, the bangers beat them both severely. Sleepy survived, but his brother did not. It was because he had watched his brother being beaten to death by Latinos that Sleepy made a profession of murdering Mexicans.

One night a young Mexican girl from Boyle Heights attended a party given by members of the Santana Blocc Crips. She liked to hang out with black gangbangers, and thought she could do so in Compton with impunity. She was wrong.

The Crips got her drunk and then slipped her some drugs. When she was totally out of control, they gang-raped her. Jackoff Sleepy was at the party, and he watched the rape with growing excitement. He did not touch the half-conscious girl; instead, when the others were done, he took out a gun and shot her in the head. Her body was dumped in the Grandee Apartments, where we found it several days later.

We had no idea who the girl was. Her body had been stripped, and the only identifying mark on it was a crude tattoo in blue ink of the letters *PF* on her right hand. After some research, I was able to determine that *PF* stood for Primera Flats, the name of a gang that had originated in

Boyle Heights in the 1920s. It was one of the oldest Latino gangs in Los Angeles, and a remnant of it still existed.

Paul Herpin and I drove to Boyle Heights, made some inquiries, and learned the identity of the girl. Her nickname was India, because she had the swarthy skin and dark features of an indigenous Mexican. We tracked down her relatives, who told us that the last time they had seen her, she was planning to attend the Santana Crips' party. That led us back to Compton, where Herpin was able to determine that it was Sleepy who had killed her. We arrested him, and he was tried for murder and sentenced to life in prison.

When I asked India's brother why she had gone into Compton to party with black gangbangers, he answered that she was addicted to rap music. Under its influence, she thought that hanging with the bangers would be cool, and that she could do so in safety. This was at a time when rap music was just beginning to emerge as a phenomenon in Compton, led by Eazy-E, Dr. Dre, and Ice Cube. These characters haunted Atlantic Drive, which was known as a center for the sale of drugs. Later, Eazy-E admitted that he had started his record label, Ruthless Records, with profits from selling cocaine.

By the early eighties, rappers had replaced the hand jivers and doo-wopers of my youth on the street corners of Compton. Rap traced back through the New York DJs to the Caribbean and ultimately to Africa. At first it seemed to be a legitimate means of expressing the realities the rappers lived on the street. Later, rap mutated into another form that was at once more cynical and more sinister.

Compton quickly became the West Coast center of rap, spawning some of its leading personalities. One of these was a Dominguez High School football player by the name of Marion Hugh Knight. His nickname was Sugar Bear, which was later shortened to the unpronounceable "Suge."

Our gang expert, Reggie Wright, identified Knight as a member of a Compton Bloods set called the Mob. He went on to play football at the University of Nevada, Las Vegas, and then as a scab in the NFL during the players' strike. In 1989 Knight entered the rap music business by, it is said, threatening to throw Vanilla Ice off a twentieth-floor balcony to secure royalty payments for one of his clients. In 1991 Suge founded Death Row records with Dr. Dre, after he and his fellow Bloods forced Dre's producer to release him from his contract by threatening them with base-ball bats. Knight owned a club in Las Vegas called the 662, which on a push-button phone spells Mob. It was to the 662 that Suge and rap star Tupac Shakur were headed the night Shakur was shot to death.

In Suge Knight's junior year, four of his buddies from the football team decided to rob a local pharmacy for drugs. They waited until the place had closed, then broke in through a back window, setting off a silent alarm.

I took two units to the location, and we surrounded the store, trapping the four inside. I walked to the rear, where I found the broken window, stuck in my head, and yelled, "Heeeeeere's Johnny!" a reference to the film *The Shining,* which had recently been in the theaters.

We could hear the four football players scurrying for cover as we moved in. Three were caught hiding lamely behind the counters, but the fourth had climbed up a ladder into the crawl space above the ceiling. We ordered him to come down, but he was too terrified to move. We did not know whether he was armed, so Officer Paul Wing cautiously climbed the ladder and doused the narrow attic with pepper spray. We could hear the kid groaning and cursing in the ceiling, but still he refused to come down.

Wing asked me what we should do. We did not want to shoot him, but we could not get him to budge. "Call for a K-9 unit," I said.

The closest canine unit was in Signal Hill, so we radioed them for as-sistance and waited at the foot of the ladder until it arrived.

"How the fuck am I supposed to get my dog up there, Sergeant?" the Signal Hill cop asked.

I shrugged. "Carry him up there."

The canine officer looked at me doubtfully. Then he picked up his German shepherd and, with some help from our officers, hauled it up the ladder and shoved it into the crawl space. The effect was immediate. We heard screaming, growling, shrieking, barking, and tearing. Dust was puffing from the light fixtures, the ceiling was vibrating, and then, sud-denly, it collapsed. Two bodies hurtled to the floor in a cloud of fluorescent lights and plaster: the thief and the dog, its teeth still sunk in his backside.

We arrested all four kids. They were suspended from school, and missed the next football game.

In 1980, Alan Parker resigned as city manager, and, to our surprise, the council chose Joe Rouzan to replace him. I suppose that, given Rouzan's and Parker's behavior at the time of Roland Ballard's run for city council, we should have known that Rouzan himself had political ambitions. The question, of course, became: Who would succeed him?

For the third time, the Police Officers Association backed Captain Manny Correa. He was by now the longest-serving member of the department, widely respected for his integrity and his administrative abilities. However, Rouzan had other ideas.

Disgusted with Tom Cochée, Lieutenant Jim Carrington had left the department and taken an administrative job with Irvine PD in Orange County. When Cochée resigned two years later, Joe Rouzan brought Carrington back at his former rank. Since then, Carrington had been promoted to director of police services and assistant chief. In his new position as city manager, Rouzan was able to, in effect, anoint his successor. He named Carrington.

We were shocked. If Manny Correa were to be passed over again, as we expected, we assumed the job would go to one of Rouzan's entourage, like Gil Sandoval or Roger Moulton. Carrington had quit the department at a critical time, and though he had contributed scathing articles to the *Communicator,* he had had no direct involvement in the removal of Cochée. Many of us saw his elevation to chief over more senior and more qualified candidates as a mystery.

Not unexpectedly, rumors began to circulate regarding Rouzan's motives for the move. One held that Rouzan owed a favor to a black newspaper for its support during his tenure and Carrington was the price the paper had named. Another was that Rouzan was repaying Carrington for some sort of service he had done while Rouzan was still at LAPD. Whatever the reason, those of us who had labored hard to rid the department of Cochée could not help but feel that Carrington was being rewarded for disloyalty in leaving when we needed him the most.

Jim Carrington would not have been the choice of the rank and file. Most of the white officers disliked him, as did all of the Latinos, and many of the black officers distrusted him because of his anonymous attacks on Cochée. In fact, shortly after Rouzan's announcement, some of the senior black officers met at the Ramada Inn to discuss whether to fight Carrington's nomination. In the end they decided that it was probably pointless to do so. Rouzan was city manager; he would ramrod Carrington's nomination through the council, and anyone who opposed it would be blacklisted.

Jim Carrington was confirmed as chief of police, the fourth I had served under, and his first act was indicative of the kind of chief he would be. Knowing the CPOA's support of Manny Correa, Carrington immediately moved to neutralize him. He took away his car and demoted him, making him head of technical services, a job that any patrolman could have done. Instead of being a field commander with inspector rank, Manny was now confined to a desk job where he supervised only three people. Carrington's treatment of Correa was a malicious attempt to humiliate a rival, and to force him out of the department. It also demonstrated that the Latino community's fear that they were becoming the victims of reverse racism was grounded.

I openly criticized Carrington's appointment, but it happened so quickly that there was simply no time to mount an organized opposition. Besides, as the black officers had decided, I knew that to protest was probably futile. The Police Officers Association had had no say in the appointment of the last three chiefs, but, unlike with Cochée and Rouzan, who were outsiders unknown to us, we knew pretty much what to expect of Jim Carrington. He was an acerbic, vindictive man who carried grudges, as his mistreatment of Manny Correa showed.

Because I had argued that there were better qualified candidates for chief, I expected that Carrington would retaliate against me, probably by taking me off the gang task force. However, an unforeseen event happened that made that impossible.

When Carrington returned to Compton, he moved into a house on the east side with his mother. I knew Mrs. Carrington fairly well; she was a pleasant, well-educated woman who was popular in the neighborhood. Next door to the Carringtons' house lived a white family, one of the last in the neighborhood; like them, a mother and son.

The son, Greg, in his midtwenties, was an unfortunate creature with a long history of mental illness. One day early in 1981, when the chief was out of town on official business, Greg got hold of a gun and began shooting over the fence into the Carringtons' home. Mrs. Carrington was terrified. She hid in the bedroom and called for the police. I was on patrol on the east side that morning, so I put on the siren and lights and raced over.

When I arrived, I found Davey Arellanes and Henry Perez, two of my watch officers, crouching in the bushes at the front of the house. They told me that they had heard shooting from inside, and when they approached the door, a shot had been fired at them through the front window.

I asked if they knew whether Mrs. Carrington was still in her house. Arellanes said she was, but he did not know whether she had been hit.

"What about Greg?"

"He says he's not coming out under any circumstances."

"You'd better call the sheriff's SWAT unit," Perez said. "It's a hostage situation."

Normally that is what would have been done; in fact, given that the hostage was the mother of the police chief, all the heavy-duty equipment in town would have been summoned. But I was damned if I was going to ask the LASO for help to rescue my own chief's mother on my watch.

I told Arellanes and Perez to remain where they were, and went back to my car and called the station. I asked the officer on duty to look up the number of Greg's house in the upside-down directory. I then went to the nearest station phone—a locked telephone for police use—and called the number. Greg answered.

"Greg, it's Sergeant Baker," I told him. "You've got to come out, Greg."

"I ain't coming out, the way things are now!" he shouted. His voice was trembling, near tears.

"Greg, where's your mother?" I asked. Silence. "Greg, is your mother in the house?"

"Yeah," he muttered. "She locked herself in the bathroom."

"Okay, Greg. You leave her alone, and you come on out. I'll be right outside."

Again he refused. I was losing patience. "Listen to me, Greg," I went on tightly. "You know me. If you don't come out, I'm coming in. And I want your gun—"

"No!" he shrieked.

"I want you to give me your gun. I want you to come into the living room, put your gun on the table, and sit down."

"Don't come in," he growled.

"I am coming in, and I won't have my gun out—"

"I'll shoot you!"

"Greg, even if you shoot me, I'll get one or two shots off, and if I don't kill you, I've got two officers out here who'll kill you on the spot. They'll shoot you down where you stand. You'll die, Greg, they'll shoot you to death. And then they'll shoot your mother and say you did it. Now you know me, Greg, and you know I'm telling the truth. Do you understand?" Again there was a long silence. "Greg . . . ?"

"Yeah."

"I'm coming in now, and I want your gun. I'm not going to shoot you, and I know you aren't going to shoot me. Here I come . . ."

I walked up onto the porch while Arellanes and Perez backed me up with their guns drawn. I had told them what I had said, and they knew I meant it. The screen door was latched. I tugged it open. At any second I expected a bullet to come ripping through the front door. There was nothing—no sound, no movement. I tried the knob—it was not locked.

I stepped to one side and pushed the door open. As I had promised, my gun was still in its holster. "Greg . . . ?"

It was dark inside, and it took a moment for my eyes to adjust. Greg was doing exactly as I had told him to do. He was sitting on the living room sofa, his gun lying on the table before him. His head was down; he was sobbing.

"I wasn't gonna hurt anybody, Sergeant Baker," he said. "I was just mad—so damn mad I didn't know what to do . . ."

"I know, Greg," I told him. "Sometimes you get real mad . . ." I moved carefully toward the table.

His head jolted up. "Yeah! I get so mad I wanna do something!" he snapped. "I wanna kill somebody!"

"But you won't," I answered. "You won't kill anybody because you know that's wrong . . ." Gingerly I reached down and grabbed the gun.

Greg watched me slip it into my waistband with a childlike curiosity. "What're you gonna do with that?"

"I'm just going to hold on to it for a while."

He smiled sheepishly. "If I promise not to do it again, can I have it back?"

"We'll see," I said.

He turned suddenly contrite. "I'm sorry I caused such a fuss. I was just mad at my mom. I'm real sorry." I told him to stand up. "Are you gonna put handcuffs on me?" he asked anxiously.

I had two guns on me, and he seemed so meek. I told him I just wanted to walk him out to my car. He frowned suddenly. "No," he pleaded. "Put handcuffs on me, like they do on *Hill Street Blues*? Okay?"

He was a poor, hapless soul to whom God or Fate or Nature had been unkind. For a moment, though he had threatened to kill me, my heart went out to him. "Okay, Greg," I said. "I'll hook you up just like on TV."

He smiled, turned his back, and clasped his wrists together. When I put the cuffs on, he thanked me.

I called outside that it was clear. Half a dozen cops rushed in through the door.

"Mrs. Carrington's in the bedroom," I told them. As they went to free her, I took Greg out of the house and put him in Arellanes's car. Davey asked me if everything had gone all right.

Suddenly I felt all my muscles relax—I had not realized how tense I had been—but I covered it. "Just another day in Compton," I said.

The incident did not make the papers, was not featured on the evening news; in fact, it was scarcely noticed. Chief Carrington told me that he was grateful to me for saving his mother, and that was that—no commendation, no accolade.

Neither was I taken off the task force. And that was sufficient reward for me.

What I had come to think of as the curse of Compton continued. One afternoon I received a phone call from the son of Officer Dick Bidwell, the man who had asked my mother how she felt about my becoming a police officer, and who had then trained me personally when my Marine Corps duties took me out of the academy for two weeks.

"I just thought you would want to know that Dad is dead," he told me.

What had happened was this:

After leaving Compton, Dick Bidwell had taken a job with a department in the San Joaquin Valley. On his retirement, he returned to Los Angeles, where he lived with his son in Oceano, near Pismo Beach. Bidwell was diagnosed with prostate cancer, and neither chemo nor experimental drugs had any effect. He was sinking, wasting away before his own eyes. Though he had been a proud man of action all his life, with a command presence that could take control of any situation, he now found himself growing helpless. Like many heroes, he did not fear death; what he feared was decrepitude.

One August afternoon, while his son was at work, Dick Bidwell put in a call of shots fired to the local police. Then, knowing that they would respond within a few minutes, he went to the living room, sat down in his favorite armchair, took out his service revolver, and shot himself in the head. He had not wanted his son to come home and find him. It was a sad but noble end to one of Compton's best and most selfless police officers. When his son told me about it, I remembered what was said about Ernest Hemingway's suicide: *Gracia*. Dick Bidwell had gone out with grace.

Our approach of playing the gangs off against one another was a delicate and potentially explosive one. Much like the global balance of power between the United States and the Soviet Union, our strategy was aimed at maintaining an equilibrium among these homicidal armies, while at the same time not provoking armed conflicts between them. We wanted the gangs divided, but not at war. Yet this is precisely what threatened to happen at, of all places, a burger joint.

It is one of the ironies of urban warfare that the battlegrounds do not have exotic names like Thermopylae or Austerlitz; instead, they are the mundane locales where ordinary people eat and work and play. Lueders Park was one, Sonny's Pool Hall was another; so were Margi's liquor store and the Glenmore Hotel. One of the most incendiary spots in Compton was the Jack in the Box at the corner of Santa Fe and Rosecrans. This fast-food joint had the misfortune to be located in the no-man's-land between the Santana Blocc Crips and the Compton Barrio Tres. Both sides coveted the turf, but they had carefully avoided each other there.

One night "Baby Gangster" Freddy Staves and some of his boys from the Santana Crips walked into the Jack in the Box, sat down, and began drinking beer and smoking spliffs. Staves had been identified to us as the cold-blooded killer who had gunned down Donald MacQuillers, and he knew that the street telegraph would spread the word quickly. In half an hour, the Tres showed up.

They were led by Max Saldana, known as Frosty, the CV3 leader. I had known Saldana since childhood, and had arrested him three years before for rape. Now in his early thirties, he was the capo of a gang of remorseless killers that terrorized the streets of North Compton. Among the others were the Fimbres brothers and Victor Granados, a six-foot-three thug whose street name was John Wayne because of his sidewinding shuffle. Granados was known as the gang's best fighter. When they swaggered into the burger joint, they were armed with garbage can lids, baseball bats, and brass knuckles.

Instantly, the Jack in the Box erupted in a ferocious gang brawl. While the clerks and burger-flippers ran for cover, the bangers tore the place and each other apart. By the time two patrol cars arrived, two Crips and three Latinos were lying on the floor in dirty slicks of blood, beaten nearly to death. There had been no shooting. For some reason, neither the Crips nor the Tres had brought guns. The cops arrested all the bangers who could walk and sent the others to the hospital.

When I heard about the fight, I was concerned. The invasion of the Jack in the Box had been a provocation, but did it signal the beginning of a new gang war? We had been lucky that no shots had been fired and that no one was killed, but if the Crips were going to take on the Tres, it might spark an all-out conflict between the black and the Latino gangs, who had not clashed head-on since Johnny Jones had killed Robert Valdez at Whaley Junior High ten years before.

We watched the situation carefully for the next three months. Nearly every weekend a few Crips would turn up at the burger joint, the Tres would respond, and there would be a bloody fight. But still, no guns were used. It was strange to me—baffling, in fact. The Crips were challenging the Tres, and, by extension, all of the black gangs were calling out the Latinos. Perhaps because of that very fact, however, neither side was willing to escalate the confrontations to killings. The Santa Fe–Rosecrans Jack in the Box was becoming the Berlin Wall of Compton. Both sides flexed their muscles there, dangerous flare-ups occurred, but neither was prepared to risk an armed conflict.

It was, I suppose, a measure of what might be called the maturity of the gangs. By now the black gangs and the Latino gangs had too much respect for and too much fear of each other to go head-to-head in a full-scale war. They knew that if one side started shooting, it would unleash a cycle of drive-bys, ambushes, and executions that would spiral into a tornado of war. They had been around long enough, and had enough to lose both in lives and money, that their self-interest curbed their more savage instincts. Like the United States and the Soviet Union, the gangs had achieved a kind of détente.

I knew this situation could not go on forever, and so, in a move reminiscent of Rutigliano's and Hall's mano a mano, I met with the leaders of Santana and the Tres and told them that either they backed off the Jack in the Box and called a truce, or the task force would come down on both of them. They put up a show of defiance, but it seemed to me that both sides were looking for just such a way of saving face. The blacks had made their statement and the Latinos had made their stand, and now they needed a way out. My ultimatum provided it, and they accepted.

A war between black gangs and Latino gangs that nobody wanted had been averted before it threatened to engulf the whole city in violence.

I have mentioned the leader of the 1-6-6 Neighborhood Blocc Crips, a shooter called Lance Singleton, and his lieutenants, Johnny Taylor and the brothers Eugene and Elgene Robinson. One day Eugene Robinson was showing off his .32 to another Crip, a thug nicknamed Fatso, when it went off. The bullet struck Fatso in the head, killing him instantly. At first Robinson and his homeys claimed the killing had been a drive-by, but I determined pretty quickly that Robinson was responsible. I busted him and charged him with negligent homicide.

It was a chance to put one of the Crips' leaders away, so I pursued the case aggressively. Robinson was represented by an ambitious attorney in the public defender's office in Compton named Mark Rosenbaum. Rosenbaum, who wore a beard and a shaggy mop of hair, was a Harvard Law School graduate, and he proved a skillful defense advocate. When the not-guilty verdict came in, he and Eugene Robinson hugged each other.

Outside the courthouse, I walked up to Rosenbaum and told him what a disservice he had done to the community. He peered at me quizzically. "What are you talking about?"

"Eugene Robinson is a sociopath," I answered. "He may have shot his friend by accident, but he'll kill someone else. And next time, it'll be on purpose."

Rosenbaum smiled. "No, no, no," he said. "I've gotten to know this boy. He has a good heart; he's just made some bad choices. But he swore to me he's learned his lesson."

"Sure he told you that, and maybe he even believes it," I replied. "But I know him, too. He's a stone-to-the-bone Crip. Killing is in his DNA."

Rosenbaum scowled at me. "Eugene says that he'll straighten himself out, and I believe him. He'll keep his nose clean. He's going to go back to school and make something of himself. I probably saved his life by getting him off."

"No," I answered. "By getting him off, you've condemned someone else to death."

Rosenbaum was getting angry now. "You're a cop," he said. "Of course you expect the worst of people—cops always do. But I guarantee you that Eugene Robinson will be a positive contributing member of society."

"Okay," I said. "I'll remind you that you said that."

Over the next three years I ran into Mark Rosenbaum in the courts, and each time, he made a point of telling me that Eugene Robinson had called him to say he was working at a job, going to school part-time, and keeping out of trouble. Rosenbaum took a smug enjoyment from proving to me that I had been wrong.

Each time, I answered, "Just give it time."

The following summer, four years after the trial, I was in court when one of the clerks said to me, "Hey, Rick, your old friend Eugene Robinson is coming up for arraignment." I asked what he had done. "Got popped for a murder down in Long Beach. Some kid."

By then Mark Rosenbaum had moved on to become the head of the Southern California ACLU. He had recently filed a lawsuit on behalf of two teenagers who claimed that they had been named in LAPD's top secret Alpha Files. This was a list of suspected gang members that the LAPD's intelligence division was assembling. Rosenbaum hoped to have such records, which we had kept for years in Compton as field investigation files, ruled unconstitutional. When it turned out that neither teenager was in the files, the suit was dismissed.

I do not know whether Rosenbaum received the news about Eugene Robinson, and I never had the chance to tell him. Another kid was dead—and there was no joy or satisfaction in my having been right.

Joe Rouzan proved as good as his word. He spoke with the members of the Guardians, and they agreed to end their schism and rejoin the CPOA. John Soisson was president, and he set two conditions for their readmission: They would have to reapply for membership, and, if readmitted, they would lose whatever seniority they had enjoyed before the split. The black officers and Terry Ebert agreed, and all were accepted back with one exception. John James, who had led the secession movement, was judged to be too disruptive of the association's goals and was refused membership. The antagonism was over; the dissension was ended. The CPOA was unified again.

Richard III, the Stardust, and Orchard Street

Because the gangs of Compton formed along racial lines, they tended to be strictly racist. Black gangs never admitted nonblack members, Samoan gangs were entirely composed of Samoans, and most Latino gangs did not allow outsiders to join. An exception was the 1-5-5, which, from its inception, had admitted whites such as the Holmes brothers, and Samoans like Saber and Pineapple, in a rare show of toleration. But the most amazing example of interracial gang membership was to be found in a black gang.

Lime Hood was one of the most vicious and homicidal sets of the Bloods. Headquartered on Lime Street on the extreme eastern side of Compton, the Lime Hoods numbered from thirty to fifty members, making them one of the Bloods' larger affiliates. They were notorious for drive-by shootings, and by the early eighties they had shot from 100 to 150 Crips. Though an exclusively black gang, by the late seventies Lime Hood's leader was a Latino named Luis Velasquez. It was the only instance I am aware of in which a Latino led a black set. In the brutally conformist world of Compton gangs, Luis Velasquez was unique.

Clever, cunning, and utterly ruthless, Velasquez had grown up not in the Latino Corridor but on Lime Street on the east side. In order to survive in the heart of the Lime Hood turf, he had had to prove he was tougher and more resourceful than any of the black bangers; necessity had turned him into a remorseless killer. At a time when black gangs took no outsiders, Luis had managed to insinuate himself into the Bloods, and had murdered, cheated, and intimidated his way to the top.

He was the Richard III of the Compton gangs, creating strategic alliances, charming and intimidating, cajoling and betraying, and systematically eliminating his rivals in a virtuoso display of malign ambition. In the process he had become more black than the black bangers, adopting their style of dress, mastering their jargon, sleeping with only black girls, and displaying a deep pathological hatred of Latinos, which he acted out in a campaign of beatings, torture, and murder. The black bangers of the Lime Street Hood idolized him.

I met him once. I was at City Hall on official business and I ran into Lorraine Cervantes, the wife of Alfredo Toledo, whom I had gone to Mexico to arrest. She remained undaunted in her role as city council gadfly, and she was there to check on the council's meeting schedule. She was accompanied by a friend, a comely middle-aged Latina named Irma Velasquez. With her was her slender, good-looking son Luis.

Lorraine introduced me to Irma, and then to Luis. It was a strange and unexpected encounter. He put out his hand, which was surprisingly small and white. "*Buenos días*, Señor Baker," he said.

I shook hands with him. His grip was gentle, almost like a girl's. In Spanish I replied, "I'm glad to meet you, Luis. I have heard of your reputation."

He smiled, a truly modest and charming smile. "And I have heard of yours, too, Detective Baker," he replied.

I did not feel it was appropriate to go any further. Luis's mother seemed pleased that we knew each other. Lorraine Cervantes was in a hurry, and she bustled Irma and her son away. In those few moments, though, I had seen in the eyes of this polite and diffident boy the soul of a killer. I knew that if I ever went up against him, one of us would have to die, for with Luis, there was no alternative.

We had a policy in the CPD of not killing gang leaders. The implications were too complex, and, besides, we found it more effective to negotiate with them, play them off against one another, or arrest them when it was possible to send them away for long prison terms. Luis Velasquez was different. He and his Lime Street Hoods were responsible for so much murder and mayhem that my task force targeted him as our most wanted man. Nevertheless, in the end, it was not we who got him.

In 1982, Luis Velasquez did a solo drive-by in Crip turf in daylight, firing with an automatic pistol out the windows of his car. It was a typically brash and flagrant act of suicidal bravado. One of our patrol cars was in the area, and the officers, Jasper Jackson and Brent Garland, gave chase.

Velasquez sped and swerved his way through traffic, shooting at Jackson and Garland, who held their fire. At last, caught in a crowded intersection, he pulled his car to a stop, jumped out, and began firing at the officers. For a moment he stood there, while drivers and pedestrians ran for cover, emptying his pistol in a final act of naked defiance. Jackson and Garland returned fire, and Velasquez was shot and killed. If he had been a soldier in a European war, his death might have been called heroic. As it was, it marked the end of an audacious villain every bit as inevitable as that of Richard Plantagenet on Bosworth Field.

Luis Velasquez's death was a turning point in the history of Compton gangs. Never again would any gang leader openly challenge the police, and never again would a Latino head a major black set. However, since the evil that men do lives after them, that was not the end of Velasquez's story.

In an act unprecedented in the history of Compton gangs, the Lime Street Hood put a bounty on Officer Brent Garland's life, declaring that he had been responsible for Velasquez's killing. The gang offered fifteen thousand dollars to anyone who killed Garland, be he Blood, Crip, or Latino. It was a perverse act of fealty to their fallen leader, and one we could not permit. No Compton gang had ever targeted a police officer, and I knew that if we allowed it, the intricate balance between bangers and cops would be destroyed and none of us would be safe.

I put the word out on the street that if so much as a hair of Officer

Garland was harmed, the CPD would retaliate on the Lime Street Hood until every one of them was in prison or the cemetery. There was no room for political correctness; I was, in effect, declaring total war on an entire gang, and they knew that I meant it. The message was clear: Harm a Compton cop, and you—all of you—will be wiped out.

From that day, all the police in Compton took it in turns to go Code 7 on Lime Street, one car after another parking in the middle of the block in relays, disrupting the gang's operations, busting their members for the slightest offense. Catfish Bailey, in particular, was relentless in hassling them, sitting in his unit with its amber lights on every night, smoking a Tiparillo. At last, after three months of this, the Lime Street Hood backed off. Their new leaders announced that the contract on Brent Garland's life was canceled.

Memories in Compton are very long, and none is longer than that of a cop.

In 1966, Officer Ray Oliver, while off duty, was doing his weekly grocery shopping at the Food Giant on Long Beach Boulevard on the east side. Two black men barged into the store, shouting and waving sawed-off shotguns at the clerks, demanding money. The supermarket was instantly echoing with screams and fearful panic. Oliver was at the back of the store, and by the time he realized what had happened, the robbers had fled.

Ray raced to the parking lot and jumped into his car. As he did, one of the shoppers, a black man named Ritterbocker, ran up to him. "I saw what happened, man," he said. "You goin' after them?" Oliver identified himself as a cop. "Let me help you," Ritterbocker insisted. "I'll do whatever I can."

He pulled open the door and climbed in beside Ray Oliver, and together they took off after the robbers.

Oliver pursued them for several blocks before they were stopped in traffic. He jumped out of the car with his service weapon drawn and moved up on the driver's side. Ritterbocker strode up on the other.

"Police officer!" Oliver shouted. "Let me see your hands!"

Mimicking him, Ritterbocker yelled, "Show me your damn hands!"

The two men surrendered, and Mr. Ritterbocker helped Ray Oliver take them into custody.

When Oliver booked the men in at the police station, he thanked Mr. Ritterbocker and told the other patrolmen on the watch what he had done. They mobbed him and congratulated him. In those days there were no awards for citizen bravery, but one of the officers who shook his hand was Dominic Rutigliano.

In 1981, Mr. Ritterbocker was arrested on some old traffic warrants by a rookie cop and brought into the police station for booking. When Rutigliano heard that he was there, he went down to the cells. They had not seen each other in fifteen years, but Rut recognized him immediately.

"Mr. Ritterbocker," he said, "what are you doing here?"

The old man smiled. "I guess my sins finally caught up with me."

Rut called over the jailer. "Do you realize who this man is?" he demanded. The jailer said no. "He's a hero who helped an officer capture two armed robbers. Turn him loose."

The jailer responded that Ritterbocker was being held on two hundred dollars' bail.

"That's okay," Rut said. "I'll take care of it."

He went to the bank, drew out the money, and delivered it to the court clerk. Mr. Ritterbocker was released, and when he came up for trial, Dominic Rutigliano appeared as his character witness. The old warrants were dismissed, and Rut treated him to lunch.

Lyn Steward was the most wanted man in Los Angeles County. He was a giant, at six foot nine and 320 pounds, and a psychopathic killer. The sheriffs were looking for him in connection with some fifty robberies, as well as two murders. In one, he had broken into a salvage yard owned by a Korean immigrant who had learned karate to defend himself. When Steward confronted him in his office, the Korean threw an overhead chop at him. Steward caught the man's arm in his meaty paw, lifted him off the ground, and sank his teeth into his stomach, ripping through the flesh like a crazed shark and tearing out the man's intestines. In the other murder, he had beaten a man to death with a sawed-off shotgun.

I had been in court all morning. Around 10:00 A.M. I went Code 7 with Davey Arellanes, who had also been testifying, and we drove down Compton Boulevard to a diner where there was a waitress I was romancing. I was wearing a three-piece suit, and I had left my gun at the station. As I turned onto Sherer Place, I noticed a towering hulk of a man on the sidewalk. He was walking toward Wilmington, carrying a brown paper bag.

"Isn't that Lyn Steward?" I said to Arellanes.

He peered at the man. "I don't know," he replied. He reached for the Wanted file we kept in the car.

"Fuck the paperwork," I told him. "Look at the size of him. Who the hell else could it be? Let's roust him."

"I don't have my gun," Arellanes said.

"Me neither."

I pulled the car to the curb, got out, and walked up behind the man. He was massive, with thick hands and a bullish neck so large that he walked stoop-shouldered.

"Hey, you," I called. "Turn around."

He came to a stop slowly, like a boxcar rolling to rest on a siding, and turned. His face was as broad as his body, fringed by wiry hair, his eyes dark and glassy.

I showed him my badge. "What's your name?"

He regarded me a long moment with a dull expression. "Jones," he answered. "Jerry Jones."

"Let me see some identification."

He shrugged heavily. "I left my wallet at home." I asked him what he had in the bag. "Just a bottle of wine."

"Your name's Steward," I said. He scowled at me; I could practically hear him growl. "You're under arrest."

"Fuck you," he grunted.

Arellanes was standing by the car, backing me up, but I knew that if

Steward tried to resist, the two of us would have a hard time taking him down. He was the biggest, most intimidating creature I had ever seen. He took a step toward me.

I reached into the waistband at the back of my jacket. "Don't move, motherfucker!" I barked. "If you take one more step, I'll drop you where you stand. I'll shoot you in the face."

He was towering over me, murder in his vacant eyes. Arellanes was also reaching under his coat. Steward hesitated.

"I swear I'll kill you," I told him. "Don't make me kill you."

He glanced slowly between us, and then he stepped back. "You ain't got to shoot me," he said.

"Turn around." He swiveled his immense frame. "Let me see your hands."

Steward reached back. His wrists were as thick as my forearms. I took the paper bag away from him, clapped a cuff onto one wrist, and pulled the other toward me. His back was so broad I could not make the handcuffs reach. I called to Arellanes to bring his. He answered that he did not have them.

"Shit," I muttered.

"We can't put him in the car like that," Davey said.

I was holding the gigantic man by the ring of one cuff, knowing that at any second he could shake me off and run, or attack me and Davey. "I've got some rope in the trunk," I said. "Go get it."

Arellanes came back with a length of nylon cord, and I used it to tie the cuffs to his free wrist. As I did, Steward said again, "You ain't got to shoot me."

I marched him to the car and put him in the back. Before I closed the door he said, "Can I have some of that?" He nodded to the paper bag, which I still held. "Where I'm goin', I won't get no more."

I hesitated. Though he barely fit into the backseat, there was something pathetic about the way he asked for his wine. I unscrewed the cap and held the bottle to his lips. He closed his eyes and took a long drink, his bulbous Adam's apple working up and down like the blunt head of a pile driver. At last, he leaned back in silence.

We turned Lyn Steward over to the L.A. Sheriff's Office. The whole time he was in custody he said not a word, a huge, brooding figure alone in the holding cell. When the deputies came to the station to pick him up, I signed over the paperwork. They took him out in leg shackles and three pairs of cuffs. As he passed me at the door, he paused. "Thank you" was all he said.

A few weeks later I was cruising down Santa Fe Avenue. When I turned left onto Alondra Boulevard I pulled up alongside a battered gray '58 Chevy flatbed pickup. In the back were mops, brooms, buckets, a folding ladder, all the paraphernalia of a custodian. As I passed, I glanced over at the driver. I was stunned.

It was Tom Cochée.

He was wearing a frayed denim navy surplus shirt; his hair was graying, and he looked aged and worn. He turned toward me, and I waved. He started to return the greeting, but when he saw who I was, the expression in his eyes deadened.

I pressed the accelerator and pulled on ahead. When I ended my shift, I said nothing to the other cops. To have done so would have been cruel and unwarranted. For when Cochée had realized who I was, I saw in his eyes the same look I had seen in those of the kids on the fire escape behind the church. It was the look of a man who has been beaten, and who knows it. Humiliation was unnecessary—Tom Cochée had gone beyond that.

Davey Arellanes asked me to be the best man at his wedding, and I accepted happily. He had become one of my closest friends on the force, a tough, intelligent, and compassionate cop who had backed me up in a lot of dangerous situations. A few days before the ceremony, a carload of Bounty Hunters, one of the most vicious of the L.A. Bloods sets, drove down from Nickerson Gardens in Watts and shot up a 166th Street Crips party. After the wedding, five cops gathered at the Garter to continue the drinking they had begun at the reception. As the liquor flowed, the conversation turned to the Bounty Hunters' raid, and, with the peculiar logic of alcohol, the cops became indignant that L.A. Bloods had crossed the border and attacked one of "our gangs." They decided to do something about it.

The five piled into a car and drove up to Watts. They were all very drunk, and they had their guns. It was late, and the long, two-story white buildings of Nickerson Gardens were quiet. The cops drove through the chain-link entrance into the courtyard and began shooting. People dived for cover behind Dumpsters and cars, or darted back inside the buildings. The Compton cops drove through the complex firing at the buildings, creating chaos. Finally someone called for the police, and in a few minutes a sheriff's unit came wailing into the compound, lights swirling. The deputies pulled the Compton car over and ordered the cops out. When they showed their badges, the deputies were perplexed.

"What the hell are you doing here?" one of them asked.

"You tell your fucking Bounty Hunters to stay the fuck outta Compton," one of the cops replied.

The deputies stared at them a moment. "You're *defending* your gangbangers?"

"Damn straight we are!"

"Was anybody hurt?" the deputy asked, bewildered.

"'Course not. We fired over their heads. Whadaya think we are—hoodlums?"

"Maybe you oughta go the fuck back to Compton," the deputy suggested.

"Maybe you oughta keep your fuckin' assholes on this side of Watts," the cop said as they got back into their car.

The deputy peered at the driver. "Are you okay to drive?"

"Certainly," he slurred, and he roared off weaving through the complex. The sheriffs escorted them as far as El Segundo Boulevard, and then turned back. No charges were filed, but the Bounty Hunters never came back into Compton. They had shot up the 1-6-6, and the CPD had retaliated. They were probably as mystified as everyone else.

The Stetner family had lived on the east side for decades. I had known the eldest son, Vernie, when I was at Compton College. After the Watts riots accelerated white flight, the Stetners had chosen to remain in their home in the 1100 block of East Marcelle Street. By 1970, they were the last white people on the block, and one of the few Jewish families remaining in the city.

Vernie Stetner became a fixture in Compton, appearing at city council meetings to grouse about crime in the neighborhood, and calling the police at the slightest provocation. Most of the cops were thoroughly sick of his continual complaining, but I had known him most of my life, and I was able to talk him down when he went on his flights of compulsive kvetching.

In the mid-1980s, a family of black Muslims, the Wahids, moved into the house directly across from the Stetners, and a whole new form of antagonism began. The Wahids complained about the Stetners and the Stetners complained about the Wahids: Their grass was uncut, they used too much water, they parked their cars across the sidewalk, their trash cans were in the wrong place. The complaints and the rhetoric escalated, and I began to fear that we would have our own Middle East crisis on Marcelle Street.

At last, the Wahid family called for an anti-Stetner rally. Some twenty-five to thirty Muslims showed up wearing white robes and Fruit of Islam fezzes, and they held a strategy session on the front lawn to decide what to do about the Jews across the street. In response, the Stetners contacted the Jewish Defense League and asked for help. A dozen JDL thugs arrived, big, tattooed biker types, led personally by the group's new chairman, Irv Rubin. As soon as the JDL appeared, the FOI returned.

I had watched this madness with growing alarm. At first it had seemed an annoying tit for tat, but now we had a dangerous situation on our hands. Two militant groups were camped out on opposite sides of Marcelle Street, shouting racial epithets and threats back and forth. Both sides were armed, and each was itching to wipe out the other. At any moment a false step or a miscalculation could ignite a shooting war.

I drove down to Marcelle to talk to the two sides. The narrow little street was clogged with cars. Twenty or thirty JDL enforcers were camped out on the Stetners' front lawn, living in makeshift tents, and they glared at me with undisguised mistrust as I made my way among them to the front door. Across the street, the Muslims looked on with malicious curiosity.

Irv Rubin was living in the Stetners' house, and Vernie introduced me to him. He was a tall, heavyset forty-year-old with thinning hair and a thick mustache, and every bit as much a fanatic as Hakim Jamal and David Hutton had been. He declared at the top of his voice that the JDL was not leaving Marcelle Street as long as the Muslims remained. I asked what he intended to do.

"Protect the Stetner family by whatever means are necessary," he stated.

"People could get hurt," I said.

Vernie Stetner snorted. "So be it."

"C'mon, Vernie, you don't mean that. You don't want to see anybody get shot."

He lowered his eyes and said nothing. Irv Rubin answered for him. "The Stetners didn't ask for this confrontation, just like the Israelis didn't ask for it! We're not backing down!"

The Arab-Israeli conflict had lasted for decades, and it showed no signs of ending. I wanted no such futile and deadly standoff in Compton. Something had to be done, and done immediately, and the more unexpected it was, the better.

"Look, Mr. Rubin," I said, "I'm going to go across the street and talk to the Muslims. And I'm going to tell them that the Compton PD is backing you up."

Rubin looked at me, startled. "You are?"

"That's right. So I want you to stay put, and tell your people to be cool, and let me handle it."

It was the last thing he expected. "Handle it how?"

"If they leave, will your people leave?"

"Only if they leave first."

"I have your word?"

"Yes."

"Okay," I said. "I'll be back."

I walked outside and glanced over the tattooed biker bodies on the lawn. I could see their weapons hidden in their tents—Uzis and automatic pistols. I crossed Marcelle Street, approached the Muslims, and identified myself. I asked to speak with Mr. Wahid. He was a short, light-complected man with a trim mustache and a distinguished and determined air.

"This situation has got to stop," I began. "I want your people off the street."

"Absolutely not," he snapped. "Not as long as those Jews remain."

"They'll leave when your people do."

Wahid pulled himself up. "They have to leave first," he stated.

The room was full of FOI militants, so I asked if we could speak privately. Wahid led me into the kitchen.

"One way or the other, those people outside are gonna leave Compton," I told him. He glared at me scornfully. "If I move them, people are gonna get hurt," I went on. "Maybe innocent people. If that happens, I'm personally gonna come down on you every day you stay in this house. I'm gonna make your life such a living hell, you'll be sorry you ever heard of Compton."

He was looking at me dumbfounded now. "Are you taking their side?" he sputtered.

"I've only got one side," I said, "and that's my city. Now you tell those people on your lawn to pack up, or I'm gonna make you wish you never came here."

He could see that I was not bluffing. "What about them?"

"They'll leave just as soon as your people do."

He nodded slowly.

By late that afternoon the Muslim militants had left, followed in a few hours by the JDL. I stood on Vernie Stetner's front porch and watched the tattooed thugs pile on their bikes and into their cars and drive away.

"You did the right thing, Rick," Vernie said to me, "backing us against those bastards."

I looked at him a long moment. "Vernie," I said, "if I ever hear another complaint from you, about anything, I'm gonna burn your fucking house down. You understand?"

He looked at me in shock. He, too, knew I was not bluffing.

One morning when I was patrolling on day watch, I saw smoke pouring from an apartment building at the corner of Willowbrook and Cedar, and I raced over. I knew the place; it was occupied mostly by elderly and indigent people. I called the fire department, and for backup, and I ran into the building. Smoke was billowing down the staircase like an angry storm cloud; the entire second floor seemed to be ablaze. I made my way from apartment to apartment on the first floor, banging on doors and yelling for the tenants to get out. By this time two units had arrived, and I ordered the men to cordon off the area, which was filling up with gapers, and to take care of the fleeing tenants. I soaked my handkerchief in water from the hose spigot and dashed back inside.

The stairs were now shrouded in thick smoke, but I made my way up to the second floor. There were still people in the apartments, some already overcome with the smoke. I kicked in doors and herded them out into the corridor, feeling along the banister to find the stairs again. I half-carried two old women and shoved the other people ahead of me. Together, we stumbled down the steps and out into the street.

The fire engines were arriving, but all I could think was that there might still be people or animals in the building, so I went in a third time. The smoke was suffocating now, but I went into every room I could reach, yelling and blowing my whistle. When I was sure the building was clear, I staggered outside again.

People were sprawled on the sidewalk, being attended to by the officers and paramedics. My eyes were streaming and I was coughing black mucus, but there was still work to do. I called for the Red Cross to come and take charge of the people, and when they arrived, I told them to make sure everyone had a decent place to spend the night. Only then did I let myself collapse. Altogether, I had gotten seventy-five people out of the building. No one was left inside.

News of the fire reached the papers, and my role was mentioned specifically. Though I doubt he enjoyed doing so, Chief Carrington recommended me to the city council for an official citation. It was worded as vaguely as possible, commending me for my "contribution to the operational success of this matter." The citation made me the most decorated police officer in Compton history. That was unimportant, however; saving those seventy-five people remains one of my most gratifying accomplishments.

At this time I was engaged to a *Penthouse* centerfold named Lenée Peake, who lived in Redondo Beach. For some time she had been begging me to take her for a ride-along so that she could boast about it to her girlfriends. Finally I capitulated, on the condition that she cover her long blond hair with a bandanna and a hat and wear an overcoat.

When she pulled into the station parking lot, I quickly transferred her to the backseat of my unmarked task force unit. "I'll take you out for an hour," I told her. "You're not to leave the car for any reason. You understand?"

"I understand," she replied eagerly. I could see her big green eyes in the rearview. She looked like a little girl on Christmas Eve.

"If anything goes down," I said as I put the car in gear, "stay quiet and keep your head down." She promised she would.

As I was pulling out of the parking lot, a call came over the radio. "Shots fired at the Uptown Motel; man with a gun. Unit 33, can you handle?" I asked whether there was anyone else available. "Negative, 33. You're the only one."

All I could think was that if I took the call and Lenée was shot, it would be the end of my career. Even so, I had no choice. "You heard what I said," I told her as I slapped the light on the dash, "whatever happens, stay down."

The Uptown was a dive on Long Beach Boulevard, a haunt of dope dealers and prostitutes. The street was parked solid, so I drove up onto the sidewalk and got out with my gun drawn. As I did, there was an explosion—a shot from behind the motel. Lenée peered over the backseat. "Get down!" I barked.

At that moment, Al Skiles's car screeched up. He was the only person I had told about Lenée's ride-along. When he heard the call, he had raced to the motel, knowing that I had her in the car.

"Where is she?" I pointed to the backseat, where she was huddled on the floor. Another shot rang out. "Holy shit."

"He's in the back," I told him.

"What about her?!"

"We gotta trap him back there."

I locked the doors of my unit. Skiles and I split up and circled around the motel. When we reached the driveway at the back, it was empty—the shooter had somehow disappeared.

Skiles looked at me. "Where the fuck did he go?"

Before I could answer there was another shot, this time from the *front* of the motel.

"Oh, fuck!" I said, and we dashed back to the street. Again, there was no one. Skiles and I glanced at each other; then I walked over to my car. There was no sign of life. I tapped on the glass. "Lenée?"

The big green eyes appeared, filled this time not with excitement but with terror.

"Are you okay?" I asked. She nodded. "Don't move."

Skiles and I searched the area around the motel, but the shooter was gone. I hurried back to the car.

"I'm taking you home," I told Lenée as I got in. I started the engine, but at that moment, another call came over the radio. "Major disturbance, Stardust Motel." Again I hesitated. "33, can you respond?"

"33 responding," I said.

"Does that mean I can't go home?" Lenée asked meekly.

"Will you be okay?"

"Uh . . . no . . ."

I turned to look at her. "What's the matter?"

"I'm bleeding," she replied.

"Oh, my God," I gasped. "Did you get shot?!"

"No," she said. "I got so scared I started my period."

What could I do? I had a menstruating centerfold model on the floor of the backseat, and a thug rampaging at the Stardust Motel. I called Al Skiles on frequency 2, the car-to-car channel. "Can you take the 415?" I asked.

"I'm on it," Al answered.

I started to pull away, then stopped. I could not leave Al on his own after he had backed me at the Uptown. It was a dilemma, but I knew what I had to do. "I've got to take this call," I told Lenée.

She started to cry. "I need a tampon," she whined.

"Okay. Try to hang on."

"I'll try," she offered bravely.

Skiles was already in the courtyard of the Stardust Motel when I pulled up next to his car. He was engaged in a shouting match with a hulking, bare-chested black thug named Abdul. He had just been released from prison, and his muscles spoke of years of determined lifting. Again I warned Lenée to stay down. When I walked up on Abdul, he started swearing and screaming at me. There was no time for negotiation; I had to get Lenée to a drugstore. "Let's take the fucker down," I said.

Skiles grabbed Abdul, twisted him around, and put him in an arm lock. Together we dragged him to Skiles's car and threw him down over the hood. When his face hit the hot metal, he began screeching like a madman.

"Shut the fuck up!" Skiles yelled. Abdul squealed louder. Skiles smacked him in the ribs with his sap gloves.

My car was alongside Skiles's, and as he cuffed Abdul, I could see Lenée's eyes peeking out at the window. She was directly opposite Abdul as he yelped and cursed. When he caught sight of her, he suddenly fell silent. "Who the fuck is that?" he said. Skiles smacked him again and threw him into the cage.

For a second time I got back into my car. Lenée was nearly in shock. "You okay?" I asked. Before she could answer, another call came over the radio. "Man with a gun," the dispatcher said, "shots fired. 33, can you respond?"

Lenée let out a pathetic groan, something between a whimper and a bleat. "Please, Rick," she panted.

By now I was losing my temper. "You asked for this," I told her.

"Please . . . take me home?"

"Damn it!" The dispatcher was calling for me again. I picked up the mike. "Unit 33—" I began. Lenée was still whimpering on the floor behind me. I threw a glance at her. She was huddled like a little girl hiding in the basement from a tornado. "My car is disabled," I answered. "I'm going Code 3 back to the station."

I drove as fast as I could, and when I got to the parking lot, Lenée staggered out of the back. I asked if she would be able to take herself home. She was pale and trembling. "You better believe it," she answered.

I did not know quite what to say. In less than ten minutes, she had been shot at and come face-to-face with a murderous ex-con. I asked, "Did you enjoy the ride-along?"

For the first time since she had dropped to the floor of the car, her face flushed. "Don't you ever ask me to do anything like that again!" she snapped, and she ran to her car as fast as her bulky overcoat and bloodied underpants would allow.

The next day she mailed her engagement ring back to me at the police station. There was a note attached. "Thanks, but no thanks," it read.

The Stardust was located in the 1700 block of North Long Beach Boulevard near Rosecrans. It was a run-down courtyard motel, and it made the Glenmore look like the Ritz-Carleton. Its eighteen units were inhabited by the dregs of Compton: crack addicts, gangbangers, thugs, pimps, winos, and whores. My task force hit the Stardust nearly every night, and it was always good for five or six arrests, but it was a running sore that festered no matter how many times we cleaned it out. Finally the owners had had enough, and they sold the place to a young Chinese entrepreneur from the exclusive suburb of San Marino.

Tom Jang was an energetic and conscientious businessman who believed in running his properties himself, so he moved into the office of the Stardust. He had no idea what he was getting into, having been told only that the motel's units were always occupied. His first night on the job, Reggie

Wright, Al Skiles, Tony Miranda, Mike Markey, and I rolled to the Stardust in two cars. We banged on doors, tossed the rooms, confiscated weapons and drugs, and began herding the occupants out into the courtyard. Since we were in civilian clothes and unmarked cars, Tom Jang had no idea who we were. He ran out of the office yelling for us to leave his customers alone, threatening to call the cops. I told him to do so.

When the patrol cars arrived, we threw half a dozen of the worst tenants into the cages, gathered up the evidence, and drove off, leaving Tom Jang cursing in Cantonese amid the debris strewn across the courtyard. We repeated the performance regularly for the next few weeks until Jang decided *he* had had enough. Instead of selling, though, he came to the police station and asked to see one of the officers who had been raiding his motel. Tony Miranda was on duty that night, and Jang took him aside.

"I want you to stop busting up my property," he said. Tony explained that that was not possible so long as the Stardust remained a cesspool. "Then I want you to clean it out." Jang lowered his voice. "Just make it so I can run a peaceful business."

Tony thought it over and agreed he might be able to help out on his own time. "But it'll cost money," he said.

"I'll pay," Jang assured him. "Whatever it costs."

Tony went to his contacts in the SOS, the Samoan gang, and recruited its biggest and baddest bangers. Then he rented a minibus, and he, Beef, Juice, Knuckles, and Carlton drove to the Stardust. They parked in the middle of the courtyard and fanned out, kicking in doors and beating the occupants with clubs and sap gloves. They hit every single room, hauled the half-conscious bodies outside, and jammed them like cordwood into the bus. Tony then drove his bruised and bleeding cargo to the border between Signal Hill and Long Beach and dumped them in the Dominguez Hills. They were discovered next morning by the Long Beach PD.

The incident caused a minor scandal. LBPD launched an investigation, which led back to Compton, the Samoans, and Tony Miranda. At that time, Tony was under investigation for having shot a Jamaican shell game hustler in the leg, and that, together with the raid, proved too much for

Chief Carrington. Tony was fired. There was no appeal. My six-man task force was now down to five.

Joe Rouzan had asked me to create the task force and had backed us up; although Jim Carrington had retained it, I was not convinced he was committed to it. He had demonstrated throughout his career that he could be vindictive and unreliable, and I began to suspect that he felt menaced by the task force in general and me in particular. Though we were carrying out the mayor's mandate to control the gangs at any cost, it was not the kind of mandate Carrington would have enforced.

Tony Miranda's off-duty escapade at the Stardust was highly irregular, but it was the sort of thing for which a Compton cop would be suspended without pay, not fired. The shooting of the Jamaican was under investigation, and, even though Tony had failed to inform the transport officer that the man was wounded (for which he should have been disciplined), it was entirely possible that the shooting would have been declared justified. I could not help but feel, therefore, that his firing was meant, at least in part, as a signal to me.

With our number reduced, the task force had to become more aggressive, and that meant we began taking more chances. Routinely we patrolled alone in unmarked cars. One night I was checking my regular hot spots and turned into Dwight-'52. At the far end, 1-5-1 bangers were congregated in the driveway of an abandoned house. Since lookouts had been posted up and down the street, I knew that a big drug deal was going down.

I had nothing but my pistol and an old Ithaca 12-gauge pump gun. I slipped out of the car and made my way through the bushes of adjoining houses until I had a clear view of the driveway. There were eight to ten gang members, all armed, all hard-core. I could not let the deal go down, but I knew that if I went in shooting and some of the bangers were killed, there would be hell to pay. I sat in the bushes, thinking.

The asphalt at the mouth of the driveway had been churned into loose gravel. I quietly cocked the Ithaca, pointed it at the gravel, and fired. There was a thunderous explosion as the buckshot slammed into the asphalt, spraying it like shrapnel at the bangers. They froze. Half a dozen of them were hit by the flying gravel, but they could not tell where the blast had come from or how many people were shooting. I fired another round, and again the gravel riddled them. They panicked and took off.

I waited in the bushes until the street was clear, then hurried back to my car. In the meantime, the neighbors had put in frantic calls of shots fired, and my radio was blaring. I grabbed the mike. "Unit 33 at the scene," I said. "Suspects are GOA"—gone on arrival.

"Okay, 33," the dispatcher replied, and she canceled the call.

It was probably the first time in history that an officer had responded to a shots fired call when he himself had been the shooter.

It had been a foolishly risky thing to do—taking on eight hard-core gang bangers by myself. Yet I did it again a few nights later, firing shotgun blasts at the feet of half a dozen bangers in Dwight Avenue, forcing them to scatter. It was madness to go into a situation like that alone, but to me, in the heightened state of urgency I had reached, it seemed perfectly sane. The odds against us were so overwhelming, and the war we were fighting so unwinnable, that no risk we took seemed excessive. With that came the inevitable sense of invincibility: I was not going to die, no matter how many chances I took. In my mind, my immortality, or at least my sense of it, more than evened the odds.

A few nights later, Mike Markey and I were given a tip that a crack dealer was operating out of a house on Cherry Street in Fruit Town, selling to high school kids. We parked at the end of the street and made our way half crouching, half running to the house. I told Markey that I would take the front door. I waited a few minutes to give him time to circle around to the back, then moved onto the porch.

I heard a thud as the back door was kicked in. I threw my weight against the front door as hard as I could, and nearly broke my shoulder. It had been reinforced with iron. No matter how I battered at it, it would not budge. Meanwhile, I could hear the muted clatter of a struggle at the back of the house, and I knew that Markey was in the middle of a fight.

I ran to the backyard fence; it was topped with razor wire. I could not climb over without tearing myself to shreds. Inside the house, the fight was getting more violent. In my experience, if a fight lasts more than a minute, you are in trouble, and Markey had been at it for nearly that long. I looked around frantically.

Crumpled in the corner of the tiny garage was a canvas tarp. I grabbed it, threw it over the concertina wire, and dived headfirst over the wall. I landed on my skull and scrambled to my feet. Markey and the drug dealer were grappling in the laundry room at the back of the house. The dealer had Mike wedged in between the washer and the dryer, and was standing over him with an iron rod in his hand.

I raced into the laundry room and threw myself at the dealer, and we hit the floor hard. I wrestled him for the rod, pried it away, and bashed him across the back of his shoulders with it. He let out a grunt and went limp. I put the cuffs on him.

Mike pulled himself to his feet.

"You okay?" I asked him.

"Yeah," he replied, panting. He motioned to the unconscious pusher. "But he's gonna get off."

"How so?"

"When he jumped me he said we were intruders."

Mike was right. We had not identified ourselves, we were not in uniform, and we drove an unmarked car. If he went to trial, his lawyer would claim that he thought we were there to rob him. The case would be thrown out, and we would probably be disciplined.

I knelt down and took the cuffs off the drug dealer. We left him lying on the floor of the laundry room, groaning, half conscious.

Maybe he had learned his lesson, I told myself as we walked back to our car. In any case, we simply did not have the time for the paperwork and legal battle that bringing him in would provoke. Better to let one guilty man go free than cripple a third of the task force. The chances were that we would get him eventually. Meanwhile, it was best for everyone that he had no idea what had hit him.

Later that week, I was cruising in a black-and-white unit down Short Avenue on the east side when a flurry of shots erupted a block away, and bullets zipped past an inch from the roof of my car. As I turned and headed in their direction, more shots were fired. I swerved around the corner into Tucker Street and saw Reggie Wright and a rookie officer, Donny Miller, crouched in the bushes at the front of a house, firing at a car in the middle of the street. The two men in the car were blasting back, and bullets were crisscrossing the street and ricocheting off the houses on both sides.

The car took off, and I raced after it. As I did, the two men pointed their pistols out the windows and began firing at me. I had no idea who they were or what they had done, but I was not going to let them get away. It was only later that I learned what had happened.

Wright and Miller, who was on his first night of patrol, had responded to a call of shots fired in Tucker Street. As they walked up to the house, a car came careening around the corner and screeched to a stop. Two Chicanos pointed guns at the house and opened fire, not realizing that the officers were on the front porch. Earlier they had bought what they thought was cocaine, only to discover that it was baking soda. They had driven back, fired shots at the house, and disappeared. It was these shots that had nearly hit my car. In the few moments it had taken Wright and Miller to reach the scene, they had circled the block for another drive-by. The two cops dived into the bushes and returned fire.

I chased the Chicanos through the narrow streets, zigzagging up onto the sidewalks and dodging cars that swerved madly to avoid us. I was right behind them, taking gunfire the whole time. They turned into Orchard Street behind the old Sears building, and the car slid to a halt. They had decided to stop running, perhaps to make a stand.

I opened my door and crouched behind it. I expected their doors to fly open and the two bangers to jump out, shooting—but they made no move. There was an odd, expectant silence.

At that moment, a patrol unit pulled up at the end of the street. I glanced back. Brent Garland and Jasper Jackson got out, the two officers who had killed Luis Velasquez.

I shouted to them, "I got this!"

I dropped to my elbows and knees and did a combat crawl toward the Chicanos' car. There was still no movement inside. I worked my way around to the passenger-side door, reached up, and yanked it open. The kid on that side sagged out, bleeding from a bullet wound in the temple, the blood seeping down his collar and onto his sleeve. He was conscious, and still clutched a .41 Magnum in his hand. I grabbed his arm and pulled him out of the car onto the street. I had to pry his fingers off the trigger of the gun. Then I glanced up into the car.

The other kid was sitting behind the wheel, a .32 lying in his palm on the seat. He seemed stunned, disoriented. I pointed my gun and yelled at him to drop his. He glanced at me with a dull curiosity, as if unsure what was happening. I called to him again to put down the gun and get out of the car.

There was a moment when he might have done anything—dropped the gun onto the floor, or raised it to shoot me. He did neither. Instead, he sat there staring at me. I could easily have shot him dead, and most cops would have, but I could see in his eyes that he was finished—his spirit had been broken.

At that moment, his door was yanked open, and Jasper Jackson hauled him out of the car by his neck. He threw him facedown on the sidewalk; Brent Garland pounded a boot onto his wrist and took the .32 away. I cuffed the kid on my side, and the whole crazy incident was over.

Again, it had been madness to chase these two killers alone, and even more to have crawled up on their car blindly as I had done. I was working on the fringes now, though, and chances few cops would have taken seemed standard procedure to me. It was no longer police work so much as a sort of vigilantism, as unorthodox as it was addictive.

I used to drive alone into the worst neighborhoods, like Dwight-'52 and Alondra and Willowbrook, in civilian clothes and an unmarked car. I carried a .38 loaded with wadcutters, practice rounds from the target range, and when I spotted a gaggle of bangers, I moved up as close to them as possible and fired the cutters over their heads, scattering them like roaches and disrupting their drug dealing for hours.

I did this a dozen times or more, being careful to scope out the locale in advance so that no citizens would be at risk. The risk to myself, however, was narcotic. I checked the surroundings and the backstop of my rounds with clinical care, then chose my hiding place, a hunting blind where I would wait sometimes for an hour or more.

On each of these occasions, neighbors made shots fired calls to the police. I responded to these calls myself, claiming that the suspects were GOA. If I had been caught doing this I would have been suspended, even fired, and if the bangers had caught me, I might well have been killed. I was beyond caring.

It was a curious confluence of insanity and humanity. Though I was being exposed to more danger than ever, though I was being shot at and using my gun more often than at any other time in my career, it had become a point of pride with me to take on the most dangerous criminals in Compton alone—without killing them. In a sense, it was the most extreme form of police work Compton Style.

I knew that if the two bangers in Orchard Street had come out of the car shooting, Jackson and Garland would have killed both of them. In my gut, I did not want that to happen. I was sure I could take them down without gunplay, as I had done with the three killers on the fire escape behind the church. The more I reflected on it, though, the more I began to suspect that I was simply becoming weary of violence, tired of seeing people killed, sick of corpses in the street. Perhaps that was how the Compton Style had evolved—not from desperation but from resignation. Perhaps over the hundred-year history of the force, Compton cops had simply grown tired of the toll.

Then I began to wonder whether a part of it might be that I was beginning to identify with these gangbangers—that I was empathizing with them. I had dealt with enough of them, knew enough about their origins, seen enough of their culture, that I felt, in a visceral way, that I understood them. With less parenting, with fewer breaks and les self-discipline, I might even have become one of them myself. Like them I lusted for adventure, thrived on danger, and craved the chance to show that I was the best, the toughest, the most cunning and skillful of my peers.

In another world, I might have been Sylvester Scott or Luis Velasquez. It might have been me in the car on Orchard Street, sagging against the door with a bullet crease in my temple, or sitting stunned behind the wheel, unable to move an inch farther, wondering where I was and who I was, and how I had come to this final solitary impasse, a gun in my hand.

This was the point to which fifteen years on the street had brought me: to an impending crisis of consciousness rigid with years of stress, soaked in the blood of the guilty and innocent, bloated with death, staring into an obscure mirror of callous self-respect. I thought of the Stinker fished out of the Compton Canal. Then I had reflected on his humanity as an intellectual proposition; now I was beginning to feel it viscerally. The only difference between us was two weeks in the water. I had had fifteen years on the street. I did not know how much more of it I could take, how much longer I could go on. I felt instinctively that I needed to find myself outside of the police work that had defined me for those fifteen years.

Yet there was so much more to be done—the tide of crime was rising, not ebbing—and, besides, I did not know any other way of life. I was reaching a turning point, morally, emotionally, spiritually, but I could not imagine another path; even if it existed, I could not envision where it would lead.

That night, I stopped at the Garter when I got off duty. It was one of those peculiar times when Vito's liquor license had been suspended pending a hearing of the Alcoholic Beverage Control Board's complaints, so I ordered a Coke and chatted with the night manager, Eddie Layton.

Eddie had formerly been the manager at the Chatterbox, a popular dive on Compton Boulevard. One night Dominic Rutigliano had come in and gotten rowdy as usual. Eddie tried to throw him out, and when Rut demurred, Eddie took a poke at him and broke his nose. Rut then beat him senseless, but a legend had been born, at least in Eddie Layton's mind: He was "the guy who broke Rutigliano's nose." Ever since, he had regaled patrons with the story, no matter how many times Rut reminded him that it had been a sucker punch, and that he had cleaned the floor with him. That one punch was the highlight of Eddie's life—his proudest boast.

On that particular night there were three Mexican illegals in the Garter, drunk and getting boisterous. The bouncer was a biker named Tony, whose nickname was No Nose since half his nose had been shot off in a gunfight. He rumbled up to the Mexicans like a Buick with a busted headlight and told them in Spanish to leave. Not wanting to tangle with Tony, they got up, and he led them to the door. As they started out, Eddie Layton yelled at them, "Get the fuck out and don't come back!" And he added an ethnic slur.

At that one of the Mexicans swung around and punched Tony in the face. He staggered back, and all three jumped him. I ran over and identified myself in Spanish as a police officer. Before I finished the sentence, one of the Mexicans punched me in the eye. I saw the blood before I felt the pain, and I went ballistic. I swung at the guy who had hit me and knocked him out, and when a second one jumped me, I threw him off and gave him three quick jabs, which put him on the floor. Tony collared the third man and threw him through the front door.

My eye was streaming blood, blinding me, so I told Eddie to call the cops, and I took myself to the hospital. The punch had opened a cut in my eyebrow that required three stitches to close. The next afternoon I reported for work with a headache and a livid mouse above my eye to find a notice from Chief Carrington that I was suspended. I grabbed it and marched into his office.

"What the hell is this?" I demanded.

Carrington scarcely glanced up from his paperwork. "You were in a fight last night," he remarked.

"Yeah? So why the suspension?"

"You left the scene of an emergency."

I was incensed. "The emergency was mine!" I pointed to the stitches over my eye. "One of those assholes clocked me. I had to go to the hospital!"

Carrington finally looked up. "You should have remained at the scene until the units arrived. Two days without pay." He returned to his papers.

I demanded a hearing before the personnel board, but in the meantime I was taken off duty. When I appeared before the board, Carrington attended, as did the city attorney, Arnett Hartsfield. Clearly they did not intend to lose this case. Hartsville repeated the charge against me, and I gave my side of the story. The board members heard us both out, and then the chairman, Johnny Heaton, who had been my boxing trainer, gave his opinion. "I think instead of suspending Officer Baker, you should give him a medal."

Carrington was shocked. "What for?" he demanded.

Heaton glared at him. "For backing up the security at the club at his own risk. And for showing amazingly good pugilistic skills." He closed the case file. "The suspension is hereby revoked. The department is directed to restore Sergeant Baker's lost pay."

It was a small victory but, to me, an important one. I had never received a suspension, and I did not want one on my record. In fact, though I thought little more about it, the event would have repercussions later in my career. For it would be cited as part of a pattern of defiance of authority on my part, tracking back to the blue flu.

Gangstas, the Carnival,
and the Ritual

Music had always been a part of the life of Compton, vibrating on its corners and echoing in its clubs and bars. From country and western to jive and doo-wop to rock and rap, Compton had either spawned or showcased the musical tastes and tensions of the time. In the mid-1980s, that tradition continued, but it took on a dark and sinister character.

Gangsta rap was a calculated perversion of the hip-hop genre that put a premium on profanity, misogyny, human degradation, and violence. One particular target of Compton gangsta rappers like N.W.A. was the police. The featured song on N.W.A.'s album *Straight Outta Compton* was entitled "Fuck tha Police." The lyrics were provocative and profane—and, far from being a reflection of the rappers' experience in Compton, they were a catalog of lies.

The song charged that cops regularly abused their authority to shoot and kill blacks, and it denigrated policemen for not having the guts to take off their badges and "go at it." If they did, the rapper declared, "I'ma fuck you up." In fact, we rarely fired our weapons, and we regarded lethal force as a last, desperate resort. Further, Compton cops readily accepted challenges to fight one-on-one, and I am unaware of any who were ever beaten in a fair fight.

Little of what the gangsta rappers said was based in reality, though the white media lionized them for their brutal honesty as poets of the streets. Meanwhile, major companies such as Warner Music were making fortunes off the rappers' glorification of rape, drug dealing, and murder. To my mind, it was a cynical and hypocritical exploitation of the young people of the inner cities. While young lives were perverted and put in danger, and while violence increased to the insistent tempo of the gangstas, the white executives who marketed their music went back to their homes in Malibu and Brentwood, where their own privileged children were forbidden to listen to the CDs they produced.

I knew many of the early rappers, and the neighborhoods they came from. Most were petty criminals, though some, like Eazy-E, were hardened drug dealers. Like the Panthers and the Malcolm X Foundation before them, the gangstas fed off drugs and violence while proclaiming to the world that they were the advocates of black cultural integrity. It was the same blatant hypocrisy we had seen in Compton for years, but this time there was an important difference.

To me, it was not the explicit and viral nature of gangsta music that posed the greatest social danger—it was the fact that the mainstream music industry embraced it so readily and marketed it so zealously. Gangsta rap remained on the edges of popular culture for only a very short while. As soon as corporations perceived the potential for quick and potent profits, they seized what should have festered as a fringe phenomenon and injected it into the mainstream.

People like Eazy-E, Snoop Dogg, and Suge Knight, who would otherwise have been nothing but scabrous, short-lived crooks, became national figures—corrosive models for the most impressionable and at-risk young people in the country. Through the mainstreaming of gangsta rap, the fetid subculture of the gangs, with its sociopathic paranoia and violence, its loathing of women, and its hatred of authority, which had previously been seen as antisocial behavior, suddenly became an accepted artifact of popular culture.

As a police officer and as a citizen of Compton, I viewed the rise of gangsta rap with growing alarm. The very behaviors and attitudes that we risked our lives to suppress were being exploited by corporate America and lionized in the media. I had dealt with the OGs and wannabes who performed the music my entire life, and I had neither respect for them nor fear of their message. The people who were new to me—the ones I truly wanted to whoop Compton Style—were the anonymous, self-satisfied music moguls and the smug, self-important critics who were pushing songs that glorified drive-bys and crack, and called women bitches and black people niggers. Gangsta was mass-market inhumanity, a degradation of the human spirit in the name of culture.

In my view, the explosive success of gangsta rap was the worst form of the abuse of the free market, and it presented a dismal prospect to those of us who were trying to protect our citizens from violence, and their kids from gangs. With gangsta rap, it was suddenly the gangs that were being thrust into the mainstream, and the police who were forced to the fringes. Its popularity threatened to reverse the relative positions of cops and criminals across the tenuous line that separated us. It imbued the bangers with sympathy and made them seem cool while it cast us in the role of villains.

I hated it; it made me angry and depressed. For the first time, I began to be fearful for the future.

The future . . . After sixteen years on the force, I began to think about my future as well as my past. This reflection was propelled by a series of events. The first and most important was my mother's death.

My mother had always been my biggest fan. It was she who had framed my athletic trophies, she who had carefully kept my commendations in a scrapbook, she who had supported me consistently throughout my career and in my turbulent personal life. Her sudden death in 1983 robbed me of a sense of groundedness and left a giant vacuum in my heart.

It also stripped me of a foundation and a touchstone on which I had depended, although I did not realize how much until she was gone. Often, in the middle of a trying day, I would stop at my parents' house and eat lunch with my mother. Just being able to talk to her, to hear her voice and watch her careful movements around the kitchen, calmed me, and reminded me of the child I had been, and the idealistic student I had grown out of.

Her neighbors and friends Minnie Jones and Betty Stafford often came over to sit with me and ask how my day was going. While I could never bring myself to tell them the truth of what I was dealing with, their simple caring, their smiles and solicitude, gave me the strength to go back onto the street, knowing who and what I was fighting for.

I was not married, and I had not forged the kind of committed relationship with a woman that means a center and a refuge in life. Now that my mother was gone, I felt cut adrift as never before. More than anything else that had happened to me, more than the carnage and the chaos in the streets, my mother's death compelled me to question my identity, and the meaning of my career.

Dick Bidwell had asked her how she felt about my becoming a Compton cop. She had answered that she was for it if it was what I wanted. I told her it was. Now, after sixteen years, I had to decide whether it was still what I wanted.

To this point I had received a dozen commendations, and only the highest performance evaluations, facts of which I was extremely proud. In 1985 that changed.

That summer, the staff of the day watch hosted a party for me at the Rodeway Inn to recognize the accomplishments of my gang task force. Despite all the odds, we had succeeded in keeping the gangs at bay, and we had broken departmental records in the number of weapons seized, the amount of drugs we had confiscated, and the number of arrests we had made. I was presented with an inscribed pen and pencil set, and the watch commanders made speeches praising me for my work. It was the sort of reinforcement a Compton cop rarely received, and I was as grateful as I was humbled.

My supervisor was Lieutenant Terry Ebert, the only white officer to have joined the Guardians. His decision, which had seemed curious at the time, had by now begun to make sense. What I had at first taken for ambitiousness was, in fact, a political appetite that was as voracious as it was cunning. Joining the Guardians had been the first step in Ebert's plan to position himself as the darling of the black establishment in the department and city government. When Jim Carrington became chief, Terry Ebert quickly attached himself to him. Then, when Carrington announced his decision to retire in 1985, Ebert made it clear that he had his own designs on the chief's job.

When it came time for Ebert to write my evaluation, I assumed his report would reflect the accolades I had received and the accomplishments of the task force. Instead, he issued a cutting indictment of my recent activities, citing my complaints that bilingual detectives were not being hired despite the fact that a growing number of crime victims were Hispanic. I had also continued to denounce the department's failure to hire more Latino officers, though the city council admitted that it had the money to do so, and this, too, he criticized.

I protested the evaluation to the personnel board. When I appeared before them I pulled no punches. "Lieutenant Ebert is nothing but a court jester performing cartwheels for the amusement of Chief Carrington," I stated.

The remark did nothing to endear me to the politicians. Ebert's report remained a part of my permanent record, a fact that devastated me. After seventeen years of unbroken praise, and despite the achievements of the task force, I had, for the first time in my career, been evaluated as being subpar.

Compton was changing again, and with it, the police department was changing. In a demographic shift that mirrored white flight, in the late 1980s blacks continued moving out of the city, to be replaced by Hispanics. The process was not hurried and hysterical as it had been in the sixties, but it was just as important a demographic shift. From their steady minority of 5 percent of the city's population, Hispanics expanded to 10 and then 20 percent. It was for this reason that I had begun to agitate for more Spanish-speaking officers. By 1986, nearly 40 percent of the victims of crime in Compton were Hispanic.

Despite this increasing trend toward parity between the two groups, the city government remained almost entirely black. I had seen it happen before—this growing incongruity between the government and the citizens—and I knew the likely consequences. As the Latino community expanded, Hispanics expected a greater role in the affairs of the city, and the blacks, who were so firmly entrenched, resisted these demands, just as the whites had resisted theirs. This would bring a new form of racial tension and, I supposed, a new wave of crime—Latino on black crime.

It was this that I dreaded more than anything. For twenty years we had managed to keep the black and Latino gangs from each other's throats, and with the exception of a few flare-ups, there had been no widespread conflict between the two. Maintaining this uneasy balance had been one of the highest priorities of the CPD. We knew that open warfare between black and Latino gangs might become uncontrollable, given their numbers and their unquenchable appetite for violence. Once started, the momentum of black versus Latino gang warfare would play itself out in a bloodbath that could bring about the very sort of anarchy of which Mayor Cade had warned.

In any event, the new tide of Latino violence did not come. What I had not anticipated was that the great majority of Latino families that were moving into Compton were not second- and third-generation Chicanos but recent immigrants to America. The difference was critical. Established Mexican Americans were schooled in the ways of American culture, for better and for worse. Chicano criminals were as hard-core and sophisticated as any in Compton. The new arrivals, however, were mostly people from rural communities who had little or no experience of urban life. They had made their way to America looking for jobs and for opportunities for their children, and for that reason they resisted the lure of the gang lifestyle. They had come seeking new lives, not early deaths.

I saw this demographic shift as a potential watershed in the history of Compton. If we could gain the trust of the new Latino residents, and befriend and help guide their children, we might be able to reduce the amount of crime significantly.

This was why I was arguing so insistently for more Latino officers. We had a chance to make the kind of lasting change in Compton that I had originally joined the force to achieve, but the mayor and city council, dependent as they were on the black vote, failed to seize this opportunity. Compton was changing before their eyes, just as it had done before the eyes of the old white establishment, and, like their predecessors, the black politicians denied and resisted that change.

Through the CPOA I shouted and cajoled, urged and reasoned, but I could not get the city's leaders to budge. I saw that they were not going to adopt a new way of thinking any more readily than the old white leaders had, at least not until it was too late. In the process, I was viewed as making a nuisance of myself. It was for this reason, in part, I assumed that I had been given a less than glowing evaluation.

The department was changing, too. The young officers who were joining had been in junior high school when we called the blue flu, and they did not understand how bad things had been or how hard we had had to fight in those days. The gains for which we had risked so much were taken for granted now, as was the political status of the CPOA. Under my leadership, and that of Roland Ballard and John Soisson, the association had successfully negotiated every contract since 1970. Ironically, all those years of labor peace engendered complacency. The young officers saw no need for a militant union. To us the blue flu had been a life-and-death struggle; to them, it was an artifact of the past.

I had served on the board of the Police Association for fifteen years, but when I ran again in 1986, I was not reelected. It was a stunning blow to me. CPOA politics had been a major part of my life; indeed, it could be argued that I had helped to create it. However, I realized I could not demand that city officials adapt to change if I myself did not. I accepted the defeat as graciously as I could, but I felt that I had been rejected by the new generation of officers for whose benefit I had struggled as a young patrolman. No matter how I tried to rationalize it, the loss was devastating to my morale.

In the mid-1980s, the sheriff's office stepped up its campaign to take over policing Compton. LASO had by now surrounded the city, patrolling in

Paramount, Carson, Lynwood, and the unincorporated areas along the border. Sheriff Sherman Block did not hide his determination to fill in the blank spot on his patrol map that was Compton. He made exorbitant claims to the city council of the money that would be saved by replacing the CPD with the LASO, and he repeated the familiar charge that Compton cops were too close to the criminal element.

What he did not mention, though he must have known, was that a gang called the Vikings had grown up inside his own department. I say that he must have known about the Vikings since we knew that they had started inside LASO in 1985, and their existence was an open secret. Eventually this Neo-Nazi gang would include dozens of deputies as well as one of Block's own assistant sheriffs. Yet he continued to insist that the Compton PD was "too close to the gangs" and ought to be disbanded. His attitude could not help but filter down to the LASO rank and file.

It was perhaps because of the growing animosity between the Compton PD and the sheriff's office that an incident occurred that, I could not help but feel, was an ominous portent of things to come.

One chilly February night, I was patrolling the northeast section in an unmarked unit with a black reserve officer named Rudy Johnson. There was a carnival on Bullis Road near the border with Lynwood, and, since such events always attracted gangbangers, I decided to drive past and check it out.

As I cruised slowly along Bullis, a sheriff's unit from Lynwood turned on its flashing lights and drove toward us. I assumed that the deputies had picked up a call about a disturbance at the carnival and had decided to "poach." This was a common practice along the border: LASO would intercept Compton calls and dart into the city to make the arrests.

I continued to drive down Bullis as the LASO car swung into the lane behind me. There were two deputies in the car. I held up my badge, and I expected that they would wave as they went past. Instead, through the loudspeaker, the driver ordered me to pull over. I did, and Johnson and I remained in the car.

"Put your hands up where I can see them and don't move!" the deputy called over the bullhorn.

We did as he directed. In the rearview, I could see his door open. He got out carrying a shotgun and walked up alongside our car. His partner also got out, and stood behind Johnson's door, a hand on his pistol.

I smiled up at the driver. "What brings you over here?"

"Get out of the fucking the car!" he ordered.

"What are you talking about?" I said. I thought he might be joking.

He pointed the snout of the riot gun at my face. "I said get out of the fucking car!"

This was no joke. The young Latino deputy was deadly serious, and what was worse, he was scared: The shotgun was trembling in his hands. All I could think was that this lunatic was going to shoot me.

"Okay, okay," I said, and I carefully opened the door and stepped out. I glanced at his name tag. "Look, Deputy Ortiz, we're Compton PD—"

He grabbed me by the elbow and pushed me toward his car.

"I'm a cop!" I growled at him. "I'm a sergeant working the gang task force—"

"Shut up and put your hands on the back of your head!" he snapped.

He had the shotgun pressed against the small of my back. I did as I was told. He shoved me down over the hood of his unit and began frisking me. He found my gun and stuck it into his belt.

"God damn it," I told him, "I'm a cop! Look at my badge if you don't believe me."

He dug it out of my pocket, glanced at it, and threw it onto the hood at my face. "Stay there and don't move." Then he yelled to his partner; "Get that asshole out of the car!"

Johnson was wearing an issue Windbreaker with the word POLICE printed plainly on the back. Nonetheless, the deputy searched him and took his weapon. All the time I was insisting that we were cops, demanding to know what the hell he was doing.

"There's a salt-and-pepper team impersonating Compton cops and jacking people up," the deputy said. "How do I know you're for real?"

"Run the damn plate," I yelled at him. "You'll see it's a city car."

"I did," he said. "It came back 'not on file.' Besides, police Novas are two-door, not four-door."

"Then get on the goddamn radio and call my watch commander. He'll tell you who I am."

He hesitated. The shotgun was still pointed at me. Johnson and I were both spread-eagled across the hood, our arms stretched out. "Okay," Ortiz said. "But you move and I swear I'll shoot you."

He climbed back into his car while the other deputy kept his gun on us. I watched through the windshield as he put in a call to Compton PD. Meanwhile, two men were approaching from the carnival across the street. Ortiz yelled at his partner to watch his back.

"U.S. Marshals," one of the men said. He reached into his pocket for his ID. The deputy warned him not to move and pointed his pistol at him.

"Frisk them," Ortiz ordered.

The deputy told both men to put their hands on the roof of the car. He took their guns away and pulled out their badges. "What the fuck are you doing at the carnival?" he demanded.

"We're off duty, working security," the marshal told him, and he started to turn around.

"You stay put!" the deputy snapped.

Now there were four of us plastered to the LASO unit while Ortiz waited for a response from my station. I was fuming and cursing, and so were the two marshals.

At last, Ortiz got out of the car. "They cleared you," he said.

I started to straighten up. Ortiz jerked the riot gun at me again. "I didn't say you could move!"

This time I lost it. I was livid. "You lousy motherfucker!" I screamed at him. "We're cops, I told you we're cops, now you know we're cops! You give us our weapons back and get the fuck outta my town!"

Ortiz was stunned by my blast. He took a step back. "I just wanna get home alive tonight," he said.

"So do I!" I shouted. "And the biggest fuckin' threat to me is you!"

He took my gun out of his belt and, instead of handing it to me, tossed it onto the hood of the car. His partner did the same with Johnson's. We snatched them up, and the deputies returned the marshals' guns.

"You're witnesses to what happened," I said to them as Ortiz drove off. "I want your names and badge numbers."

I was still furious when I got back to the station, where I filed a formal complaint against Deputy Ortiz. When the other members of the task force heard about the incident, they were nearly as angry as I.

After much bureaucratic wrangling, the LASO investigator admitted that Ortiz's behavior had been uncalled for, though no apology was offered. This was Compton, though, so that was not the end of the affair.

Four days later, we were alerted that the sheriffs would be conducting a surveillance at the Uptown Motel on Long Beach Boulevard. They had traced a fugitive who was wanted on half a dozen county warrants to the motel and were planning to stake him out and arrest him. That night, Mike Markey and Al Skiles were on duty. They drove to the Uptown, spotted the deputies' unmarked car, and walked up on it with guns drawn.

"Get the fuck out of the car!" Skiles commanded. When the deputies answered that they were on a stakeout, Markey and Skiles pointed their guns at them. "Get out!"

The deputies climbed out cursing and protesting. Mike and Al threw them over the hood of their car, frisked them, and took their guns away. When the suspect arrived at the motel, he saw them sprawled over the hood of the car, guarded by two men with guns. As the deputies watched, he took off. Markey and Skiles made them stay where they were until an LASO supervisor came to identify them.

"We informed CPD about the stakeout," the supervisor huffed.

"Really?" Mike Markey replied. "Nobody told us."

At the end of my complaint I had stated that, if such incidents continued to occur, relations between CPD and LASO, which were already deteriorating, would reach an all-time low. The sheriff's insistent campaign to take over Compton had created an institutional animosity between us that had penetrated to the rank and file. The sheriffs saw us as obstacles to their plan to expand their territory and influence, and we saw them as a threat to our very existence. The situation could not continue forever: One side or the other would have to capitulate. I knew that it would take only a sufficiently weak or corrupt administration to make the difference. In Compton, those were not hard to come by.

I could not help but feel that, after its 112-year history of service, the days of the Compton PD were numbered.

I was now starting my eighteenth year as a police officer—eighteen years of adrenaline, pressure, and unbroken battles against the criminals and the politicians. Sooner or later, such stress was bound to take a toll on my health.

In 1986, I began experiencing stomach pain. At first I tossed it off as indigestion, but the longer I tried to ignore it, the worse the pain became. Finally, unable to sleep or eat, sometimes even to walk, I went to see my doctor. I was hoping that some form of medication would get me back on my feet. He prescribed painkillers and antibiotics and recommended that I take some time off and rest.

I had accumulated six months of sick time, but when I applied for two weeks' leave, my request was denied. Instead, the risk management officer ordered me to consult a specialist in Century City. I did so, underwent a number of tests, and was informed that I was suffering from acute stomach ulcers.

The ulcers were debilitating, making it almost impossible for me to do my job. Since they were considered to be an injury incurred in the line of duty, I was entitled to take disability retirement. Quitting was the last thing I wanted to do, though. I had lived, worked, and breathed the police force for nearly two decades, and I knew exactly how much there was yet to do. Though I protested that I could still do my job, the department's risk management officials refused to allow me to return to the street.

I had few options. I could continue to struggle on, occasionally backing up other officers as Ron Malachi had done after the loss of his leg, or I could remain in an administrative or training capacity. This last idea had some appeal for me. Training would give me an opportunity to infuse new recruits with the spirit of the early seventies, perhaps resuscitate the Dirty Dozen and reinvigorate the CPOA. On reflection, I decided that my defeat in the board election represented a signal that the new generation of officers no longer related to the old department values. I felt that it was best to let them go their own way.

Then one bright spot appeared. Commander Ivory Webb had been a solid supporter of my work in the task force; even though our tough form of police work was not his style, Webb was a native Comptonite, and he understood the importance of what we were doing. He was clearly next in line to be chief, and when he heard that I was eligible for disability retirement, he approached me and asked me not to retire before he took office.

He told me he was planning to create a new program to be called "*Aquí,* Officer," aimed at improving the department's relations with the Latino community, and he offered me the job as director. It was a tempting prospect. I had been arguing for years that we needed to reach out to the growing Latino population, and here was a chance to take the lead in doing so.

However, the events of the past few years—the death of my mother, the association setbacks, the subpar evaluation by Ebert, whose star was rising in the department, the increasing pressure from the LASO—were taking their toll as much as the ulcers. I was beginning to see my illness as a physical manifestation of the mental, emotional, and spiritual debility I was increasingly feeling. My stomach was screaming what my brain did not want to admit: I was burned out. Eighteen years on the streets of Compton was as much as I could take. It was time for me to stop worrying about my city and start taking care of myself.

When the risk management officer concluded that my ulcers had rendered me no longer fit for duty, I acceded to the inevitable.

I retired from the police force.

Clearing out my locker was an experience filled with meaning for me. I performed the end of watch ritual, giving my equipment to the officers who had come to say good-bye. I arranged my personal possessions carefully in a cardboard box. As I did, I could hear echoes of the past eighteen years: Dave Hall declaring in his booming voice that we were "gonna kick some ass tonight"; Vince Rupp strapping on the helmet that saved his life; Griff Chase sharing a raucous joke; Julio Hernandez telling me how excited he was that Sergeant Stover had teamed us up; Rutigliano polishing his buttons and belts.

Rut was long gone. He had resigned from the department shortly after Jim Carrington became chief. Rut had always despised Carrington, whom he regarded as a backstabbing opportunist. When Joe Rouzan, after serving as city manager, became chief of the Inglewood PD, Rut went with him. After one year on the job, he suffered a massive heart attack. Though he survived, it meant the end of his career.

As I closed the box I recalled him telling me at his own ritual that he had nothing to give me—but he had. He had given me an example of what a police officer should be. He had made me want to be the best cop I could. He had inspired me.

"Dime con quien andas y te diré quien eres," my mother had always said to me. "Tell me who you walk with and I'll tell you who you are." I had walked with Rut; he had made me the cop I was. Now it was important to me that I go out with dignity.

I walked out the front door of the station house for the last time on August 15, 1986. It was not, as I had expected, with melancholy and regret. It was with pride. Pride that I had done my job for the people of Compton as well and as honorably as I could. Pride that I had given everything I had to the city I served. Pride that I had, after all, made a difference.

Pride that I had been part of the finest police force in the nation.

Aftermath

When your life has driven in fifth gear for two decades, it is very hard to slow down. Nothing had prepared me for retirement. I missed the daily routine of police work, the comradeship of my fellow officers, the challenges of the streets. My departure from the department left a hole in my heart almost as big as the death of my mother had. It left something else as well—something I had not anticipated: a craving.

I was so used to danger, and my system had been so saturated with adrenaline for so long, that when it stopped, I felt like a crack addict on a crashing descent. In the months after my retirement, I experienced an insatiable need to satisfy my hunger for action, and I did so in ways that can only be described as manic.

Longing for excitement and the need to vent years of pent-up rage, I would go into bars in the meanest parts of Los Angeles looking for a fight. If I could not find one, I would start it. I was chronically agitated, irritable, and short-tempered. I watched myself turning into something like a shadow of the criminals I had spent eighteen years combating.

One night while driving on the freeway with my girlfriend, I found myself alongside a new Honda sports car. I admired it, and I gave the thumbs-up signal to the driver. He evidently mistook it for a vulgar gesture, and he tried to run me off the road. I swerved to avoid him, but he kept coming at me. He was on the passenger side, and my girlfriend was panicking. I reached under my jacket, took out a .38, stretched my arm across her chest, and fired three shots into the Honda's fender. The driver darted off the freeway at the next exit.

On another occasion, we were double-dating with a buddy and his girlfriend. After dinner we went to the Blue Bayou in Paramount to hear some live music. There were four rednecks in the bar, and when they became too rowdy, I told them to quiet down. Later, as we were pulling out of the parking lot, they blocked my car with their pickup truck and climbed out carrying tire irons. As they moved on my car, I took out a .45 automatic and cranked half a dozen rounds into the engine of their truck. The rednecks stopped in their tracks and watched as the engine hissed and burbled and fluids began spewing onto the sidewalk.

One night in Hollywood I had what was probably the closest call of my life. A friend of mine, Vincent Lora, and I were at a strip club on Sunset Boulevard when a member of the Rolling 60s, the largest of the Crip sets, challenged Vincent to fight. A tall, skinny kid, he wore baggy pants, a Pendleton shirt, and a do-rag. He snarled at Vincent to "step outside."

I got in between them and told the banger to be cool. What I did not know was that the night before, Vincent had hassled the banger's girlfriend, a stripper in the club. He ignored me. "I got a bullet for you," he told Vince.

Vince clearly was intimidated, so I answered, "He doesn't want to dance, but I'll go outside with you."

The moment we got to the sidewalk, the owner locked the door. Before I could make a move, the banger reached under his shirt and pulled out a 9mm pistol. He was not more than a foot from me. He raised the gun, pointed it at my face, and fired—and missed. My reaction was instantaneous. I yanked the pistol away from him and tossed it onto the roof of the club. Then I grabbed the banger by his collar, spun him around, kicked him in the ass, and threw him into the middle of Sunset Boulevard.

Such encounters were not unfortunate coincidences. I sought them out or did what I could to manufacture them. As time went on, however, and I had a chance to observe and reflect on my behavior, I began to realize that what I was lacking was not danger but a definition. Police work had defined me most of my life; now I would have to replace it with something else. To do that, I would have to answer some very basic questions: Who was I? Who had I become? Who did I want to be?

I was Rick Baker, the altar boy and idealistic sociology major, the ex-marine and starry-eyed rookie cop, the political policeman, the husband, father, and detective. I had been hardened by years on the streets of Compton, an experience that had impelled me through a trajectory whose milestones I recognized, but had nonetheless brought me to a point where I was no longer sure I recognized myself. What I had lived through was searingly clear to me; what lay ahead was not.

I would spend the next few years working out the answers to those questions. The process was, for me, like coming back to Earth after a near-death experience. It required redefining my life, rechanneling my energies, retooling my emotions, rediscovering my soul.

My lifelong passion for working out helped, as did my love of reading and writing. Without those avenues of expression, I might have stoppered up my feelings until they exploded in a self-destructive outburst the nature of which I could neither have predicted nor controlled—like Griff Chase on his front porch, or Dick Bidwell in his armchair. The need to be of service, which I had felt since my childhood, and the urgent sense that the story of what my fellow officers and I had lived through and accomplished had to be told, kept me going. My life had not ended when I left the police force: It just needed to begin again in a new form and with a new purpose.

Before that could happen, like Bobby Erlanger, I required healing. For his, he had turned to the fey little girl called Shell. I, too, had such a creature in my life—a fairylike princess named Tiffany.

My healing started with a phone call to Oregon.

Compton Coda

Compton, during the years I lived and worked in it, was a microcosm of America. It was a city in continual and profound transition, a community of contradictions, hopes, and dreams, and a reality that was sometimes inspiring, often brutal, always complex. Compton was a community searching for its soul. That search went on long after I left the police department.

As the twentieth century ended, a new phase in the life of Compton began. The Latino migration continued, and by the arrival of the new millennium, Hispanics made up nearly 55 percent of the population. Compton was no longer a black city. Nonetheless, the city's government continued to be dominated by black politicians. Mayor Walter Tucker Jr. served honorably until his sudden death in 1990, when he was succeeded in a special election by his son, Walter Tucker III. His brief tenure was marked by accusations of corruption and by the civil unrest following the Rodney King trial. After only a year in office, Tucker ran for and was elected to Congress. In 1995, he was forced to resign his seat after being indicted for having taken bribes while he was mayor of Compton. He was convicted and sentenced to twenty-seven months in prison for extortion and tax evasion. It was the beginning of the worst era of political corruption in Compton's history.

Led by Councilwoman Patricia Moore, a group of city council members began to lay the groundwork for the dismembering of the Compton Police Department. This clique proposed a "golden handshake," whereby all CPD officers with twenty years of service or more would be allowed to retire at full pension. Labeled as a cost-cutting measure, the move was, in effect, an attempt to gut the department—the first step on the road to its dissolution. Many of the veteran officers who had been on the force when we declared the blue flu took early retirement. Among them was the chief, Ivory Webb. The CPD's leadership was being decapitated.

After Webb resigned in 1990, Terry Ebert realized his goal of becoming chief. It had been a long and cunning climb up the ladder for Ebert, who had had to overcome not only the fact that he was white but also his involvement in one of the worst scandals in the history of the detective division.

In a case that made headlines, a young white female security officer at a strip mall on the north side was kidnapped, tortured, and raped. The case was assigned to Ebert. He did nothing for more than a month, and when at last he began his investigation he bungled it so badly that it was taken away from him and given to Detective Steve Finch. Finch, the rookie who had given me a cup of coffee after the blue flu, solved the case in ten days. Ebert was humiliated.

Nonetheless, he had continued his inexorable rise. When Webb announced his intention to retire, the CPOA again argued for a Latino chief. This would have made eminent sense since the city was now largely Hispanic. Instead, the city council named Terry Ebert as chief. Ebert's lust for the top job had finally been satisfied. It was a short-lived victory, however. Two years later, he was forced to resign rather than face indictment for having embezzled money from the department's narcotics fund to pay off gambling debts.

After his resignation in disgrace, Terry Ebert was succeeded by my old friend Hourie Taylor. Taylor was a popular and effective chief who retained something of the old spirit of the department. When the Rodney King riots broke out in Los Angeles in 1992, Taylor instructed his line officers to protect the city at any cost. As the rioters surged toward Long Beach Boulevard in the northeast section, officers were told to shoot anyone who attempted to cause destruction. In fact, one rioter was killed, shot by Stone Jackson when the man attacked him with a broken bottle. Knowing the CPD meant business, no other rioters crossed the border. As it had done during the Watts riots, the CPD had kept the city from chaos. It was perhaps the final example of police work Compton Style.

Several years after I resigned, I received a call from Tiffany's mother, Shannon. She was desperate, near tears. Her husband, a well-to-do food supplier, had become involved in a tawdry financial scam and was under investigation by the Riverside district attorney's office. Over the phone, she recounted to me the details of her husband's reckless business dealings, and his harebrained plans for escaping justice. A few days later, the DA subpoenaed me to appear before the grand jury to answer questions about what Shannon had told me.

Once again I was being asked to testify against someone close to me. I considered taking the Fifth, but that would leave Shannon at the mercy of the DA, who had sworn he would send not only Shannon's husband to prison but her as well. When I appeared before the grand jury, therefore, I refused to be baited by the DA, stating that, in my opinion, Shannon had had nothing to do with her husband's crazy schemes. The DA was furious.

I assumed that the matter would end there, but I could not have been more wrong. The DA declared that he had found my name in the rolodex of a murdered highway patrolman, and he named me a suspect in the case. With no other evidence, he issued a warrant for me, and I was arrested and jailed. It seemed that I had at last fallen victim to the curse of Compton.

Though my attorney, Steve Finch, the rookie who had given me a coffee after the blue flu, protested and filed motions for my release, the Riverside DA would not relent. He was determined to force me to testify against Shannon, and to keep me in prison until I agreed to do so. When I refused, he ordered me held in solitary confinement, claiming it was for my own protection. Weeks went by, then months, as the legal wrangling wore on. The solitary confinement in which I spent twenty-two hours a day alone in an eight-by-ten-foot cell was wearing on my psyche, but I refused to buckle. Only my Marine Corps training, and my years on the streets of Compton, enabled me to survive the isolation and crushing loneliness.

Finally, the judge in the case ruled that there was no evidence on which to hold me, and he ordered me released. Reprimanding the DA for his misconduct, he further ordered that the charge against me be dropped, and that the record of my arrest and incarceration be expunged, as if the whole rotten mess had never happened. Acting Chief Ramon Allen then issued a memo to the CPD bureau commanders notifying them that I had been cleared of all charges, restoring my reputation in the department. Two years later, I assisted the Orange County Cold Case Team in solving the murder of the highway patrolman.

The damage had been done, however. The effect on my psyche and the offense to my honor could never be expunged. I was furious and bitter. I had lost weight, my skin was pale, and I felt that I had aged a dozen years. What was more, I had been engaged to be married to a model and former *Playboy* centerfold, Kara Styler, but after the arrest, she broke off our engagement.

When I was released from jail, a familiar figure was waiting for me: Dominic Rutigliano. He was standing by a new Lincoln Town Car in a three-piece suit and shades, smoking a cigar. When the guard who let me out saw him he said, "I shoulda known you'd be picked up by a gangster."

As I walked to Rut's car, he shook his head. "I see they finally caught up with the infamous Rosecrans Rick. How much time did you do?"

"Nine fucking months," I growled.

Rut grinned. "I'm surprised they let you out so soon."

"I was damned if that asshole DA was gonna break me."

"Justice is a bitch," he said. "Come on, let's get you a burger at Denny's."

The simple, kindly gesture broke the hard crust of my anger. I could not help but smile. "I got no money," I told him.

"It's on me," he said as we walked to his car. "They've got a senior citizens' discount. The way you look, you might just qualify."

Walter Tucker's departure for Congress was followed by one of the most vitriolic mayoral elections in Compton's history. Patricia Moore and Councilman Omar Bradley fought furiously for the job, shunting aside the city's first Latino candidate, Pedro Pallan. Bradley won by a mere 349 votes, largely with the support of the Latino community. During his campaign, he had pledged to pay special attention to the needs of Latinos, and to appoint Pallan to replace him on the council. No sooner had he been elected than those promises were forgotten, and Bradley began appointing political cronies to office.

Though he had not said so publicly, Bradley was determined to cash in on the LASO's persistent offers to take over the policing of Compton. The CPD was costing the city eighteen million dollars a year, and the new sheriff, Leroy Baca, claimed he could do the job for twelve million. Omar Bradley, Patricia Moore, and the council's antipolice clique eyed that six-million-dollar difference hungrily.

Meanwhile, John Soisson and the last of the old CPOA officers had retired. With no friends in the Bradley administration and a leadership devastated by the golden handshake, the association lost its clout. The only obstacle that remained was Chief Hourie Taylor. He was quickly dispensed with. The mayor's cronies concocted accusations of official misconduct against him, and he was suspended. Bradley named Ramon Allen to replace him.

Allen was highly qualified and experienced, and he had compiled a record of accomplishments that has never been equaled. In the late 1980s, Allen's narco strike force had raided over 1,000 rock houses, seized millions of dollars in drugs, made over 1,200 arrests, and achieved an astounding 99 percent conviction rate in the cases it brought. On the surface his appointment appeared to be an enlightened move. In fact, Mayor Bradley knew that, since Allen was from West L.A. and a leader of the bourgeois faction, his appointment would be resented by the remaining Compton-born cops, further dividing the department. In a development reminiscent of the defection of the Guardians, the animosity over Allen's appointment erupted into an open split that crippled the CPOA.

It was in this poisonous atmosphere of scandal, divisiveness, and low morale that the Bradley administration opened negotiations with the LASO. What Ramon Allen had not been told was that he was intended only as an interim chief, a figurehead to fill in while the negotiations continued. The way was now open for the sheriffs to take over.

The Compton Police Department was disbanded in 2000, and the Los Angeles County Sheriff's Office replaced it. In a move calculated to solidify the LASO's control, no Compton police officer was offered a job in the city. Instead, the detectives and rank and file were dispersed among departments across the county. Most accepted jobs elsewhere, but some of the veterans chose simply to retire. They were Compton cops; no other police work had any meaning for them.

In 2004, Mayor Omar Bradley was indicted on charges of misappropriating city funds for personal use. He was convicted and sentenced to three years in prison. The city manager and three members of the council— the clique that had engineered the LASO deal—were also arrested on corruption charges. All went to jail. Councilwoman Patricia Moore, the author of the golden handshake, became the target of a federal sting operation and was arrested. Convicted of embezzling city funds, she was sentenced to thirty-three months in prison.

All of those who had orchestrated the demise of the CPD had thus been found to be criminals. It was too late, though: The deal was done. The Compton Police Department was gone.

One day, a few years after the CPD was dissolved, I received a call from Dominic Rutigliano. He had, he said, a favor to ask me.

That night we met at a coffee shop in Lynwood. He looked older; he had put on weight, and his movements were slow and deliberate. Even so, as we talked, I caught glimpses of the old fire. Rut was still Rut, though the burden of the years was beginning to weigh on him, as no doubt it was on me. Finally I asked what I could do for him.

"You remember Joe MacAuliffe?" he asked me. I assured him I did. It was MacAuliffe who had led the drive to force Rut to resign. "He called me a couple of weeks ago. Poor bastard was dying of prostate cancer."

I said that I was sorry to hear it.

"He told me he wanted to get something off his chest," Rut continued. "He admitted that he set me up, that his two witnesses against me were phonies. He said he wanted to set the record straight before he died."

I told him that I had never doubted it.

Rut took a long, meditative sip of his coffee. "He was crying, Rick. He begged me to forgive him. He said, 'Rut, before I die, I need to know that you forgive me for what I did.'"

"What did you say?" I asked.

"I told him I appreciated it, that it meant a lot to me." Then he grinned devilishly, and in that grin I saw the old brazen Rut spirit. "But I told him, 'I'm still gonna piss on your grave.' He died a few days ago."

That night we drove to the cemetery in Lynwood. While I kept watch, Rut hauled himself over the wall and made his way to Joe MacAuliffe's grave, where he settled his debt.

Life may be short in Compton, but memory is long.